History of the Qur'ān

APPROACHES & EXPLORATIONS

Edited by F. Redhwan Karim

History of the Qur'an: Approaches and Explorations

First published in England by

Kube Publishing Ltd, Markfield Conference Centre, Ratby Lane,
Markfield, Leicestershire LE67 9SY, United Kingdom.

Distributed by

Kube Publishing Ltd.

Tel: +44(0)1530 249230
Email: info@kubepublishing.com
Website: www.kubepublishing.com

Cataloguing-in-Publication Data is available from the British Library.

ISBN 978-1-84774-235-3 Hardback
ISBN 978-1-84774-234-6 Paperback
ISBN 978-1-84774-236-0 ebook

Cover design: Nasir Cadir
Typesetting: LiteBook Prepress Services
Cover Image: istock
Printed by: Elma Basim, Turkey

CONTENTS

Acknowledgements

There are many people who were instrumental in the publishing of this book. Zahid Parvez for his facilitation to allow this volume to come into fruition at the Markfield Institute of Higher Education (MIHE). Haroon Bashir for our many long discussions. Mariam Attia for sourcing Arabic works from the Cairo Book Fair. Haris Ahmed and Salman al-Azami at Kube Publishing for ensuring the smooth publication of the volume. Raihan Karim for his proofreading of the manuscript. Mustafa Shah and Marijn van Putten for their kind reviews of the volume. Finally, I must thank all the contributors to this volume. You will no doubt read their articles, but it is only proper that I name them once more: François Déroche, Éléonore Cellard, Yousry Elseadawy, Nazir Khan, Ammar Khatib, M.A.S Abdel Haleem, Zahed Fettah, Yasir Qadhi, Khairil Husaini Bin Jamil, Stephen Cúrto, Meysam Kohantorabi and Afsan Redwan.

Stylistic Conventions

The Arabic transliteration generally follows the standard of the *International Journal of Middle East Studies* (IJMES). Names and terms have been transliterated into English, although the final discretion has been left to the authors. Hence at places, the Arabic text without transliteration is also adopted. Dates in Islamic History are indicated in both *hijrī* and Common Era forms. The salutation for the Prophet Muhammad is adopted only for the first occurrence in each chapter.

List of Contributors

Afsan Redwan is a PhD candidate in Theology and Religious Studies at Cardiff University.

Ammar Khatib is the Director of Education and Religious Affairs at the Manitoba Islamic Association (MIA). He completed his PhD in Islamic Sciences at the Université Privée Africaine Franco-Arabe (UPAFA).

Éléonore Cellard is an Independent Scholar of Ancient Qur'ānic Manuscripts. She completed her PhD in Arabic Language and Literature at the Institut National des Langues et Civilisations Orientales and École Pratique des Hautes Études.

F. Redhwan Karim is a Lecturer in Islamic Studies at the Markfield Institute of Higher Education. He completed his PhD in Islamic Studies at SOAS, University of London.

François Déroche is Professor at the Collège de France where he holds the 'History of the Quran, Text and Transmission' Chair. He completed his PhD in Arab-Islamic Studies at Paris-Sorbonne University.

Khairil Husaini Bin Jamil is an Associate Professor of Islamic Scriptural Sciences at the International Islamic University Malaysia. He completed his PhD at SOAS, University of London.

M.A.S Abdel Haleem is Professor of Islamic Studies at SOAS, University of London and Editor-in-Chief of the Journal of Qur'anic Studies. He completed his PhD at the University of Cambridge.

Meysam Kohantorabi is an Associate Professor of Qur'an and Hadith Studies at Bozorgmehr University of Qaenat. He completed his PhD at Usul Al-Din University of Tehran.

Nazir Khan is an Assistant Professor in the Faculty of Health Sciences at McMaster University. He is a PhD candidate in Islamic Theology at the University of Nottingham.

Stephen Cúrto is Adjunct Professor of Arabic and Philosophy at Union College of Union County, NJ. He is a PhD student at Claremont Graduate University.

Yasir Qadhi is the Dean of The Islamic Seminary of America and Chair of the Fiqh Council of North America. He completed his PhD in Islamic Studies from Yale University.

Yousry Elseadawy is an Independent Scholar of Medieval Arabic Manuscripts. He completed his PhD at the Free University of Berlin.

Zahed Fettah is a Lecturer in Islamic Studies at the Markfield Institute of Higher Education. He is a PhD candidate at the University of Swansea.

CHAPTER ONE

Towards a History of the Qur'ān

F. Redhwan Karim

Within Islam, there are multiple areas that are a source of contention and disagreements, whether that be theology, history or law. However, the Qur'ān alone remains unique among all Muslims as an agreed-upon source of revelation and the focal point for all other auxiliary Islamic sciences. Being the focal point of Muslims around the world, both past and present, the contents of the Qur'ān have been the source of earnest examination. Indeed, the exegeses of the Qur'ān, numbering into the thousands, seek to elucidate various facets of the Qur'ān's content, such as language, historical background of verses, and interpretation. However, the Qur'ān's journey in history as a book and as scripture remains understudied. In this present volume, the transmission and understanding of the Qur'ān in history is explored, through the adoption of various methodological approaches whether that be through manuscript studies and codicology, or literary analysis and intellectual history. In doing so, this present volume hopes to provide and contribute towards the construction of the history of the Qur'ān. The overarching nature of the Qur'ān is represented in the makeup of the volume by drawing upon the expertise of scholars, not just based in the West, but throughout the world.

To reconstruct the Qur'ān's historical journey to the modern period, the most precious physical source we have at our disposal are the actual vessels of the Qur'ānic text itself – Qur'ānic manuscripts. François Déroche, who has already produced pioneering work in this field,[1] begins by providing an overview of early Qur'ānic manuscripts, and in particular draws attention to the earliest extant manuscripts in our possession. These extant manuscripts were composed primarily on parchment, or animal skin, and to a lesser extent, papyrus, and stored in depositories where manuscripts which were no longer in use were stored in the various heartlands of the Muslim world such as Damascus, Qayrawān, Fustat and Ṣanʿā'. Through radiocarbon (C14) dating, these early manuscripts can be roughly dated from the middle of the first/seventh century to the middle of the second/eighth century. Various parchments, for example have been dated to originate within the range of 606 to 55/675.[2]

Déroche looks at the history of the discovery and study of these early manuscripts in the West. The figures that were involved in this process, the activities they undertook with these manuscripts, and the current state of the field. He discusses some of the problems that working with these manuscripts entails, such as the process of dating these manuscripts, and the role palaeography and radiocarbon dating have played in this process of the eventual dating of these manuscripts to as far back as the second half of the first/seventh century. The difficulties in reconstructing where these actual manuscripts were produced is also considered, since even if they were found in depositories in Damascus, Qayrawān, Fustat or Ṣanʿā', this does not entail that they were originally produced in these regions. The chapter

1 François Déroche, *La Transmission Écrite Du Coran Dans Les Débuts de l'islam. Le Codex Parisino-Petropolitanus* (Leiden: Brill, 2009); François Déroche, *Qur'āns of the Umayyads: A First Overview* (Leiden: Brill, 2014); François Déroche, *The One and the Many The Early History of the Qur'ān*, trans. Malcom DeBevoise (New Haven: Yale University Press, 2021).

2 Michel Marx and Tobias Jocham, 'Radiocarbon (14C) Dating of Qur'ān Manuscripts', in *Qur'ān Quotations Preserved on Papyrus Documents, 7th-10th Centuries, and the Problem of Carbon Dating Early Qur'āns*, ed. A Kaplony and M Marx (Leiden: Brill, 2019), 188–221.

then looks closely at some of the technical material aspects of these early Qur'ānic manuscripts, including the kind of writing surfaces and ink that were used, the size and format of the manuscript, the types of quires and bindings which were used, and the setting and ruling of the pages. The chapter also gives a broad overview of the technical typology that is adopted in categorising the various styles of scripts which were utilised in writing the Qur'ān, such as *Ḥijāzī*, late *Ḥijāzī*, BI, A and OI. The chapter then includes a comprehensive overview of the internal features of these specific Qur'ānic manuscripts, more specifically, looking at orthographical practice and the way various letters and words were copied by these scribes, the development of verse and chapter division, and the use of illuminations. The chapter finally considers early modes of editing the Qur'ānic text, and the way potential variant readings of the Qur'ān were incorporated into the manuscript tradition.

Book production, in general, was a popular enterprise in early and medieval Islamic societies and the Qur'ān as a codex holds pride of place in its production. Indeed, some of the oldest and most ornate examples of books in Muslim societies are copies of the Qur'ān and close analysis of such manuscripts not only give a deeper understanding of the Qur'ān, but also of early calligraphic practices and bookmaking in general in the Muslim world. From among the oldest corpus of the Qur'ān in existence are the Ṣanʿā' manuscripts, which were discovered in Yemen in 1972 during a renovation at the Great Mosque of Ṣanʿā'. However, what is more remarkable is that on closer inspection, the corpus was discovered to be a palimpsest, meaning that the parchment had been reused and re-written. Hence, the manuscripts actually contain 'two texts'. The 'lower' original version of the text – which was scraped off and erased – and an 'upper' version of the text, the actual visible text which was written over the 'lower' text. This practice in general was not altogether uncommon in the early period due to the cost and value of parchments. Hence, it was common practice to reuse parchments as palimpsests. While the 'upper' text is the text of the Qur'ān which is visible on the parchment with the naked eye, the 'lower' text can also be seen through enhancement and reconstruction with the use of ultraviolet light and image processing. Collating the various fragments together show the Ṣanʿā' manuscripts to consist of approximately 40% of the Qur'ān.[3]

Despite work that has already been conducted on the Ṣanʿā' manuscripts, their fragmentary nature and their early ascription means there is much we still do not know about them and their production. For example, the manuscripts carry no dating nor any indication of where they were actually produced geographically. Neither do we know anything about the scribes that actually wrote the text, nor the impetus or conditions that led them to do so. In chapter three, Éléonore Cellard focuses specifically on the material aspects of the Ṣanʿā' manuscripts and attempts to uncover the scribal practices of the copyists who composed this corpus. Cellard pays close attention to the various fragments of the Ṣanʿā' manuscripts in order to describe the corpus's original book form. From this she also reconstructs the manner in which the scribes worked by examining aspects such as the way they laid out the various pages, and the scribal rules they adopted and adhered to. She also examines the way this group of scribes worked collaboratively to compose the manuscripts. Specific scribal practices that were adopted such as the way various chapters and verses were separated are also broached upon. Although Cellard focuses on the Ṣanʿā' manuscripts she also adopts a comparative approach by comparing scribal practices of other early Qur'ānic corpuses such as the Codex Parisino-Petropolitanus, which were

3 See, Behnam Sadeghi and Mohsen Goudarzi, 'Ṣan"ā" 1 and the Origins of the Qur'ān', *Der Islam* 87, no. 1–2 (2012): 1–129; Asma Hilali, *The Sanaa Palimpsest The Transmission of the Qur'ān in the First Centuries AH* (Oxford: Oxford University Press/Institute of Ismaili Studies, 2017).

originally found in Fustat, but later acquired, with the bulk now primarily being housed in the Bibliothèque Nationale de France. The fact that similar features can be extracted from these two corpuses allow us to better understand the scribal practices and approaches that guided the production and transcription of the Qur'ān in the very earliest period of Islam.

The history of the Qur'ān is accompanied by a whole host of ancillary sciences which developed alongside the Qur'ān, shaping its understanding and engagement. This includes genres such as exegesis, grammar, and works dealing with the various Qur'ānic sciences. The third/ninth century was a particularly crucial period for Islamic knowledge production since it coincided with the widespread use of paper as a medium for written text, a far more accessible and practical material over parchment. This period also coincided with the growing legal discussions of the various schools of law and the translation of foreign books into Arabic, further leading to a boom in knowledge production.[4] Yousry Elseadawy, focuses on this crucial period and looks closely at the codicological practices of scribes working on works related to Qur'ānic studies to highlight the practices they adopted to ensure that the manuscripts were clear and accurate which in turn would facilitate access to knowledge of the Qur'ān. Elseadawy draws upon representative genres of Qur'ānic studies manuscripts from the third/ninth century in the field of exegesis, variant readings, and philology of the Qur'ān. This includes the *Tafsīr al-Bustī*, of Abū Muḥammad al-Bustī (d. 307/919), the *Kitāb al-Ḥujjah li A'immah al-Sab'ah min Qurrā' al-Amṣār* of al-Fārisī (d. 377/987), the *Kitāb Al-Badī'* of ibn Khālawayh (d. 370/980), the *Mushkil al-Qur'ān* of ibn Qutaybah (d. 276/889) and the *Ma'ānī al-Qur'ān* of al-Zajjāj (d. 311/923).

4 Dimitri Gutas, *Greek Thought, Arabic Culture: The Graeco-Arabic Translation Movement in Baghdad and Early 'Abbasaid Society (2nd-4th/5th-10th Centuries)* (New York: Routledge, 1998).

In order to ensure clarity in the copying process, Elseadawy elaborates upon the types of scripts which were employed in this period, such as the Abbasid Book Hand, the New Abbasid Style, *Naskh* and the *Maghribī* script. All of these were utilised diligently and consistently to ensure that the writing and hence the contents of such works were uniform and clear. We see that there is also a clear preponderance towards maintaining the aesthetic quality of the script and a consistency in ensuring that the script contained vowel markings and dotting. Elseadawy also elaborates upon other codicological practices that were used by scribes in this period such as the use of *ihmāl* signs to distinguish between the dotted and undotted letters.[5] Other practices include distinguishing between the different sections of the book through the use of word elongation, or the practice of underlining key words in different coloured ink. The page layout was also an important aspect of scribal practice and Elseadawy shows how scribes would ensure that they left sufficient spacing between lines to allow accidentally omitted words to be inserted during the collation process at the end of the manuscript's completion. The collation process is where the copied manuscript would be compared to the original in order to ensure that the copy accurately reflected the original. As Elseadawy shows, in many cases, an omitted word would be reinserted between the lines. However, sometimes the omitted word would be inserted in the margin instead, with a marking known as the *aftah*, being drawn at the place of the omitted word.

Alongside clarity, accuracy was also equally important for the scribes of these important manuscripts. Elseadawy highlights a whole host of scribal practices which were used by scribes to ensure precision, such as the use of catchwords, where the last

5 *Ihmāl* signs are markings that are attached to undotted letters to further emphasise their distinction from their dotted counter parts. For example, the *rā* would have a marking to distinguish it from the *ḍād*. For an handy overview of scribal practices of Arabic manuscripts in general see, Adam Gacek, *Arabic Manuscripts A Vademecum for Readers* (Leiden: Brill, 2012).

word of a page would be repeated on the next page, to indicate continuation and highlight that pages were not missing. Although scribes are often the silent transmitters of a text, they would sometimes also communicate their personal thoughts on the text, by for example, indicating when a wording was potentially problematic. An example of this would be a *ḥadīth* quoted in the text that was composed of variant wordings. Scribes would also stress the correctness of a passage if they could potentially be interpreted as being incorrect and provide legible versions of illegible texts. All of these practices underscore the diligent nature of scribal practice in relation to Qur'ānic studies manuscripts to ensure that the contents of these manuscripts and hence knowledge of the Qur'ān was clear and accurate.

The codification and standardisation of the Qur'ān is perhaps one of the most important aspects of the Qur'ān's history. The traditional narratives hold that the Qur'ān was revealed to the Prophet Muhammad over a period of twenty-three years. During this period, its various verses and chapters were memorised and transmitted orally among the first generation of Muslims. Alongside this oral tradition, the Qur'ān's various parts were also written on materials such as "palm stalks and thin white stones".[6] However, at least at the time of the Prophet Muhammad's death in 632, these discrete parts were not yet compiled into a single codex. What is conspicuous in histories of the Qur'ān is that its eventual codification is attributed to the efforts of the third Caliph 'Uthmān ibn 'Affān. However, various *ḥadīth*, as well as early Arabic historical texts speak of a codification process taking place prior to this with the first Caliph Abū Bakr. These narrations and accounts are significant since this would rather make this codification the very first in the Qur'ān history. Despite this, this event is eclipsed in focus of scholarly attention to 'Uthmān's codification.

6 *Ṣaḥīḥ al-Bukhārī*, no. 4986.

Furthermore, there is a tendency to dismiss the plausibility of this earlier codification since the evidence for this event relies solely on narrations and historical reports, of which 'Uthmān's codification is more widely attested. The specifics of Abu Bakr's codification also mirror the codification of 'Uthmān, such as the process of codification and the people involved. The early nature of the Abū Bakr's codification also precludes us from engaging in any material analysis. In chapter five, Ammar Khatib and Nazir Khan argue for the plausibility of this early codification and by using an expansive range of narrations and accounts, provide a comprehensive and unified account of the compilation. They discuss the context in which this codification is said to have occurred, namely the Battle of Yamāma in 632, where a significant number of those who had memorised the Qur'ān (*ḥuffāẓ*) are said to have perished thereby providing the urgency and impetus for the Qur'ān's codification. The selection and role of Zayd ibn Thabit is broached upon as well as the process he adopted in finalising the compilation. Sources state for example that Zayd collected the scattered written material of the Qur'ān, which were then corroborated with two witnesses. The witnessing process was understood to mean those who had witnessed the Qur'ān's documentation in the presence of the Prophet.

The chapter goes beyond merely providing an account of this codification but also examines multifaceted issues relating to this compilation, such as the issue of a verse from Sūrah al-Tawba (Q.9), where Zayd purportedly only found one witness. Khan and Khatib also deal with the issue of the narrations which speak of Abu Bakr's codification being equally applicable to 'Uthmān's codification, of which the peculiar similarities in the process and mechanism of the codifications led some to completely dismiss the occurrence of the former. Khan and Khatib explore the various narrations and attempt to reconcile both narratives. They discuss the ways different scholars understood the function of the two codifications, showing how Abu Bakr's collection had more to do with ensuring that parts of the Qur'ān were not lost due to the Battle of Yamāma, while the Uthmānic codification was to ensure unity and restrict the use of multiple variant recitations. Other factors are also explored such as the potential structure of both codifications, and theorisations on the way Abu Bakr's codex incorporated the variant recitations of the Qur'ān. The chapter finally considers the fate of Abu Bakr's codex.

'Uthmān's codification of the Qur'ān holds primary importance in the Qur'ān's history. In fact, this standardisation is so important that the Qur'ānic text is sometimes also referred to as the Uthmānic codex. Traditional sources state that sometime during 'Uthmān's Caliphate in 23/644 – 35/656, disputes began to emerge among the Muslim soldiers as to the correct way of reciting the Qur'ān. The Muslim world had grown considerably during this period, and now encompassed regions and cultures as diverse as modern-day Iraq, Iran, Syria, and Egypt. Prompted by Ḥudhayfah ibn al-Yamān, 'Uthmān appointed Zayd ibn Thābit to oversee this process of codification. This codified Qur'ān was then subsequently copied and sent to the various centres of the Muslim world, including Kufa, Baṣra and Damascus. All other variant copies of the Qur'ān were then ordered to be destroyed. The orthography (*rasm*) of the 'Uthmānic codex came to be seen as the correct way of writing the Qur'ān, termed as *al-rasm al-'Uthmānī* or *rasm al-muṣḥaf*. Studies which have retraced this archetypal text have shown it to be highly uniform, despite some regional variances, which in turn can be traced to regional archetypes.[7] However, this mode of writing the Qur'ān differs in many ways from the way the Arabic script in general

7 Hythem Sidky, 'On the Regionality of Qur'ānic Codices', *Journal of the International Qur'ānic Studies Association* 5, no. 1 (2020): 133–210; See also, Michael Cook, 'The Stemma of the Regional Codices of the Koran', *Graeco-Arabica* 9–10 (2004): 89–14. For more on the Arabic language tradition and the Qur'ān see, Marijn van Putten, *Qur'ānic Arabic From Its Hijazi Origins to Its Classical Reading Traditions* (Leiden: Brill, 2022).

is written due to the fact that the Arabic language itself was still in a process of development. In particular, the two main differences include the lack of distinction between letters that have a similar shape and the lack of vowel markers. Such deficiencies did not mean that the early Qur'ānic manuscripts could not be read, since the emphasis on oral transmission mitigated against such difficulties. However, in time, traditional sources speak of the eventual steps that were taken to facilitate the reading of the Qur'ānic *muṣḥaf*, such as the widespread use of dots to distinguish between letters, and the inclusion of vowel markers with figures such as Abū-l-Aswad al-Du'alī (d. 69/688) and Nasr ibn 'Āsim (d. 89/707) being ascribed as playing pivotal roles in this process. The initial practice of such differentiation techniques included the use of different coloured ink. For example, using red dots to distinguish vowels and yellow dots for the *hamza*. Eventually, particular symbols were adopted to represent the vowel markers instead of dots, with this process being attributed to Al-Khalīl ibn Aḥmad (d.170/786).[8]

Eventually, Arabic orthography, in general, developed through time and increasingly came to differ from the Qur'ān's orthography. In fact, we see certain early authorities such as Mālik ibn Anas being asked about the permissibility of writing the *muṣḥaf* in the new orthography as opposed to the old one, to which Malik is reported to have replied in the negative.[9]

8 For early vocalisation practices with the use of coloured dots see, Yasin Dutton, 'Red Dots, Green Dots, Yellow Dots and Blue: Some Reflections on the Vocalisation of Early Qur'ānic Manuscripts – Part I', *Journal of Qur'ānic Studies* 1, no. 1 (1999): 115–40; Yasin Dutton, 'Red Dots, Green Dots, Yellow Dots and Blue: Some Reflections on the Vocalisation of Early Qur'ānic Manuscripts – Part II', *Journal of Qur'ānic Studies* 2, no. 1 (2000): 1–24; Alain George, 'Coloured Dots and the Question of Regional Origins in Early Qur'āns (Part I)', *Journal of Qur'ānic Studies* 17, no. 1 (2015): 1–44; Alain George, 'Coloured Dots and the Question of Regional Origins in Early Qur'āns (Part II)', *Journal of Qur'ānic Studies* 17, no. 2 (2015): 75–102.

9 Jalāl al-Dīn al-Suyūṭī, *Al-Itqān Fi 'ulūm Al-Qur'ān*, vol. 2 (Beirut, 1987), 470.

The adoption of this initial orthography of the Qur'ān has continued to this day. The increasing difference between Arabic orthography in general, and the Qur'ān's led to the latter having a branch of its own orthographical style known as *ʿilm al-rasm*. In chapter six, M.A.S Abdel Haleem, explores the history of the Qur'ān's orthography and examines the various ways classical scholars articulated the peculiar features of the Qur'ān's orthography drawing upon figures such as Jalāl al-Dīn al-Suyūṭī (d.909/1503). This includes a close exposition of the Qur'ān's specific orthographical features such as the addition and deletion of the *wāw*, *alif*, and *yā* or the differing way the *hamza* is written in various contexts. Abdel Haleem also elucidates other orthographical features such as the way certain letters morph into other letters, such as the *alif* becoming a *wāw* or a *yā*, or the closed *tā* (*tā marbūta*) being written as an open *tā* (*tā maftuḥa*), the joining or separation of particles, the accommodation of variant readings, and the use of full vocalisation.

In the modern world, when thinking of Qur'ānic orthography, or perhaps even the physical form of the Qur'ān in general, one is almost certainly referring to the 1924 Cairo edition, also known as the *Amīrī Muṣḥaf*. Undertaken by a group of scholars from al-Azhar, and under the patronage of Fuad I, the *Amīrī Muṣḥaf* would come to be the most utilised and widespread written version of the Qur'ān. In this chapter, Abdel Haleem also pays close attention to this critical edition and the specific orthographical features associated with it. Finally, the chapter ends by considering the debates around the adoption of potential changes to the Qur'ān's classical orthography.

Although the codification of ʿUthmān was largely successful, variances did still exist, and there were some prominent detractors to ʿUthmān codification efforts. Most notably, ʿAbdullah ibn Masʿūd, who is described as one of the leading companions with regards to knowledge of the Qur'ān. Despite this, in the story of the Qur'ān's codification, he is described as a prominent dissenting figure. When 'Uthmān commands the Muslim community to burn copies of the Qur'ān that were not in conformity with his version, ibn Mas'ūd vehemently refuses. Hence, it would seem that ibn Mas'ūd's version of the Qur'ān contained significant enough differences from 'Uthmān's codified version for him to refuse to do so. However, more egregiously, the variances in ibn Mas'ūd's version of the Qur'ān were far greater than changes in word or pronunciation. Rather, traditional sources relay his version to have excluded the final two chapters of the Qur'ān – Sūrat al-Falaq and Sūrat al-Nās. Instead of seeing these as legitimate chapters of the Qur'ān, ibn Mas'ūd is depicted as seeing these two chapters as mere supplications the Prophet would recite to seek protection from harm. In fact, certain traditions go even further in depicting ibn Mas'ūd as scraping these two chapters out of the Qur'ān exclaiming, "do not mix the Qur'ān with which is not from it."[10]

Ibn Mas'ūd also voices concerns against the appointment of younger companions in the codification process, most notably, Zayd ibn Thābit, who ibn Mas'ūd states "was in the loins of a disbelieving man", while he, ibn Mas'ūd, was a Muslim.[11] In another report, ibn Mas'ūd chides the selection of Zayd as "a boy playing with children while he had recited seventy chapters to the Prophet."[12] In being faced with such reports we find classical Muslim scholars adopting various mechanisms in order to make sense of ibn Mas'ūd position, from rejecting such reports outright, to attempting to contextualise them. In chapter seven, Zahed Fettah critically examines and evaluates the various ways such Muslim scholars understood ibn Mas'ūd's objections. In particular, Fettah looks closely at the chains of transmissions

---

10 Muhammad ibn Idrīs al-Shāfi'ī, *Kitāb Al-Umm*, vol. 7 (Beirut: Dār al-Fikr, 1990), 199.

11 *Sunan al-Tirmidhī*, no. 3104.

12 *Sunan al-Nasā'ī*, no. 5063.

which encapsulate ibn Masʿūd's objections arguing that simply dismissing such narrations, although convenient, raises other methodological issues since these chains of transmission have traditionally been seen as authentic. Ibn Masʿūd's objections also raise questions around the Qur'ān's transmission in general and notion of mass-transmission (*tawātur*) of the Qur'ān especially when considering his prominent standing as a scholar of the Qur'ān. If the Qur'ān was widely transmitted as traditionally understood during the time of the companions and thereafter, then ibn Masʿūd should not have any difference of opinion with regards to the status of Sūrat al-Falaq and Sūrat al-Nās being the last two chapters of the Qur'ān. However, if we take ibn Masʿūd's objections as sound, this would then call into question the notion of *tawātur*. Fettah considers these questions and evaluates the positions of various Muslim scholars on this important figure in the Qur'ān's history.

One cannot speak on the history of the Qur'ān, without making mention of the important notion of the *aḥruf* and the *qira'āt*. Although the vast majority of Muslims recite the Qur'ān in the mode of ʿĀṣim through the transmission of Ḥafṣ – in no small part due to its adoption in the influential 1924 Cairo edition of the Qur'ān – there are other multiple accepted ways of reciting the Qur'ān. Most notably, the seven modes of recitation (*qiraāt*) that were championed by Abu Bakr ibn Mujāhid (d.936/324) in the eighth/second century. In fact, in many ways we can speak of ibn Mujāhid's efforts as a second step in the Qur'ān's codification or canonisation after ʿUthmān. To this seven, another three were later championed by ibn al-Jazarī (d.1429/833), bringing the total number of recitations that came to be seen as canonical to ten, with each of these ten recitations being diffused by two primary transmitters.[13] The sole theological justification for the

13 The seven reciters championed by ibn Mujāhid include: ʿĀṣim, Nāfiʿ, ibn Kathīr, ibn ʿĀmir, Abū ʿĀmir, al-Kisā'ī and Ḥamza al-Zayyāt. For a

multiple ways of reciting the Qur'ān stem from narrations that speak of the Qur'ān as being revealed according to 'seven *aḥruf*'.[14] The precise meaning of which has been the focus of much contention and debate throughout history. Different scholars have postulated what the differences between the *aḥruf* represent, from variations in language and syntax to synonymous word changes to differences stemming from the various dialects of the various Arab tribes. From this, further questions are then raised as to the relationship between the *aḥruf* and the Qur'ān's history. How did ʿUthmān's codification relate to these *aḥruf*? Did he preserve all of them, or some of them, or as much as the script would allow? This also raises other questions such as to the relationship between the *aḥruf* and the actual widely accepted codified recitations, the *qiraāt*.

Overwhelmingly, the most common way the notion of the *aḥruf* has been understood is through what is termed as the 'Dictation Model'. According to this model, the Qur'ān was revealed in seven different ways and the Prophet Muhammad then recited the Qur'ān in these different ways. The ten canonical recitations then stem back and encapsulate and relate to these various ways the Qur'ān was revealed. On the other hand, recent scholarship has sought to champion a slightly different model, termed as the 'Divine Permission Model' (or *qirā'ah bi-l-maʿnā*). According to this model, the seven *aḥruf* and the narrations that reference it, refer to a divine concession that was granted to the early Muslim community to recite the Qur'ān in their own dialect and to the best of their ability as long as the meaning of the Qur'ān was

---

comprehensive overview and analysis see, Shady Nasser, *The Second Canonization of the Qur'ān (324/936) ibn Mujāhid and the Founding of the Seven Readings* (Leiden: Brill, 2020). See also, Christopher Melchert, 'Ibn Mujāhid and the Establishment of Seven Qur'ānic Readings', *Studia Islamica* 91 (2000): 5–22. The three additional reciters championed by ibn al-Jazarī include Abū Jaʿfar, Yaʿqūb al-Ḥaḍramī and Khalaf.

14 *Ṣaḥīḥ al-Bukhārī*, no. 3074; *Ṣaḥīḥ Muslim*, no. 819.

conveyed correctly. According to this model, the Qur'ān was only revealed in one way and the Prophet recited the Qur'ān in one way, even though the companions were given permission to deviate slightly from this in consideration of dialectical and practical differences. Hence, the codification of 'Uthmān preserved this original recitation of the Qur'ān and restricted the concession that was given. However, some of the dialectical variances of the companions were still in circulation, which is reflected in the differences in the various *qira'āt*.[15] In chapter eight, Yasir Qadhi focuses on this critical issue and provides an encyclopaedic overview and analysis of how the 'Divine Permission Model' has been articulated, and the strengths and challenges it provides. The chapter draws upon fifteen points of contention that are raised in the adoption of the 'Dictation Model', the concerns they raise and subsequently, the way they are resolved by the 'Divine Permission Model'. The chapter draws upon an expansive array of narrations to encapsulate and give a clear picture of how the notion of the *aḥruf* was represented in the earliest sources. Qadhi also draws upon intellectual history to show how previous Muslim authorities either alluded to the 'Divine Permission Model' or even adopted it themselves. The chapter then ends by examining five possible objections to the 'Divine Permission Model' and the potentialities of its adoption.

When examining the field of Qur'ānic studies in general, and from the perspective of classical Islamic literature, one finds a plethora of works which detail various aspects of the Qur'ān's historical compilation, its variant readings and its transmission.

15 For discussions of the two models adopted for the Qur'ān transmission, but more specifically the 'Divine Permission Model' see, Ṣaliḥ al-Rājḥī, *Al-Masā'il al-Kubrā Allatī Khālafa Fīhā Qurrā' al-Muta'akhirūn Ijmā' al-Mutaqaddimīn Min al-Qurrā'* (Riyadh: Dār al-Ṣumay'ī, 2021); Tarek Moqbel, 'The Emergence of the Qirā'āt : The Divine Permission Hypothesis', *Journal of Islamic Studies* 33, no. 3 (2022): 299–330; Yasin Dutton, 'Orality, Literacy and the "Seven Aḥruf" Ḥadīth', *Journal of Islamic Studies* 23, no. 1 (2012): 1–49.

In particular, with regards to the Qur'ān's transmission, many works adopt the position of the Qur'ān's dissemination being *mutawātir*, meaning that the transmission of the Qur'ān is overwhelmingly widespread and mass-transmitted.[16] A consequence of adopting this position meant that collecting the chains of transmission of specific individual verses was not the overwhelming concern of classical Muslim scholars. Despite this, there are some examples of this genre and in chapter nine, Khairil Husaini Bin Jamil provides a topography of such sources from the eighth-century up until the nineteenth-century which focus exclusively on the contents and transmission of solitary verses.

These classical studies which examine and highlight the chains of transmission of specific verses and chapters of the Qur'ān restrict themselves to the field of Qur'ānic studies. However, the centrality of the Qur'ān in the everyday lives of Muslims, meant that the transmission of its verses could also be found in a plethora of non-Qur'ānic sources, including but not limited to works of *ḥadīth*, legal manuals, Sufī epistles and theological tracts. Here, Khairil Husaini Bin Jamil draws attention to these oft-neglected 'silent transmissions' of the Qur'ān. In the field of exegesis (*tafsīr*) for example, the exegesis of a specific verse may establish an additional line of transmission for a specific verse. Even if the emphasis in this body of literature is the interpretation of that verse, the transmission of the verse is inadvertently also recorded. In a similar way, legal works may focus on the legal implications of a specific verse in various ways, yet implicitly also encapsulate the transmission of this verse, providing another chain of transmission for the verse. The most important genre

---

16 For a traditional articulation see, Muhammad Mustafa al-Azami, *The History of the Qur'ānic Text, from Revelation to Compilation: A Comparative Study with the Old and New Testaments* (London: U.K Islamic Academy, 2003). For a contemporary re-evaluation see, Shady Nasser, *The Transmission of the Variant Readings of the Qur'ān: The Problem of Tawātur and the Emergence of Shawādhdh* (Leiden: Brill, 2012).

in this regard is the *ḥadīth* literature, which provide explanations and contextualisation of numerous verses, but at the same time also provides a chain of transmission for that stated verse. The same can also be said of theological and Sufī works. These various genres may not deal with the transmission of the Qur'ān in its entirety, yet a close examination of such extraneous literature brings to light a wide plethora of transmission chains for solitary or groups of verses.

Husaini presents a comprehensive examination of the immense potential of extracting additional chains of transmission for verses in the Qur'ān, from a diverse range of non-Qur'ānic works and in particular the way they may be used in relation to questions of *tawātur*. In particular, he focuses on Sūrat al-Kawthar as a case study and pinpoints the diverse non-Qur'ānic contexts in which this short chapter of the Qur'ān occurs. Finally, this chapter also highlights the importance of Jalāl al-Dīn al-Suyūṭī's *al-Durr al-Manthūr* (The Scattered Pearls), as a means of exploring the transmission of individual verses further, since al-Suyūṭī's work explains the different passages of the Qur'ān through narrations and reports from the Prophet Muhammad, his companions, and the generation after that.[17] Husaini conducts a close comparative analysis of the identified extraneous narrations of Sūrat al-Kawthar with those that are stated in al-Suyūṭī's work.

When looking at the history of the Qur'ān's transmission, there is a question of whether to accord primacy to the Qur'ān's textuality or its orality. In chapter ten, Stephen Cúrto critically re-examines the presuppositions which inform the conceptual paradigm of the ontological category of 'Qur'ān' and from this the methodological underpinnings which inform Qur'ānic textual and historical criticism. In particular, this chapter looks at

---

17 Jalāl al-Dīn al-Suyūṭī, *Al-Durr al-Manthūr Fī al-Tafsīr al-Ma'thūr*, 8 vols (Beirut: Dār al-Fikr, 2011).

the way the Qur'ān is narrowly identified and conflated with the singularity of the Prophetic archetypical "autograph" or with the delimited category of *'muṣḥaf'*. Cúrto draws upon the works of Gary D. Martin and D.C. Parker and their approaches to text-critical theory arguing that the paradigm of what has been referred to as a static and invariable origin of a text or "Urtext," is largely untenable for the textual traditions of Antiquity and Late Antiquity and hence also for the Qur'ān as is commonly adopted and in understanding its transmission. Adopting a transdisciplinary approach and drawing upon Qur'ānic textual criticism and Biblical text-critical study Cúrto argues that the adoption of *Ausgangstext* (initial text) is more apt and provides a more coherent accounting of the dynamic modes of the Prophetic articulation, represented in both oral and textual Qur'ānic transmission. Finally, Cúrto argues for the importance of borrowing and drawing open some of the principles of the CBGM (Coherence Based Genealogical Method) in light of this conversation.

A history of the Qur'ān will remain incomplete if we only examine its history from the perspective of Sunnī Islam. In chapter eleven, Meysam Kohantorabi examines some of the most crucial aspects relating to the history of the Qur'ān in Shīʿah intellectual history and in particular, the way the variant readings of the Shīʿah Imams have been understood and interpreted. From classical sources, we know that the Shīʿah Imams adopted modes of recitations that were different from the predominant modern recitation of *Ḥafṣ 'an 'Āṣim*. The different readings attributed to the Imams can be broadly bifurcated in two ways. Firstly, differences that relate to wording, for example, the addition of certain words or phrases. An example can be seen from Q. 4:168, which conventionally reads, "God will not forgive those who have disbelieved and do evil, nor will He guide them to any path." However, the sixth Imam, Jaʿfar al-Ṣādiq, is reported to have read this as "God will not forgive those who have disbelieved and do evil *to the family of the Prophet Muhammad*, nor will He guide them to any path."[18] Or secondly, the differences that relate to the internal structure of verses, which could relate to factors such as pronunciation, morphology or syntax. This would then lead to variances in recitation.

The differences that relate to additional wording are particularly important and have been the focus of intense discussion within Shīʿah Islam. Does the attribution of additional wordings to the Imams mean that the standard Qur'ān in existence is somehow incomplete or has been the product of distortion (*taḥrīf*)? Most Shīʿah scholars vehemently opposed this and saw these additions not as recitations *per se* but rather as interpretative statements or exegesis. This would be in accord with early exegetical practice where explanations would merely be in the form of additional wordings. Hence, the additional wordings attributed to the Imams are merely their explanations of the Qur'ān and not the actual Qur'ān. On the other hand, when taking into consideration the narrations within both Sunnī and Shīʿah sources attributing a particular codex ʿAlī, and the additional words associated to the recitations of the Imams, a minority of Shīʿah scholarship did ascribe to the notion of the Qur'ān's distortion.[19] Kohantorabi looks closely at this issue. This chapter also looks at the way the recitation of the Qur'ān is tied to eschatology within Shīʿah Islam. Certain narrations attributed to the various Imams, portray the Imams as ordering their followers to adopt the widespread reading of the Qur'ān over their own variances up until the emergence of the promised Mahdi. How does one make sense of this issue, as well as other issues relating to a codex attributed to the first Imām and fourth Caliph, ʿAlī ibn Abī Ṭālib, sometimes described as the actual first collection of the

18 ʿAlī ibn Ibrahīm al-Qummī, *Tafsīr Al-Qummī*, vol. 2 (Qum: Dār al-Kitāb, 1987), 159.

19 See for example, Aḥmad al-Sayyārī, *Revelation and Falsification The Kitāb Al-Qirā'āat of Aḥmad b. Muḥammad al-Sayyārī*, ed. Etan Kohlberg and Mohammad Ali Amir-Moezzi (Leiden: Brill, 2009).

Qur'ān? Kohantorabi examines these various issues in Shī'ah intellectual history taking into consideration both classical and modern scholarship.

The vast majority of Muslims around the world do not speak, nor understand Arabic, the language of the Qur'ān. It is here that translations of the Qur'ān are pivotal to the dissemination and spread of its contents and hence any history of the Qur'ān remains incomplete without consideration of its translation. In the final chapter, Afsan Redwan conducts a broad historical survey of Qur'ān translations. From the onset, the methodological process of translating the Qur'ān in the first place is a critical question. How does one translate what is understood as the divine word of God into another vernacular? We find echoes of this question stretching all the way back to the earliest period of Islam with the early conquests which led to a multitude of non-Arabs being exposed to Islam, each with their own language systems and cultures. In fact, we can expand this question further due to the centrality of the Qur'ān in the ritual worship of prayer (*ṣalāh*). Indeed the importance of encapsulating the Qur'ān's message was such that it lead certain jurists, most notably Abū Ḥanīfa, to hold that the recital of the Qur'ān in Persian was permitted in prayer.[20] Abū Ḥanīfa's discussion on this topic and subsequent debates in the Ḥanafī School by his followers is discussed by Redwan. This important initial theoretical debate then leads to an examination of a global history of Qur'ān translation.

20 One of Abū Ḥanīfa's primarily students, Muḥammad al-Shaybānī (d.189/805) asks him for his opinion on "a man who recites in Persian during the prayer while he is able to do so in Arabic". To which, Abū Ḥanīfa replies that this person's prayer is valid, Muḥammad al-Shaybānī, *Kitāb Al-Aṣl*, vol. 1 (Beirut: Dār ibn Ḥazm, 2012), 219. See also, Omar Qureshi, 'The Shifting Ontology of the Qur'ān in Ḥanafism: Debates on Reciting the Qur'ān in Persian', *Journal of the International Qur'ānic Studies Association* 8, no. 1 (2023): 72–99.

The chapter explores the history of the very first complete translations of the Qur'ān in Islamic history into Persian, the most dominant language after Arabic in the Muslim world. Redwan goes into detail charting the mechanisms of early translations and identifies the main figures who participated in this endeavour. The chapter then moves on to South Asia, which provides an interesting case study of translation since the region and its Muslim population consists of multiple languages each requiring their own translations, from Bengali, to Tamil, to Urdu. The chapter looks at the importance of Shah Walī Ullah, who was especially concerned with the decline of the Muslim community identifying its cause to a lack of Qur'ān literacy and hence composed multiple works on the Qur'ān to make it accessible to Muslims in South Asia. The impact of colonialism in South Asia also played an important role in Qur'ān translation by now including the English language as a focus of translation. However, the history of Qur'ān translations in English trace their roots to the translation of the Qur'ān into Latin in Medieval Europe.[21] Redwan examines these earliest European translations and the motivations behind them. This includes important figures such as Robert of Ketton in the twelfth-century, who is said to have composed the first Latin translation of the Qur'ān. Despite the fact that these translations were dubious due to these translators either being outrightly hostile and polemical, or having a poor grasp of the Arabic language, they were nevertheless pivotal since they were the main avenue through which the Qur'ān, and hence Islam, was accessed in Europe. From Latin translations we have the very first English translation with the very first attributed to Alexander Ross, chaplain to Charles I. Redwan charts the process that gave way to more accurate translations by scholars such as Marracci and Sale. The chapter ends

21 See also, Bruce Lawrence, *The Koran in English: A Biography* (New Jersey: Princeton University Press, 2017).

by looking at modern English Qur'ān translations conducted by Muslims themselves by figures such as Yusuf Ali and Pickthall. The importance of large bodies such as Al-Azhar and the Saudi state is also broached upon and the impact they have had on Qur'ān's translation in the modern world.

It is hoped therefore that this current volume will contribute in some way towards the reconstruction of some of the most crucial aspects and moments in the Qur'ān's history, from an examination of early Qur'ānic manuscripts, to the study of the development of Qur'ānic orthography (*rasm*), to examinations of crucial moments in the Qur'ān's transmission, such as the collection of Abū Bakr, controversies surrounding ibn Masʿūd's codex, or through an evaluation of the precise meaning of the *aḥruf*. Further still, it is hoped that the volume offers distinctive ways of looking at the Qur'ān's history and transmission, whether that be through the theoretical exploration of the 'Qur'ān' as a category of analysis, the re-examination of extraneous non-Qur'ānic transmission, the investigation of the place and practice of the Shīʿah Imams to the Qur'ān's history or through consideration of the history of Qur'ān translation. In doing so, it is hoped that our knowledge of the Qur'ān, the central focal point of Muslims around the world, both past and present, will be further advanced.

Bibliography

Azami, Muhammad Mustafa al-. *The History of the Qur'ānic Text, from Revelation to Compilation: A Comparative Study with the Old and New Testaments*. London: U.K Islamic Academy, 2003.

Cook, Michael. 'The Stemma of the Regional Codices of the Koran'. *Graeco- Arabica* 9–10 (2004): 89–14.

Déroche, François. *La Transmission Écrite Du Coran Dans Les Débuts de l'islam. Le Codex Parisino-Petropolitanus*. Leiden: Brill, 2009.

———. *Qur'āns of the Umayyads: A First Overview*. Leiden: Brill, 2014.

———. *The One and the Many The Early History of the Qur'ān*. Translated by Malcom DeBevoise. New Haven: Yale University Press, 2021.

Dutton, Yasin. 'Orality, Literacy and the "Seven Aḥruf" Ḥadīth'. *Journal of Islamic Studies* 23, no. 1 (2012): 1–49.

———. 'Red Dots, Green Dots, Yellow Dots and Blue: Some Reflections on the Vocalisation of Early Qur'ānic Manuscripts – Part I'. *Journal of Qur'ānic Studies* 1, no. 1 (1999): 115–40.

———. 'Red Dots, Green Dots, Yellow Dots and Blue: Some Reflections on the Vocalisation of Early Qur'ānic Manuscripts – Part II'. *Journal of Qur'ānic Studies* 2, no. 1 (2000): 1–24.

Gacek, Adam. *Arabic Manuscripts A Vademecum for Readers*. Leiden: Brill, 2012.

George, Alain. 'Coloured Dots and the Question of Regional Origins in Early Qur'āns (Part I)'. *Journal of Qur'ānic Studies* 17, no. 1 (2015): 1–44.

———. 'Coloured Dots and the Question of Regional Origins in Early Qur'āns (Part II)'. *Journal of Qur'ānic Studies* 17, no. 2 (2015): 75–102.

Gutas, Dimitri. *Greek Thought, Arabic Culture: The Graeco-Arabic Translation Movement in Baghdad and Early 'Abbasaid Society (2nd-4th/5th-10th Centuries)*. New York: Routledge, 1998.

Hilali, Asma. *The Sanaa Palimpsest The Transmission of the Qur'ān in the First Centuries AH*. Oxford: Oxford University Press/ Institute of Ismaili Studies, 2017.

Lawrence, Bruce. *The Koran in English: A Biography*. New Jersey: Princeton University Press, 2017.

Marx, Michel, and Tobias Jocham. 'Radiocarbon (14C) Dating of Qur'ān Manuscripts'. In *Qur'ān Quotations Preserved on Papyrus Documents, 7th-10th Centuries, and the Problem of Carbon*

Dating Early Qur'āns, edited by A Kaplony and M Marx, 188–221. Leiden: Brill, 2019.

Melchert, Christopher. 'Ibn Mujāhid and the Establishment of Seven Qur'ānic Readings'. *Studia Islamica* 91 (2000): 5–22.

Moqbel, Tarek. 'The Emergence of the Qirā'āt: The Divine Permission Hypothesis'. *Journal of Islamic Studies* 33, no. 3 (2022): 299–330.

Nasser, Shady. *The Second Canonization of the Qur'ān (324/936) Ibn Mujāhid and the Founding of the Seven Readings*. Leiden: Brill, 2020.

———. *The Transmission of the Variant Readings of the Qur'ān: The Problem of Tawātur and the Emergence of Shawādhdh*. Leiden: Brill, 2012.

Putten, Marijn van. *Qur'ānic Arabic From Its Hijazi Origins to Its Classical Reading Traditions*. Leiden: Brill, 2022.

Qummī, ʿAlī Ibn Ibrahīm al-. *Tafsīr Al-Qummī*. Vol. 2. Qum: Dār al-Kitāb, 1987.

Qureshi, Omar. 'The Shifting Ontology of the Qur'ān in Ḥanafism: Debates on Reciting the Qur'ān in Persian'. *Journal of the International Qur'ānic Studies Association* 8, no. 1 (2023): 72–99.

Rājḥī, Ṣaliḥ al-. *Al-Masāʾil al-Kubrā Allatī Khālafa Fīhā Qurrāʾ al-Mutaʾakhirūn Ijmāʿ al-Mutaqaddimīn Min al-Qurrāʾ*. Riyadh: Dār al-Ṣumay'ī, 2021.

Sadeghi, Behnam, and Mohsen Goudarzi. 'Ṣan"ā" 1 and the Origins of the Qur'ān'. *Der Islam* 87, no. 1–2 (2012): 1–129.

Sayyārī, Aḥmad al-. *Revelation and Falsification The Kitāb Al-Qirā'āat of Aḥmad b. Muḥammad al-Sayyārī*. Edited by Etan Kohlberg and Mohammad Ali Amir-Moezzi. Leiden: Brill, 2009.

Shāfiʿī, Muhammad Ibn Idrīs al-. *Kitāb Al-Umm*. Vol. 7. Beirut: Dār al-Fikr, 1990.

Shaybānī, Muḥammad al-. *Kitāb Al-Aṣl*. Vol. 1. Beirut: Dār Ibn Ḥazm, 2012.

Sidky, Hythem. 'On the Regionality of Qur'ānic Codices'. *Journal of the International Qur'ānic Studies Association* 5, no. 1 (2020): 133–210.

Suyūṭī, Jalāl al-Dīn al-. *Al-Durr al-Manthūr Fī al-Tafsīr al-Ma'thūr*. 8 vols. Beirut: Dār al-Fikr, 2011.

———. *Al-Itqān Fi 'ulūm Al-Qur'ān*. Vol. 2. Beirut, 1987.

CHAPTER TWO

Early Qur'ānic Manuscripts: An Overview

François Déroche

The name "early manuscripts of the Qur'ān" will be applied here to a group of manuscripts that were written on parchment or papyrus and were mostly found within larger depositories where Qur'ān manuscripts that were no longer in use were kept -roughly until the nineteenth and twentieth centuries CE. Either partial or complete copies of the Qur'ān that were said to have belonged to Caliph ʿUthmān himself, or else to have been made under his direction – and thus became relics – are not necessarily included here. The chronology of these early manuscripts of the Qur'ān is not completely clear cut; they were produced roughly between the middle of the first/seventh century and the middle of the following century. They shared the fate of most of the ancient copies on parchment produced before the fourth/tenth century, sometimes beyond that date, that have been preserved in the Islamic world. They were discarded and stored rather carelessly and in a disordered manner in depositories like those of Damascus, Fusṭāṭ, Qayrawān or Ṣanʿā'. Physical deterioration, broken bindings for example, or difficulties in reading an obscure script led to this situation. In addition, the importance of orality and the availability of more recent and more precise copies did not contribute to keeping them in use. For a long time, scholarship did not take seriously -with some exceptions- these early fragments either. It is no wonder that some scholars, like Estelle

Whelan and Sheila Blair,[1] came to think that nothing remained from the earliest handwritten tradition of the Qur'ān and that John Wansbrough could put forward the hypothesis of a compilation of the text in the third/ninth century.[2]

The State of the Material

The Discovery of the Early Manuscripts

In the seventeenth century CE, a few ancient Qur'ānic manuscripts on parchment were already in Europe, none of them from the category of early copies discussed here, but the first attempt at studying them only took place at the end of the eighteenth-century CE. The results were somehow disappointing and the next effort in this field by the middle of the next century failed to get proper scholarly attention for circumstantial reasons. At the same time, collectors brought an increasing number of folios to Europe: the major collections, those of Jean-Joseph Marcel, Jean-Louis Asselin de Cherville,[3] Ulrich Seetzen, Johann Gottfried Wetzstein[4] or Edward Henry Palmer and Charles Tyrwhitt Drake, were acquired by libraries in Saint Petersburg, Paris, Gotha, Berlin and Tübingen as well as Cambridge. However, although some early manuscripts were

1 Sheila Blair, *Islamic Calligraphy* (Edinburgh: Edinburgh University Press, 2006), 108.

2 John Wansbrough, *Qur'ānic Studies: Sources and Methods of Scriptural Interpretation* (Oxford: Oxford University Press, 1977), 43–52.

3 François Burger, 'Asselin de Cherville, Agent consulaire et collectionneur de manuscrits orientaux', *Dix-Huitième Siècle* 28 (1996): 125–33; François Déroche, *La Transmission écrite du Coran dans les débuts de l'islam. Le Codex Parisino-Petropolitanus* (Leiden: Brill, 2009), 13–16.

4 François Déroche, 'The Qur'ānic Collections Acquired by Wetzstein', in *Manuscripts, Politics and Oriental Studies. Life and Collections of Johann Gottfried Wetzstein (1815-1905) in Context*, ed. Boris Liebrenz and Christoph Rauch (Leiden: Brill, 2019), 92–115.

among them, the scholarly milieu was still discussing the date of the material and its interest for science. Palaeography was from the start an obvious reason to study this material, even if the approach was mainly relying on the information gathered from literary sources.

With the publication by Gotthelf Bergsträsser and Otto Pretzl of the third volume of the second edition of the revised and enlarged *Geschichte des Qorans* of Theodor Nöldeke,[5] the situation had gradually changed, and the importance of the earliest copies for research on the Qur'ān in general came to be more widely appreciated. A systematic study of the holdings of the Bibliothèque nationale de France (the Asselin de Cherville collection from Fusṭāṭ and other manuscripts and fragments of various provenances) was undertaken between 1979 and 1983 in connection with the preparation of a new catalogue of Arabic manuscripts.[6] This made it possible to clarify the paleography of a period extending from the second half of the first/seventh century until the fourth/tenth while laying the basis for a more general approach to codicology (the historical study of manuscripts as cultural artifacts) and typology of the scripts in this field. In the interval, the Ṣanʿāʾ trove acted as a stimulus to further investigation, with the discovery of a copy with a text deviating from the vulgate, the famous palimpsest.

The new and fundamental points of reference that emerged from these advances allowed other researchers to make progress more quickly than had been anticipated. As a result, a number of papers and books, particularly on the Qur'ānic text itself, were published in rapid succession. Scholarly attention has since been concentrated largely on the oldest copies, the "early manuscripts

5 Theodor Nöldeke, Gotthelf Bergsträsser, and Otto Pretzl, *Geschichte Des Qorâns von Theodor Nöldeke*, Second Edition, vol. III (Leipzig, 1938).

6 François Déroche, *Les Manuscrits Du Coran: Aux Origines de la calligraphie coranique [Catalogue des Manuscrits arabes, 2e Partie, Manuscrits musulmans, I/1]* (Paris: Bibliothèque Nationale, 1983).

of the Qur'ān", and this in parallel with a deeper exploration of Muslim tradition regarding readings [*qirā'āt*],[7] and, more generally, of Qur'ānic sciences as a whole. In a significant evolution, the rich manuscript heritage of Islam in its early years is now incorporated globally in research on the Qur'ānic text and more generally in studies on the beginnings of Islam. A growing number of facsimiles of manuscripts[8] and the availability of digital images in libraries and collections (see Corpus Coranicum or Gallica) provide easier access to this material.

The State of the Material and the Problems it Entails

Most of the early Qur'ān manuscripts that have been preserved are fragmentary in the sense that we have only part of the original volume. However, although they were kept under conditions that were certainly not optimal, some measure of protection was assured to folios, bound sheets, even whole volumes found inside a

7 Shady Nasser, *The Transmission of the Variant Readings of the Qur'ān: The Problem of Tawātur and the Emergence of Shawādhdh* (Leiden: Brill, 2012); Marijn van Putten, 'Arabe 334a. A Vocalized Kufic Qur'ān in a Non-Canonical Hijazi Reading', *Journal of Islamic Manuscripts* 10, no. 3 (2019): 327–75.

8 François Déroche and Sergio Noja-Noseda, *Le Manuscrit Arabe 328 (a) de la Bibliothèque nationale de France [Sources de la transmission manuscrite dutTexte coranique I, Les Manuscrits de style hijâzî, 1]* (Lesa, 1998); François Déroche and Sergio Noja-Noseda, *Le Manuscrit Or. 2165 (f. 1 à 61) de la British Library [Sources de la transmission manuscrite du texte coranique, I: Les Manuscrits de style higâzî]* (Lesa, 2001); Tayyar Altıkulaç, *Al-Muṣḥaf al-Šarīf (in Arabic). Al-Muṣḥaf al-Sharīf Attributed to 'Uthmān Bin 'Affan (The Copy at the Topkapı Palace Museum)* (Istanbul, 2007); Tayyar Altıkulaç, *Hz. Osman'a Nisbet Edilen Mushaf-ı Şarif. Türk ve Islâm Eserleri Nüshası. Al-Muṣḥaf al-Šarīf al-Mansūb ilā 'Uthmān ibn 'Affān (in Arabic)*, 2 Vols. vols (Istanbul, 2007); Tayyar Altıkulaç, *Al-Muṣḥaf al-Šarīf (in Arabic). Al-Muṣḥaf al-Sharīf Attributed to 'Uthman Bin 'Affan (The Copy at al-Mashhad al-Husaynī in Cairo)*, 2 Vols. vols (Istanbul, 2009); Eléonore Cellard, *Codex Amrensis 1* (Leiden: Brill, 2018).

building; the fact that they were copied on parchment undoubtedly improved their resistance to the elements. The situation is therefore quite different from what can be observed with papyri which are mostly fragments, that is remains of the original leaves; however, various collections with Qur'ānic material contain fragments in this sense, for example, the Seymour Ricci collection at the Bibliothèque nationale de France,[9] or of certain items now at the Institute for the Study of Ancient Cultures in the University of Chicago.[10] However, in the great majority of cases it is possible to work out how the book to which a group of leaves initially belonged was made and, by sequentially ordering them, to identify a particular codex structure.

The risk that confusion may arise from the use of the same term to designate, on the one hand, the fragmentary form in which the revelations were given to Muhammad, in brief, relatively independent segments, and, on the other, the fragmentary state of certain physical manuscripts, itself the result of a more or less advanced process of decomposition, needs to be kept in mind as well.

These manuscripts do not contain the date of their production. Even if literary sources quote a colophon from a certain date,[11] nothing similar has been found so far on manuscripts of the first three centuries of Islam – leaving aside the spurious colophons by ʿUthmān or ʿAlī. If colophons existed during the ancient period, they must have disappeared. New techniques of analysis were brought to establish the chronology of these copies; paleography, in particular, has played an important role in identifying distinct sets of copies, known as *Ḥijāzī* manuscripts

---

9 Déroche, *Les Manuscrits du Coran*, 151–55.

10 Nabia Abbott, *The Rise of the North Arabic Script and Its Ḳur'ānic Development* (Chicago: University of Chicago Oriental Institute Publications, 1939), 59–68.

11 al-Dānī, *Al-Muqniʿ fī Maʿrifa Marsūm Maṣāḥif Ahl al-Amṣār*, ed. M.A Dahmān (Damascus, n.d), 88.

after the style of their script. This first attempt at classification was made more precise by various means. Codicological and orthographical analysis, supplemented by carbon-14 (C14) dating, made it possible to place the earliest of these copies in the second half of the first/seventh century, which is to say that they supply evidence very near in time to Muhammad's apostolate and close to the period when Muslim tradition maintains that the Qur'ān was first put into written form. Radiocarbon dating of nine manuscripts has given results comprised between 606CE and 798CE, four of them being dated between 606CE and 675CE.[12] The C14 results thus suggest that manuscripts with a text quite similar to the 'Uthmānic text of modern editions was already compiled at an early date. I leave aside the MS Birmingham, Cadbury Research Library, Mingana 1572a which was dated by the Oxford Lab to 568CE-645CE -and the excitement that followed.

The geographical origin of the material is similarly problematic. Most of it was found in the four large deposits already mentioned: Damascus, Fusṭāṭ, Qairawān and Ṣanʿāʾ, but this does not entail that the manuscripts found there were ever locally produced. Of course, a quantity must have been prepared in large cities like Damascus and Fusṭāṭ, but which ones? In the Fusṭāṭ collection in Paris, we do have explicit evidence of manuscripts transferred from another place (which may or not be the place of production).[13] It should also be noted that the Ṣanʿāʾ deposit is the easternmost of the four; we presently know nothing similar for the Eastern part of the Umayyad empire – with a possible exception in Mashhad. Conversely, it seems surprising that the name of Fusṭāṭ is not mentioned in the sources covering the early written transmission of the Qur'ān when the mass of

12 Michel Marx and Tobias Jocham, 'Radiocarbon (14C) Dating of Qur'ān Manuscripts', in *Qur'ān Quotations Preserved on Papyrus Documents, 7th-10th Centuries, and the Problem of Carbon Dating Early Qur'āns*, ed. A Kaplony and M. Marx (Leiden: Brill, 2019), 216.

13 Déroche, *Les Manuscrits du Coran*, 86, 91, 126.

fragmentary manuscripts found there include a few ones from the first/seventh century and leave open the possibility of a local activity of copy but also of oral transmission of the text.

Then, of course, the study of the written transmission of the Qur'ān is open to questions. It may be objected that it could only have been a secondary element by comparison with the oral one, as Muslim tradition also maintains. The surviving record makes it clear that there was a deliberate effort by the authorities, beginning in the first/seventh century, and later by private persons, to produce enormous quantities of copies of the sacred text. The Bibliothèque nationale de France keeps parts of 250 copies of the Qur'ān from the first/seventh to the fourth/tenth centuries that were found in the Mosque of ʿAmr in Fusṭāṭ, some of them containing hundreds of leaves – proof of the great expense their production entailed.[14] The collection found in Ṣanʿāʾ, according to one estimate, comprised 926 parchment copies. The very circumstances under which the Qur'ān was written down, as they are reported by Muslim tradition, make it clear that the various factions that grew up within the Muslim community following Muhammad's death attached the greatest importance to literacy and the possession of manuscript copies. Literary sources record information about various individuals who were actively transcribing the Qur'ān at an early date.[15]

Material Aspects

Writing Surfaces

Parchment is largely predominant in the material that has come down to us. The animal species used for the preparation

14 Déroche, *Les Manuscrits du Coran*.

15 Estelle Whelan, 'Evidence for the Early Codification of the Qur'ān', *Journal of the American Oriental Society* 118 (1998): 1–14.

of parchment has not been systematically identified, but a few results indicate that sheep and goat were commonly used in the Islamic world. The size of the parchment sheets varies, the larger dimensions being 50 x 43 cm.[16] One of the advantages of parchment was its sturdiness. It was possible to modify the text written on the sheet by scraping it locally in order to correct a mistake. It was also possible to wipe out the text completely and write another text over it: in that case, we can speak of palimpsest. This technique is not attested by many manuscripts and the Ṣanʿāʾ palimpsest is one of them. Papyrus was also used: there is an example of a small monobible codex, P.Hamb.Arab.68, and seven fragments with Qur'ānic content which cannot be considered as serving other purposes like amulet or quotation. Instances of tainted parchment seem to belong to a later period.

The inks used for the copy of the text itself were probably metallo-gallic, but their exact composition should be investigated. Carbon based inks do not strongly adhere to the parchment and could be washed away. Red ink seems also to have been in use from an early date, although not on the manuscripts that are supposed to be the most ancient ones.

Quires and Format

The earliest codices are vertical ones, similar to those found in the prevailing tradition in the Eastern part of the Mediterranean. They were made by sewing together various quires which were mainly quaternions or quinions, that is to say four or five bifolios folded together. The Codex Parisino-Petropolitanus, Late *Ḥijāzī* and A style manuscripts (see below) seem to favour quaternions arranged according to Gregory's rule – that is to say with sides

16 MS Raqqada, MIA R 38

of the same nature, flesh or hair, facing each other.[17] This was no longer the case later, when quinions became the rule, with sides of different nature facing each other. The preference for a kind of quire over another one may reflect local uses.

In the first/seventh century, the largest copies of the Qur'ān, like the Codex Parisino-Petropolitanus, were quarto volumes. Then, at the beginning of the next century, folio volumes like MS Ṣanʿāʾ, DaM Inv. 20-33.1 began to be produced. Whereas a sheet of parchment was folded twice in order to produce four folios in the older manuscripts, folio copies relied on sheets folded once, thus providing only two folios per sheet of parchment. This did not eliminate the production of smaller manuscripts, but some communal copies in Umayyad times were of fair size. The use of isolated folios with a stub seems to have been initially quite reduced, contrarily to what was later the case.

The coexistence of two formats of *muṣḥaf*, vertical and oblong, seems to have been the case already by the end of the first/seventh century, with a few examples in *Ḥijāzī* style.[18] The oblong format, with the manuscript's width being larger than its height, was present in manuscripts from Umayyad times.[19] It later became the rule during a good part of the second/eighth century and all of the third/ninth, before slowly receding during the fourth/tenth.

---

17 Déroche, *La Transmission écrite du Coran dans les débuts de l'islam. Le Codex Parisino-Petropolitanus*, 24; Eléonore Cellard, 'The Written Transmission of the Qur'ān during Umayyad Times: Contextualizing the Codex Amrensis 1', in *The Umayyad World*, ed. Andrew Marsham (Abingdon: Routledge, 2021), 451–52.

18 François Déroche, *Qur'āns of the Umayyads: A First Overview* (Leiden: Brill, 2014), 58–59.

19 Cellard, *Codex Amrensis 1*; MSS Istanbul, TIEM ŞE 4321 and ŞE 3591; Déroche, *Qur'āns of the Umayyads: A First Overview*, 97.

Page Setting and Ruling

All the manuscripts have been written in long lines, be they in vertical or oblong format. Only a few of them exhibit traces of ruling. In most of the cases, a frame helped the copyist to keep a measure of regularity over the folios. In a few fragments, the horizontals were traced, like in Codex Amrensis 1.[20] The tools were predominantly an iron point, rarely a lead point. Pricking seems also to have been in use.[21] In spite of the ruling, the number of lines to the page was varying throughout the earliest copies as can be seen in the Codex Parisino-Petropolitanus,[22] but a tendency towards regularity can be detected in the later production. The *scriptio continua* adapted to the conditions of the Arabic script (that is to say taking into account the connected and unconnected letters) is commonly used by the copyists during the period under consideration. As a consequence, words including unconnected letters can be cut at the end of a line.

In the earliest copies, there are almost no margins as can be seen by the traces of the natural edges of the parchment sheets visible on the side of some folios. Over the period, the margins become more important.

Scripts

The earliest layers of manuscript production cover a period which roughly coincides with the Umayyad period. Before offering a very short description of the main features of the scripts, which are the guiding line for the identification of these manuscripts since they are explained elsewhere in more detail, I shall first

20 Cellard, *Codex Amrensis 1*, 4.

21 Déroche, *Les Manuscrits Du Coran*, 20; Cellard, *Codex Amrensis 1*, 4.

22 Lines 21-28 see, Déroche, *La Transmission Écrite Du Coran Dans Les Débuts de l'islam. Le Codex Parisino-Petropolitanus*, 27.

make a few remarks on terminology. Two names are widely used for the material from the period, but although they seem to cover the situation, they are very different in their origin and their use. *Ḥijāzī* is a word coined by Michele Amari by the middle of the nineteenth century (he actually spoke of écriture du Ḥijāz, i.e., script of Ḥijāz) on the basis of ibn al-Nadīm's description of the earliest Arabic scripts in his *Fihrist*:

> The first of the Arab scripts was the script of Makkah, the next of al-Madīnah, then of al-Baṣrah, and then of al-Kūfah. For the alifs of the scripts of Makkah and al-Madīnah there is a turning of the hand to the right and lengthening of the strokes, one form having a slight slant.[23]

Kūfī or Kufic is borrowed from Medieval Arabic sources and refers to the script(s) of Kufah – see above. It has been applied to various kinds of bold scripts from the first centuries. In order to take into account more precisely the diversity of these scripts, a typology of the Qur'ānic scripts of the first four centuries of Islam has been devised on the basis of the collection in the Bibliothèque nationale de France.[24] It endorses the definition of *Ḥijāzī*, but rejects the *Kūfī* denomination.[25] The problems faced by the use of this traditional name are illustrated in a paper by M. Marx and T. Jocham.[26] Applying it on top of the typology and defining the 22 types which are not *Ḥijāzī* as *Kūfī*, they write that "manuscripts like Ma VI 165 (Tübingen) and We. II 1913 (Berlin) … are

23 Ibn al-Nadīm, *The Fihrist of al-Nadîm, A Tenth-Century Survey of Muslim Culture*, trans. B Dodge, vol. 1 (New York/London: Columbia University Press, 1970), 10.

24 Déroche, *Les Manuscrits du Coran*; François Déroche, *The Abbasid Tradition, Qur'āns of the 8th to the 10th Centuries [The Nasser D. Khalili Collection of Islamic Art]*, vol. 1 (London, 1992).

25 Déroche, *Les Manuscrits du Coran*, 14; Déroche, *The Abbasid Tradition, Qur'āns of the 8th to the 10th Centuries*, 1:34.

26 Marx and Jocham, 'Radiocarbon (14C) Dating of Qur'ān Manuscripts'.

to be classified as a script known as Kufic B" or that the present writer "classifies the writing of Arabe 331 as Kufic B Ia" – which is not the case.[27] In the pages devoted to the description of the various types, the word *Kūfī* is found only twice, one about Group D,[28] the other about NS with reference to the same Group D.[29] As a result of this confusion, Marx and Jocham find themselves in a chronological quagmire when they write about the script of Paris, BnF Arabe 331 that "the C14 dating questions the fragments' classification as Kufic", a classification which is of their making.[30] The typology includes groupings which, like *B*, cross the boundary between *Ḥijāzī* and so-called *Kūfī* in order to reflect closely the evolution of the script and to escape this binary stalemate.

Ḥijāzī

The oldest Qur'ānic texts are written in *Ḥijāzī*. In his study of the early Qur'ān manuscripts and fragments in the Paris collection, Amari was able to identify those of the fragments which offered the various features appearing in ibn al-Nadīm's statement; unfortunately, his work remained largely ignored and research on these manuscripts did not advance significantly until Nabia Abbott's contribution to the subject.[31]

The name of the script (*Ḥijāzī*) does not mean that these manuscripts were transcribed in the Ḥijāz. The bulk of the material known to this day comes from the three repositories of old Qur'ān codices previously mentioned (Damascus, Fusṭāṭ and Ṣanʿāʾ), which cannot either be taken as a conclusive argument as to their origin which remains for the moment uncertain.

---

27 Marx and Jocham, 193, 206. Underlining mine.

28 Déroche, *Les Manuscrits du Coran*, 41.

29 Déroche, 45.

30 Marx and Jocham, 'Radiocarbon (14C) Dating of Qur'ān Manuscripts', 211.

31 Abbott, *The Rise of the North Arabic Script and Its Ḳur'ānic Development*.

On the other hand, the fact that the collection in Qayrawān does not contain such material only has the value of an argument *a silentio*. A preliminary survey shows that the *Ḥijāzī* script varies widely as if the peculiarities of the individual hands were of little concern to the scribes, the patrons or the readers. This diversity might be ascribed to regional habits, but such an explanation does not seem satisfactory in view of the fact that in manuscripts written in teamwork, the hands of the various copyists are so different from one another that they can be recognized at first glance (e.g., MSS Paris, BNF arabe 328 a, f. 28 a and b, or Ṣanʿāʾ, DaM, Inv.Nr. 01-21.1). A common standard concerning the script had probably not yet developed and it would thus be safer to speak of *Ḥijāzī* style, rather than *Ḥijāzī* script.

The dating of this material relies mainly on palaeographic arguments: slant and shape of the *alif*, elongation of the shafts, but also the similarities with the script of the earliest papyri as pointed out by Amari and later by Adolf Grohmann.[32] The script is slender and regularly spread out on the page. The spaces are always identical between the segments, regardless of their being part of a word or not. Words can be divided at the end of a line. Vowels are not recorded and diacritical dots are used in varying degrees by the copyists; when they happened to work jointly in two or three to copy the text, they did not agree on common rules but dotted the letters according to their own habits.[33] The defective writing of the long /a/ (see below) adds weight to the early dating of these manuscripts and fragments, some of which count the *basmala* as a verse.[34] As no direct evidence,

32 Adolf Grohmann, 'The Problem of Dating Early Qur'āns', *Der Islam* 33 (1958): 221–22.

33 Déroche, *La Transmission écrite du Coran dans les débuts de l'islam. Le Codex Parisino-Petropolitanus*, 44.

34 See MS Paris, BNF arabe 328 a: Déroche, 79. Also, MS London, BL Or. 2165: Déroche and Noja-Noseda, *Le Manuscrit Or. 2165 (f. 1 à 61) de la British Library*.

for instance a colophon, has been found so far, the dating to the second half of the first/seventh century based on these criteria can therefore only be tentative, although already three C14 datings between 606 and 665 CE of the parchment of *Ḥijāzī* or *Ḥijāzī*-related fragments provide an indication of this style's antiquity.[35] Future research might throw more light on the chronology of these codices.

The Sequels of Ḥijāzī
Late Ḥijāzī

Some of the features of *Ḥijāzī* remained present in later styles which developed in Umayyad times in an environment of increasing sophistication of the copies of the Qur'ān. Next to the *O I* and *O II* scripts which correspond probably to a production under the patronage of the Umayyad elite (see below), other scripts, like the one exemplified by the Codex Amrensis 1 which Eléonore Cellard suggested to call Late *Ḥijāzī*,[36] or *B Ia* (see below) show that some circles wanted to retain some of the hallmarks of the earliest manuscripts, but with more constant or stable shapes, a possible result of an increasingly professionalization of the copyists.

The Late *Ḥijāzī* script is mainly characterized by long strokes, such as *alif* and *lām*, as well as large, curved tails (final/isolated *nūn*, *alif maqsūra* or final/isolated *qāf*). Except for the stroke of the emphatic letter *ṭā'*, systematically bent to the right, the degree of bending of the shafts can vary among the manuscripts, and also within one manuscript. In isolated position, the lower return of *lām* is set on the base line. The final *ṭā'* has a more or less accentuated appendage at the bottom of the shaft. Another feature

35 Marx and Jocham, 'Radiocarbon (14C) Dating of Qur'ān Manuscripts', 201, 216.

36 Cellard, *Codex Amrensis 1*, 7.

of this script are the optional shapes for the *jīm* (and associated letters) and *ʿayn* in isolated and/or final position.

B Ia and B Ib

Another script which keeps some relationship with *Ḥijāzī* is *B I* -with its two variants, *a*, then *b*. *B Ia* maintains the bending of the shafts, but in a more subdued way than in the *Ḥijāzī* style. As is commonly the case in the latter, the strokes are usually thin.[37] The letters like initial and medial *hā'* and *mīm* are set on the base line, slightly protruding below. The shape of the final *nūn* seems to vary slightly, from a somewhat rounded to a more angular one. MSS Berlin, SB We. II 1913, Leiden, UB Cod. or.14.545b and Tübingen, UB Ma VI 165 are examples of *B Ia*. The results of C14 analyses (respectively 662-765 CE, 652-763 CE and 649-675 CE)[38] seem to support an early date for the diffusion of *B Ia* and I would suggest the first half of the second/eighth century – the dating of the Tübingen manuscript to the third quarter of the first/seventh century seems too early with regard to other elements like orthography and I would prefer a date towards 700.

B Ib seems to reflect an evolution towards verticality for the shafts of letters like *alif* or *lām*. The shapes of the letters remain basically similar to those of *B Ia*, with the exception of *nūn* in final position (and of the letters with a similar ending like *sīn* or *ṣād*). The production of *B Ib* manuscripts could overlap with Late *Ḥijāzī*, *B Ia*, *A* and *O I* and might also have extended later into the second/eighth century. MSS Leiden, UB Cod. or.14.545a, Saint Petersburg, OI E 20 and Stuttgart, Sig. isl.18 are dated

37 Déroche, *Les Manuscrits du Coran*, 37–38.

38 Marx and Jocham, 'Radiocarbon (14C) Dating of Qur'ān Manuscripts', 216.

respectively 652-763 CE, 775-995 CE and 690-877 CE.[39] Manuscripts in *B Ia* and *B Ib* scripts were discovered in Fusṭāṭ,[40] Damascus and further East in Mashhad[41] or Katta Langar.[42] This does not mean that they were transcribed in these same places, but it may be indicative of a large diffusion.

New Orientations
A

Among the scripts which can be dated to the period under consideration, one notes developments which contrast with the scripts described above which can be palaeographically related directly to the *Ḥijāzī* style. A first one, already mentioned, is *A*. It shows a change in the conception of the script, not only in the evolution towards verticality, but also in the general aesthetics and more precisely in the relationship between the thickness of the strokes and the height of the line module. Whereas the scripts described previously tend to keep a slender appearance, *A* is stouter but maintains at the same time a more spacious distribution of the text on the page.

O I and O II

The two Umayyad scripts, *O I* and *O II*, are of particular interest as they show a radical change in the aesthetics. In fact, they herald the development of calligraphy and are the forerunners

39 Marx and Jocham, 216; Efim Rezvan, 'Yet Another "'Uthmānic Qur'ān" on the History of Manuscript E 20 from the St. Petersburg Branch of the Institute of Oriental Studies', *Manuscripta Orientalia* 6, no. 1 (2000): 49–68.
40 Déroche, *Les Manuscrits du Coran*, 67–69.
41 Morteza Karimi Nia, *Codex Mashhad. An Introduction to its History and Contents* (Qom: The Alulbayt Islamic Heritage Institute, 1445/2023).
42 François Déroche, 'Note sur les fragments coraniques anciens de Katta Langar (Ouzbékistan)', *Cahiers d'Asie Centrale* 7 (1999): 65–73.

of the bold scripts that will blossom during the early Abbasid period. Both cases indicate that the copyists were trained in order to produce copies in scripts that were looking alike.

O I retains a link with the *Ḥijāzī* style.[43] On some copies like Saint Petersburg, NLR, Marcel 13 or Istanbul, TIEM ŞE 321, the *alif* is still slightly bent to the right, but the stroke is bolder and very regular. Some letters exhibit the same tendencies and the final *mīm* is usually written without any tail. The size of the lines is quite homogeneous, despite the dimensions of the various manuscripts which exhibit *O I* style – from octavo to quarto – as if the script had been conceived for a specific module of line. It seems possible to distinguish two stages in the development of *O I*. Copies like MSS Istanbul, TIEM ŞE 4321 and ŞE 3591, both in oblong format, seem still very close to *Ḥijāzī* style, with the shafts leaning to the right, although the script is clearly more slender than the script of MS London, BL Or. 2165. The *Ḥijāzī* style's influence is less definite in Marcel 13 or Istanbul, TIEM ŞE 321, both in vertical format. The first stage could be called *O Ia* and the second *O Ib*. On various copies, the *basmala* stands alone on the first line of the sura.[44] Copyists seem to have made experiments in the use of coloured inks. Fragments in *O I* style were found mainly in the Damascus and Fusṭāṭ deposits.

Much more impressive is *O II* which is associated with folio volumes with twenty lines to the page, like MSS Dublin, CBL Is 1404, Ṣanʿāʾ, DaM 20-33.1 and 01-29.2, or Cairo, DaK Maṣāḥif 387.[45] The script is bold, and its thickness could be associated with a change of writing tool. The shafts are now vertical – even that of the *ṭāʾ*. Inv. 20-33.1 has been C14 dated to 657-690 CE, but it has been suggested that the manuscript was more

43 Déroche, *Qur'āns of the Umayyads: A First Overview*, 79–80.

44 Déroche, 102–4.

45 Déroche, 107–21.

consonant with al-Walid b. ʿAbd al-Malik's reign.[46] MS Qayrawan, MIA R 38, another folio manuscript with 20 lines to the page which can be related to the series to which MS Inv. 20-33.1 belongs, has also been dated to the same period (648-691 CE),[47] but its script is slightly different.

Bindings

No binding of a Qur'ān manuscript of the period seems to have come down to us, with the possible exception of MS Istanbul, TIEM ŞE 80. Its "binding-cum-case" could be the earliest example of its kind. It has wooden boards covered with decorated leather and still has fragments of the leather protective wall on the three outer sides.[48] The fastenings which kept the book tightly closed have been preserved. More expensive bindings were probably known: there is a reference in one of our sources to a silver binding.

State of the Text

Orthography

The opposition between the *scriptio defectiva* (meaning roughly the sparing use of *alif* to denote the long /*a*/) and the *scriptio plena* (where the long /*a*/ is more consistently indicated) has been used as an indicator of the state of development of the orthography and the chronology of the copies, although it should always

46 Hans-Caspar von Bothmer, 'Architekturbilder Im Koran. Eine Prachthandschrift Der Umayyadenzeit Aus Dem Yemen', *Pantheon* 45 (1987): 4–20.
47 Déroche, *Qur'āns of the Umayyads: A First Overview*, 125.
48 Déroche, 132; T. Altıkulaç et al ed, 1400. *yılında Kur'an-ı Kerim.* no. 4 (Istanbul: Antik A.Ş. Kültür Yayınları. 2010), 148-9.

be used with care.[49] It has been argued that the copyists were responsible for the introduction of an increasing number of elements, mainly *alif*, that were aiming at giving more precision to the written text by eliminating ambiguities of the *rasm*.

The study of the Codex Parisino-Petropolitanus which was transcribed by five copyists working together led to a comparative study of the way in which each copyist was writing each of five words that occur sufficiently frequently to make an assessment of the variations.[50] The analysis of the forms taken by these five words alone has shown that the solutions adopted vary according to the copyists of the manuscript. Indeed, by considering the different contributions individually, it is possible to identify the general orientations of each of them, it being understood that the disparities in terms of textual volume between the five contributors introduce distortions. The relative homogeneity observed in each case invites us to assume that these were options taken by the copyists and not variations of a possible original that were carefully maintained.

It was also possible to conclude that the five copyists had obviously not tried to define a common position that could have been maintained from the beginning to the end of the Qur'ānic text. The contribution of some of them contains inconsistencies that betray the individual - and undoubtedly autonomous - character of their interventions. In view of this evidence, the present writer suggested that the written transmission was characterized in the first decades of Islam by a process of improvement of the orthography which was not homogeneous: within the same manuscript, the same word could be written in *scriptio plena* thanks to the addition of an *alif* for instance, while it was

49 Déroche, *La Transmission écrite du Coran dans les débuts de l'islam. Le Codex Parisino-Petropolitanus*, 137.

50 Déroche, *La Transmission écrite du Coran dans les débuts de l'islam. Le Codex Parisino-Petropolitanus*, 54–59.

still in *scriptio defectiva* a few lines later.[51] A comparison between the manuscripts also supports the hypothesis that their orthography was not upgraded at the same pace and might reflect various circumstances. We know for instance that some authorities were opposed to the change of orthography of the *muṣḥaf*.[52]

The improvement of orthography is not limited to the addition of *alif* in specific places. In some cases, letters found in the old spelling of some words were suppressed or replaced. The plural of the word *āya*, either alone or with the possessive suffixes, shows particular variations when it is preceded by the preposition *bi-*. In *bi-āyati-nā*, for instance, the copyists used a "four denticles" orthography, the first two denticles being *yā*ʾ-s, the second of which denoting the long vowel later indicated by an *alif*. The dominant spelling of *shay*ʾ involves an *alif* between the *shīn* and *yā*ʾ– except when the word is in the indeterminate direct case (*shay*ʾ*an*). The spelling that has become established and that the Cairo edition features seems to be a later feature. *Dhū* is written with an *alif* after the *wāw* which is difficult to explain.

The comparison of the Codex Parisino-Petropolitanus with the Cairo edition allows us to see that the discrepancies are mainly a defective notation of /ā/. While the long vowels /ū/ and /ī/ are on the whole regularly indicated in the *rasm* respectively by the *wāw* and by a denticule which, despite the absence of diacritical marks, can be presumed to be a *yā*ʾ, the notation of /ā/ is characterised by a strong irregularity in the use of the *alif* to mark this vowel. It is thus extremely frequent to find the active participle of form I, *fāʿil*, transcribed without the *alif* after the

---

51 Déroche, 54–59. Also about other manuscripts see, Déroche, *Qur'āns of the Umayyads: A First Overview*, 47.

52 Abdelouahed Jahdani, 'Du Fiqh à la codicologie. Quelques opinions de Mālik (m. 179/796) sur le Coran-Codex', in *Mélanges de l'Université Saint-Joseph [Actes de La Conférence Internationale sur les manuscrits du Coran]*, 56 (Bologna, 2006), 273.

first radical. Common feminine plural forms are also affected by the omission of this *mater lectionis*.[53] This could be traced to the use attested in pre-Islamic spelling.[54] Actually, a hypothesis posits that a reform in the use of *matres lectionis* occurred in Medina in the decades that followed Muhammad's death.

The word *Qur'ān* has two forms depending on whether it is indeterminate in the direct case or not. In the first case, it is written *Qur'ānan*; in the others, we find a form with an *alif* between *rā'* and *nūn*. What does this *alif* note? In view of the modern form and the propensity of the copyists not to note the /ā/, it could be understood as the support of a *hamza*; but it could also be seen as the notation of the long vowel by pointing to a similar alternation in relation to *ʿadh(ā)b* found in the Codex Parisino-Petropolitanus. The study of the manuscript discarded the possibility of an exemplar irregularly employing the *scriptio plena* since the alternation of hands associated with different uses of *scriptio plena* would have implied a complex organization to follow faithfully these irregularities and suggested that they were individually upgrading the orthography.[55]

In a paper aiming at demonstrating that the early copies derive from a written model, Marijn van Putten shows that various orthographic peculiarities can only be explained by a dependence on a written original. He adds:

> Even if we assume … that scribes were essentially "upgrading" the orthography of the exemplar from which they were copying, we cannot assume that, whenever

53 Déroche, *La Transmission écrite du Coran dans les débuts de l'islam. Le Codex Parisino-Petropolitanus*, 62.

54 Christian Robin, 'La Réforme de l'écriture à l'époque du Califat Médinois', *Mélanges de l'Université Saint-Joseph* 59 (2006): 319–64.

55 Déroche, *La Transmission écrite du Coran dans les débuts de l'islam. Le Codex Parisino-Petropolitanus*, 75.

> early manuscripts are in disagreement with each other, the spelling without ʾalif is the older one.[56]

Although in some cases it is possible to distinguish a pattern going from the early manuscripts to the Cairo edition,

> word-internal ʾalifs that do not obviously denote ā are not controlled for in the scribal tradition that produced these early Qur'ānic manuscripts. However, scholars are in general agreement that the spelling with the ʾalif in miʾah and shayʾ is the more archaic spelling, while one without is innovative.[57]

The use of diacritics is attested in the earliest manuscripts and evolves over the period. They are infrequent in the former and they do not seem to answer specific purposes like helping to identify an ambiguous word. There is currently no study of the development of their use over the period under consideration. The distinction between *fāʾ* and *qāf* is not yet unanimous and the two letters are identified in various ways. *Qāf* is usually marked by two dots/strokes above the letter, but also by a single dot. In the second case, *fāʾ* may be recognisable either by a dot below or without any dot at all.[58] In MS Ṣanʿāʾ, DaM Inv. 20-33.1, *qāf* is distinguished from *fāʾ* by a stroke below the letter, the latter being marked by a stroke above.[59] In the Codex Amrensis 1, the *lām-alif* is marked sometimes with either one or two strokes in the lower part of the letter.[60] The short vowels are not indicated at all

56 Marijn van Putten, '"The Grace of God" as Evidence for a Written Uthmanic Archetype: The Importance of Shared Orthographic Idiosyncrasies', *Bulletin of the School of Oriental and African Studies* 82, no. 2 (2019): 283.

57 van Putten, 284.

58 Déroche, *Les Manuscrits Du Coran*, 21; Cellard, *Codex Amrensis 1*, 9.

59 Déroche, *Qur'āns of the Umayyads: A First Overview*, 113.

60 Cellard, *Codex Amrensis 1*, 10.

on the oldest copies. The system using red dots begins to be used in *O Ib* and *O II* copies.

Verse and Sura Divisions, Illuminations

Clusters of dashes in triangular shape or in columns are used in a first moment in *Ḥijāzī* manuscripts to separate the verses. There seems to have been a tendency to opt for a column of parallel strokes, set at an angle, in later manuscripts. Groups of five or ten are only marked off on later manuscripts, but many cases of addition of these signs to earlier copies of the Qur'ān are found.

Contrary to what has been stated, the graphic identification of verse endings is thus a distinctive feature of the oldest manuscripts of the Qur'ān. The Codex Parisino-Petropolitanus is far from being a unique case: in both the MS London, BL Or. 2165 and a manuscript from Ṣanʿāʾ (MS DaM 01-25.1), for example, verses are clearly separated. What was the origin of this practice? In the Jewish manuscript tradition, in the second or first century BCE, isolated instances of the use of a dicolon -one dot superimposed on another [:] -to separate verses is found in an Aramaic manuscript from the Dead Sea, whereas a blank space was used for the same purpose in copies of Greek translations. After a long period in which scribal practice is obscure, verse endings began once more to be precisely indicated in manuscripts of the third/ninth to fifth/eleventh centuries. In the great uncial codices of the Christian Bible in Greek, for example the Codex Sinaiticus, which dates from the middle of the fourth century CE, the dicolon is sometimes employed along with other symbols in order to separate verses from one another. A tradition therefore existed in this connection that might have been known to the first Qur'ān copyists.

In the Qur'ān tradition, the fragmented character of the revelations themselves no doubt gave rise in part to the habit of specifying verse limits, which took root when the revelations first were put in writing -records that may have been more akin to the ones that Richard Bell had in mind than what Keith Small calls "authoritative text-forms".[61] The importance of rhyme in the Qur'ān text probably reinforced this tendency. Exactly when such signs, inspired quite obviously by the customary practice of other manuscript traditions, were introduced remains an open question. From the earliest manuscripts, we know that meticulous care was taken to indicate verse endings, though the verses themselves remained unnumbered; later copies, mainly from the third/ninth century, ceased to indicate verses endings, while yet still marking off verses in groups of five or ten. After the third/ninth century, noting where each verse ended became the rule. Traditional accounts of the writing down of the Qur'ān do not tell us when these signs were inserted into the text. References in legal literature to verse separations first appeared in the second/eighth century, but they only concern the markers for five and ten verses which do not seem to have been originally singled out. The groups of ten are indicated in manuscript Saint Petersburg, NLR, Marcel 13 by gilded *abjad* letters, perhaps the oldest instance of this practice.

In the classical Qur'ān sciences, this aspect constituted a separate topic, and different traditions (Damascus, Kufa, Basra, Medina and Mekka), were distinguished from one another by their manner of dividing up the *rasm*.[62] The ancient manuscripts as a whole, it should be emphasized, do not exactly correspond to any particular tradition. Even when a tendency to follow a specific tradition can be discerned, there is no exact coincidence as will be the case later.

---

61 Keith Small, *Textual Criticism and Qur'ânic Manuscripts* (Lanham: Lexington Books, 2011), 152–53.

62 Anton Spitaler, 'Die Verszählung des Koran nach islamischer Überlieferung', in *Sitzungsberichte Der Bayerischen Akademie Der Wissenschaften, Phil.-Historische Abteilung. Jahrgang*, vol. 11 (Munich, 1935).

Between the suras, a blank space is left in copies like MSS London, BL Or. 2165 or Paris, BnF Arabe 328 a, but some of the fragments suggest that crude decorations in ink were already allowed (if they do not belong to a second stage of the *Ḥijāzī*-codices). The sura titles found on these manuscripts are often in red ink and are a later addition. Soon ornaments were inserted, ranging from simple designs to sophisticated illuminations. In a *B Ia* copy like MS Tübingen, Ma VI 165, some of them are inspired by vegetal components drawn in ink. In *O Ib* manuscripts like MS Saint Petersburg, NLR Marcel 13, illuminations are part of the initial project. They rely on a complex repertory involving architecture, vegetal shapes, geometry as well as specific Umayyad ornaments and use gold, red, blue and green. The sura titles written in red in the space between the illumination and the first line of the next sura were added later.[63] In *O II* manuscripts, there is evidence of more sophisticated illuminations at the beginning and/or end of the manuscript. In MS Ṣanʿāʾ, DaM Inv. 20-33.1 for instance, the sequence of full-page illuminations followed by framed pages witnesses the complexity of decorative programs for copies on the Qur'ān in Umayyad times. In this manuscript as well as in MS Qayrawan, MIA R 38, the illuminations between the suras do not contain a title (those in the Ṣanʿāʾ copy are an addition). MSS R 38 and Ṣanʿāʾ, DaM Inv. 01-29.2 suggest that frames were becoming a common feature at that time in the most luxurious copies of the Qur'ān.[64]

There are a few instances of division of the text into seven parts, with the indication within the written area itself –in MS London, BL Or. 2165 in green ink – instead of being in the margin as will be the case later; they are also necessarily additions, but the shortness of these marks makes it impossible to assess how much time elapsed after the copy of the Qur'ānic text itself.

63 Déroche, *Qur'āns of the Umayyads: A First Overview*, 83.

64 Déroche, 120–21.

Text

The text found on most of the manuscripts from the period under consideration seems to be basically 'Uthmanic – the Ṣanʿā' palimpsest being an exception. The Codex Parisino-Petropolitanus, for instance, agrees very largely with the ʿUthmānic recension.[65] In a few cases, however, one finds signs of later editorial intervention, probably spread out over time and generally involving passages where what had been written originally was scratched out and sometimes replaced by new text.[66] Some of these corrections may have been prompted by the distinctive orthographical practice that characterized the earliest stages of manuscript transmission or, in a certain number of very specific cases, by variants that are similar to some of those that subsequently were considered as canonical by the tradition. In the manuscript, a dozen variants not registered by the tradition survived. We may provisionally assume that they were remnants of a now forgotten version that flourished during an ancient phase of the manuscript (and possibly also oral) transmission of the 'Uthmānic recension.[67]

These variants raise two further questions: when did the attempt to categorize them in relation to other variants take place, and what criteria were applied? Included among the canonical variants, tradition tells us, are ones that occur in the *maṣāḥif al-amṣār*, the copies sent by Caliph 'Uthmān to the great cities of his empire, which differ from one another in respect of the readings *qāla* and *qul*. This is what one finds in Q. 21:4, 21:112, and 23:114, where the manuscripts associated with one tradition have *qāf* + *alif* + *lām* (*qāla*), whereas those associated with another tradition have *qāf* + *lām* (*qul*). Now, if the copyists of

65 Déroche, *La Transmission écrite du Coran dans les débuts de l'islam. Le Codex Parisino-Petropolitanus*, 162.

66 Déroche, 105, 144.

67 Déroche, 107, 144.

the Codex Parisino-Petropolitanus, like others active during this period, are scarcely familiar with this difference and write *qāf* + *lām* for both the past *qāla* ("he said") and the imperative *qul* ("say!"), one may wonder whether the lists that were drawn up to catalogue the variants of the *rasm* have their origin in events that unfolded around the middle of the first/seventh century, under the reign of ʿUthmān, or whether they were not instead part of an initiative that was undertaken only when the graphic distinction between the two forms had been definitively established. If the latter, the flexibility that characterizes the Codex Parisino-Petropolitanus, with regard both to the additional variants that it originally contained and the orthographic changes that were entered subsequently, suggests that corrections to the consonantal skeleton of the ʿUthmānic text may have continued to be made as late as the end of the first/seventh century, and perhaps even the early second/eighth century. These modifications were not unanimously approved. In the late second/eighth century, the Medinan jurist Mālik b. Anas expressed his dismay at the modernization of Qur'ān spelling – a further proof, if any more were needed, of the controversies to which the written transmission of the text lastingly gave rise to.[68]

The manuscript probably can be dated to the third quarter of the first/seventh century on the basis of its archaic orthography and its script; with respect to the latter, the phenomenon of several or more different hands working on a single codex gradually disappeared as scribal practice became more sophisticated. The copy, transmitting the ʿUthmānic version, exhibits a certain number of interesting variations. Some are synchronic and show that different attitudes toward orthography and so forth coexisted within the same *muṣḥaf*. Others are diachronic; although the points at issue may seem to us minor,

---

68 Jahdani, 'Du Fiqh à la codicologie. Quelques opinions de Mālik (m. 179/796) sur le Coran-Codex', 273.

the assiduousness with which certain variants were erased and corrected by later readers indicate that they had ceased to be acceptable at a time when other Qur'ān manuscripts displaying a more developed system of notation had come into circulation or a doctrinal corpus had emerged that set stricter limits on permissible transmission.

Two slightly later manuscripts provide us with reason to believe that the 'Uthmānic canon had not yet been completely fixed in the second/eighth century and that copyists and their sponsors were still allowed a certain freedom of opinion, preferring one formulation of the Qur'ānic text rather than another without fear of official censure. The first of these manuscripts was discovered in Fusṭāṭ. Its eighty-four leaves are dispersed among MSS Paris, BnF Arabe 331 (fifty-six leaves), St. Petersburg, NLR Marcel 3 (twenty-six leaves), Leiden, UL Or. 14.545b/c (one leaf), and Chicago, Oriental Institute 1 [= A 6959] (one leaf). This is a copy in large folio format whose dimensions (41 x 35 centimeters [16 x 13.75 inches]) are comparable to those of the de luxe copy found at Ṣan'ā' (44 x 46.5 centimeters [17.25 x 18.25 inches]), which fits twenty lines to the page, as against nineteen in the one we are concerned with here. The writing in the Fusṭāṭ manuscript places it among those of group *BI a* in the present writer's classification, of which we possess many specimens – proof of its success. The orthography is more developed than in the Parisino-Petropolitanus, but signs for noting short vowels are still lacking. Palaeographic and codicological examination justifies us in dating it to the first half of the second/eighth century; C14 analysis of the parchment yields an interval more than twice as great, extending from 652 to 763, with a 2σ confidence level of 95.4%.[69]

69 Marx and Jocham, 'Radiocarbon (14C) Dating of Qur'ān Manuscripts', 203, 216.

The manuscript, which presents a text conforming in almost every detail to the vulgate, would not be of interest were it not for a word missing from verse Q. 2:137. Here one reads:

fa-in amanū bi-mā amantum bi-hi,

whereas the canonical text is:

fa-in amanū bi-mithli mā amantum bi-hi
[If they believe as you do....].

If the copyist had omitted to copy *bi-mithli* (an uninterrupted sequence of letters in the canonical text), and had inadvertently skipped from *amanū* to *mā*, we would find:

fa-in amanū mā amantum bi-hi,

which would be grammatically incorrect; yet the reading of the manuscript, *bi-mā*, is perfectly idiomatic. What does this textual divergence signify? It could not be the result of inattention; nor is it likely to be due to the copyist's own initiative, for this formulation is attested in the specialized literature and attributed to ibn Masʿūd. Along with ibn ʿAbbās, ibn Masʿūd felt that the use of the term *mithl* could not be countenanced in this context, because God has no equal. In the early second/eighth century, then, a time when the authorities sought to prohibit the production and distribution of copies containing discrepant recensions, it was still nonetheless possible to incorporate a reading from another version in an otherwise canonical copy.

A similar situation is found in another manuscript known as a "Qur'ān of ʿUthmān", the largest part of which (eighty-one leaves) is held by the Institute of Oriental Studies in St. Petersburg (MS E 20); the remainder, sixteen leaves, has long been conserved in Uzbekistan, twelve of them in an isolated sanctuary in Katta Langar, the rest in collections in Tashkent and Bukhara. Efim Rezvan has made a close study of the manuscript and dated it to the late second/eighth century or the early third/ninth on the basis of a C14 analysis of the parchment.[70] The type of writing and the vertical format are more in keeping with the style of manuscript production current in the first half of the second/eighth century.

The manuscript was originally bound in two volumes and was transcribed by two copyists, the number of lines per page varying from twenty-four to thirty-one lines, as is the case of the Codex Parisino-Petropolitanus. The text is everywhere identical with the ʿUthmānic vulgate, except for four variants identified by Rezvan that tradition associates with ibn Masʿūd:

1. Q. 4:34 (fol. 4r): *al-maḏjaʾ*;
2. Q. 26:42 (fol. 32v): omitting *idhā*;
3. Q. 33:68 (fol. 47r): *kathiran*;
4. Q. 48:15 (fol. 65v): *kalima*.

An editor later corrected these places, so that the text would completely agree with the ʿUthmānic vulgate, while at the same time making the spelling uniform throughout the whole of the copy.

A possibly related case is found on the only papyrus codex with a Qur'ān text we know today, P.Hamb.Arab.68 which only contains s. 2. Here, four verses are modified by an omission which does not deeply affect them as far as the correctness of the sentence is concerned. However, one of these omissions is quite conspicuous since the part of Q 2:219 related to the prohibition

---

70 Efim Rezvan, 'The Qur'ān and Its World: VI. Emergence of the Canon: The Struggle for Uniformity,' *Manuscripta Orientalia* 4, no. 2 (1998): 13–51; Rezvan, 'Yet Another "ʿUthmānic Qur'ān" on the History of Manuscript E 20 from the St. Petersburg Branch of the Institute of Oriental Studies'.

of wine has been suppressed. It is not clear whether they represent a copyist's mistake, the dependence on a model also without this part or a choice by the copyist.[71]

Like the Codex Parisino-Petropolitanus, but in a different manner, these three copies allow us to appreciate the malleability of the Qur'ānic text in the mid-second/eighth century. Notes in MS Arabe 331 indicate that it was bequeathed in perpetuity to an undesignated mosque, perhaps that of ʿAmr in Fusṭāṭ. This folio edition is unlikely to have been made for someone's personal use; it is far more probable that it was originally meant to be deposited in a particular place of worship, in keeping with a practice that is attested during this period, and therefore perfectly acceptable by contemporary standards, notwithstanding the textual peculiarities that MS Arabe 331 exhibits. The missing word was entered later, exactly when is impossible to say. It is reasonable to suppose that what we observe in both cases came about when a copyist, seeking to satisfy either the wishes of a sponsor or those of a part of a Muslim community, occasionally preferred the text of a different version than the one that he generally respected - in the event, the one that came to be considered canonical. Further exploration of the Qur'ānic manuscript tradition during the first/seventh century and the first half of the second/eighth may be expected to uncover similar cases, strengthening the evidence we presently have of a quite different approach to the text than the literalism that later came to be strictly enforced.

---

71 Matthieu Tillier and Naïm Vantieghem, *The Book of the Cow, An Early Qur'ānic Codex on Papyrus (P.Hamb. Arab.68)*, (Leiden-Boston: Brill, 2024), p. 32-35, 115 and 145.

Production

Copy or Dictation?

Interestingly, various copies of the earliest layer of production coincide in showing that the copy from an exemplar was the rule, rather than dictation: this is the case for the Codex Parisino-Petropolitanus,[72] for the various copies analyzed by Marijn van Putten[73] and for the P.Hamb.Arab.68.[74] This is again a point in support of the importance of the handwritten transmission during the first century of the handwritten transmission of the Qur'ān.

Diffusion: Public and Private Copies

During the second half of the seventh century, according to traditional authorities, Qur'ānic manuscripts were used in various contexts. Some copies no doubt were meant for private use. Mālik b. Anas, for example, tells us that his grandfather possessed a personal copy of the sacred text.[75] But probably more copies were meant for public use. One thinks in the first place of the ones that were prepared on 'Uthmān's orders to be sent to the different regions of his empire. Later, the revision of the 'Uthmānic version made by al-Ḥajjāj b. Yūsuf under the reign of the Umayyad caliph 'Abd al-Malik was followed by the production

72 Déroche, *La Transmission écrite du Coran dans les débuts de l'islam. Le Codex Parisino-Petropolitanus*, 152.

73 van Putten, '"The Grace of God" as Evidence for a Written Uthmanic Archetype: The Importance of Shared Orthographic Idiosyncrasies'.

74 Tillier and Vantieghem, *The Book of the Cow, An Early Qur'ānic Codex on Papyrus (P.Hamb. Arab.68)*, 30.

75 Michael Cook, 'A Koranic Codex Inherited by Mālik from His Grandfather April-5 May 1996', in *Proceedings of the Sixth International Congress on Graeco-Oriental and African Studies. Nicosia 30 April-5 May 1996*, ed. V. Christides and T. Papadopoulos, *Graeco-Arabica* 7-8, 1999, 93–105.

of copies sent to major cities.[76] Now, the account reported by al-Samhūdī specifically says that the copy sent to Medina was used for readings that took place on both Thursdays and Fridays.[77] In Fusṭāṭ, the governor was angered by al-Ḥajjāj's move and decided to have his own copy made.[78]

Conclusion

The early manuscripts of the Qur'ān have still much to teach us and we are fortunate in having so many early witnesses to fuel this new field of research. In spite of some progress in our understanding of the manuscript production chronology, our knowledge of its geography and sociology is still insufficient to fully grasp the diffusion of the various manuscripts and the scripts they bear. Over roughly one century, the features of the early manuscripts of the Qur'ān evolved dramatically. We can expect that there was some overlapping depending on the geography or the identity of the copyists/patrons; some of the scripts, the layout of the manuscripts or their orthography may have been different at a given moment. These changes probably reflect shifts in the intellectual sphere -as can be deduced from the progress in the notation of the text- but also in the society -as shown by the material features of some copies which seem to have been produced under the patronage if not of the caliph himself, at least by his circle. The control of the centre over the production seems however still rather unequal. All the early manuscripts which have been mentioned here transmit the 'Uthmānic version, in

---

76 Omar Hamdan, *Studien zur Kanonisierung des Korantextes. Al-Ḥasan al-Baṣrīs Beiträge zur Geschichte des Korans* (Wiesbaden, 2006), 172–73.

77 al-Samhūdī, *Kitāb Wafā' al-Wafā' bi-Akhbār Dār al-Muṣṭafā,* ed. M 'Abd al-Ḥamīd, vol. 2 (Beirut, 1984), 668.

78 Ibn Duqmāq, *Description de l'Egypte, Part 1*, ed. K. Vollers (Cairo, 1893), 72–74.

some cases with variants. There is no doubt that it was more or less established, but it did not supersede all the rival versions. The Ṣanʿāʾ palimpsest is one proof of that, but we know from the sources that copies of ibn Masʿūd's recension were still circulating for instance. The manuscript evidence we have today reflects probably the authorities' effort to eliminate these dissident versions -but not some readings. On the other hand, the Vulgate did not either reach the status of *ne varietur* version within its own line of transmission. The three copies mentioned above show that even a manuscript which was basically in accordance with the *rasm* traditionally attributed to ʿUthmān could still include non-canonical variants. Further research on the early layer of manuscript transmission of the Qur'ān will certainly yield new examples and new insights into this history.

Bibliography

Abbott, Nabia. *The Rise of the North Arabic Script and Its Ḳur'ānic Development*. Chicago: University of Chicago Oriental Institute Publications, 1939.

al-Dānī. *Al-Muqniʿ Fī Maʿrifa Marsūm Maṣāḥif Ahl al-Amṣār*. Edited by M.A Dahmān. Damascus, n.d.

al-Samhūdī. *Kitāb Wafāʾ al-Wafāʾ Bi-Akhbār Dār al-Muṣṭafā*. Edited by M. ʿAbd al-Ḥamīd. Vol. 2. Beirut, 1984.

Altıkulaç, Tayyar. *Al-Muṣḥaf al-Šarīf (in Arabic). Al-Muṣḥaf al-Sharīf Attributed to ʿUthman Bin ʿAffan (The Copy at al-Mashhad al-Husaynī in Cairo)*. 2 vols. Istanbul: IRCICA, 2009.

Altıkulaç, Tayyar et al. 1400. *yılında Kur'an-ı Kerim*. no. 4 (Istanbul: Antik A.Ş. Kültür Yayınları. 2010).

———. *Al-Muṣḥaf al-Šarīf (in Arabic). Al-Muṣḥaf al-Sharīf Attributed to ʿUthmān Bin ʿAffan (The Copy at the Topkapı Palace Museum)*. Istanbul: IRCICA, 2007.

———. *Hz. Osman'a Nisbet Edilen Mushaf-ı Şarif. Türk ve Islâm Eserleri Nüshası. Al-Muṣḥaf al-Šarīf al-Mansūb Ilā ʿUthmān Ibn ʿAffān (in Arabic)*. 2 vols. Istanbul: IRCICA, 2007.

Blair, Sheila. *Islamic Calligraphy*. Edinburgh: Edinburgh University Press, 2006.

Bothmer, Hans-Caspar von. 'Architekturbilder Im Koran. Eine Prachthandschrift der Umayyadenzeit aus dem Yemen'. *Pantheon* 45 (1987): 4–20.

Burger, François. 'Asselin de Cherville, Agent Consulaire et Collectionneur de Manuscrits Orientaux'. *Dix-Huitième Siècle* 28 (1996): 125–33.

Cellard, Eléonore. *Codex Amrensis 1*. Leiden: Brill, 2018.

———. 'The Written Transmission of the Qur'ān during Umayyad Times: Contextualizing the Codex Amrensis 1'. In *The Umayyad World*, edited by Andrew Marsham. Abingdon: Routledge, 2021: 438-463.

Cook, Michael. 'A Koranic Codex Inherited by Mālik from His Grandfather'. In *Proceedings of the Sixth International Congress on Graeco-Oriental and African Studies. Nicosia 30 April-5 May 1996*, edited by V. Christides and V. Papadopoulos, 93–105. Graeco-Arabica 7-8, 1999: 93-105.

Déroche, François. *La Transmission écrite du Coran dans les débuts de l'islam. Le Codex Parisino-Petropolitanus*. Leiden: Brill, 2009.

———. *Les Manuscrits du Coran: Aux Origines de la calligraphie coranique [Catalogue Des Manuscrits Arabes, 2e Partie, Manuscrits Musulmans, I/1]*. Paris: Bibliothèque Nationale, 1983.

———. 'Note sur les fragments coraniques anciens de Katta Langar (Ouzbékistan)'. *Cahiers d'Asie Centrale* 7 (1999): 65–73.

———. *Qur'āns of the Umayyads: A First Overview*. Leiden: Brill, 2014.

———. *The Abbasid Tradition, Qur'āns of the 8th to the 10th Centuries [The Nasser D. Khalili Collection of Islamic Art]*. Vol. 1. London: Azimuth Press in Collaboration with OUP, 1992.

———. 'The Qur'ānic Collections Acquired by Wetzstein'. In *Manuscripts, Politics and Oriental Studies. Life and Collections of Johann Gottfried Wetzstein (1815-1905) in Context*, edited by Boris Liebrenz and Christoph Rauch. Leiden: Brill, 2019: 92-115.

Déroche, François, and Sergio Noja-Noseda. *Le Manuscrit Arabe 328 (a) de la Bibliothèque nationale de France [Sources de la transmission manuscrite du texte coranique I, Les Manuscrits de style Hijâzî, 1]*. Lesa: Fondazione Ferni-Noja Noseda, 1998.

———. *Le Manuscrit Or. 2165 (f. 1 à 61) de la British Library [Sources de la transmission manuscrite du texte coranique, I: Les Manuscrits de style Higâzî]*. Lesa: Fondazione Ferni-Noja Noseda, 2001.

Grohmann, Adolf. 'The Problem of Dating Early Qur'āns'. *Der Islam* 33 (1958): 213–31.

Hamdan, Omar. *Studien zur Kanonisierung des Korantextes. Al-Ḥasan al-Baṣrīs Beiträge zur Geschichte des Korans*. Wiesbaden: Harrassowitz, 2006.

Ibn Duqmāq. *Description de l'Egypte, Part 1*. Edited by K Vollers. Cairo, 1893.

Jahdani, Abdelouahed. 'Du Fiqh à la codicologie. Quelques opinions de Mālik (m. 179/796) sur le Coran-Codex'. In *Mélanges de l'Université Saint-Joseph [Actes de La Conférence Internationale sur les manuscrits du Coran, Bologna]* 56 (2006): 269–79.

Karimi Nia, Morteza, *Codex Mashhad. An Introduction to its History and Contents*. Qom: The Alulbayt Islamic Heritage Institute, 1445/2023.

Marx, Michel, and Tobias Jocham. 'Radiocarbon (14C) Dating of Qur'ān Manuscripts'. In *Qur'ān Quotations Preserved on Papyrus Documents, 7th-10th Centuries, and the Problem of Carbon Dating Early Qur'āns*, edited by A Kaplony and M Marx. Leiden: Brill, 2019, 188–221.

Nadīm, Ibn al-. *The Fihrist of Al-Nadîm, A Tenth-Century Survey of Muslim Culture*. Translated by B Dodge. Vol. 1. New York/London: Columbia University Press, 1970.

Nasser, Shady. *The Transmission of the Variant Readings of the Qur'ān: The Problem of Tawātur and the Emergence of Shawādhdh*. Leiden: Brill, 2012.

Nöldeke, Theodor, Gotthelf Bergsträsser, and Otto Pretzl. *Geschichte des Qorâns von Theodor Nöldeke*. Second Edition. Vol. III. Leipzig, 1938.

Rezvan, Efim. 'The Qur'ān and Its World: VI. Emergence of the Canon: The Struggle for Uniformity'. *Manuscripta Orientalia* 4, no. 2 (1998): 13–51.

———. 'Yet Another "Uthmānic Qur'ān" on the History of Manuscript E 20 from the St. Petersburg Branch of the Institute of Oriental Studies'. *Manuscripta Orientalia* 6, no. 1 (2000): 49–68.

Robin, Christian. 'La Réforme de l'écriture à l'époque du califat médinois'. *Mélanges de l'Université Saint-Joseph* 59 (2006): 319–64.

Small, Keith. *Textual Criticism and Qur'ânic Manuscripts*. Lanham: Lexington Books, 2011.

Spitaler, Anton. 'Die Verszählung des Koran nach islamischer Überlieferung'. In *Sitzungsberichte der Bayerischen Akademie der Wissenschaften, Phil.-Historische Abteilung. Jahrgang*, Vol. 11. Munich, 1935.

Tillier, Matthieu, and Naïm Vantieghem. *The Book of the Cow, An Early Qur'ānic Codex on Papyrus (P.Hamb. Arab.68)*. Leiden-Boston: Brill, 2024.

Van Putten, Marijn. 'Arabe 334a. A Vocalized Kufic Qur'ān in a Non-Canonical Hijazi Reading'. *Journal of Islamic Manuscripts* 10, no. 3 (2019): 327–75.

———. "The Grace of God" as Evidence for a Written Uthmanic Archetype: The Importance of Shared Orthographic Idiosyncrasies'. *Bulletin of the School of Oriental and African Studies* 82, no. 2 (2019): 271–88.

Wansbrough, John. *Qur'ānic Studies: Sources and Methods of Scriptural Interpretation*. Oxford: Oxford University Press, 1977.

Whelan, Estelle 'Evidence for the Early Codification of the Qur'ān'. *Journal of the American Oriental Society* 118 (1998): 1–14.

CHAPTER THREE

Ancient Scribes and Qur'ānic Manuscripts: Uncovering Scribal Practices in the Ṣanʿāʾ Palimpsest

Éléonore Cellard

Arab and Islamic culture have accorded a crucial place to the art of the book and calligraphy. Among the books produced during the fourteen centuries of this civilization and in the geographical areas that extend from Spain to India, the Qur'ān is obviously central. The extremely close attention paid by the craftsmen of these books, as much to the aesthetics of the books as to their sturdiness, as well as the scrupulous care of the individuals who preserved the books for so many centuries today allows us to appreciate the diversity of traditions of the book over the ages.

The many manuscripts that have found their way through history reveal that the Qur'ān has taken a wide variety of forms over the years. Copied onto a broad range of materials, in sizes ranging from miniature manuscripts to monumental tomes, the Qur'ān has also given rise to a multitude of scribal innovations, including calligraphic styles including calligraphic styles, various formats and endlessly renewed ornamental traditions. and endlessly renewed ornamental traditions.

Qur'ānic manuscripts also offer a rare opportunity to return to the very origins of the arts of the book and calligraphy. Indeed, a large number of extremely old fragments, certainly contemporary or nearly contemporary to the original handwritten versions of the Qur'ān have been preserved. These fragments pose a number of problems, however, for those who seek to trace the history of the Qur'ān and calligraphy. First, these manuscripts carry no dates or signs of their geographical origins; nor do we know who wrote or ordered them, or the conditions or reasons for which they were produced. To this dilemma, a second difficulty must be added. All, or nearly all, of these manuscripts are fragmentary. Only rare copies, probably made later, preserve the majority of the original writing.[1] Typically, only a few sheets remain, complicating any effort to discern the book's original shape and dimensions, and to study the rules that governed the copying and layout.

Indeed, the present chapter concerns one of these archaic exemplars of the Qur'ān: the Ṣanʿāʾ palimpsest. My first goal is to describe the book's original form based on preserved fragments. The second objective of the chapter is to describe aspects of how the copyists worked and laid out the pages. The fact that other manuscripts from the same period display a number of similar features may broaden our understanding of the scribal practices and aesthetic norms that guided the manufacture of Qur'ānic books during Islam's first century.

The Ṣanʿāʾ Palimpsest

One particularity of the Ṣanʿāʾ palimpsest – or Codex Ṣanʿāʾ 1 – derives from the fact that it consists of not one but two Qur'ānic texts that were sequentially copied onto the same material

1 Some existing manuscripts – which were probably manufactured as early as the first half of the 2nd H/8th CE – are nearly complete, with 99% of the text. Most are attributed to eminent figures from the beginning of Islam, particularly ʿUthmān ibn ʿAffān himself. It is possible that this attribution – which in most cases is based on oral tradition – helped encourage the preservation of the integrity of these manuscripts (and, naturally, restoration attempts).

(Figure 1). The oldest text was erased, but the imprint of the earlier ink remains sufficiently visible for it to be deciphered. The two texts are thus two different entities that will be labelled respectively the "first codex" (the underlying or bottom text) and the "second codex" (the upper text).

According to its script type, which is referred to as the "*Hijazi*" style, the first codex may date from the first Hijra/7th century CE. This date has been roughly corroborated by Carbon 14 testing of the parchment that situates the manuscript in the first half of the 7th century CE.[2] The second, upper text appears to be only slightly younger, possibly only a few decades. No dating technique presently allows the accuracy of this estimate to be improved upon.

---

2 Several carbon dating studies suggest this date. The Stanford '07 folio, which was carbon-dated at the University of Arizona, has a 68% (1σ) probability of belonging to the period between 614 CE to 656 CE, and a 95% (2σ) probability of belonging to the period between 578 CE and 669 CE (see Behnam Sadeghi, and Uwe Bergmann, "The Codex of a Companion of the Prophet and the Qur'ān of the Prophet," Arabica 57 (2010): 353). Three further samples from DAM 01-27.1 were dated by different laboratories (as part of the CORANICA Project). The following are the results published by Christian J. Robin, "L'Arabie dans le Coran" in *Les origines du Coran, le Coran des origines*, ed. François Déroche, Christian J. Robin, and Michel Zink (Paris: De Boccard, 2015), 65. The results obtained in the Lyon laboratory were assigned a 68% (1σ) probability: F.2: 543-643 CE; F.11: 433-599 CE and F.13: 388-535 CE. These were submitted to dating by three additional laboratories. Oxford obtained 1423 ± 23 BP, while the Zurich result was 1437 ± 33 BP, which after calibration corresponds to 595-650 CE (1σ) or 565-660 (2σ), and Kiel obtained 1515 ± 25 BP, which corresponds to 430-495 (18.5%) and 530-610 (76.9%) (2σ).

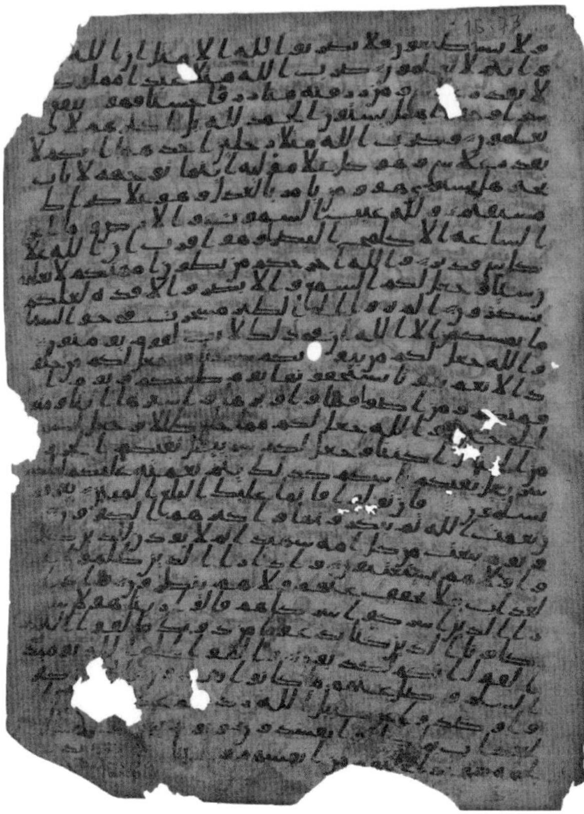

Figure 1. The Codex Ṣanʿāʾ 1 (Ṣanʿāʾ, DaM 01-27.1, f.5a). Courtesy: CNRS-DATI

Fragmentary Evidence

The Codex Ṣanʿāʾ 1 is an extensive set of folios that constitute over 40% of a complete Qur'ān codex. Reuniting the folios necessitates careful examination of the palaeography, codicology, and text of folios that potentially belong to the same manuscript. For the purposes of the present study, palaeographical and codicological evidence have allowed eighty folios and some additional fragments dispersed among different collections to be identified as belonging to the Codex Ṣanʿāʾ 1, including:

- Thirty-five folios discovered above the mosque ceiling in 1973 and stored in the collection of the Dār al-maḫṭūṭāt (DAM) in proximity to the Great Mosque of Ṣanʿāʾ, under the shelfmark DAM 01-27.1.
- Forty folios are stored in the Eastern Library (*al maktaba al-šarqiyya*) of the Great Mosque of Ṣan'ā', also known as the *awqāf* Library. Their identification was made possible by the 2004 Master's thesis of Razan Ghassan Ḥamdūn, who provided images of nearly all of the folios, as well as a transcription and analysis of the second (upper) text.[3] At least two other small, fragmented folios that were not included in Ḥamdūn's work have subsequently been identified.[4]
- Five additional, isolated folios circulated on the antiquities market, all of which complement those stored in the Eastern Library. One is in the David collection in Copenhagen (David 86/2003),[5] another is preserved by the Abu Dhabi Louvre museum,[6] and the other three were sold to private collectors.

---

3 See Ghassan Ḥamdūn, "Al-maḫṭūṭāt al-qur'āniyya fī Ṣan'ā' min al-qarn al-awwal al-hiğrī" (MA diss., Al-Yemenia University, 2004).

4 Personal communication, Dr. ʿAlī ad-Dawla, Assistant Curator of the awqaf Library.

5 Images available on: https://www.davidmus.dk/en/collections/islamic/materials/calligraphy/art/86-2003 (most recent access: 05.18.2021).

6 This final folio has recently been identified, although only a photograph of its reverse side is currently available (https://fridaymagazine.ae/life-culture/to-do/20-must-see-pieces-at-the-louvre-abu-dhabi-1.2146523, most recent consultation on 05.19.2021)

Table 1. The Ṣan'ā' 1 Codex and its Fragments

Location	Number of Folios	Textual Sequences of the Upper Text
Ṣanʿāʾ Great Mosque, Eastern Library (*al maktaba al-šarqiyya*)	40 + 2?	Q. 2, 246 – 5, 111 (with lacunae) Q. 7, 40 – 12, 49 (with lacunae)
Copenhagen, David 86/2003	1	Q. 2, 265 – 2, 277
Stanford '07	1	Q. 2, 277 – 286
Bonhams 2000	1	Q. 4, 33 – 56
Christie's 2008	1	Q. 4, 171 – 5, 9
Abu Dhabi Louvre	1	Q. 5, 9 – 32
Ṣanʿāʾ Great Mosque, DAM	35	Q. 6, 49 – 7,11 (with lacunae) Q. 9, 112 – 127 Q. 14, 32 – 60, 1 (with lacunae)

Material Characteristics: The Book/Codex

The Codex Ṣanʿāʾ 1 is written on medium-quality parchment with a high degree of opacity and slight irregularities consistent with the manufacture of parchment during the early period of Qur'ānic manuscripts. Similar, sometimes more apparent anomalies are frequently found in other early Qur'ānic manuscripts, including the Codex Parisino-Petropolitanus.[7]

The manuscript is oriented vertically and is quite large, although it would originally have been even larger. The largest folios currently measure between 365 mm high x 280 mm long and 371 x 280 mm. Before being trimmed, however, they would have measured at least 380 x 290 mm. It is possibly even larger than other early volumes, including Codex Parisino-Petropolitanus (330 x 240/48 mm) or Paris BnF Arabe 328c (330 x 245 mm).

Codicological analysis of the folios reveals that they originally formed two successive (primary and secondary) books – or codices – composed of small, regular units or groups of folios (quires) that were bound together after fabrication. Reassembling the quires provides valuable insight into the work habits and scribal rules behind the Codex Ṣanʿāʾ 1.

Scribal Rules in *Hijazi* Manuscripts

Copying a Qur'ānic manuscript in early times
The copyists of the Codex Ṣanʿāʾ 1

The primary Codex Ṣanʿāʾ 1 was written by at least two scribes – A(SI) and B(SI) – who collaborated throughout the copy.[8] Specific traits of two scribes' work enable us to distinguish between their writing (see Table 2). Copyist A(SI) wrote with a thicker, stockier nib than B(SI) and made vertical strokes that were slightly angled to the right. However, their script styles were similar, somewhat like the *Hijazi* style, and sometimes intersected because they did

7 François Déroche, *La transmission manuscrite. La transmission manuscrite du Coran dans les débuts de l'islam. Le Codex parisino-petropolitanus* (Leiden: Brill, 2009).

8 Distinguishing between hands was impossible on the other leaves because they are not sufficiently clear to determine this level of palaeographic detail. As a consequence, the folios in the Eastern Library and the folio in the Abu Dhabi Louvre have not been taken in account.

not adhere to a fixed script typology. These similarities may be due to shared training or a deliberate effort to write as uniformly as possible.

I was able to identify the scribes of nearly 75% of the thirty-nine most readable folios whose respective contributions were roughly equal (i.e., thirty-two pages[9] were written by Hand A and twenty-six pages by Hand B). They systematically alternated between recto and verso sides of the same folio.[10] It is worth noting that on seven occasions the change of hands occurs within a verse rather than corresponding to the end of a verse (such as Stanford '07 recto and DAM 01-27.1, f.23A).[11] This practice may suggest that the scribes were copying from a written original rather than from dictation, in which case one would not expect them to relay each other in the midst of a unit of text.

9 The term page refers here to the recto or verso of a sheet. The term folio refers to both recto and verso sides. One folio thus consists of two pages.

10 Copyist A(SI) wrote the Stanford '07 recto, Bonhams 2000, Christie's 2008 verso, and DAM 01-27,1, ff.2, 3B, 4, 5A, 6B, 7, 10, 11, 16, 17A, 19, 20, 21, 23A, 24B, 32A, 33, 36B and the copyist B(SI) wrote the others. Some folios remain unidentified: DAM 01-27.1, ff.1 (presence of lower text?), 3B, 12, 15, 18, 22, 25, 24A, 34A, 35, 37, 38A.

11 This phenomenon is clear in DAM 01-27.1, ff.5A-5B, 6A-6B and in Christie's 2008 recto-verso. This could also be the case in the fragmentary folios DAM 01-27.1, ff.32A-32B and f.36A-36B.

Table 2. The Scribes of the primary Codex Ṣanʿā 1 (Lower Text)

Copyist A(SI)	**Copyist B(SI)**
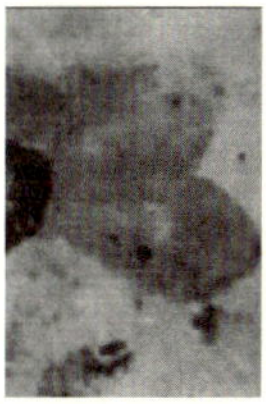 The letter *hā'* displays a heart-shape (image: DAM 01-27.1, f.23A)	 The letter *hā'* has a rounded or pear shape, with the vertical bar bent to the left (image: DAM 01-27.1, f.23B).
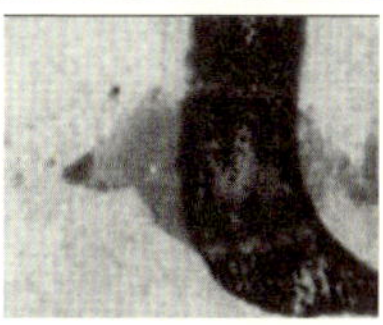 The final *mīm* has an almost non-existent tail (image: Stanford '07 recto).	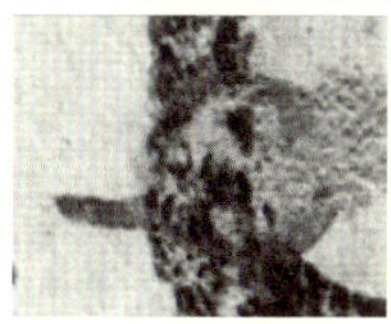 B(SI) prefers a clear upward tail (image: Stanford '07 verso).
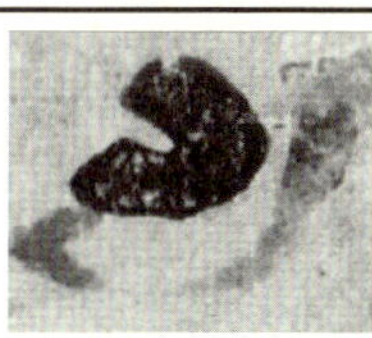 The *nūn* has a semi-circular shape and tends to incorporate the dots used to mark the verses (image: Stanford '07 recto)	 The *nūn* has a straighter, longer stroke that ends with a short return (image: Stanford '07 verso)

Copyist A(SI)	Copyist B(SI)
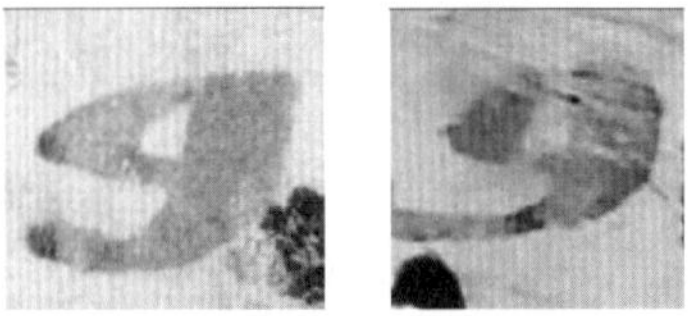	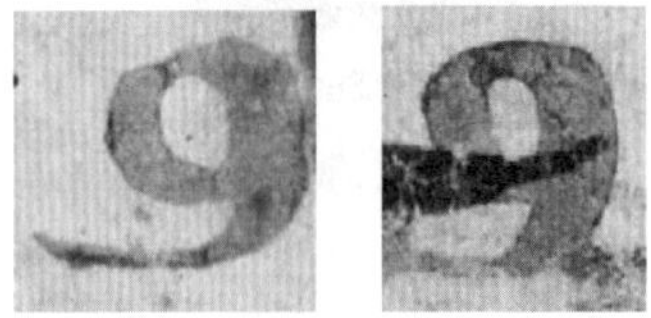
Wāw and *fā'/qāf* have a triangular head (image: Stanford '07 recto).	*Wāw* and *fā'/qāf* have a more rounded head (image: Stanford '07 verso).

The secondary Codex Ṣan'ā' 1 (upper layer) was also written by two copyists. The first hand, A (see Figures 2), has a broad script – the folios contain between nineteen and twenty-five lines per page – and shows straight vertical strokes, smooth angles – more in accordance with documentary scripts – and a slight accentuation in the treatment of the curves.[12] However, the letter shapes are not significantly different from those of the other copyist. Copyist B (see Figure 3) employs a writing density that primarily varies between quires, ranging from twenty-three to thirty-seven lines per page. His script exhibits a hybrid, professional style, including certain tendencies of the *Hijazi* style, particularly in the leading strokes and the shapes of medial *hā'* and final/isolated *ṭā*, ended with a short tail. According to Déroche's classification, however, it tends to reveal a more elaborate angular script similar to C.I.[13]

12 Note the particular treatment of *lām-alif*, with strokes curved toward each other and the final *kāf* shaped like a hairpin.

13 François Déroche, *Catalogue des manuscrits arabes. Deuxième partie: Manuscrits musulmans*, *Tome I, 1* (Paris: Bibliothèque Nationale de France, 1983), 39–40. The shapes of several letters may indeed be consistent with C.I. First, the medial *ğīm*, does not cross the baseline but is laid down, implying a shift in the baseline. Second, the final or isolated *nūn* is crescent shaped, with all three parts well-defined. Third, the final or isolated *qāf* has a long, oblique tail before a U-shaped return.

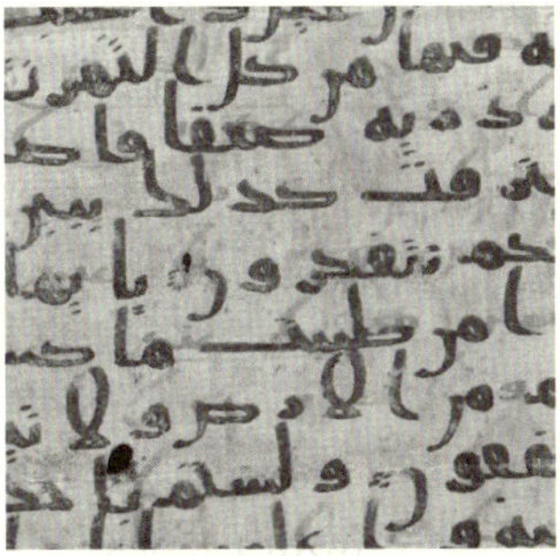

Figure 2. Stanford '07. Hand A of the *scriptio superior* (Courtesy of B. Sadeghi and U. Bergmann)

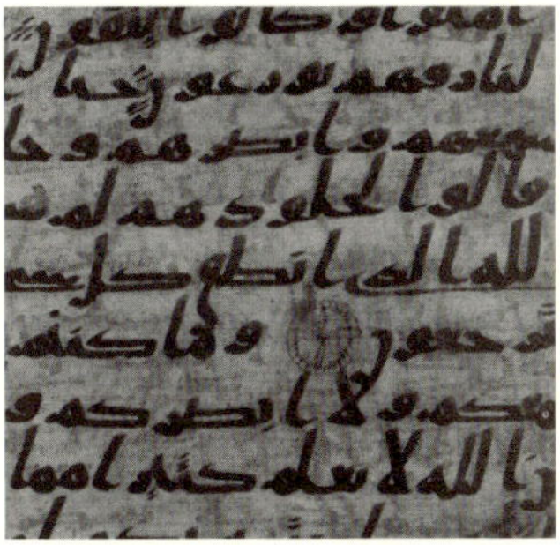

Figure 3. DAM 01-27.1, f.30A. Hand B of the *scriptio superior* (Courtesy CNRS-DATI)

Unlike the primary codex Ṣanʿāʾ 1, the scribes of the upper layer collaborated in a different manner that could reflect a series of copyists instead of a collaborative process. The first copyist may have written the beginning of the codex[14] and left his work to Copyist B at the end of a folio, in mid-quire (Ḥamdūn, MS f.4b). Copyist B wrote the other seventy-four existing folios of the codex. Unexpected events may explain Copyist A's limited contribution and his mid-quire departure.

Writing Hijazi Manuscripts: A Working Collaboration?

Collaborative scribal practices are often observed in early Qur'ānic texts. As noted above, the Codex Ṣanʿāʾ 1 presents two different copying scenarios. The second layer reveals a sequence of scribes, perhaps due to unexpected events. The primary layer may instead illustrate effective collaboration in which scribes

14 His contribution is now confirmed only in the first six existing folios (Ṣanʿā', Eastern Library, Ḥamdūn, MS ff.1-2, Stanford '07, David 86/2003 and Ḥamdūn, MS ff.3-4).

alternated throughout the copying process. Is this consistent with other *Hijazi* manuscripts? The evidence presented below sheds additional light on how the scribes organized the copying process.

Division of labour has been observed in a number of handwriting cultures, including Latin manuscripts from the 9th-10th centuries CE that show evidence of several scribes working simultaneously.[15] In the Qur'ānic handwritten tradition, some early manuscripts – in *Hijazi* and early Kufic styles – also indicate the participation of multiple scribes. The fragmented condition of the earliest manuscripts does not permit definitive conclusions concerning the number of writers involved in the original project or the distribution of labour. Manuscripts with the longest preserved sequences such as Codex Parisino-Petropolitanus and the British Library codex, however, may offer significant insights into scribal practices, although they should be considered with caution.

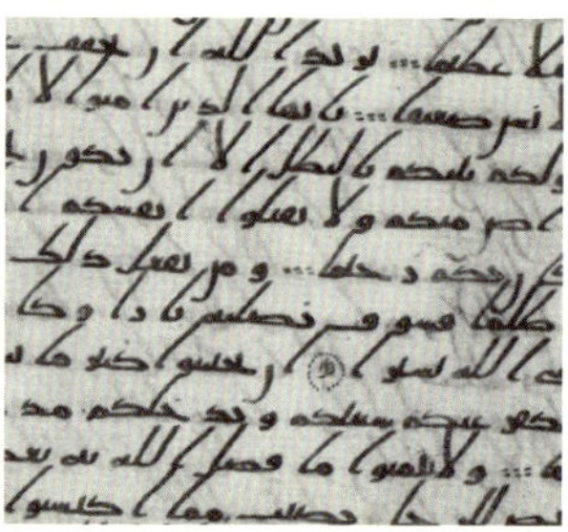

Figure 4. The Codex Parisino-Petropolitanus, Hand A (Paris, BnF Arabe 328, f.12a). Courtesy: BnF.

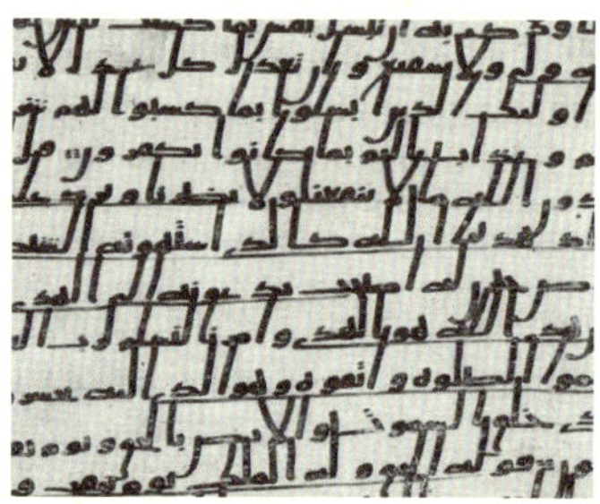

Figure 5. The British Library codex, Hand A (Paris, BnF Arabe 328, f.94a). Courtesy: BnF.

Scribal teams and the distribution of labour. Based on current knowledge, teams varied from two to five or even more scribes, as in

15 Jean Vézin, "La répartition du travail dans les "scriptoria" carolingiens," *Journal des Savants* 3 (1973): 212-227.

Codex Parisino-Petropolitanus, on which at least five scribes worked together, and Ṣanʿāʾ DAM 01-29.1, for which at least fifteen scribes have been identified in the thirty-three remaining folios.[16] It is difficult at times to distinguish between scribes, however, because of individual stylistic variations, probably depending on their levels of skill. The five scribes who copied the Codex Parisino-Petropolitanus, for example, are easily distinguishable from one another, whereas the styles of the three British Library codex (Or.2165) scribes are similar to each other and are identifiable only based on a few distinct parameters.[17]

Despite the often fragmentary nature of most manuscripts, the division of labour between scribes is an additional phenomenon that can be investigated. The ninety-eight currently available folios of the Codex Parisino-Petropolitanus, for example, comprise nearly 45% of the complete Qur'ānic text.[18] Hand A copied 68% of these folios, significantly out-copying his four fellow scribes (See Figure 4). The length of his interventions is irregular, however, and range from thirty pages to as few as two pages. On occasion, Hand A's passages are briefly interrupted by five short sequences of between two and six pages written by Hands B, D and E. After Q.41:31, a different scribe, Hand C, copied the remaining sixteen leaves.

The other *Hijazi* example that preserves a significant percentage of the complete original is the British Library codex, which consists of 129 folios and is currently dispersed between several collections.[19] Constituting more than 60% of the original

16 Éléonore Cellard, "Un nouveau témoignage sur la fixation du canon coranique dans les débuts de l'Islam: le manuscrit Ṣanʿāʾ DAM 01-29.1," *Compt-es-Rendus de l'Académie des Inscriptions et Belles-Lettres* 2018/2: 1112.

17 For additional details, see Déroche, *Transmission*, 127–130.

18 Distributed into two principal sections, from Q.2:275 to 10:78 and from Q.23:15 to 31:23, with brief lacunae.

19 London, BL Or.2165 has 121 leaves, Paris, BnF Arabe 328e has six leaves (ff.90-95). Two additional leaves, LNS19CA, can be consulted in the National

(from Q.5:7 to Q.43:71), these folios have small gaps in the first portions of the sequence that represent the equivalent of eight folios. The division of labour between the three scribes is highly uneven: the first scribe, Hand A (Figure 5), copied nearly all of the folios, and the remaining two scribes copied a total of six folios.[20]

As these two examples illustrate, the uneven distribution of work seems to suggest a different approach than the primary Codex Ṣanʿāʾ 1. It is possible that the pattern of the Codex Parisino-Petropolitanus and the British Library codex indicate the presence of a master scribe (or possibly two master scribes in the case of the Codex Parisino-Petropolitanus, Hands A and C) who copied the majority of the text but may have been briefly substituted by other scribes. Other, more fragmentary *Hijazi* manuscripts, such as Ṣanʿāʾ DAM 01-25.1 reflect a similarly patterned division of labour.[21] The Codex Ṣanʿāʾ 1, however, seems to have involved equal participation by two similarly-skilled scribes. A comparable approach appears to have been used in another manuscript, referred here to as Codex Amrensis 11, in which the short existing sequence of twenty-eight leaves was copied by four scribes alternating with each other nineteen times (see Figure 6).[22]

Museum in Kuwait. See Marilyn Jenkins, *Islamic Art in the Kuwait National Museum. The al-Sabah Collection* (London: Sotheby, 1983), 18.

20 Changes between scribes occurred in two locations: between the recto and verso sides of f.90 of BnF Arabe 328e. In this case, the second scribe, Hand B, copied only two pages – 90v and 91r – before leaving the work to hand A. Hand A copied the next seven folios, but the sequence is fragmented, with eight missing folios. Hand A copied the text through the middle of verse Q.7:101 (BL Or.2165, f.3a) before again leaving the work to another scribe – Hand C – who wrote ten pages (from f.3b to f.8a) before the final return of Hand A, who copied the remaining 225 pages.

21 The twenty-nine remaining folios of DAM 01-25.1 were written primarily by a single copyist, A (forty-eight pages). He was replaced by a less skilled copyist who copied ten folios on seven different occasions.

22 The Codex Amrensis 11 includes eleven leaves that are held in the Russian National Library in Saint Petersburg (NLR, Marcel 17), seven leaves in the

It is possible that this pattern of distribution indicates a project of inferior quality that was not supervised by a master scribe, as appears to be the case of the Codex Parisino-Petropolitanus, the British Library codex, and perhaps other manuscripts. Identifying the scribes in the remaining leaves of the Codex Ṣanʿāʾ 1 remains a critical step towards confirmation of this hypothesis. Further investigations of other *Hijazi* manuscripts will undoubtedly provide a better understanding of the work practices of Qur'ānic scribes in the 1st century of Islam.

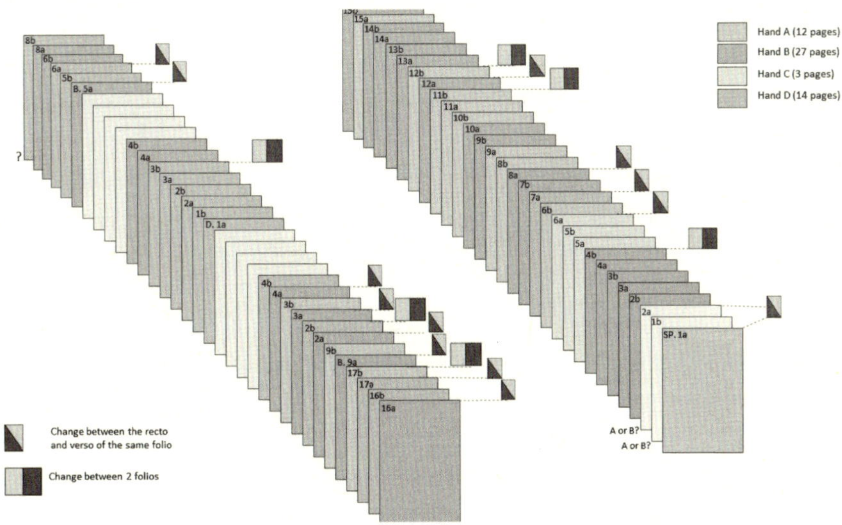

Figure 6. Distribution of labour in Codex Amrensis 11 (drawing by the author)

Cadbury Research Library of the University of Birmingham (MS Mingana Islamic Arabic 1572b), and four leaves in the Museum of Islamic Art in Doha (MS.67.2007.1). The identification of the scribes is based on Alba Fedeli's dissertation, "Early Qur'ānic Manuscripts" (PhD diss. University of Birmingham, 2015), 61–66. My personal observation of the Russian portion of this manuscript in 2019 raised doubts about the role of Hand C, who may in fact be a later corrector who erased and recopied three pages.

Changing hands

The scribes of *Hijazi* manuscripts also alternated between recto and verso sides on the same folio, as in the primary Codex Ṣan'ā' 1. Sixteen changes of hands have been documented for the Codex Parisino-Petropolitanus where Déroche found that this rule was systematically followed: "in no case does the reader see two different hands when the manuscript is open."[23] The same rule appears to govern the four changes of hands in the British Library codex. More fragmentary manuscripts appear to follow the same rule, although changes between two folios have been observed.[24] Alternating between recto and verso sides of the same folio is clearly inconsistent with simultaneous labour because it would require scribes to interrupt the writing process at the end of a page and hand the sheet to another scribe.

Déroche contends that this singular practice denotes adherence to a principle of symmetry and aesthetic rules regarding open double pages. *Hijazi* styles vary so significantly between scribes that it would presumably have been disconcerting to leave a book open with two dissimilar pages facing each other.[25] Another important concrete detail may also be the drying time of the ink. Indeed, a lapse of time after completing a page was needed for the ink to dry before the page could be turned, a potentially suitable moment for scribes to alternate with each other. In any event, this practice – which merits further investigation in other *Hijazi* manuscripts[26] – might indicate that a manuscript

23 See Déroche, *Transmission*, 172

24 In the Codex Amrensis 11, thirteen of a total of nineteen changes occur between recto and verso sides of the same folio. The scribes take turns only six (or five) times on different folios. Both practices are almost equally observable in the thirty folios of Ṣan'ā', DAM 01-25.1, where the two copyists alternated seven times on the same folio and six times between two folios.

25 Déroche, *Transmission*, 118

26 In some *Hijazi* manuscripts such as Saint-Petersburg, Marcel 17, and Ṣan'ā' DAM 01-25.1, copyists appear to have occasionally taken turns

was copied from a written model rather than from dictation, in which case one would not expect copyists to relieve each other in the middle of a unit of text.

Separating Sūras: Blank spaces, Ornamentation, Titles?

Titles and ornaments in the Codex Ṣanʿāʾ 1

In the primary Codex Ṣanʿāʾ 1, both copyists shared a similar approach to tracing the ornamental headers that separate *sūras* as well as hundred-verse groups. For the groups, they drew medallions on Q. 2, 101 (DAM 01-27.1, f.2B) and Q. 2, 203 (Stanford '07 verso).[27] When copyists reached the end of a *sūra*, they always wrote a subscript title formula (*haḏihi ḫatima sūra*...) before drawing a sometimes elaborate ornament using the same black ink (Figures 7 and 8). A single exception between *sūra* 8 and *sūra* 9 contains the title after the *Basmala* of the following *sūra* rather than before the ornament.[28] In several instances, the *Basmala*

---

between the recto and verso sides of the same folio, sometimes on two different pages, showing dissimilar pages facing each other.

27 The typology of the medallions – close to 1.A.II in Déroche, *Catalogue*, 29 – resembles other early manuscripts such as Codex Amrensis 1, see Cellard, *Le Codex Amrensis 1* (Leiden: Brill, 2018). It is worth noting, however, that every other manuscript uses medallions to separate groups of ten verses but not hundred-verse groups.

28 DAM 01-27.1, f.5A. According to Elisabeth Puin's reading, the title formula of *sūra* 9 is written on lines 8 and 9. At the beginning of line 9, the end of the title "*[a]l-anfal*" is followed by a short *Basmala*, used to separate contents. See Elisabeth Puin, "Ein früher Koranpalimpsest aus San'a' (DAM 01-27.1) – Teil III: Ein nicht-'utmanischer Koran," in *Die Entstehung einer Weltreligion I: Von der koranischen Bewegung zum Frühislam*, ed. Markus Groß and Karl-H. Ohlig (Berlin: Verlag Hans Schiler, 2010), 272. My own reading supports this interpretation. Puin's reading, like mine, does not include any reading instruction "*lā taqul bi-smi llāhi*" on line 9 as assumed by Asma Hilali in *The Sanaa palimpsest* (London: Oxford University Press, 2017), 39–40, and Déroche in *Le Coran,*

is not placed at the beginning of a new line but, where there is adequate space, is inserted immediately following the ornament.

Figure 7. DAM 01-27.1, f.20B, lower text: Ornament traced by A(SI). Courtesy CNRS-DATI

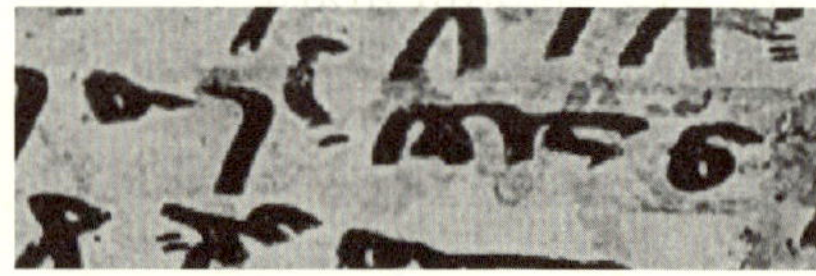

Figure 8. Christie's 2008, recto, lower text: Ornament traced by B(SI). Courtesy Christie's

Unlike the lower text, the secondary Codex Ṣanʿāʾ 1 reflects the intervention of one or more illustrators who were responsible for adding headbands between *sūras* and medallions to mark groups of verses. Headbands and medallions were not drawn during the actual writing process but were added later, although copyists left a larger space to accommodate them.[29] The ornaments are highly variable. One sequence of folios (DAM 01-27.1, ff.30-38) belonging to a single quire features a different approach to separating *sūras* in which coloured headers were inserted into the blank spaces (See ff.35-38).[30] One possible explanation is that

une histoire plurielle. Essai sur la formation du texte coranique (Paris: Seuil, 2019), 208, or, with a slight difference, by Behnam Sadeghi, and Mohsen Gourdarzi in "Ṣanʿāʾ 1 and the Origins of the Qur'ān," *Der Islam* 87/1-2 (2012): 53, note 157. According to the editors, the copyist "wanted to write *lā taqul bi-smi llāhi*" here but confused the grapheme with the similar *[a]l-anfal*).

29 In many instances, medallions were not added in the intended spaces, but elsewhere (see, for example, DAM 01-27.1, f.11B, in which the original space is left on Q.20, 105; while the medallion appears on Q.20, 102). These medallions were clearly added by a different hand.

30 Another header, sketched only in pencil, can be seen in the folios preserved in the Eastern Library (Ḥamdūn, MS f.11A). The ornamental vocabulary used in these headers recalls that of several Qur'ānic manuscripts in C.I script. See Éléonore Cellard, "La Transmission manuscrite du Coran. Étude d'un corpus de manuscrits datables du 2e s. H./8e s. ap. J.-C." (PhD diss., INALCO, 2015).

the illustrator began with the final quires of an overly-ambitious project and later reduced his work to only medallions. Such variations in ornamentation can also be seen in another manuscript written in early Kufic, probably from the Umayyad period, about which Déroche notes that "there seems to be a connection between the quire structure of the manuscript and the illuminated sura headers, as though the illustrator had been working on loose quires."[31] Whatever the explanation, the structure of the quires offers important clues to the process of writing and illustrating a manuscript on parchment.

Separations between sūras in Hijazi manuscripts

Past scholarship has generally accepted that the oldest Qur'ānic manuscripts contained no rubrics for separating the *sūras*. Craftsmen began using ornamental headings before subsequently introducing titles and the number of verses.[32] By contrast with this assumed linear pattern of development of ornamentation over time, however, a number of currently available manuscripts, including the primary Codex Ṣanʿā' 1, demonstrate that blank spaces, titles, and/or ornaments were in use as early as the 1st H./7th century CE.

The greatest difficulty is estimating the interval of time between when the text and titles were copied and the ornaments were added. The inks used for such embellishments typically differ from the ink used in the body of the text, but there are exceptions that include the primary Codex Ṣanʿā' 1, whose titles and ornaments were added in the same ink by the scribes themselves.

31 Déroche, *Qur'āns of the Umayyads*, (Leiden: Brill, 2014), 84.

32 See Arthur Jeffery "Book review," review of *The Rise of the North Arabic Script*," by Nabia Abbott, *The Moslem World*, 30 (1940): 196, and Estelle Whelan, "Writing the Word of God: Some Early Qur'ān Manuscripts and Their Milieux, Part I." *Ars Orientalis* 20 (1990): 113, http://www.jstor.org/stable/4629403.

Another early fragment in the Istanbul Museum reveals a title formula written continuously by the same scribe as the title of the text.[33] In other situations, parallels can be drawn between the script style used to write a title and that used for the ornamental vocabulary, which supports the hypothesis that the text, titles, and/or ornaments were contemporary or were not separated from the copying itself by a long interval. The ornamental motif of wavy or zigzag lines that can be observed in several Hijazi manuscripts, such as Birmingham, Add. 1572a or Ṣanʿāʾ DAM 01-29.1 (Figure 9), may thus represent one the earliest forms of decoration of the 1st H./7th century CE.

Figure 9. Ṣanʿāʾ DAM 01-29.1, f.13b. Courtesy: CNRS-DATI

33 See, for example, Déroche, *Qur'āns*, Figure 16, Istanbul, TIEM, ŞE12827/1.

Conclusion

The extensive corpus of folios that currently constitute the Codex Ṣanʿāʾ 1 – and that represent nearly half of a full Qur'ān – allows us to reconstruct the codicological structure of the secondary codex, the upper text, while also supporting assumptions about the original structure of the primary codex. Further, material analysis has provided clear insights into the scribal rules that guided the composition of the manuscript. Several characteristics of the primary codex of Codex Ṣanʿāʾ 1 suggest a planned, professionally executed scriptural project.

The various patterns of work distribution between scribes described here indicate that copying the Qur'ān during this long-ago period was a collaborative project that implicated a number of scribes and a range of writing settings, as well as a variety of approaches to visually highlighting textual divisions such as sūras. In addition to the particularities of Codex Ṣanʿāʾ 1, notably on the textual level, that may reflect a highly specific local context, there is genuine visual coherence between this manuscript and others in the *Hijazi* style. Despite the inherent difficulties of analysing this highly varied and fragmentary corpus, one clear observation emerges: Early Qur'ānic scribes shared a common set of aesthetic rules that guided their writing and illustration of these manuscripts. I am confident that future research into these scribal traditions will further enrich our understanding of these early phases in the development of the art of Qur'ānic books and calligraphy.

Bibliography

Cellard, Eléonore. "La Transmission manuscrite du Coran. Étude d'un corpus de manuscrits datables du 2e s. H./8e s. ap. J.-C." PhD diss., INALCO, 2015.

Le Codex Amrensis 1. Leiden: Brill, 2018.

"Un nouveau témoignage sur la fixation du canon coranique dans les débuts de l'Islam: le manuscrit Ṣanʿāʾ DAM 01-29.1." *Comptes-Rendus de l'Académie des Inscriptions et Belles-Lettres*, 2018/2 (2020): 1107–1119. Paris: De Boccard, 2020.

Déroche, François. *Le Coran, une histoire plurielle. Essai sur la formation du texte coranique*. Paris : Seuil, 2019.

Qur'āns of the Umayyads. Leiden: Brill, 2014.

La transmission manuscrite du Coran dans les débuts de l'islam. Le Codex parisino-petropolitanus. Leiden: Brill, 2009.

Catalogue des manuscrits arabes. Deuxième partie: Manuscrits musulmans, Tome I, 1, Paris: Bibliothèque Nationale de France, 1983.

Fedeli, Alba. "Early Qur'ānic Manuscripts." PhD diss. University of Birmingham, 2015.

Grohmann, Adolf. "The Problem Of Dating Early Qur'āns." *Der Islam*, 33 (1958): 213–231.

Ḥamdūn, Razan Ghassan. "Al-maḫṭūṭāt al-qur'āniyya fī Ṣanʿāʾ min al-qarn al-awwal al-hiǧrī." MA diss., Al-Yemenia University, 2004.

Hilali, Asma. *The Sanaa palimpsest*. London: Oxford University Press, 2017.

Jeffery, Arthur. "Book review N. Abbott, The Rise of the North Arabic Script." *The Moslem World*, 30 (1940): 191–198.

Jenkins, Marilyn, ed. *Islamic Art in the Kuwait National Museum. The al-Sabah Collection*. London: Sotheby, 1983.

Maṣāḥif Ṣan'ā', 19 March – 19 May 1985, Kuwait: Kuwait National Museum: 1985.

Puin, Elisabeth. "Ein früher Koranpalimpsest aus San'a' (DAM 01-27.1) – Teil III: Ein nicht-'utmanischer Koran." In *Die Entstehung einer Weltreligion I: Von der koranischen Bewegung zum Frühislam*, edited by Markus Groß and Karl-H. Ohlig, 233–305. Berlin: Verlag Hans Schiler, 2010.

Robin, Christian Julien. "L'Arabie dans le Coran." In *Les origines du Coran, le Coran des origines*, edited by François Déroche, Christian J. Robin and Michel Zink, 27–74. Paris: De Boccard, 2015.

Sadeghi, Behnam, and Mohsen Goudarzi. "Ṣan'ā' 1 and the Origins of the Qur'ān." *Der Islam* 87/1-2 (2012): 1–129.

Sadeghi, Behnam, and Uwe Bergmann. "The Codex of a Companion of the Prophet and the Qur'ān of the Prophet." *Arabica* 57 (2010): 343–436.

Vézin, Jean. "La répartition du travail dans les "scriptoria" carolingiens." *Journal des Savants* 3 (1973): 212–227.

Whelan, Estelle. "Writing the Word of God: Some Early Qur'ān Manuscripts and Their Milieux, Part I." *Ars Orientalis* 20 (1990): 113–47. Accessed on July 28, 2021. http://www.jstor.org/stable/4629403.

CHAPTER FOUR

Writing About the Qur'ān: Scribal Practices of Qur'ānic Studies Manuscripts from the Fourth/Tenth century

Yousry Elseadawy

Between the third/ninth centuries, there were significant advancements in education and scholarship in the Islamic world. This environment led to an increase in book production, which was driven by various factors, such as the widespread use of paper as a medium for written texts,[1] the growing legal discussions within the Sunnī schools of law,[2] and the translation of foreign books into Arabic.[3] All of these factors contributed to the

1 On the introduction and the widespread of paper, see, Jonathan M. Bloom, *Paper before Print: The History and the Impact of Paper in the Islamic World* (New Haven, London: Yale University Press, 2001), 42-89. For more literature on paper, see Beatrice Gruendler, *The Rise of the Arabic Book.* (Cambridge, Massachusetts: Harvard University Press, 2020), 177-8, note 47.

2 On this, see Christopher Melchert, *The Formation of the Sunni Schools of Law, 9th-10th Centuries C.E* (Leiden: Brill, 1997). On the formation of the Shāfiʿī school in particular, see Ahmed El Shamsy, "From Tradition to Law: The Origins and Early Development of the Shāfiʿī School of Law in Ninth-Century Egypt." (PhD diss., Harvard University, 2009).

3 On the translation movement, see Dimitri Gutas, *Greek Thought, Arabic Culture: The Graeco-Arabic Translation Movement in Baghdad and Early Abbasid Society (2nd-4th/8th-10th Centuries)* (London: Routledge, 1998), see particularly pp. 2- 129.

flourishing of scholarly activities during this period. A particular area of development in this milieu of knowledge production in the fourth/tenth was the study of the Qur'ān. In a previous study, I drew upon a particularly interesting corpus of Qur'ānic studies manuscripts from this period which merit closer scrutiny for the codicological practices we can extract from them.[4] An initial examination of these manuscripts shows great care on behalf of the scribes in preserving the clarity and correctness of the text of the manuscripts. In other words, copyists seem to have exerted great effort into making sure that the text was easily readable and stylistically legible. Looking further at these manuscripts, we ask a specific question: What specific scribal practices were employed in the fourth/tenth century to make Qur'ānic studies manuscripts easy to use?

This paper focusses on specific scribal practices from four Qur'ānic studies manuscripts from the fourth/tenth century and in doing so presents a codicological analysis of extant manuscripts from this timeframe. The scribal practices that we focus on overwhelmingly show an attention and concern on part of the copyists in presenting knowledge of the Qur'ān in a clear and correct manner. Previously understudied manuscript specimens were collected and examined in order to analyse scribal practices of Qur'ānic studies works. These manuscripts are charted (see appendix 1).

The manuscripts under examination underscore three topics that were of particular interest to Qur'ānic studies scholars in the fourth/tenth century: Qur'ānic exegesis, Qur'ānic readings, and philology of Qur'ān (see Appendix 1). MS BA 233 (Alexandria, Maktabat al-Iskandariyyah, MS Baladiyyat al-Iskandariyyah 233) is representative of the *tafsīr bi-l-ma'thūr*

4 Yousry Elseadawy, "Arabic Scribal Practices in the 3rd-4th/9th-10th Centuries: Normative Sources and Manuscript Evidence." (PhD diss., Freie Universität Berlin, 2022).

(traditional) genre of exegesis.[5] The author of the manuscript, Isḥāq ibn Ibrāhīm ibn Ismā'īl Abū Muḥammad al-Qāḍī al-Bustī (d. 307/919-20),[6] clarifies the various intricacies of the various verses of the Qur'ān by quoting the sayings of earlier Muslim exegetes and prophetic traditions. Another group of manuscripts that represents this particular school of exegesis is the voluminous and famed fourth/tenth-century work of Muḥammad ibn Jarīr al-Ṭabarī (d. 310/923).[7] On the other hand, MS Şehid 27 (Istanbul, Süleymaniye Yazma Eser Kütüphanesi, MS Şehid Ali Paşa 27), which is part of a larger manuscript, and MS Ch. B. Ar. 3051 (Dublin, Chester Beatty Library, Ar. 3051) are both devoted to the various Readings of the Qur'ān.[8] Finally, MS DK 663 Tafsīr (Cairo, Dār al-Kutub

---

5 On the traditional exegesis in comparison with rational exegesis (*al-tafsīr bi-l-ra'y*), see , Hussein Abdul-Raof, *Schools of Qur'ānic Exegesis: Genesis and development* (London and New York: Routledge, 2010).

6 On his bio-bibliography with a special attention to his book of *Tafsīr*, see, 'Uthmān Mu'allim Maḥmūd Shaykh Alī, "Tafsīr Isḥāq ibn Ibrāhīm al-Bustī al-mutawaffā sanat 307 H. Taḥqīq wa-dirāsah min awwal sūrat al-naml ilā al-āyah 12 min sūrat al-najm." (PhD diss., al-Jāmi'ah al-Islāmiyyah bi al-Madīnah al-Munawwarah, 1416/1995),11-50. He was also mentioned in ibn Ḥibbān, *Kitāb al-Thiqāt*, edited by Muḥammad 'Abd al-Mu'īd Khān, 9 vols (Hyderabad: Dā'irat al-Ma'ārif al-'Uthmāniyyah, 1973), 8: 122.

7 MS Maktabat al-Qarawiyyīn (Qar.) 791 (Jīm 31), 403 (illus. 4.8), MS Qar. 912 (Jīm 2), 65, MS Qar. 912 (Jīm 4), 66, MS Qar. 912 (Jīm 8), 66, MS Qar. 912 (Jīm 12), 66, MS Qar. 912 (Jīm 19), 66, MS Qar. 912 (Jīm 31), 67, MS Qar. 912 (Jīm 36), 67, MS Qar. 912 (Jīm 42), 67, MS Qar. 912 (Jīm 47), 6. On al-Ṭabarī, see *The Encyclopaedia of Islam*. New Edition, edited by P. Bearman et al. 12 vols (Leiden: Brill, 1954-2004), s. v. "Al-Ṭabarī, Abū Ja'far Muḥammad b. Jarīr b. Yazīd."; Carl Brockelmann, *History of the Arabic Written Tradition*, edited by Maribel Fierro et al.; translated by Joep Lameer. 5 vols (Leiden: Brill, 2016-2019), vol. 1:128-9; Fuat Sezgin, *Geschichte des arabischen Schrifttums*, 13 vols. Leiden: Brill; Frankfurt am Main: Institut für Geschichte der Naturwissenschaften and der Johann Wolfgang Goethe Universität, 1967-2007, 1: 323-8.

8 On the variant reading of the Qur'ān, see, Shady Hekmat Nasser, *The Transmission of the Variant Readings of the Qur'ān: the Problem of Tawātur and the Emergence*

al-Miṣriyyah, 663 Tafsīr) and MS Fazil 43 (Istanbul, Süleymaniye Yazma Eser Kütüphanesi, MS Fazil Ahmed Paşa 43) belong to a genre of Qur'ānic studies works that deal with philological commentaries on the Qur'ān.[9]

In our discussion of these manuscripts, we argue that the scholars who produced such works on the Qur'ān in the fourth/tenth century were keen on presenting the contents of these manuscripts in a clear and correct manner. To support our contention, we carefully scrutinise the manuscripts in light of certain scribal elements (elaborated later on) that deal with clarity and correctness. These elements underscore the extent to which scribes were keen on preserving knowledge of the Qur'ān in a clear and correct manner.

Clarity

The manuscripts under examination show that the copyists of these manuscripts were keen on presenting knowledge of the Qur' ān in a clear and well-defined manner. Taking care in preserving the clarity of the text is reflected through the utilisation of the following scribal practices: clear scripts to facilitate ease of reading; drawing the reader's attention by using underlining and elongation in order to highlight particularly important places in the text; and adopting a well-organised page layout (including the use of catchwords to connect the pages). We will now go on and deal with these specific elements in detail.

---

of Shawādhdh (Leiden: Brill, 2013).

9 On the philological commentaries, see Raoul Villano, and Giuliano Lancioni. "Arabic Grammar and Qur'ānic Scholarship in 2nd/8th Century's Basra: A Comparative Analysis of the Qur'ānic Material Found in the Kitāb Sībawayhi and in al-'Aḫfaš al-'Awsaṭ's Ma'ānī al-Qur'ān,". in *The Foundations of Arab Linguistics V* (Leiden: Brill, 2022), 72.

Clear Script

The manuscripts under examination show a clear preponderance towards maintaining a well-defined script and well-executed handwriting. The copyists of these manuscripts employed a range of script styles: the Abbasid book hand,[10] New Abbasid Style,[11] *naskh*,[12] and *Mahghribī*.[13] We can see that all of these various scripts are executed in a neat and clear manner (see figs 1-4 and fig 7). It appears that five of the six manuscripts under scrutiny were created by calligraphers who prioritise the aesthetic aspects of writing (see figs. 1-4 and appendix 1). Moreover, the text in all of these six manuscripts carefully utilize dots[14] and vowel signs (see figs.1-4).[15] This is important in that different scribal traditions have varying degrees of dotting and vowel signs usage.[16]

---

10 On Abbasid book hand, see, François Déroche et al.,*Islamic Codicology: An Introduction to the Study of Manuscripts in Arabic Script*, translated by Deke Dusiberre and David Radzinowicz; edited by Muhammad Isa Waley (London: Al-Furqān Islamic Heritage Foundation, 2005), 217; Adam Gacek, *Arabic Manuscripts: A Vademecum for Readers* (Leiden: Brill, 2009), 1-2.

11 On the "New Style", see François Déroche, *The Abbasid Tradition: Qur'āns of the 8th to 10th Centuries AD* (New York: Nour Foundation in association with Azimuth Editions and Oxford University Press, 1992), 132-83.

12 On *naskh* script, see Gacek, *Vademecum*, 162-5.

13 On *Maghribī* script, see Gacek, *Vademecum*, 147-50.

14 On dots, see Andreas Kaplony, "What Are Those Few Dots for? Thoughts on the Orthography of the Qurra Papyri (709- 710), the Khurasan Parchments (755-777), and the Inscription of the Jerusalem Dome of the Rock (692)." *Arabica* 55 (2008); Gacek, *Vademecum*, 144-5.

15 On vowel signs, see Gacek, *Vademecum*, 288-90.

16 Gacek, *Vademecum*, 145, 288-90.

Figure 1. MS BA 233, fol. 74r, Abbasid book hand, elongating *qāla* (he said).

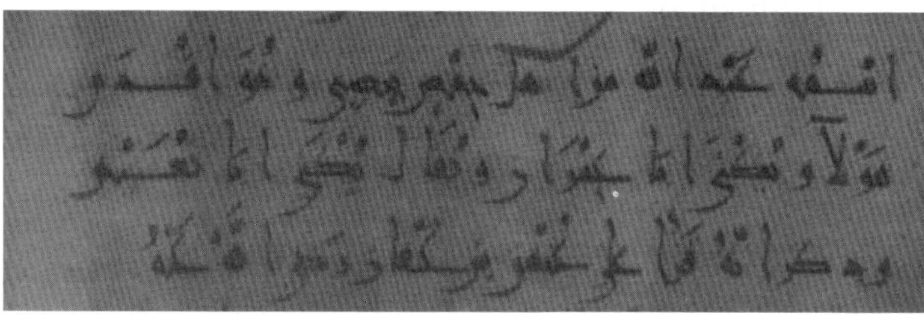

Figure 2. MS Ch. B. Ar. 3051, fol. 5r, New Abbasid Style.

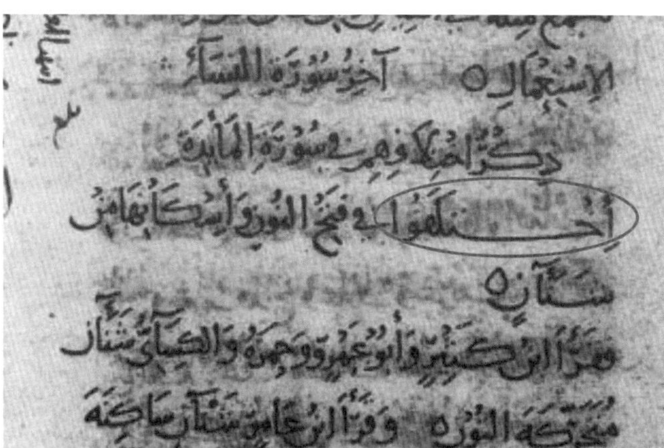

Figure 3. MS Şehid 27, fol. 5r, *naskh* similar to the unique Qur'ānic MS of ibn al-Bawwāb (MS Chester Beatty Is 1431) and the elongation of *ikhtalafū* (they disagreed)

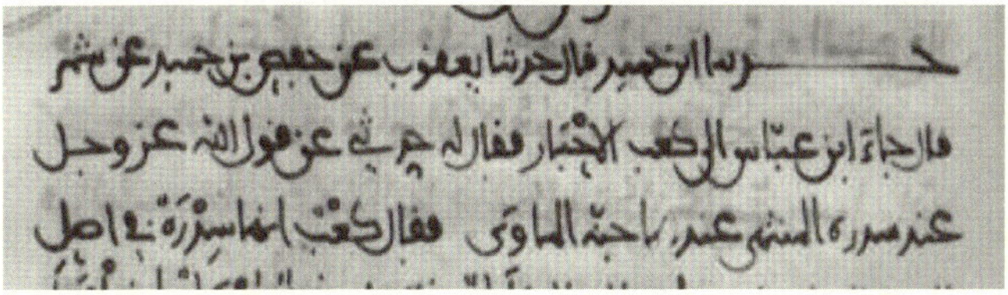

Figure 4. MS Qar. 912 (Jīm 47), 67 p. 252, Maghribī script

Furthermore, our scribes consistently utilise the practice of the *ihmāl* mark to further provide clarity to the writing in order to distinguish between the dotted and undotted letter.[17] For example, (see fig. 5), the *rā'* ر is marked with a v-like shape above it to distinguish it from the *zāy* ز. Similarly, the *ṣād* is marked with either a v-like shape above it or the head of *ṣād* ص underneath it to distinguish it from the *ḍād* ض. The *ṭā'* ط is drawn with a dot underneath it to distinguish it from the *ẓā'* ظ. The *'ayn* ـعـ is marked with another small *'ayn* underneath to differentiate it from the *ghayn* ـغـ. Likewise, a small *ḥā'* is drawn underneath the *ḥā'* ح in order to prevent confusion with the *khā'* خ or *jīm* ج.

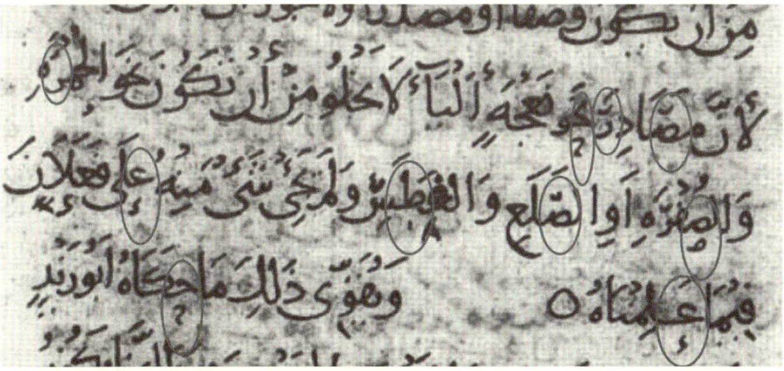

Figure 5. MS Şehid 27, fol. 9r, *ihmāl* marks.

17 On ihmāl, see Gacek, *Vademecum*, 286; Jan Just Witkam. "The Neglect Neglected: To point or not to point, That is the Question," *Journal of Islamic Manuscripts* 6 (2015)

Underlining and Elongation

The scribes of our examined manuscripts do not leave the reader alone with the text without aiding them through scribal elements that help the reader navigate the text. For example, in MS Fazil 43, the scribe underlines the most crucial information in the text using red ink (see fig. 6). Additionally, in MS BA 233, we can see the scribe elongating words that begin a new section of a text. For example, the scribe elongates the word *qāla* (he said) which indicates a new saying of a scholar, or *ḥaddathanā* (he told us) which indicates the beginning of a new prophetic tradition (see fig. 1 and fig. 7). In MS Şehid 27, the scribe elongates the word *wa-ikhtalafū* (they disagreed) to highlight the places of the disagreement amongst the different readers of the Qur'ān (see fig. 3).

Figure 6. MS Fazil 43, fol. 22r, Underlying key information.

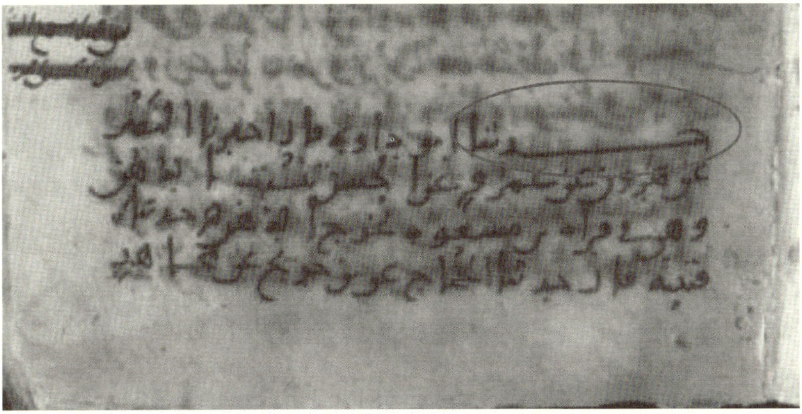

Figure 7. MS BA 233, fol. 51r, elongating *ḥaddathanā* (he told us) and Abbasid book hand.

Page Layout

Our corpus of manuscripts shows well-executed page layouts.[18] The reader can notice precise alignment at the beginning and the ending of lines. In addition, spaces are intentionally left around the text to allow the scribes to insert omissions from the text and write legible versions of illegible words. The scribes do not rule the space of the text on the page with a *misṭarah* or any other tool since no traces of ruling are found in the manuscripts. Nevertheless, even without the aid of tools, it is apparent that the scribes place considerable effort in keeping lines straight (see fig. 8).

Catchwords

A catchword is the first word from a left-hand-sided page which corresponds to the last word of the previous right-hand-sided

18 On page layout, see Gacek, *Vademecum*, 177-9.

page. The word itself is usually placed at the bottom left corner of the right-sided page to show the reader that the texts are connected and that there is no missing part in between.[19] The catchwords, which were uniquely used in the early centuries (the third/ninth and fourth/tenth centuries), can be seen in one of our examined manuscripts (see for instance MS Ch. B. Ar. 3051, fol. 5r, see fig. 8).

Figure 8. MS Ch. B. Ar. 3051, fol. 5r, well-executed page layout and catchword *lara'ūf.*

19 On catchwords, see Déroche et al. *Islamic Codicology*, 97-9; Gacek, *Vademecum*, 50-1.

Correctness

In order to preserve the authenticity and correctness of the text, the scribes of our examined manuscripts insert omitted words and correct any mistakes in wording. Furthermore, they take measures to prevent any misunderstandings of text.

Insertion of Omissions

Omitted words from the texts in manuscripts are inserted either between two lines or in the margin.[20] The actual place of omission is marked with a mark called '*'aṭfah*', which indicates the reader to the margin for the omitted word (see figs 9, 10, 11, 12). Inserting accidentally omitted words of a text is usually undertaken during the collation of copied text with the original text. In longer omissions, in order to distinguish the inserted omission in the margin from comments in the text, scribes either mark the end of insertion with the mark *ṣaḥḥ* (see fig 10) or with a word or words that follows the missing part of the main text (see figs 11

---

20 On insertions of omissions, see Adam Gacek,. "Technical Practices and Recommendations Recorded by Classical and Post-Classical Arabic Scholars concerning the Copying and Correction of manuscripts," in Les manuscrits du Moyen-Orient. Essais de codicologie et de paléographie: Actes du Colloque d'Istanbul (Istanbul, 26-29 mai 1986). Istanbul/Paris 1989, edited by François Déroche (Paris / Istanbul: Institut français d'études anatoliennes et Bibliothèque Nationale, 1989), 57-9 "Taxonomy of Scribal Errors and Corrections in Arabic Manuscripts," in Theoretical Approaches to the Transmission and Edition of Oriental Manuscripts: Proceedings of a Symposium Held in Istanbul March 28-30, 2001, edited by Judith Pfeiffer and Manfred Kropp (Würzburg: Ergon Verlag, 2007), 223-4; *Vademecum*, 170-1; 'Ābid Sulaymān al-Mashūkhī, *Anmāṭ al-tawthīq fī al-makhṭūṭ al-'Arabī fī al-qarn al-rābi' al-Hijrī* (Riyadh: Maktabat al-Malik Fahd al-Waṭaniyyah, 1414/1994), 69-70; al-Ḥalwajī, 'Abd al-Sattār. *Al-Makhṭūṭ al-'Arabī* (Cairo: al-Dār al-Miṣriyyah al-Lubnāniyyah, 2011), 170, 172-3.

and 12). Inserting omissions underscores the copyists' efforts in producing correct copies of these manuscripts.

Figure 9. MS BA 233, fol. 19v: Marking the missing parts with *'aṭfah* and inserting the omitted parts in the margin

Figure 10. MS Şehid 27: Marking the missing parts with *'aṭfah* and inserting the omitted parts in the margin and marking the end of the insertion with *ṣaḥḥ*

Figure 11. MS Dār al-Kutub al-Miṣriyyah, 663 Tafsīr, fol. 43r

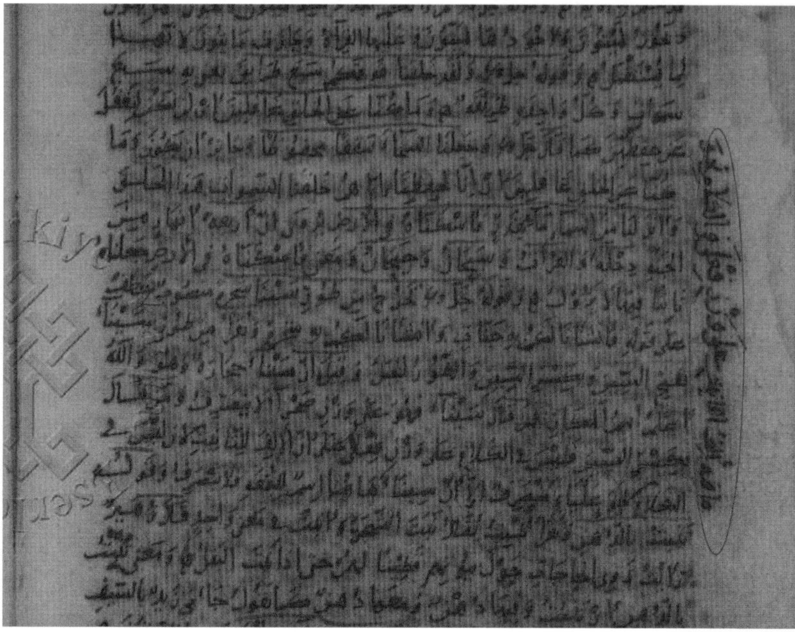

Figure 12. MS Fazil 43, fol. 96v: Marking the missing parts with *'atfah* and inserting the omitted parts in the margin and marking the end of the insertion by writing two words that follows the missing part in the main text

Correcting and Preventing Mistakes

Our manuscripts show that the scribes of these manuscripts are careful to not only correct the text but also take measures to prevent misunderstanding of the text.[21] These practices include: correcting mistakes, indicating that a text is problematic

21 On correcting mistakes and preventing misinterpretation, see Franz Rosenthal, *The Technique and Approach of Muslim Scholarship* (Roma: Pontificum Institutum Biblicum, 1947), 15; Gacek, "Technical Practices," 57-8; "Taxonomy," 219, 225-7; *Vademecum*, 266, 80, 81; al-Mashūkhī, *Anmāṭ*, 70-3; al-Ḥalwajī, *al-Makhṭūṭ al-'Arabī*, 168-9, 171-2.

(*tamrīḍ* or *taḍbīb*), stressing the correctness of a text, and providing a legible version for an illegible text.

Correcting Mistakes

The scribes correct mistakes by striking out the wrong text and placing the correct text either above the incorrect text (see figs. 13 and 15) or in the margin (see figs. 12 and 14).

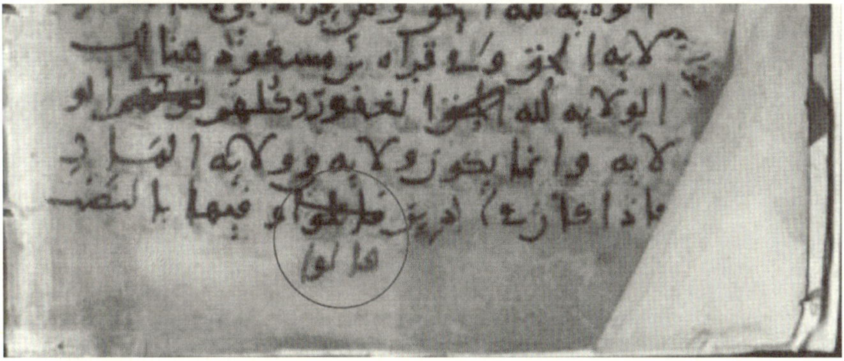

Figure 13. MS BA 233, fol. 4v. correcting the mistakes by striking the wrong text and giving the correct text in the margin.

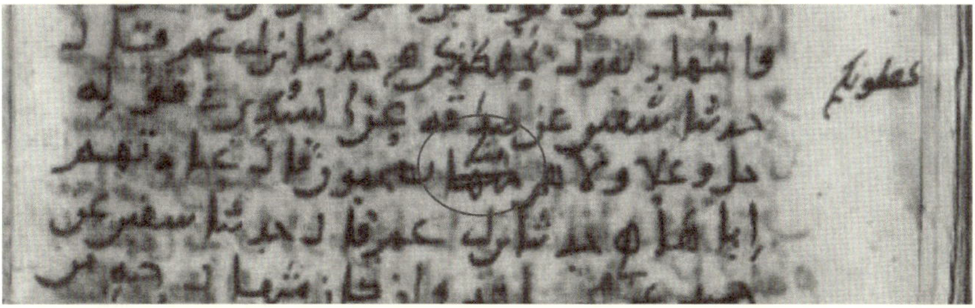

Figure 14. MS BA 233, fol. 33v: Correcting the mistakes by striking the wrong text and giving the correct text above it.

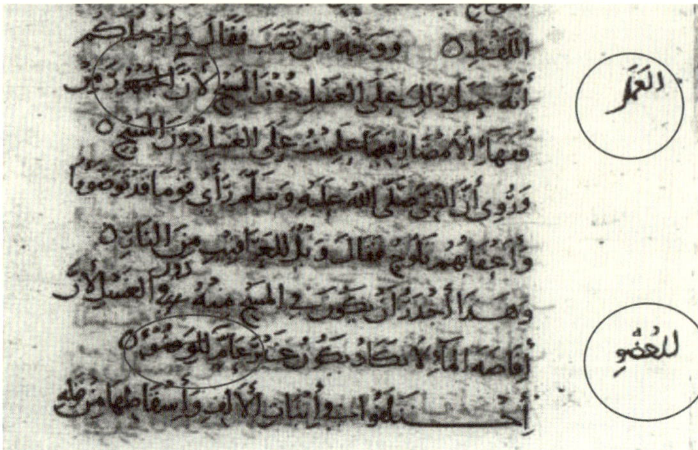

Figure 15. MS Şehid 27, fol.14v: correcting the mistakes by striking the wrong text and giving the correct text in the margin.

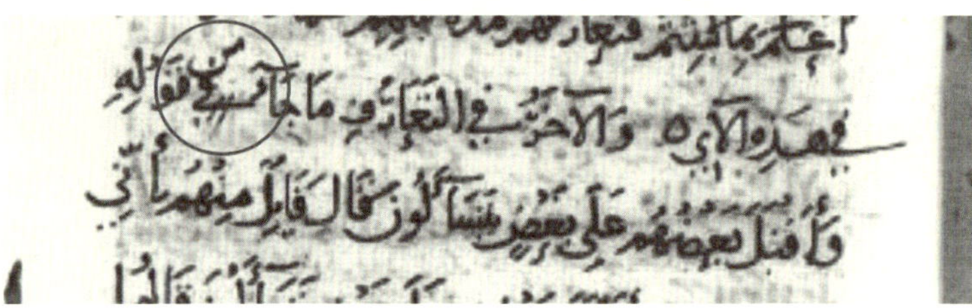

Figure 16. MS Şehid 27, fol.14v: Correcting the mistakes by striking the wrong text and giving the correct text above it.

Indicating Text as Problematic

We can see our scribes marking out any parts of text they find problematics such as in terms of language (for instance, a text having variant wording of a *ḥadīth*).[22] As our manuscripts show,

22 For details on this practice through the investigation of normative sources and the examination of manuscript evidence, see Elseadawy, "Scribal

the mark that is used in this regard is the initial form of the *ṣād* صـ placed above the problematic text (see fig. 16). Al-Qāḍī 'Iyāḍ, calls this mark a *ḍabbah* (door bolt), which is the beginning letter of *ṣaḥḥ* صح, meaning "correct". The term itself is used to stress the correctness of a particular text.[23] The *ḍabbah* (صـ) being an incomplete form of *ṣaḥḥ*, which marks correctness (see more below), underscores the incompleteness of the text that it marks.[24] The scribe uses this mark when he personally finds the text problematic or incorrect, yet cannot simply change it since it may actually be correct from a different perspective.[25] Hence, he indicates that the text may be problematic through the *ḍabbah*. This practice in other sources, is also called the *tamrīḍ*, which literally means "declaring to be sick".[26] When doubts about a marked text with the *ḍabbah* are dispelled, the *ḍabbah* is subsequently turned into *ṣaḥḥ* صح (see fig. 17).

Figure 17. MS BA 233, fol. 41r: Marking with *ḍabbah*.

Practices," 311.

23 Al-Qāḍī 'Iyāḍ. *Al-Ilmā' ilā ma'rifat uṣūl al-riwāyah wa-taqyīd al-samā'*, edited by al-Sayyid Aḥmad Ṣaqr (Cairo: Dār al-Turāth; Tunis: al-Maktabah al-'Atīqah, 1970), 166.

24 Al-Qāḍī 'Iyāḍ, *al-Ilmā'*, 166-7.

25 Al-Qāḍī 'Iyāḍ, *al-Ilmā'*, 167.

26 Al-Qāḍī 'Iyāḍ, *al-Ilmā'*, 166.

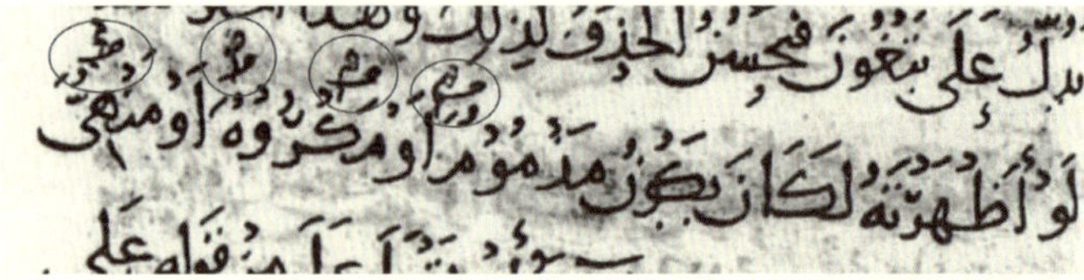

Figure 18. MS Şehid 27, fol. 263r: changing the *ḍabbah* to *ṣaḥḥ*.

Stressing the Correctness of a Text

When a word can potentially be mistakenly understood by a reader, the scribes mark the word to stress its correctness.[27] They mark the word with *ṣaḥḥ* صح to tell the reader that this word is indeed correct even if it may seem to be incorrect to the reader. This practice is called *al-taṣḥīḥ*.[28] The aim of this practice is to prevent readers from changing the actual correct word to another incorrect one they think is correct.[29] As fig. 18 shows, the scribe adds the mark *ṣaḥḥ* to the words *mushajjajan/mushajjaj* (tent peg). The scribe marks the word to prevent a potential reader who assumes it to be wrong (since the word is potentially more difficult to understand for a less educated reader) from amending it.

27 For details on this practice through the investigation of normative sources and the examination of manuscript evidence, see Elseadawy, "Scribal Practices," 313.

28 Al-Qāḍī 'Iyāḍ, *al-Ilmā'*, 166-8. On *ṣaḥḥ* and *taṣḥīḥ*, see Gacek, "Taxonomy," 224-7; Gacek, *Vademecum*, 283.

29 Al-Qāḍī 'Iyāḍ, *al-Ilmā'*, 166-8.

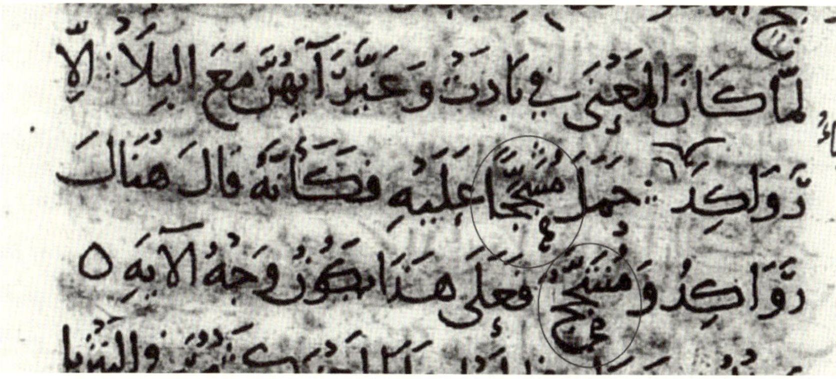

Figure 19. MS Şehid 27, fol. 19r: Marking with *ṣaḥḥ*.

Providing Legible Version

When a word is illegible, scribes rewrite a more legible version of this word.[30] For instance, as figure 19 shows, the scribe of this manuscript finds the word *yanfa'anī* (it benefits me) written in a way that can potentially appear unclear to the reader. Therefore, the scribe writes another clearer version of this word in the margin. The legible version in the margin is not only better written than the one in the main text, but additionally, for further clarity, is written with *shakl* and *ihmāl* marks. This practice contributes to underscoring the text's clarity and prevents confusion. A further practice of supporting legibility, can be seen in fig. 20. Here the scribe, restates the letter to be a *dhāl* in the margin: *Bi al-dhāl al-mu'jamah* ("with the dotted *dāl*"). Doing so, the scribe prevents a possible reader from confusing the *dhāl* with a *dāl* and hence

30 For details on this practice through the investigation of normative sources and the examination of manuscript evidence, see Elseadawy, "Scribal Practices," 313-4.

read the word as *al-khad'*, "cheating," as opposed to *al-khadha'* ("the obliqueness").

Figure 20. MS Şehid 27, fol.14v:
Providing a legible version of an illegible word.

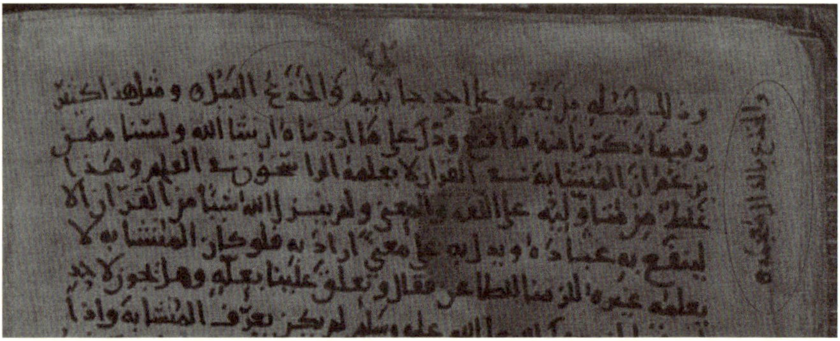

Figure 21. MS Dār al-Kutub al-Miṣriyyah, 663 Tafsīr, fol. 43r.

Conclusion

In conclusion, the scribes of Qur'ānic Studies works from the fourth/tenth century, and in particular, works of Qur'ānic exegesis, Qur'ānic readings, and philology, took considerable care in preserving the quality, correctness and integrity of these manuscripts. The clarity and correctness of the text are preserved through various noticeable scribal practices. The implementation of these practices can be widely seen in our examined manuscripts.

With regards to clarity, scribes take care to present a clear text by maintaining a clear script with well-executed handwriting. They also help the reader navigate the text by underlying in red ink key words and phrases, and by elongating words at the beginning of a text. A further two elements of establishing clarity are by maintaining a neat page layout and providing catch words.

Scribes expend great effort to provide readers with a text that is as correct as possible and take care to prevent misunderstandings. For example, scribes insert any omitted words either in the interlines or in margins. They write the omissions in a way that enables readers to recognize them as insertions of omissions amongst other notes in the marginalia. In addition to correcting mistakes that occur in the text, scribes allude to potentially problematic parts of the text. They mark such places with a *ḍabbah* (the head of the *ṣād*) instead of completely amending it since it may be correct from a different perspective. Concomitantly, they also stress the correctness of a text when they expect a reader to potentially misread and therefore incorrectly 'correct' a word. Finally, scribes are careful to add legible versions of any illegible words. In utilizing such practices, the scribes of these manuscripts were keen in transmitting Qur'ānic knowledge in these manuscripts as clearly and correctly as possible.

Bibliography

Manuscripts

Alexandria, Maktabat al-Iskandariyyah, MS Baladiyyat al-Iskandariyyah 233.
Cairo, Dār al-Kutub al-Miṣriyyah, 663 Tafsīr.
Dublin, Chester Beatty Library, Ar. 3051. https://viewer.cbl.ie/viewer/object/Ar_3051/220/. [Accessed May 6, 2021].
Istanbul, Süleymaniye Yazma Eser Kütüphanesi, MS Fazil Ahmed Paşa 43
Istanbul, Süleymaniye Yazma Eser Kütüphanesi, MS Şehid Ali Paşa 27.
Fez, Maktabat al-Qarawiyyīn, 791(Jīm 31).
Fez, Maktabat al-Qarawiyyīn, 912 (Jīm 2), 65.
Fez, Maktabat al-Qarawiyyīn, 912 (Jīm 4), 66.
Fez, Maktabat al-Qarawiyyīn, 912 (Jīm 8), 66.
Fez, Maktabat al-Qarawiyyīn, 912 (Jīm 12), 66.
Fez, Maktabat al-Qarawiyyīn, 912 (Jīm 19), 66.
Fez, Maktabat al-Qarawiyyīn, 912 (Jīm 31), 67.
Fez, Maktabat al-Qarawiyyīn, 912 (Jīm 36), 67.
Fez, Maktabat al-Qarawiyyīn, 912 (Jīm 42), 67.
Fez, Maktabat al-Qarawiyyīn, 912 (Jīm 47).

Printed Sources

Abdul-Raof, Hussein. *Schools of Qur'ānic Exegesis: Genesis and development*. London and New York: Routledge, 2010.
Bearman, P et al(ed). *The Encyclopaedia of Islam*. New Edition, 12 vols. Leiden: Brill, 1954-2004.
Bloom, Jonathan M. *Paper before Print: The History and the Impact of Paper in the Islamic World*. New Haven, London: Yale University Press, 2001.

Brockelmann, Carl. *History of the Arabic Written Tradition*, edited by Maribel Fierro et al.; translated by Joep Lameer. 5 vols. Leiden: Brill, 2016-2019.

Elseadawy, Yousry. "Arabic Scribal Practices in the 3rd-4th/9th-10th Centuries: Normative Sources and Manuscript Evidence." PhD diss., Freie Universität Berlin, 2022.

El Shamsy, Ahmed. "From Tradition to Law: The Origins and Early Development of the Shāfiʿī School of Law in Ninth-Century Egypt." PhD diss., Harvard University, 2009.

Gacek, Adam. *Arabic Manuscripts: A Vademecum for Readers*. Leiden: Brill, 2009.

Gacek, Adam. "Taxonomy of Scribal Errors and Corrections in Arabic Manuscripts." In *Theoretical Approaches to the Transmission and Edition of Oriental Manuscripts: Proceedings of a Symposium Held in Istanbul March 28-30, 2001*, edited by Judith Pfeiffer and Manfred Kropp. Würzburg: Ergon Verlag, 2007: 217-235, 313-319.

Gacek, Adam. "Technical Practices and Recommendations Recorded by Classical and Post-Classical Arabic Scholars concerning the Copying and Correction of manuscripts." In *Les manuscrits du Moyen-Orient. Essais de codicologie et de paléographie: Actes du Colloque d'Istanbul (Istanbul, 26-29 mai 1986). Istanbul/Paris 1989*, edited by François Déroche. Paris / Istanbul: Institut français d'études anatoliennes et Bibliothèque Nationale, 1989: 51-60.

Déroche, François et al. *Islamic Codicology: An Introduction to the Study of Manuscripts in Arabic Script*, translated by Deke Dusiberre and David Radzinowicz; edited by Muhammad Isa Waley. London: Al-Furqān Islamic Heritage Foundation, 2005.

Déroche, François. *The Abbasid Tradition: Qur'āns of the 8th to 10th Centuries AD.* New York: Nour Foundation in association with Azimuth Editions and Oxford University Press, 1992.

Gruendler, Beatrice. *The Rise of the Arabic Book*. Cambridge, Massachusetts: Harvard University Press, 2020. Gutas, Dimitri. *Greek Thought, Arabic Culture: The Graeco-Arabic Translation Movement in Baghdad and Early Abbasid Society (2nd-4th/8th-10th Centuries)*. London: Routledge, 1998.

Ibn Ḥibbān. *Kitāb al-Thiqāt*, edited by Muḥammad 'Abd al-Mu'īd Khān, 9 vols. Hyderabad: Dā'irat al-Ma'ārif al-'Uthmāniyyah, 1973.

al-Ḥalwajī, 'Abd al-Sattār. *Al-Makhṭūṭ al-'Arabī*. Cairo: al-Dār al-Miṣriyyah al-Lubnāniyyah, 2011 (reprint: Jiddah: Maktabat Miṣbāḥ, 1989).

Kaplony, Andreas. "What Are Those Few Dots for? Thoughts on the Orthography of the Qurra Papyri (709- 710), the Khurasan Parchments (755-777), and the Inscription of the Jerusalem Dome of the Rock (692)." *Arabica* 55 (2008): 91-112. https://www.jstor.org/stable/25162268. [Accessed September 15, 2020].

al-Mashūkhī, 'Ābid Sulaymān. *Anmāṭ al-tawthīq fī al-makhṭūṭ al-'Arabī fī al-qarn al-rābi' al-Hijrī*. Riyadh: Maktabat al-Malik Fahd al-Waṭaniyyah, 1414/1994.

Melchert, Christopher. *The Formation of the Sunni Schools of Law, 9th-10th Centuries C.E.* Leiden: Brill, 1997.

Nasser, Shady Hekmat. *The Transmission of the Variant Readings of the Qur'ān: the Problem of Tawātur and the Emergence of Shawādhdh*. Leiden: Brill, 2013.

Rosenthal, Franz. *The Technique and Approach of Muslim Scholarship*. Roma: Pontificum Institutum Biblicum, 1947.

al-Qāḍī 'Iyāḍ. *Al-Ilmā' ilā ma'rifat uṣūl al-riwāyah wa-taqyīd al-samā'*, edited by al-Sayyid Aḥmad Ṣaqr. Cairo: Dār al-Turāth; Tunis: al-Maktabah al-'Atīqah, 1970.

Sezgin, Fuat. Geschichte des arabischen Schrifttums, 13 vols. Leiden: Brill; Frankfurt am Main: Institut für Geschichte der Naturwissenschaften and der Johann Wolfgang Goethe Universität, 1967-2007.

Shaykh Alī, 'Uthmān Mu'allim Maḥmūd. "Tafsīr Isḥāq Ibn Ibrāhīm al-Bustī al-mutawaffā sanat 307 H. Taḥqīq wa-dirāsah min awwal sūrat al-naml ilā al-āyah 12 min sūrat al-najm." PhD diss., al-Jāmi'ah al-Islāmiyyah bi al-Madīnah al-Munawwarah, 1416/1995.

Villano, Raoul, and Giuliano Lancioni. "Arabic Grammar and Qur'ānic Scholarship in 2nd/8th Century's Basra: A Comparative Analysis of the Qur'ānic Material Found in the Kitāb

Sībawayhi and in al-'Aḫfaš al-'Awsaṭ's Ma'ānī al-Qur'ān". In *The Foundations of Arab Linguistics V.* Leiden: Brill, 2022: 52-96.

Witkam, Jan Just. "The Neglect Neglected: To point or not to point, That is the Question." *Journal of Islamic Manuscripts* 6 (2015): 376-408.

Appendix 1: Charting the corpus

Case Number	Shelfmark	Date of Copying	Author	Title	Copyist	Corrections & Notes	Layout	Script	Topic
1	MS BA 233	Ṣafar 358/ [December 968 - January 969]	Isḥāq ibn Ibrāhīm ibn Ismāʿīl Abū Muḥammad al-Qāḍī al-Bustī (d. 307/919-20)	A fragment of *Tafsīr al-Bustī* ("Commentary of al-Bustī")	Khalaf ibn Ḥakam (professional copyist; for a patron)	Few corrections and notes	- Plain layout - No title page - No frame - Catchwords: e. g. 23v. - Chapter **division**: titles marked by a separate line - **New chapter** marked by new line	- Abbasid book hand - Two hands (one hand: fol. 1r-177v, 219r-231r; the second: 178r-218v, 231v-233r) - Professional - Medium thickness (neither thick nor thin line) - Medium size (neither large nor small) - Narrow line spacing	Qur'ānic exegesis

Case Number	Shelfmark	Date of Copying	Author	Title	Copyist	Corrections & Notes	Layout	Script	Topic
							- Text **division**: circles provided with stroke; small space - **Text highlighting**: elongation	- Narrow word spacing - First hand: Vertical script (oblique stroke: *ṭā'* / *ẓā'*); second hand: all oblique script - Script moving from the baseline - Stable stroke thickness	
2	MS Ch. B. Ar. 3051	Rabīʿ I 370/ [September-October 980]	Abū ʿAbd Allāh al-Ḥusayn ibn Khālawayh (d. 370/980-1)	*Kitāb Al-Badī'* ("The Wonderful Book")	Ghabzīn ibn ʿAbdullah al-Rūdbārī	Few corrections and many marginal notes		-New Abbasid Style	Qur'ānic Readings
3	MS Şehid 27	Shaʿbān 374/ [December 984-January 985]	Al-Ḥasan ibn Aḥmad ibn ʿAbd al-Ghaffār al-Fārisī al-Naḥwī (d. 377/987)	*Kitāb al-Ḥujjah li-l-a'immah al-sabʿah min qurrā' al-amṣār*	Al-ʿAbbās ibn Aḥmad ibn Mūsā ibn Abī Mawwās al-Kātib (d. 401/1010 -11)	Many corrections and notes	- Plain layout	- *Naskh* similar to the unique Qur'ānic MS of Ibn al-Bawwāb (MS Chester Beatty Is 1431)	Qur'ānic Readings

(*Contd.*)

Case Number	Shelfmark	Date of Copying	Author	Title	Copyist	Corrections & Notes	Layout	Script	Topic
				("The Book of Evidence of the Seven Most Eminent [Qur'ān] Readers of the Capital Cities")			- Title page - No frame - No catchwords - **Chapter division**: titles marked by a separate line - **New chapter** marked by new line - **Text division**: circle; small space - **Text highlighting**: elongation of the words *qāla; ikhtalafū* ("they had different views") to highlight different opinions	- One hand - Professional - Thick line - Large script - Wide line spacing - Narrow word spacing - Vertical script	

Case Number	Shelfmark	Date of Copying	Author	Title	Copyist	Corrections & Notes	Layout	Script	Topic
								- Script moving from baseline - Stable stroke thickness	
4	MS DK 663 Tafsīr (p. 55/ illus.3.18, 3.33, 3.51, 4.1)	Rabī' II 379/ [July-August 989]	Ibn Qutaybah (d. 276/889)	*Mushkil al-Qur'ān* ("Difficulties in the Qur'ān")	Muḥammad ibn Aḥmad ibn Yaḥyā	Many corrections and notes	- Plain Layout - Title page - No frame - No catchwords - **Chapter division**: titles marked by thick pen - New chapter marked by new line - Text **division**: small space; dotted circle	- Abbasid book hand - One hand - Professional - Medium thickness (neither thick nor thin line) - Medium size (neither large nor small) - Narrow line spacing - Narrow word spacing	Qur'ānic philology

(*Contd.*)

Case Number	Shelfmark	Date of Copying	Author	Title	Copyist	Corrections & Notes	Layout	Script	Topic
								- Vertical script -Script tends to be adhering to the baseline - Stable stroke thickness	
5	MS Qar. 791 (Jīm 31), 403 (illus. 4.8), MS Qar. 912 (Jīm 2), 65, MS Qar. 912 (Jīm 4), 66, MS Qar. 912 (Jīm 8), 66, MS Qar. 912 (Jīm 12), 66, MS Qar. 912 (Jīm 19), 66, MS Qar. 912 (Jīm 31), 67, MS Qar. 912 (Jīm 36), 67, MS Qar. 912 (Jīm 42), 67, MS Qar. 912 (Jīm 47), 6 al-Ṭabarī, *Jāmiʿ al-bayān ʿan taʾwīl āy al-Qurʾān*	391/[1000-1001]						-Maghribī script	Qur'ānic exegesis

Case Number	Shelfmark	Date of Copying	Author	Title	Copyist	Corrections & Notes	Layout	Script	Topic
6	MS Fazil 43	Jumādā I 395/ [March-April 1005]	Ibrāhīm ibn al-Sarī al-Zajjāj (d. 311/923)	Ma'ānī al-Qur'ān ("Meanings of the Qur'ān")	Not given	Few corrections and notes	- Plain Layout - Title page (added later) - No frame - No catchwords - **Chapter division**: titles marked by a new line and thick pen; three dots before and after the heading (likely added later) - **New chapter** marked by new line - **Text division**: small space; circle with a stroke	- Naskh? - One hand - Routined? - Medium thickness (neither thick nor thin line) - Medium size (neither large nor small) - Narrow line spacing - Narrow word spacing	Qur'ānic philology

(Contd.)

Case Number	Shelfmark	Date of Copying	Author	Title	Copyist	Corrections & Notes	Layout	Script	Topic
							- **Text highlighting**: underlying with a red line (likely added later)	- Vertical script - Script tends to be adhering to the baseline - Stable stroke thickness	

CHAPTER FIVE

The Compilation of the Qur'ān during the Reign of Abu Bakr

Ammar Khatib and Nazir Khan

How exactly did the Qur'ān come to be preserved in writing? The Islamic tradition provides a considerably detailed narrative of the Qur'ān's textual preservation. The Qur'ān was written down by scribes during the lifetime of the Prophet on various materials. It was the first caliph of Islam, Abū Bakr al-Ṣiddīq who compiled the earliest complete official codex of the Qur'ān, according to the traditional narrative found in canonical hadith sources.[1] Despite this, for a variety of reasons, the compilation of Abū Bakr remains understudied as considerably greater academic attention has been paid to the codices assembled by the third caliph, ʿUthmān ibn ʿAffān. Yet, Abū Bakr's compilation was a major event in the history of the Qur'ān's preservation. It brought together all the written fragments on which the Qur'ān was previously written during the Prophet's lifetime in order to produce a single official unified compilation. The present chapter analyses what the hadith literature and historical sources tell us about the nature of this compilation, the reasons and circumstances that led to it, the process by which it was compiled,

1 For an overview, see Muhammad Mustafa al-Azami, *The History of the Qur'ānic Text, from Revelation to Compilation: A Comparative Study with the Old and New Testaments* (Leicester: UK Islamic Academy, 2003), 77–86. Cf. Theodor Nöldeke, Friedrich Schwally, Gotthelf Bergsträßer, and Otto Pretzl, *The History of the Qur'ān* (Leiden: Brill, 2013), 223–34.

and some of the scholarly differences of opinion concerning it. Through examining these narratives, a clear picture emerges as to the precision and meticulous detail with which the Qur'ān has been preserved.

The initial challenge confronting researchers is that there is considerably more information available for the codices compiled by the third Muslim Caliph, ʿUthmān, in comparison to Abū Bakr's compilation. For the ʿUthmānic codices, a list has been recorded in the Islamic tradition of approximately forty total differences between the codices and this can be correlated precisely with the surviving material evidence in the form of Qur'ānic manuscripts.[2] With respect to the compilation of Abū Bakr, there was only a single codex and no reports concerning variant readings. There is no data that can be used to analyse manuscripts in relation to Abū Bakr's compilation. The task of a historian interested in Abū Bakr's compilation is therefore largely confined to analysing the content of narrations recorded in the works of hadith, Qur'ānic sciences, and Islamic history, as well as the discussions of Muslim scholars. Nonetheless, the historicity of Abū Bakr's compilation may also be argued for on the basis of considerations beyond these literary sources.

Given the Qur'ān's centrality in the spreading and teaching of Islam, it would be highly improbable for Muslims to forgo having any official written copy of the Qur'ān during the reigns of Abū Bakr and ʿUmar bin al-Khaṭṭāb.[3] Given that congregational night prayers in Ramadan became organised and regularly practiced under the reign of ʿUmar, the presence of an authoritative

2 See for instance, Hythem Sidky, "On the Regionality of Qur'ānic Codices," *Journal of the International Qur'ānic Studies Association* 5 (2020):133–210; Ala Vahidnia, "Whence Come Qur'ān Manuscripts? Determining the Regional Provenance of Early Qur'ānic Codices," *Der Islam* 98, no. 2 (2021): 359–93.

3 See for instance the argument of Gregor Schoeler in "The Codification of the Qur'ān: A Comment on the Hypotheses of Burton and Wansbrough," in *The Qur'ān in Context* (Leiden, The Netherlands: Brill, 2009), 779–94, 784–85.

written copy of the Qur'ān could potentially be viewed as a prerequisite. Moreover, the efficiency with which the 'Uthmānic codices were produced with minimal variation and rapidly disseminated throughout the Muslim world is better accounted for if the companions were already familiar with the process of producing a codex, having undertaken the process during Abū Bakr's reign. That the 'Uthmānic codex was based upon, or verified with, Abū Bakr's codex would also boost its authority, one of many factors in its widespread acceptance. Taken collectively, the historical factors lend credence to the account presented in the Islamic literary sources concerning the historicity of Abū Bakr's compilation, as shall be detailed below.

In addition to the canonical hadith literature, there are quite a few additional historical sources at our disposal that mention Abū Bakr's compilation. These include Abū 'Ubayd al-Qāsim bin Sallām (d. 224/838), ibn Sa'd (d. 230/845),[4] al-Fasawī (d. 277/890),[5] al-Ya'qūbī (d. 284/897),[6] Baḥshal (d. 292/905),[7] and ibn Abī Dāwūd (d.316/928),[8] in addition to numerous authorities from later centuries. While individual historical reports must be treated with caution, elements that are attested across sources can be taken with greater confidence. These sources collectively provide details that corroborate and elaborate on the accounts found in the primary hadith literature. Harald Motzki has noted that most Western academics do not accept the

4 Ibn Sa'd, *al-Ṭabaqāt al-kubrā* (Cairo: Maktabat Khānjī, 2001), 5:311. Note that other editions of the text are incomplete and do not include mention of the compilation of Abū Bakr.

5 Ya'qūb b. Sufyān al-Fasawī, *al-Ma'rifa wa al-tārīkh* (Baghdad: Maktabat al-Irshād, 1974), 1:410.

6 Al-Ya'qūbī, *Tārīkh al-Ya'qūbī*, ed. 'Abd al-Amīr Mihanna (Beirut: al-A'lamī li-l-Maṭbū'āt, 2010), 2:22.

7 Abū al-Ḥasan Aslam b. Sahl Baḥshal, *Tārīkh Wāsiṭ*, ed. Kurkīs 'Awwād (Beirut: 'Ālam al-Kutub, 1406 AH/1986), 251.

8 Ibn Abī Dawūd, *Kitāb al-maṣāḥif*, ed. Abū Usāma Salīm al-Hilālī (Kuwait: Mu'asassat Gharās li-l-Nashr wa al-Tawzī', 2006), 139–54.

historicity of Abū Bakr's compilation because of scepticism concerning the details of such accounts.[9] However, on closer scrutiny many of these objections appear unfounded. Rather, a close reading of the Islamic sources alongside the elaborations provided by Muslim scholars allows one to reconstruct a coherent account that resolves the perceived discrepancies. These objections will be discussed under the circumstances preceding the compilation. Moreover, reports transmitted from ibn Shihāb al-Zuhrī (d. 124/742) which provide a detailed account of Abū Bakr's compilation were shown by Motzki to reliably date back to the first Islamic century using an *isnād-cum-matn* analysis.[10] He concludes that claims in Western scholarship that the compilation of Abū Bakr was a later fabrication can therefore be dismissed as untenable. Furthermore, a review of hadith reports on the subject demonstrates that, in addition to the famous account from ibn Shihāb al-Zuhrī–ʿUbayd bin Sabbāq–Zayd bin Thābit, narrations on Abū Bakr's compilation have also been transmitted through independent chains, including ibn Abī al-Zinād–Hishām bin ʿUrwah–ʿUrwah bin al-Zubayr and al-Suddī–ʿAbd Khayr–ʿAlī bin Abī Ṭālib, among others.[11] The contents of these accounts and reports will be analysed below. Given the existence of mutually corroborating independent reliable chains of transmission for reports that describe Abū Bakr's compilation, as well as the ability to reconcile any perceived discrepancies between such reports, the historicity of Abū Bakr's compilation can be confidently established.

---

9 Harald Motzki, "Alternative Accounts of the Qur'ān's Formation," in *The Cambridge Companion to the Qur'ān* (Cambridge: Cambridge University Press, 2008), 62.

10 Harald Motzki, "The Collection of the Qur'ān: A Reconsideration of Western Views in Light of Recent Methodological Developments," *Der Islam* 78 (2001): 1–34. *Isnād-cum-matn* is a method of analysis that collects all the various iterations for a particular hadith as transmitted by each narrator in order to determine the history of its transmission.

11 Akram ʿAbd Khalīfa al-Dalīmī, *Jam ʿal-Qur'ān: Dirāsa taḥliliyya li-marwiyyātihi* (Beirut: Dār al-Kutub al-ʿIlmiyya, 2006), 129–74.

Reports indicating it was the first codex

A number of sources have compiled the narrations concerning the first compilation of the Qur'ān under the supervision of Abū Bakr.[12] However, there are also narrations that suggest that other companions also possessed personal codices of the Qur'ān, which they wrote during the life of the Prophet.[13] This therefore requires some explanation.

The famous account by Zayd b. Thābit related in *Ṣaḥīḥ Bukhārī* describing his involvement in Abū Bakr's compilation indicates that Abū Bakr was taking on a task that had not been previously undertaken during the Prophet's time.[14] In this narration, when the idea is suggested to him, Abū Bakr asks, "How can you do something that the Messenger of Allah did not do?" If such a compilation had already been undertaken by other companions during the Prophet's life, then Abū Bakr's question would not make sense.[15]

It is also narrated from ʿAlī bin Abī Ṭālib, "May God have mercy upon Abū Bakr. He was the first to gather the Qur'ān between two covers (*huwa awwal man jamaʿa al-Qur'ān bayna*

12 See Ibn Abī Dawūd, *Kitāb al-maṣāḥif*, 153–69; Abū ʿAmr al-Dānī, *al-Muqniʿ fī maʿrifat marsūm maṣāḥif ahl al-amṣār* (Riyadh: Dār al-Tadmurrīya, 2010), 134; Makkī b. Abī Ṭālib al-Qaysī, *al-Ibānah ʿan maʿanī al-qiraʾāt*, ed. ʿAbd al-Fattāḥ Ismāʿīl Shalabī (Cairo: Dar Nahdat Misr, 1977), 157–61.

13 See for instance, Muḥammad b. ʿAbd al-Raḥmān al-Ṭāsān, *al-Masāḥif al-manṣuba li-l-ṣaḥāba wa-al-radd ʿalā al-shubuhāt al-muthāra ḥawlahā* (Riyadh: Dār al-Tadmuriyya, 2016), 88–89.

14 Al-Bukhārī, *Ṣaḥīḥ al-Bukhārī, kitāb faḍāʾil al-Qur'ān, bāb jamʿ al-Qur'ān*, no. 4986.

15 One may counter that perhaps he was unaware of the personal copies other companions had, or perhaps he was aware of them and did not agree with them. However, the first possibility seems unlikely given that there is no reason for these copies to have been kept a secret. The second possibility also appears unlikely as one would expect that it would have generated some debate. These scenarios are speculative; however, the most probable scenario suggested by the description found in the hadith is that the first complete copy was indeed Abū Bakr's.

al-lawḥayn)."[16] The authenticity of this report was deemed reliable by ibn Kathīr (d. 774/1373) and ibn Ḥajar (d. 852/1449), among others.[17] A similar report records the statement from ʿAlī as, "The greatest of people in terms of reward for their service to the complete codices (sing. *muṣḥaf*) is Abū Bakr, for he was the first to gather it between two covers."[18] The early Islamic scholar al-Layth bin Saʿd (d. 175/791) also said, "The first to compile the Qur'ān was Abū Bakr and Zayd transcribed it. The people would come to Zayd bin Thābit and he would not write a single verse except with two witnesses."[19]

There are some narrations, however, that state that the first to compile the Qur'ān was other than Abū Bakr. One report states that 'Alī bin Abī Ṭālib was the first to collect the Qur'ān, immediately after the passing of the Prophet.[20] Another report states that after the events of the Battle of al-Yamāma (11/632), ʿUmar was the first to compile the Qur'ān.[21] Yet another report states that Sālim, the tribal client (*mawlā*) of Abū Ḥudhayfa, was the first to compile the Qur'ān.[22] These reports do not

16 Ibn Abī Dawūd, *Kitāb al-maṣāḥif*, 140. Similar narrations from 140–43.

17 See Ibn Abī Dawūd, *Kitāb al-maṣāḥif*, 140. The editor, Salīm al-Hilālī, concurs with ibn Ḥajar's and ibn Kathīr's assessment. The report is transmitted by Ismaʿīl b. ʿAbd al-Raḥmān al-Suddī (d.127/745) from ʿAbd Khayr b. Yazīd al-Hamadānī (d. 81/700) from ʿAlī.

18 Ibn Abī Dawūd, *Kitāb al-maṣāḥif*, 141.

19 Reported in the no longer extant work by ibn Ashtah (d. 360/971), *al-Maṣāḥif*, as cited by al-Suyūṭī, *al-Itqān fī ʿulūm al-Qur'ān* (Beirut: Mu'assasat al-Risāla, 2008), 131.

20 Ibn Abī Dawūd, *Kitāb al-maṣāḥif*, 161–62. See editor notes concerning the narration's inauthenticity.

21 Ibn Abī Dawūd, *Kitāb al-maṣāḥif*, 162. See editor notes concerning the narration's inauthenticity.

22 Reported in ibn Ashtah, *al-Masahif*, as cited by al-Suyūṭī, *al-Itqān*, 130. Note that al-Suyūṭī suggests this could mean Sālim was one of those who compiled the Qur'ān under Abū Bakr, but this cannot be correct if Sālim died during the Battle of al-Yamāma, which was the event that motivated the compilation under Abū Bakr. See ʿAlī al-Jaʿfarī, *Jamʿ al-Qur'ān al-karīm fī ʿahdi Abī Bakr al-Ṣiddīq* (Kuwait: Dār al-Ẓāhiriyya 2022), 23.

possess reliable chains of transmission.[23] However, it is important to note that there were many companions, like ibn Masʿūd,[24] the Prophet's wife ʿĀ'isha,[25] and Ubayy bin Kaʿb, who had personal codices in which they had written some of the Qur'ānic chapters (sing. *sūrah*) they had learned during the lifetime of the Prophet. Abū Shahbah, for instance, notes that even if the reports concerning ʿAlī's compilation are taken as authentic, this would simply entail that he wrote a personal copy of the Qur'ān (whether complete or partial), which does not carry the same reliability and authority as Abū Bakr's compilation which enjoyed unanimous consensus (*ijmāʿ*) and was compiled through an official and public process.[26] Moreover, if personal copies were written down during the lifetime of the Prophet, the sequence of chapters may have been chronological, unlike the ʿUthmānic order. They may also have included abrogated verses, in addition to personal notes regarding abrogation as well as exegesis (*tafsīr*). Therefore, Abū Bakr's effort was a landmark event in preparing the first official copy of the Qur'ān.

The circumstances preceding the compilation

Although the Qur'ān had been written down by many scribes during the lifetime of the Prophet,[27] a complete compilation had not yet been assembled when he passed away. This has been

23 Al-Jaʿfarī, *Jamʿ al-Qur'ān*, 17–28.

24 Al-Bukhārī, *Ṣaḥīḥ al-Bukhārī, kitāb faḍā'il al-Qur'ān, bāb ta'līf al-Qur'ān*, no. 4996.

25 Al-Bukhārī, *Ṣaḥīḥ al-Bukhārī, kitāb faḍā'il al-Qur'ān, bāb ta'līf al-Qur'ān*, no. 4993.

26 Muḥammad Muḥammad Abū Shahba, *al-Madkhal li-dirāsāt al-Qur'ān al-karīm* (Riyadh: Dār al-Liwā' li-l-Nashr wa al-Tawzīʿ, 1987), 273. Cf. Akram Dalīmī, *Jamʿ al-Qur'ān*, 174.

27 See for instance, Muhammad Mustafa al-Azamī, *The Scribes of the Prophet* (London: Turath Publishing, 2020).

stated by none other than the Prophet's chief scribe, Zayd bin Thābit, who also played a central role in both Abū Bakr and 'Uthmān's compilations. Zayd said, "The Messenger of Allah (peace be upon him) passed away and the Qur'ān was not yet collected. It was written on palm branches, trunks, stalks, and leaves."[28] In other narrations there is evidence that the compiling of verses within chapters did take place at the instruction of the Prophet. Zayd said, "We were with the Messenger of Allah (peace be upon him) compiling the Qur'ān from parchment."[29] Al-Bayhaqī (d. 458/1066) commented, "This seems to mean that he intended by this the compilation of what was revealed from the book, the verses scattered in its chapters, and collecting them together based on instruction from the Prophet."[30] Gregor Schoeler notes that the narrations suggest that the majority of the Qur'ān had already been compiled into sheets of parchment while it was likely the later revelations just before the Prophet passed away that remained on scattered materials. Schoeler writes:

> [T]he traditional reports about the state of the Qur'ān at the time of the Prophet's death are not unbelievable if one assumes that part of it—perhaps the greater part of it—had already been written down on sheets of the same format and material, while another, and possibly smaller, part had not yet been committed to writing in this form. This latter part, perhaps consisting of the more recent revelations, may have been written on disparate materials and not yet been transferred to sheets of the same format.[31]

---

28 Aḥmad b. Ḥanbal, *Faḍā'il al-ṣaḥāba*, ed. Waṣī Allāh 'Abbās (Mecca: Mu'assasāt al-Risāla 1983), 1:390.

29 Ibn Ḥibbān, *Ṣaḥīḥ ibn Ḥibbān*, no. 114.

30 Al-Bayhaqī, *Dalā'il al-nubuwwa* (Cairo: Dar al-Rayyān, 1988), 7:147.

31 Schoeler, "Codification of the Qur'ān," 782.

Muhammad Muṣṭafā al-Azami explains that the continuous nature of Divine revelation during the Prophetic period precluded transforming the loose fragments of writing into a single volume until after the Prophet passed away. He writes:

> Setting up a master volume might have proved challenging; any divine *naskh* (abrogation) revealed subsequently, affecting the legal provisions or wordings of certain verses, would have required proper inclusion. And a loose page format greatly simplified the insertion of new verses and new suras, for the revelations did not cease until a short time before the Prophet's death. But with his death the [revelation] *waḥy* ended forever: there would be no more verses, abrogations or rearrangements, so that the situation lent itself perfectly for the compilation of the Qur'ān into a single unified volume.[32]

When Abū Bakr assumed leadership of the fledgling Muslim state after the Prophet passed away, he was immediately confronted with political turmoil in the form of secession, apostasy, multiple rebellions, and fierce battles. One of the most significant battles was the Battle of Yamāma, in which the Muslims fought against the self-proclaimed prophet Musaylima b. Ḥabīb, or Musaylima the Liar. The early historian Khalīfa bin Khayyāṭ al-ʿUṣfurī (d. 240/854) records from Saʿīd bin al-Musayyib (d. 97/715) that the total number of Muslims martyred in the battle was 500, of which 30 or 50 were *ḥamalat al-Qur'ān* (lit. carriers of the Qur'ān), a designation typically used for those who had memorised the Qur'ān.[33] Note that ibn Kathīr says instead that approximately *500 reciters of the Qur'ān* (*qurrāʾ*) were

32 Al-Azami, *History of the Qur'ānic Text*, 77.

33 Khalīfa ibn Khayyāṭ b. Abū Hubayra, *Tārīkh Khalīfa b. Khayyāṭ*, ed. Akram Ḍiyā' al-ʿUmarī (Riyadh: Dār Ṭaybah, 1985), 111.

martyred that day,[34] which likely represents a conflation of the two numbers mentioned by Saʿīd bin al-Musayyib, unless ibn Kathīr was using the term 'reciter' generically for every Muslim martyred. We find among those martyred in Yamāma none other than Sālim, the tribal client (*mawlā*) of Abū Ḥudhayfa.[35] Sālim was a prolific teacher of the Qur'ān, and one of four individuals from whom the Prophet specially instructed people to learn the Qur'ān (the others were ʿAbd Allāh bin Masʿūd, Muʿādh b. Jabal, and Ubayy bin Kaʿb (rA), rA).[36] Moreover, Sālim used to lead the prayers for the earliest Muslim migrants to Medina from Mecca (*muhājirūn*) in a location close to Qubā'.[37]

According to the report of Zayd bin Thābit, the martyrdom of many Qur'ān reciters during the battle of Yamāma was the direct reason for the compilation of the Qur'ān, as suggested by ʿUmar to the caliph Abū Bakr. ʿUmar said, "Indeed a large number of reciters (*qurrā'*) have been killed on the Day of Yamāma, and I fear that more reciters will be killed on other battlefields, whereby a large part of the Qur'ān may be lost (*fayadhhab kathīrun min al-Qur'ān*). Therefore, I am of the opinion that you should order that the Qur'ān be compiled."[38] This narration appears to comport well with the aforementioned reports that the Qur'ān was mostly transcribed on scattered fragments at the time, which adds to the weight and urgency of ʿUmar's request. Although the entire Qur'ān had been written in the Prophetic era,[39] the

---

34 Ibn Kathīr, *Faḍā'il al-Qur'ān*, ed. Abū Isḥāq al-Ḥuwaynī (Cairo: Maktaba b. Taymiyya, 1416 AH/1995), 58.

35 Ismāʿīl ibn Kathīr, *al-Bidāya wa-l-nihāya*, ed. ʿAbd Allāh b. ʿAbd al-Muḥsin al-Turkī (Riyadh: Dar ʿĀlam al-Kutub, 2003), 9:496.

36 Al-Bukhārī, *Ṣaḥīḥ al-Bukhārī, kitāb manāqib al-Anṣār, bāb manāqib Muʿādh b. Jabal*, no. 3806.

37 Al-Bukhārī, *Ṣaḥīḥ al-Bukhārī, kitāb al-ādhān, bāb imāmat al-ʿabd wa al-mawlā*, no. 692.

38 Ṣaḥīḥ al-Bukhārī, *kitāb faḍā'il al-Qur'ān, bāb jamʿ al-Qur'ān*, no. 4986.

39 This is the conclusion that has been argued by many Muslim scholars and can be inferred from Zayd's report concerning the compilation process

written fragments had not yet been formally compiled into an official codex. Since a large number of the Qur'ān reciters had been martyred, ʿUmar's concern was directly related to ensuring the textual preservation of the Qur'ān. Hadith master and exegete, al-Baghawī (d. 516/1122) comments, "They were afraid that some of it [i.e., the Qur'ān] would be lost with the deaths of those who had memorised it, so they rushed to the 'Successor of Allah's Messenger' (i.e., Abū Bakr), and asked him to collect it. He agreed with their opinion, so he ordered its collection in one place."[40] Ibn Kathīr writes similarly.[41]

One could ask why the companions would devote so much effort to preserving the Qur'ān after Allah had promised to preserve it. Muslim scholars viewed the companions' efforts as an instrument of the Divine Will to fulfil the promise of the Qur'ān's preservation. Al-Wāḥidī (d. 468/1076) wrote:

> If it is asked: "Why were the Companions preoccupied with collecting the Qur'ān in *ṣuḥuf* (parchment sheets), when Allah already promised to preserve it, given that one need not fear (losing) what Allah has preserved?"

---

under Abū Bakr. The fact that he sought testimony for each verse from those who had written the verse in the presence of the Prophet indicates that all the verses had been transcribed. Yousef Wahb also observes: "the organized scribal activities, the appointment of scribes, the encouragement of education through writing, the Divine command to preserve the text, and the authentically reported reliance on written materials transcribed during the time of the Prophet in the subsequent textual compilations of the Qur'ān—plainly substantiate the thesis that the entire Qur'ān was recorded before the Prophet's passing." See Yousef Wahb, "How the Qur'ān Was Preserved During the Prophet's Time: Mechanisms of Oral and Written Transmission," *Yaqeen*, December 5, 2022, https://yaqeeninstitute.org/read/paper/how-the-qur'ān-was-preserved-during-the-prophets-time-mechanisms-of-oral-and-written-transmission.

40 Al-Baghawī, *Sharḥ al-sunna*, ed. Zuhayr al-Shāwīsh and Shuʿayb al-Arnāūṭ (Damascus: al-Maktab Islamī, 1983), 4:521.

41 Ibn Kathīr, *Faḍāʾil al-Qur'ān*, 58.

> The response is as follows: Their collection of the Qur'ān was one of the means by which Allah preserved it. When He intended to preserve it, He appointed them for this purpose. Ibn al-Anbārī said: They wanted to facilitate learning the Qur'ān for people and make it accessible through what they did, so that it would be easy for anyone who wanted to memorise it and read it when they saw it collected in a scroll. Even if they had not done what they did, it would not have been lost, as Allah guaranteed its preservation.[42]

It is also worth noting that some scholars interpreted 'Umar's statement differently. Al-Bāqillānī (d. 403/1013) offers an interpretation that suggests that the textual preservation of the Qur'ān was not what 'Umar believed to be at stake. Al-Bāqillānī writes:

> It is possible that what was meant by this is that they (i.e., those who were martyred) used to study the Qur'ān extensively, recite it, and perform night prayers (*tahajjud*) with it. So, 'what would be lost from the Qur'ān' from what they possessed is interpreted to mean that most of the Qur'ān's study and recitation would be lost, along with the abandonment of its recitation in night prayers and supplication. And this is what was intended.[43]

Al-Bāqillānī argued that since many senior companions were alive, there was no basis to fear that the Qur'ān could be lost. However, if we examine 'Umar's statement closely, we note that 'Umar did not only reference the Battle of Yamāma but also expressed concern that future battles would result in similar casualties among the reciters of the Qur'ān. Therefore, it remains

---

42 Al-Wāḥidī, *al-Tafsīr al-basīṭ* (Riyadh: al-Īmām University, 1430H/2009), 12:547.

43 Al-Bāqillānī, *al-Intiṣār li-l-Qur'ān* (Beirut: Dār ibn Ḥazm, 2001), 1:400.

entirely plausible that ʿUmar would raise such a concern to ensure the textual preservation of the Qur'ān.

A number of Western scholars, including Theodor Nöldeke, Richard Bell, and William Montgomery Watt, also raise some contentions against the idea that the martyrdom of Qur'ānic reciters in Yamāma was a motivation for compiling the Qur'ān.[44] They cite an argument from Leone Catani that the names of those who died in the battle of Yamāma largely included new Muslims and the number of those who knew the Qur'ān by heart was too few to have been cause for alarm.[45] Certainly, this argument is readily reconcilable with al-Bāqillānī's interpretation of ʿUmar's statement discussed above. A significant number of casualties of any Muslims could motivate the concern that there would be fewer adherents of Islam to devote themselves to the study of the Qur'ān. Therefore, investing the community's efforts in collectively assembling a codex of the Qur'ān would certainly reinvigorate study and recitation of the sacred text.

But aside from al-Bāqillāni's interpretation, it is not clear that Catani's argument undermines even the conventional interpretation of ʿUmar's statement. We know that a Qur'ānic teacher as prolific as Sālim was among the martyrs in the battle. His loss alone would have certainly impacted the companions at a time when Qur'ān teachers were direly needed to educate the large numbers of tribes that had newly embraced Islam. Other Qur'ān teachers who were martyred in the battle may simply not have been recorded by name. There is precedence for this in the massacre of the 'well of Maʿūna' that took place in 4/625 during the lifetime of the Prophet, where seventy companions from

---

44 Noldeke et al., 229–30 and Richard Bell, *Introduction to the Qur'ān* (Edinburgh: University Press, 1953), 39; cf. Richard Bell and William Montgomery Watt, *Bell's Introduction to the Qur'ān* (Edinburgh: Edinburgh University Press, 2022), 41.

45 Leone Catani, *Annali dell'Islam* (Milano: Hoepli, 1907), 2:713, 739–54.

the Medinan Helpers (*anṣār*) were martyred.[46] The companions martyred in the incident are left unnamed and are simply described as Qur'ān reciters. Moreover, 'Umar's concern was realised with the deaths of those who had memorised any significant portion of the Qur'ān, not only those who had memorised the Qur'ān in its entirety. Ibn Ḥajar, for instance, mentions that "it could mean that they had collectively memorised the Qur'ān, not that every individual had memorised it in its entirety."[47]

Secondly, Noldeke et al. argue that since the compilation involved gathering materials that had already been written down, there was no way that this could have been jeopardised by the death of any number of reciters of the Qur'ān. However, this is overly simplistic. While it is true that the death of those who have memorised the Qur'ān does not cause written copies of the Qur'ān to vanish, it does increase the importance of those written copies for the continued memorisation and teaching of the sacred text, and therefore requires that they be consolidated into a unified text. After all, the fragments on which the Qur'ān was written could have been lost or damaged. On the basis of these considerations, there is consequently no reason to doubt the traditional narrative concerning the motivation of Abū Bakr's compilation.

Based on this narrative, the compilation of Abū Bakr can be plausibly dated to 12/633, between the Battle of Yamāma in 11/632 and prior to his death in 13/634.[48]

46 Al-Bukhārī, *Ṣaḥīḥ al-Bukhārī, kitāb al-maghāzī, bāb ghazwat al-Raji' wa al-Ri'l wa al-Dhakwan wa Bi'r Ma'una*, no. 4090.

47 Ibn Ḥajar, *Fatḥ al-Bārī* (Riyadh: Dar al-Ṭaybah, 2005), 11:167.

48 Khalīfa b. Khayyāṭ, *Tārīkh Khalīfa b. Khayyāṭ*, 107, 121. On the date, see also Ghānim Qaddūrī al-Ḥamad, *Aṣālat al-naṣṣ al-Qur'ānī waḥyan wa rasman wa lughatan wa qirā'atan* (Istanbul: Dār al-Ghawthānī, 2019), 99 and 'Alī al-Ja'farī, *Jam' al-Qur'ān*, 31.

The process and method of compiling the Qur'ān

Zayd bin Thābit was chosen by Abū Bakr to lead the task of compiling the Qur'ānic text. At the time when he was selected for this task, he would have been 22 years old, given that he was 11 years old at the time of the Prophet's migration.[49] Abū Bakr himself gave the reasons for selecting Zayd when he said, "You are a wise young man (*shābun ʿāqilun*), we have no aspersions against you (*lā nattahimuk*), and you used to write down the revelation for the Messenger of Allah."[50] Ibn Ḥajar comments:

> He mentioned four qualities about him which detailed his unique suitability for the task: being young so that he would have the energy for what was demanded of him, being intelligent so he would be more cognisant in his approach, being beyond reproach so that others could trust him, and having been a scribe of revelation, so he possessed the requisite experience. These qualities that he possessed could also be found in others but separately (rather than combined in one person).[51]

Although not explicitly mentioned by Abū Bakr, there are two other qualities that scholars have often added to Zayd's credentials. The first is that Zayd himself had memorised the entire Qur'ān by heart, as mentioned by Abū Bakr bin al-Anbārī (d. 328/940).[52] This is unsurprising given his role as the foremost

---

49 Ghānim Qaddūrī al-Ḥamad, *Rasm al-muṣḥaf: Dirāsah lughawīyya tārīkhīyya* (Baghdad: al-Lajnah al-Waṭanīyya, 1982), 112.

50 Al-Bukhārī, *Ṣaḥīḥ al-Bukhārī, kitāb faḍāʾil al-Qur'ān, bāb jamʿ al-Qur'ān*, no. 4986.

51 Ibn Ḥajar al-ʿAsqalānī, *Fatḥ al-Bārī*, 11:169.

52 Cited in Abū ʿAbd Allāh al-Qurṭubī (d. 671/1272), *al-Jāmiʿ li-aḥkām al-Qur'ān* (Beirut: Mu'assasāt al-Risāla, 2006), 1:88.

scribe of the Prophet Muhammad. A second credential that is often mentioned by scholars is that Zayd witnessed the "final review" (*al-ʿarḍa al-akhīra*) between the Prophet and the Angel Jibrīl (as).[53] The Prophet used to review the entire Qur'ān annually with Jibrīl in the month of Ramadan and during the last year of his life, the Prophet completed the review with Jibrīl twice.[54] Al-Baghawī states:

> It is said that Zayd bin Thābit attended the final review in which it was clarified what was abrogated and what remained. Abū ʿAbd al-Raḥmān al-Sulamī said, "Zayd recited the Qur'ān twice to the Prophet during the year in which he passed away, and this recitation is called the reading (*qirāʾa*) of Zayd because he transcribed it for the Prophet and recited it to him and witnessed *al-ʿarḍa al-akhīra*, and he taught its recitation to people until he passed away. That is why Abū Bakr and ʿUmar relied upon him in its compilation and ʿUthmān appointed him in charge of writing the *muṣḥaf*s—may God be pleased with them all."[55]

Aside from the statement of al-Sulamī, there are in fact no reports corroborating that Zayd attended the final review.[56] Qur'ānic

53 ʿAlī al-Jaʿfarī, *Jamʿ al-Qur'ān al-Karīm fī ʿahdi Abī Bakr al-Ṣiddīq*, 35–36; al-Azami, *History of the Qur'ānic Text*, 79.

54 Saḥīḥ al-Bukhārī, *kitāb al-manāqib, bāb ṣifat al-nabī*, no. 3554; see also *kitāb faḍāʾil al-Qur'ān, bāb kāna Jibrīl yaʿriḍu al-Qur'ān ʿalā al-nabī*, no. 4998.

55 Al-Baghawī, *Sharḥ al-sunna* (Beirut: Al-Maktab al-Islāmī, 1983), 4:525–26.

56 For a detailed discussion concerning the "final review," refer to the following studies: Usāma al-Ḥayānī, "*al-ʿArḍa al-akhīra li-l-Qur'ān al-Karīm wa-al-aḥadīth al-wārida fīhā jamʿan wa dirāsa*," *al-Majallat Jāmiʿat al-Amīr ʿAbd al-Qādir*, no. 10; Muhammad Bāzmūl, "*al-Aḥādīth al-wārida fī al-ʿarḍa al-akhīra*," *Majallah Jāmiʿat Umm al-Qurra li-l-ʿUlūm al-Sharīʿa wa al-Dirāsāt al-Islāmiyya* 62 (Shaʿbān 1435): 83; Nāsir b. Saʿūd al-Qithamī, "*al-ʿArḍa al-akhīra: Dalālatuhā wa atharuhā*," *Majallat Maʿhad al-Imām al-Shaṭibī li-Dirasāt al-Qur'āniyya* 15 (2013): 1–69.

philologist, Abū Ja'far al-Naḥḥās (d. 338/950), said that the reading of Zayd was the one confirmed in the final review.[57] Similarly, ibn Taymiyya (d. 728/1328) said, "And the final review is the *qirā'ah* of Zayd bin Thābit and others, and it is the one that the rightly-guided caliphs—Abū Bakr, 'Umar, 'Uthmān, and 'Alī—instructed to be written in the *maṣāḥif*."[58]

On the other hand, we have reports from ibn 'Abbās indicating that it was in fact 'Abd Allāh bin Mas'ūd who attended the final review,[59] which he mentioned to explain why ibn Mas'ūd's reading differed from the 'Uthmānic codex and the reading of Zayd Al-Ṭāsān dismisses ibn 'Abbās' report as inauthentic for several reasons. However, he suggests that, even if one were to assume the report was authentically transmitted, it was simply a confusion on the part of ibn 'Abbās.[60] Nonetheless, the relevance of the "final review" was never mentioned by the companions during the compilation process of Abū Bakr nor of 'Uthmān. Moreover, given that there is no definite and clear evidence to confirm the claim that Zayd attended the final review, mentioning it as a credential is speculative at best.

With respect to the process by which Zayd gathered the Qur'ān, the evidence indicates that he undertook a stringent process that utilised both written materials in addition to memorisation of the text. He said, "I gathered it from the bark of palm trees, thin white stones, and the men who knew it by heart."[61]

---

57 Al-Naḥḥās, *al-Nāsikh wa-al-mansūkh* (Riyadh: Dār al-'Āsima, 2009), 2:407.

58 Ibn Taymiyya, *al-Fatāwā al-kubrā* (Beirut: Dār al-Kutb al-'Ilmiyya, 1987), 4:418.

59 Imām Aḥmad, *Musnad Aḥmad*, no. 3422. This was also mentioned by al-Ṭaḥāwī and al-Māturīdī.

60 Muḥammad b. 'Abd al-Rahmān al-Ṭāsān, *Taḥqīq mawqif al-ṣaḥābī al-jalīl 'Abdullāh ibn Mas'ūd min al-jam' al-'Uthmānī* (Riyadh: Kursī al-Qur'ān al-Karīm wa 'Ulūmuh bi-Jāmi'at al-Malik Su'ūd, 1435 AH/2014), 58–67.

61 Al-Bukhārī, *Ṣaḥīḥ Bukhārī, kitāb faḍā'il al-Qur'ān, bāb jam' al-Qur'ān*, no. 4986.

During the process of compiling the Qur'ān, Zayd famously sought corroboration from two witnesses for each verse. As cited earlier, al-Layth b. Saʿd said, "The first to compile the Qur'ān was Abū Bakr and Zayd transcribed it. The people would come to Zayd bin Thābit and he would not write a single verse except with two witnesses."[62]

Zayd did not transcribe verses from memory despite the fact that he and other companions had memorised them. Nor did he simply transcribe the Qur'ān from existing written copies. Rather, he followed a meticulous process to ensure that the transcription of every verse was backed by both direct written testimony and memory. ʿAlam al-Dīn al-Sakhāwī (d. 643/1245) explained that the requirement for 'two witnesses' meant two people who possessed it in writing and could testify to having written down the verse from the Prophet precisely as they had learned it.[63] This interpretation is favoured by the majority of Muslim scholars.[64] Another interpretation mentioned by ibn Ḥajar takes the "two witnesses" as meaning "memory" and "writing."[65] While it is certainly true that both memory and writing were involved, the evidence does suggest that the meaning of two witnesses was two individuals who had learned the verses directly from the Prophet. This is particularly confirmed by the story of Abū Khuzayma discussed below. Thus, the compilation process for each verse in

62 As cited by al-Suyūṭī, *al-Itqān*, 131.

63 See al-Sakhāwī, *Jamāl al-qurrā' wa kamāl al-iqrā'* (Beirut: Mu'assasat al-Kutub al-Thaqāfiyya, 1999), 302–3.

64 See al-Azami, *History of the Qur'ānic Text*, 80; Muḥammad Ḥasan Jabal, *Wathāqat naql al-naṣṣ al-Qur'ānī min Rasūl Allāh ṣallā Allāhu ʿalayhī wa sallam ilā ummatihī* (Tanta: Dar al-Ṣaḥāba li-l-Turāth bi-Ṭanṭā, n.d.), 182; al-Judayʿ, *Muqaddima asāsīyya fī ʿulūm al-Qur'ān* (Beirut: Mu'assasat al-Rayān, 2001), 97; Muṣṭafā al-Bughā and Muḥyī al-Dīn Mistū, *al-Wāḍiḥ fī ʿulūm al-Qur'ān* (Damascus: Dār al-Kalim al-Tayyib, 1998), 84; Muḥammad Ṭāhir al-Kurdī, *Tārīkh al-Qur'ān al-Karīm* (Jeddah: al-Fatḥ, 1946), 49; ʿAlī al-Jaʿfarī, *Jamʿ al-Qur'ān*, 40.

65 Ibn Ḥajar, *Fatḥ al-Bārī*, 11:171–73.

the Qur'ān was backed by the combined attestation of written materials, memorisation, and direct testimony.

The story of a missing verse

During the compilation of Abū Bakr, while seeking two witnesses for each passage, Zayd bin Thābit came across a passage for which he found only one witness. Zayd reports, "Abū Bakr sent for me, so I collected the Qur'ān until I found the last part of *Sūrah al-Tawba* (9:128–129) with Abū Khuzayma al-Anṣārī and did not find it with anybody else."[66] This narration, found in *Ṣaḥīḥ al-Bukhārī*, explicitly notes that this took place during the first compilation, and that the witness was Abū Khuzayma. Again, one must clarify that this does not mean that Abū Khuzayma was the only one who knew this verse, as all the companions who had memorized the Qur'ān knew it. However, they were seeking a witness who had documented the verse in the presence of the Prophet Muhammad.[67] The very reason they knew exactly which verse was missing was because they had memorised it.

Another narration, also from Zayd bin Thābit and narrated in *Ṣaḥīḥ al-Bukhārī*, mentions the same incident but with the name Khuzayma al-Anṣarī:

> So I started locating Qur'ānic material and collecting it from parchments, scapulae, leaf-stalks of date palms, and from the memories of men [who knew it by heart].

---

66 Al-Bukhārī, *Ṣaḥīḥ al-Bukhārī, kitāb al-tawḥīd, bāb wa kāna ʿarshuhū ʿalā al-māʾ wa huwa rabb al-ʿarsh al-aẓīm*, no. 7425.

67 Abū Shāma, *al-Murshid al-wajīz*, 61; Ibn Ḥajar, *Fatḥ al-Bārī*, 11:171–73; al-Bāqillānī, *Nukat al-intiṣār li-naql al-Qur'ān*, ed. Muḥammad Zaghlūl Sallām (Alexandria: Munshaʾat al-Maʿārif, 1971), 333. See also al-Sakhāwī, *Jamāl al-qurrāʾ*, 307 for the alternate explanation that Zayd was looking for others who had a copy of the verse to confirm the different possible readings of the verse.

> I found with Khuzayma al-Anṣārī two verses of *Sūrah al-Tawba* that I had not found with anybody else [he cites Qur'ān 9:128–129].[68]

Such a minor difference in the name (Abū Khuzayma vs Khuzayma) would typically not raise any questions, except that we have a third narration, also in *Ṣaḥīḥ al-Bukhārī*, about an identical incident involving a different verse with Khuzayma.

> When we wrote the Holy Qur'ān, I missed one of the verses of *Sūrah al-Aḥzāb* which I used to hear Allah's Messenger reciting. Then we searched for it and found it with Khuzayma b. Thābit al-Anṣārī. The verse was "Among the Believers are men who have been true to their Covenant with Allah, Of them, some have fulfilled their obligations to Allah [i.e., they have been killed in Allah's cause], And some of them are [still] waiting." [33:23] So we wrote this in its place in the Qur'ān.[69]

Notice that this narration does not explicitly mention whether this occurred during Abū Bakr's or 'Uthmān's compilation.[70] In another narration, Zayd states "I compiled the written materials into codices" (*nasakhtu al-ṣuḥuf fī al-maṣāḥif*), which implies it was during the 'Uthmānic project which involved multiple codices.[71] In that narration he mentions verse 33:23 and Khuzayma bin Thābit al-Anṣārī. There are other narrations of this incident in other sources that use either name for each incident.[72]

---

68 Al-Bukhārī, *Ṣaḥīḥ al-Bukhārī*, no. 4679.

69 Al-Bukhārī, *Ṣaḥīḥ al-Bukhārī*, no. 4049.

70 Ghanim Qaddūrī al-Ḥamad, *Rasm al-Muṣḥaf*, 118–19.

71 Al-Bukhārī, *Ṣaḥīḥ al-Bukhārī*, no. 2807.

72 Ibn Abū Dāwūd, *Kitāb al-maṣāḥif*, 1:146, 148, 154, 203 (which mentions Khuzayma with 9:128 during Abū Bakr's compilation), 1:149 (which mentions Khuzayma with 33:23 during Abū Bakr's compilation), 1:198 (which mentions Khuzayma or Abū Khuzayma for 33:23), 2:221 (which mentions

Al-Bāqillānī argues that these narrations may be dismissed as contradictory and conflicting with more reliable evidence or may be reinterpreted in various ways.[73]

Ibn Ḥajar al-ʿAsqalānī and others reconciled the narrations by stating that the first incident took place during the compilation of Abū Bakr,[74] and that it was the verse from *Sūrah al-Tawbah* that was found with Abū Khuzayma bin Aws bin Yazīd bin Aṣram. Meanwhile, the second incident took place during the compilation of ʿUthmān with the verse from *Sūrah al-Aḥzāb*, which was found with Dhū al-Shahādatayn Khuzayma bin Thābit al-Anṣārī, a different person from Abū Khuzayma.[75] al-Azami uses this as evidence for his argument that ʿUthmān repeated the process of summoning witnesses for each verse; otherwise there is no reason they would not be able to find the verse from *al-Aḥzāb* if the compilation of Abū Bakr was in front of them.[76] Al-Jaʿfarī

Khuzayma with 33:23 during ʿUthmān's compilation), and 2:225 (which mentions Khuzayma with 9:128 during ʿUthmān's compilation). See also Abū ʿUbayd al-Qāsim b. Sallām, *Faḍāʾil al-Qurʾān wa maʿālimuhu wa adābuhu*, ed. Aḥmad ʿAbd al-Wāḥid al-Khayyāṭī (Rabat: Wizārat al-Awqāf wa al-Shuʿūn al-Islāmiyya, 1995), 2:93, 96.

73 Al-Bāqillānī, *Nukat al-intiṣār*, 331.

74 Ibn Ḥajar, *Fatḥ al-Bārī*, 11:172. See also Badr al-Dīn al-ʿAynī, *ʿUmdat al-qārī*, 20:19.

75 Abū Shāma, *al-Murshid al-wajīz*, 61; Ibn Ḥajar, *Fatḥ al-Bārī*, 11:172; see also ibn ʿĀshir, *Fatḥ al-Mannān al-marwī bi-mawrid al-ẓamān*, ed. ʿAbd al-Karīm Bū Ghazāla (Egypt: Dār ibn al-Ḥafṣī 2016), 417–18.

76 Al-Azami writes, "These two have caused confusion among some scholars, mainly due to the proximity of the two names. Note that the two are distinct: Khuzaima and Abu Khuzaima. Now if we read the hadiths carefully we see that Zaid used the word *ṣuḥuf* for the collection during Abū Bakr's reign, and the word *muṣḥaf* or *maṣāḥif* (pl. of *muṣḥaf*) for the work he did under ʿUthmān's supervision. Thus we may safely conclude that these are two different instances of compilation....If we consider the second compilation to be Zaid's work on an independent copy of the *muṣḥaf*, then everything becomes clear. On the other hand, if we assume that Zaid was simply making a duplicate copy for ʿUthmān based on Abū Bakr's, not an autonomous copy, then we

meanwhile suggests that it is not inconceivable that the written parchment of one verse may have gone missing during the time interval between the two compilations, which exceeded a decade.[77]

On the other hand, scholars like ibn Kathīr[78] and others[79] held that both incidents happened during the time of Abū Bakr. While Muḥammad Ḥasan Jabal agrees with ibn Ḥajar's analysis that the incidents described by Zayd refer to two different people, he also concurs with ibn Kathīr's opinion that both occurred during the compilation of Abū Bakr.[80]

Ghānim Qaddūrī al-Ḥamad adduces additional evidence suggesting that the incident of the lost verse happened only during the time of Abū Bakr, but also that both incidents are in fact one incident that involved the same person. He cites the following narration from the introduction to *Kitāb al-Mabānī*, in which Zayd describes the compilation during the time of Abū Bakr:

> I completed one review and I noticed I was missing this verse [33:23] so I asked the Meccan migrants (*Muhājirīn*) and the Medinan Helpers (*Anṣār*) and I did not find it [in written form] with any of them, although I knew the verse and the Prophet had dictated it to me, however

---

must confront the awkward question of why Zaid was unable to locate verse no. 23 from *Sūrah al-Aḥzāb*, since all the verses should have been right in front of him. Of interest also is that Zaid uses the first person singular pronoun in the first narration and the plural "we," indicating group activity, in the second. All of this strongly bolsters the view that the second compilation was indeed an independent endeavor." Al-Azami, *History of the Qur'ānic Text*, 92.

77 ʿAlī al-Jaʿfarī, *Jamʿ al-Qur'ān fī ʿahd ʿUthmān* (Kuwait: Dar al-Ẓāhiriyya, 2022), 44–45.

78 Ibn Kathīr, *Faḍā'il al-Qur'ān* (Cairo: Maktabah ibn Taymiyya, 1416 AH/1996), 86.

79 Burhān Ibrāhīm al-Jaʿbarī, *Jamīlat arbāb al-marāṣid fī sharḥ ʿaqīlat atrāb al-qaṣā'id*, ed. Muḥammad Ilyās Anwar (Amman: Arwiqa, 2017), 340. See also Ahmad Ali al-Imam, *Variant Readings of the Qur'ān* (London: IIIT, 2006), 45.

80 Jabal, *Wathāqat naql*, 185, 201–204.

> I disliked to establish it until someone else testified alongside me. And then I obtained it from Khuzayma bin Thābit al-Anṣārī whose testimony the Prophet had made equal to that of two witnesses. So I wrote the verse and then I conducted another review. And I found that I was missing two verses although I knew them [9:127–128]. So I inquired about them from the *Muhājirīn* and the *Anṣār* and I did not find them with any of them except with Khuzayma b. Thābit al-Anṣarī whose testimony the Prophet had endorsed. So I wrote them at the end of Barā'a [*Sūrah al-Tawbah*].[81]

Ghānim Qaddūrī al-Ḥamad states that this account alleviates some of the confusion found in other sources. He also notes that "the similarity between the two names (i.e., Abū Khuzayma and Khuzayma) and their mention in different narrations using the very same phrasing indicates that they are both names referring to the same companion and that is Khuzayma bin Thābit al-Anṣārī."[82] This is the simplest and easiest explanation for what would otherwise seem to be a rather striking coincidence of the exact same circumstances involving two different individuals with almost identical names. Nonetheless, other ways of reconciling the narrations, such as that of ibn Ḥajar, were also accepted by many scholars. Finally, it should be mentioned that the verses in question have been attested in the earliest manuscripts, and it is not reported that a single companion's codex omitted them.[83]

81 Arthur Jeffery, ed., *Muqaddimatān fī 'ulūm al-Qur'ān: Wa-humā muqaddimāt Kitāb al-mabānī wa muqaddimāt ibn 'Atiyya* (Cairo: Maktabat al-Khānjī, 1954), 20–22. On the identity of the author, see Aron Zysow, "Two Unrecognized Karrāmī Texts," *Journal of the American Oriental Society* 108, no. 4 (1988): 577–87, https://doi.org/10.2307/603146.

82 Ghānim Qaddūrī al-Ḥamad, *Rasm al-muṣḥaf*, 119.

83 Behnam Sadeghi and Mohsen Goudarzi, "*Ṣanʿā'* 1 and the Origins of the Qur'ān," *Der Islam* 87, nos. 1–2 (2012): 23. They write: "There are

Differences between the compilations of Abū Bakr and 'Uthmān

Scholars have provided a number of explanations for why the codex of 'Uthmān differed from the compilation of Abū Bakr.[84] First, the reasons for undertaking the projects differed. The compilation of Abū Bakr was meant to record the Qur'ān in its entirety to ensure that verses of the Qur'ān would not be lost with the death of those who had memorised them.[85] The 'Uthmānic codex, meanwhile, was meant to unite the entire Muslim nation upon a single text to eliminate confusion caused by Muslims reciting variant readings of the Qur'ān.[86] Eminent scholar and polymath, Imam al-Ṣuyūṭī (d. 911/1505), cited this explanation of the differences as follows:

> Ibn al-Tīn and others have said: The difference between Abū Bakr's compilation and 'Uthmān's is that Abū Bakr compiled the Qur'ān out of fear that parts of it might be lost with the loss of those who had memorised it, as it was not collected in one place. So, he gathered it into parchments, arranging the verses of its surahs as the Prophet had directed. 'Uthmān's compilation, on the other hand, was due to the growing disagreement

some traditions about 'Uthmān's team finding the last two verses of sūra 9 with a man named Khuzayma, or Abū Khuzayma, or ibn Khuzayma. C-1 [(San'ā' undertext)] has these verses in the expected place. Since they are also found in the 'Uthmānic Qur'ān, and since it is not reported that any Companion codex was without them, these verses must have belonged to the prototype from which the C-1 and 'Uthmānic text types emerged. Therefore, one should not read too much into the report."

84 See also 'Abd al-Fattāh al-Qāḍī, *Tārīkh al-muṣḥaf al-sharīf* (Cairo: Maktabat Jindī, 1951), 27; al-Juday', *Muqaddimāt aṣāsīya*, 100–101.

85 Al-Dānī, *al-Muqni'*, 137.

86 Makkī, *al-Ibāna*, 62–64; 'Abd al-Qayyūm al-Sindī, *Jam' al-Qur'ān al-Karīm fī 'ahd al-khulafā' al-rāshidīn* (Medina: Majma' al-Malik Fahd li-Tiba'at al-Muṣḥaf al-Sharīf, 1421 AH), 380; Ghānim Qaddūrī al-Ḥamad, *Aṣālah al-naṣṣ*, 105.

> in the ways of recitation, to the extent that they recited it in their own dialects, given the diversity of dialects. This led some to mistake others' readings. Fearing the exacerbation of this matter, ʿUthmān transcribed those parchments into a single *muṣḥaf* (codex), arranging its surahs, and limited the dialects to the dialect of Qur'āysh. His argument was that it was revealed in their dialect, even though the recitation was broadened to dialects other than theirs initially to ease difficulty and hardship. He saw that the need for that had ended, and thus he restricted it to one dialect.[87]

Since the reason for the compilations differed, the use of the compilations differed as well. During the time of Abū Bakr, the compilation was simply kept in safekeeping while Muslims continued to read the Qur'ān according to the way they had been taught and according to the personal copies that they had in their possession.[88] Adhering to the ʿUthmānic codex, however, was compulsory, and copies were sent to major cities in the Islamic empire. Any written copies of the Qur'ān that did not conform to the ʿUthmānic codex were burned or corrected. These are the fundamental differences between the two compilations.

Some scholars also distinguish between the compilation of Abū Bakr and the ʿUthmānic codex on the basis of the fact that the former is termed *ṣuḥuf* and the latter is termed *muṣḥaf.* These scholars understand the former term to refer to loose sheets of parchment and the latter term to refer to written sheets of parchment bound together between two covers, i.e., a codex.

It has been further suggested that Abū Bakr's compilation was not arranged according to chapter sequence.[89] Al-Ḥākim al-Naysābūrī (d. 405/1014), provides an interesting comment in

87 Al-Suyūṭī, *al-Itqān fī ʿulūm al-Qur'ān*, 133.

88 Al-Kurdī, *Tārīkh al-Qur'ān*, 49.

89 See Abū Shahba, *al-Madkhal*, 273.

this regard after citing a hadith indicating that some compilation took place at the time of the Prophet himself.[90] Al-Ḥākim writes:

> The hadith provides clear evidence that the compilation of the Qur'ān was not a single event. Some of it was compiled in the presence of the Messenger of Allah, peace be upon him, then some of it was compiled in the presence of Abū Bakr as-Ṣiddīq. The third compilation, which involved arranging the surahs, occurred during the Caliphate of the Commander of the Faithful, 'Uthmān bin 'Affān, may Allah be pleased with them all.[91]

This brief comment expresses the opinion that 'Uthmān's compilation involved arranging the surah sequence, and implies that Abū Bakr's compilation did not. Ibn 'Aṭiyya (d. 541/1147), an authoritative Sunni exegete, is more explicit in stating that the compilation of Abū Bakr was "not arranged by surah sequence" (*ghayr murattab al-suwar*).[92] Abū Shāma al-Maqdisī (d. 665/1268) explains this with reference to the term *ṣuḥuf* used to describe Abū Bakr's compilation:

> It appears that Abū Bakr, may Allah be pleased with him, compiled one, two, or more surahs onto a sheet of parchment, depending on the length of the surah. Hence it is

90 The hadith is as follows: Zayd bin Thabit, may Allah be pleased with him, reported: We were with the Messenger of Allah, peace be upon him, compiling the Qur'ān from fragments, when the Messenger of Allah, peace be upon him, said: "Blessings upon Syria." We asked, "Why is that?" He said, "Because the angels of the Merciful are spreading their wings over them."

91 Al-Ḥākim al-Naysābūrī, *al-Mustadrak 'alā al-ṣaḥīḥayn*, ed. Muṣṭafā 'Abd al-Qadir 'Aṭṭā (Beirut: Dar al-Kutub al-'Ilmiyya, 1990), 2:249.

92 'Abd al-Ḥaqq b. Ghālib ibn 'Aṭiyya, *al-Muḥarrar al-wajīz*, ed. 'Abd al-Salām 'Abd al-Shāfī Muḥammad (Beirut: Dār al-Kutub al-'Ilmiyya, 1422H/2001), 1:49.

> said that he compiled the Qur'ān in *ṣuḥuf*,[93] and similar expressions that indicate plurality. Then 'Uthmān, may Allah be pleased with him, copied from those sheets (*ṣuḥuf*) into a *muṣḥaf* which included them together, arranging the surahs in their current order.[94]

Ibn Ḥajar writes:

> The difference between the *ṣuḥuf* and the *muṣḥaf* is that the *ṣuḥuf* are the separate parchment sheets on which the Qur'ān was compiled during the era of Abū Bakr. They contained the surahs [chapters] separately, each surah arranged independently with its verses, but the surahs were not arranged sequentially. When they were copied and arranged in a sequence, they became a *muṣḥaf*.[95]

On the other hand, Ghānim Qadduri al-Ḥamad does not find the evidence sufficient to conclude that Abū Bakr's compilation lacked arrangement by surah sequence, and he points to the existence of reports that mention that Abū Bakr compiled the Qur'ān 'between two covers.'[96]

There is also some discussion concerning the suitability of the term *jamʿ* (gathering or compilation) for the compilation of Abū Bakr versus the 'Uthmānic codex. While listing the differences between Abū Bakr's compilation and 'Uthmān's codex, Ahmed al-'Abd al-Karīm writes, "The compilation by Abū Bakr was the closest to the conventional meaning of 'compilation' in the Arabic language, which implies bringing together what is

---

93 The word in the text is *muṣḥaf*, which appears to be in error since it is not plural, see al-Ṭāsān, *al-Masāḥif al-manṣuba*, 29.

94 Abū Shāma, *al-Murshid al-wajīz ilā 'ulūm tata'allaq bil-Kitāb al-Aziz*, ed. Ibrāhim Shams al-Dīn (Beirut: Dar al-Kutub al-'Ilmiyya, 2003), 76.

95 Ibn Ḥajar, *Fatḥ al-Bārī*, 11:177–178.

96 Ghānim Qadduri al-Ḥamad, *Rasm al-muṣḥaf*, 123.

scattered and connecting parts to each other."[97] For those scholars who consider the ʿUthmānic codex to simply be a direct copy of the *ṣuḥuf* of Abū Bakr, ʿUthmān's project did not involve gathering or compiling any textual materials; it was rather a gathering or unifying of people upon a single text, and thus may be more appropriately called a project of standardisation. However, the ʿUthmānic codex may be considered a compilation of a compilation, in that Abū Bakr's loose sheets of parchment (*ṣuḥuf*) were combined into a bounded codex. Indeed, the scholars of hadith listed narrations concerning the ʿUthmānic project under the title "the compilation (*jamʿ*) of the Qur'ān," which indicates that they considered it to be part of the compilation process rather than a separate process.[98] Moreover, as will be explained in a subsequent section, some scholars considered the ʿUthmānic codex to be an autonomously assembled text that was later checked against the *ṣuḥuf* of Abū Bakr; hence, it could also be appropriately termed a compilation as per that view.

The variant readings and Abū Bakr's compilation

The Islamic tradition recognizes a multiplicity of correct ways to recite the Qur'ān which relates to the hadith that the Qur'ān has been revealed according to seven *aḥruf* (ways of reciting, lit. 'letters,' sing. *ḥarf*).[99] The narrations discussed earlier do not provide any direct indications on whether Abū Bakr's compilation

97 Ahmed al-ʿAbd al-Karīm, "*Al-Farq bayna jamʿ Abī Bakr wa ʿUthmān*," 15.
98 Al-Ṭāsān, *al-Masāḥif*, 514.
99 For a more detailed discussion on the meaning of the seven *aḥruf*, refer to the discussion on the nature of the *aḥruf* in Ammar Khatib and Nazir Khan, "The Origins of the Variant Readings of the Qur'ān," *Yaqeen*, August 2019, https://yaqeeninstitute.ca/read/paper/the-origins-of-the-variant-readings-of-the-Qur'ān.

contained more than one reading; however, this was a topic on which Islamic scholars theorised. For instance, Abū ʿAmr al-Dānī (d. 444/1053) replies to a question concerning why ʿUthmān compiled the Qur'ān when it was already compiled in Abū Bakr's codex (*muṣḥaf*) beforehand:

> If someone were to say, "Now that you have clarified what you were asked about in interpreting these two reports, then explain to us the reason that prompted ʿUthmān, may God be pleased with him, to compile the Qur'ān in the *maṣāḥif*, although it was already compiled in the *muṣḥaf*, as you have narrated to us in the previous hadith of Zayid bin Thābit." I would respond that the reason for this is clear, based on the report and the opinion of some scholars. It is that Abū Bakr, may God be pleased with him, first compiled the Qur'ān according to the seven *aḥruf* [i.e., recitations] that God, the Almighty, allowed the Ummah to recite and he did not specify a particular *ḥarf*. Thus, when it was ʿUthmān's time, and a disagreement arose between the people of Iraq and the people of Shām about the recitation, and Hudhayfa informed him of this, he, along with the companions in Madīnah, decided to unite the people on a single *ḥarf* of those *aḥruf*, and to drop the others. This would eliminate the differences and produce agreement.[100]

Interestingly, al-Dānī prefaces this explanation by noting that it is the opinion of some scholars, indicating that there were perhaps differing views on this matter in his time as well. However, the view al-Dānī selected does seem to have become popular and we find his contemporary, ibn ʿAbd al-Barr (d. 463/1071) echoing a similar view:

100 Al-Dānī, *al-Muqniʿ*, 613.

> As for Abū Bakr's compilation of the Qur'ān, he was the first to gather it between two covers. 'Alī bin Abī Ṭālib also compiled the Qur'ān after the death of the Prophet, peace be upon him, and during Abū Bakr's caliphate. All of this was in accordance with the seven *aḥruf*, unlike 'Uthmān's compilation based on a single *ḥarf*, the *ḥarf* of Zayd bin Thābit, which is what is in the hands of the people between the covers of the *muṣḥaf* today.[101]

The hadith commentator, Badr al-Dīn al-'Aynī (d. 855/1451), similarly wrote:

> Abū Bakr's aim was to compile the Qur'ān with all its *aḥruf* and ways in which it was revealed, which are based on the dialect of [the Meccan tribe of] Qur'āysh and others. 'Uthmān's aim, however, was to isolate the dialect of Qur'āysh from those other readings.[102]

Other scholars who made similar statements concerning the inclusion of seven *aḥruf* in Abū Bakr's collection include al-Shāṭibī (d. 590/1193),[103] al-Sakhāwī (d. 643/1245),[104] and al-Ja'barī (d. 732/1332).[105] Many contemporary scholars also endorsed the view that Abū Bakr's compilation contained the seven *aḥruf* while 'Uthmān's compilation did not.[106] However, if this opinion

---

101 Ibn 'Abd al-Barr, *al-Istidhkār* (Beirut: Dār al-Kutub al-'Ilmiyya, 2000), 2:485.

102 Badr al-Dīn al-'Aynī, *'Umdat al-Qārī* (Beirut: Dār Iḥyā' Turāth al-'Arabī, n.d.), 18:281.

103 Al-Shāṭibī, *'Aqīlat atrāb al-qaṣā'id*, ed. Ayman Suwayyid (Jeddah: Dār Nūr al-Maktabāt, 2001), 3.

104 Al-Sakhāwī, *al-Wasīlah ilā kashf al-'aqīla* (Riyadh: Maktaba al-Rushd, 2003), 63.

105 Al-Ja'barī, *Jamīlat arbāb al-marāṣid*, 334.

106 See for instance al-Kurdī, *Tārīkh al-Qur'ān al-Karīm*, 48, 64; al-Ja'farī, *Jam' al-Qur'ān fī 'ahd 'Uthmān*, 56; Abū Shahba, *al-Madkhal*, 273; Aḥmed al-'Abd

were taken literally it would mean that Abū Bakr's compilation had to include the same verse or word written multiple times to accommodate all possible readings. Suffice it to say, this would be a convoluted process if logistically feasible at all. In his doctoral dissertation, the Egyptian Azhari scholar ʿAbd al-Ḥayy al-Faramāwī (d. 2017) theorised that since Abū Bakr's compilation was not intended to reduce readings as the ʿUthmānic codex was, it is theoretically possible that it included multiple readings of the same verse, either above or below the word or in the margins.[107] Ghānim Qaddūrī al-Ḥamad on the other hand dismisses al-Faramāwī's suggestion along with the claim that Abū Bakr's compilation contained the seven *aḥruf*, due to the absence of any evidence that such a task was undertaken.[108] Nonetheless, even if Abū Bakr's compilation did not include multiple *aḥruf* for the same passage, it remains a possibility that it contained some passages according to one *ḥarf* and other passages according to another, since fixation of one reading was not an express goal of the compilation. This is a plausible way of interpreting the scholarly comments that Abū Bakr's *muṣḥaf* contained the seven *aḥruf*; it did not contain them in their entirety, but rather incorporated combinations of readings from each of them.

al-Karīm, "*al-Farq bayna jamʿ Abī Bakr wa ʿUthmān raḍiya Allāh ʿanhumā li-l-Qur'ān al-karīm: dirāsa waṣfiyya*," *Majallat al-Jāmiʿa al-ʿIrāqiyya* 2, no. 50 (n.d.): 11–20.

107 ʿAbd al-Ḥayy al-Faramāwī, *Rasm al-muṣḥaf wa nuqṭuhu*, 108.

108 Ghānim Qaddūrī al-Ḥamad, *Rasm al-muṣḥaf*, 145. See also the discussion in Sālim Qaddūrī al-Ḥamad, *Athar rukhṣat al-aḥruf al-sabʿa fī tadwīn al-naṣṣ al-Qur'ānī* (London: al-Furqan Islamic Heritage Foundation Centre for the Study of Islamic Manuscripts, 2018), 316–17.

The subsequent use and ultimate fate of the compilation

If we return to the narrations concerning the ʿUthmānic compilation, we may note multiple indications that the process consisted of not only transcription and dictation but several stages of review and verification. The narration in *Ṣaḥīḥ al-Bukhārī* makes clear that ʿUthmān requested Abū Bakr's compilation to be used in the process of transcribing the new codex. Recall that the manuscript of Abū Bakr had been verified through an extremely meticulous process, not simply relying on the companions who had memorised the Qur'ān in its entirety, but also ensuring that each verse had two witnesses who had written it down in the presence of the Prophet in a manner that matched the way the companions had memorised it.[109] With Abū Bakr's passing, the compilation passed into the hands of ʿUmar bin al-Khaṭṭāb, and then, after his passing, into the hands of his daughter Ḥafṣa bint ʿUmar , the widow of the Prophet Muhammad.[110]

> ʿUthmān sent a message to Ḥafṣa saying, "Send us the manuscripts of the Qur'ān so that we may copy the Qur'ānic materials in perfect copies and return the manuscripts to you." Ḥafṣa sent it to ʿUthmān. ʿUthmān then instructed Zayd bin Thābit, ʿAbdullāh bin Al-Zubayr, Saʿīd bin Al-ʿĀṣ and ʿAbd al-Raḥmān bin al-Ḥārith bin Hishām to rewrite the manuscripts in perfect copies.[111]

From this narration, one might be inclined to state, as many scholars did,[112] that ʿUthmān's compilation was assembled by

---

109 Al-ʿUbayd, *Jamʿ al-Qurʾān al-Karīm*, 506–7.

110 Ibn ʿĀshir, *Fatḥ al-Mannān al-marwī bi-mawrid al-ẓamān*, 415.

111 *Ṣaḥīḥ al-Bukhārī*, no. 4987.

112 Al-Jaʿbarī, *Jamīlat arbāb al-marāṣid*, 353.

simply copying the manuscript compiled by Abū Bakr. However, Muḥammad Muṣṭafā al-Azami argues that combining the above account with other narrations paints a more complete picture in which ʿUthmān's compilation was assembled independently of Abū Bakr's compilation, which was only used during the verification process *after* ʿUthmān's committee had finished transcribing the *muṣḥaf*.[113] The first narration that al-Azami cites in support of this narrative comes from Muṣʿab bin Saʿd:

> ʿUthmān delivered a sermon and said, "The people have diverged in their recitations, and I am determined that whoever holds any verses dictated by the Prophet himself must bring them to me." So the people brought their verses, written on parchment and bones and leaves, and anyone contributing to this pile was first questioned by ʿUthmān, "Did you learn these verses [i.e., take this dictation] directly from the Prophet himself?" All contributors answered under oath, and all the collected material was individually labeled and then handed to Zayd b. Thābit.[114]

The second narration al-Azami cites comes from Mālik bin Abī ʿĀmir (one of the committee members and the grandfather of Imam Mālik bin Anas), who states:

---

113 Note that this was also mentioned as a possibility by Abū Shāmah al-Maqdisī, *al-Murshid al-wajīz*, 76.

114 As translated by al-Azami, *History of the Qur'ānic Text*, 90. One may note that al-Azami has taken some liberties in the translation and paraphrasing and the interested reader may consult the original text in ibn Abū Dāwūd, *Kitāb al-maṣāḥif*, 210. The chain of transmission is declared authentic by the editor, Salīm al-Hilālī, and was also declared authentic by ibn Kathīr. Note that Muhammad Ḥasan Jabal, following al-Bayhaqi, discounts this narration as evidence on the grounds that Muṣʿab did not hear directly from ʿUthmān and that the compilation process had already taken place during the time of Abu Bakr. See Jabal, *Wathāqah naql al-naṣṣ al-Qur'ānī*, 197–99.

> I was among those upon whom the *muṣḥaf* was dictated [from the written sources], and if any controversies arose concerning a particular verse they would say, "Where is the scribe [of this parchment]? Precisely how did the Prophet teach him this verse?" And they would resume scribing, leaving that portion blank and sending for the man in question to clarify his transcription.[115]

These narrations indicate that the *muṣḥaf* of ʿUthmān was prepared autonomously and gathered through an independent process in addition to corroboration with the compilation of Abū Bakr. Another narration that highlights this is the report of Hānī al-Barbarī that Ubayy bin. Kaʿb performed additional verification of certain words during the ʿUthmānic compilation.[116]

One can further strengthen al-Azami's argument by noting that ʿUthmān's instructions to the committee on what to do if they differed concerning a verse only make sense if they were conducting an independent compilation process. If they were simply copying the text of Abū Bakr's compilation, then there would be no occasion for them to differ in the first place. There is also the testimony of one of the scribes of the ʿUthmānic codex, Kathīr bin Aflaḥ.[117] He stated that if the scribes differed over something during the process of writing the ʿUthmānic codex, they would delay writing it. The transmitter of this report, Muḥammad bin. Sirīn (d. 110/729), hypothesized that it was because they would first examine who was closest to the time of the final review (i.e., in terms of when they had learned it from the Prophet) so that they could write it according to that reading.

115 As translated by al-Azami, *History of the Qur'ānic Text*, 90. As in the previous narration, al-Azami takes some liberties in paraphrasing; cf. Ibn Abū Dāwūd, *Kitāb al-maṣāḥif*, 206. The chain of transmission to Malik bin Abī ʿĀmir is declared authentic by the editor, Salīm al-Hilālī.

116 Abū ʿUbayd, *Faḍā'il al-Qur'ān*, 2:102.

117 Ibn Abū Dāwūd, *Kitāb al-maṣāḥif*, 213.

This lends more weight to the view that the ʿUthmānic codex was not a simple transcription of the compilation of Abū Bakr.

Furthermore, narrations indicating that Zayd transcribed while Saʿīd dictated also suggest a process more involved than mere copying.[118] Finally, we have an account which, in spite of its weaknesses, mentions that ʿUthmān requested Ḥafṣa's copy after the compilation by Zayd was completed, which was then reviewed and compared with the ʿUthmānic codex and confirmed to be in agreement.[119] As for those reports suggesting ʿUthmān asked Ḥafṣa for the manuscripts first, the wording of such reports provides only an abbreviated description. Perhaps, Ḥafṣa's copy was requested at the outset but primarily used in the final stage of producing the codices as a source of verification.

The question that emerges is why ʿUthmān would undertake this exhaustive process when he could have readily copied the manuscripts already compiled by Abū Bakr. al-Azami offers the following reasoning:

> One may wonder why Caliph ʿUthmān took the trouble to compile an autonomous copy when the end product was to be compared with the [compilation of Abū Bakr] anyway. The likeliest reason is a symbolic one. A decade earlier thousands of Companions, engaged in the battles against apostasy in al-Yamāma and elsewhere, were unable to participate in the Ṣuḥuf's compilation. In drawing

118 Some scholars also point out that the narrations do not mention a committee assisting Zayd in the time of Abū Bakr, while he was assisted by a committee in the time of ʿUthmān in order to assist in writing the Qur'ān according to one *ḥarf*. See al-Kurdī, *Tārīkh al-Qur'ān*, 61–62.

119 ibn Jarīr al-Ṭabarī, *Tafṣir al-Ṭabarī*, 1:56. Note that parts of this account contain interpolations mixing between the collection at the time of Abū Bakr and ʿUthmān; however, the point of evidence is the detail at the very end of the account which mentions the final review of ʿUthmān's codex using Abū Bakr's compilation. See also Khaṭīb al-Baghdādī, *al-Fasl li-l-wasl al-mudraj fi al-naql* (Riyadh: Dār al-Hijra, 1997), 1:399.

> from a larger pool of written materials, 'Uthmān's independent copy provided these surviving Companions with an opportunity to partake of this momentous endeavor.
>
> In the above account, no inconsistencies were found between the [compilation of Abū Bakr] and the independent *muṣḥaf* and from this two broad conclusions emerge: first, the Qur'ānic text was thoroughly stable from the earliest days and not (as some allege) fluid and volatile until the third century; and second, the methods involved in compilation during both reigns were meticulous and accurate.[120]

If al-Azami's conclusion is correct, one must note that rather than merely having a 'symbolic' reason for conducting an independent compilation, 'Uthmān also had a very practical and tangible reason: reducing differences in the ummah's readings entailed elimination of some of the variant readings from the seven *aḥruf*. Since the goal of Abū Bakr's compilation was simply to preserve the text of the Qur'ān, arbitrating between variant readings and different dialects was never a stated goal or component of the process. This relates to what was previously mentioned concerning the possibility that Abū Bakr's compilation included a combination of a greater number of readings from the seven *aḥruf*. Therefore, the advantage of repeating the collection process and independently reviewing every verse from written sources in addition to memory afforded the committee the opportunity to affirm with the highest degree of confidence and certainty that the reading they selected for the writing of the *muṣḥaf* was the reading taught and recited by the Prophet Muhammad himself.

Al-Ja'barī notes that the compilation passed from Abū Bakr to 'Umar because Abū Bakr himself designated 'Umar as his

120 Al-Azami, *History of the Qur'ānic Text*, 93.

successor. On the other hand, ʿUmar did not designate a successor but appointed a committee to consult (*shūrā*) and decide on the successor, and therefore the compilation was inherited from him by Ḥafṣa.[121]

The compilation of Abū Bakr, which remained in the possession of Ḥafṣa, was not erased or burned by ʿUthmān. However, the compilation was later requested by Marwān bin al-Ḥakam, who at that time was the governor of Medina before later becoming an Umayyad caliph. Ḥafṣa refused. However, when she passed away, Marwān retrieved it and had it destroyed.[122] Marwān stated, "I only did that because whatever was in it was already written and preserved in the [ʿUthmānic] *muṣḥaf*. And I feared that time would pass and people would start to have misgivings about this [Ḥafṣa's] *ṣuḥuf* or would say, "It contained something that has not been written.""[123]

Conclusion

In the quest to understand the timeline of the Qur'ān's textual preservation, the compilation efforts led by the first caliph Abū Bakr al-Ṣiddīq hold substantial significance, although they have been considerably understudied compared to the codices assembled by the third caliph, ʿUthmān). This chapter, through an in-depth exploration of Muslim literary sources and scholarly interpretations, aimed to illuminate the process, purpose, and

---

121 Al-Jaʿbarī, *Jamīlat arbāb*, 344. See also Al-Kurdī, *Tārīkh al-Qur'ān*, 44; M. Mohar Ali, *The Qur'ān and the Orientalists* (Ipswich: Jamʿiyat 'Iḥyaa' Minhaaj al-Sunnah, 2004), 237; ʿAlī al-Jaʿfarī, *Jamʿ al-Qur'ān*, 50.

122 Abu ʿUbayd, *Kitāb al-imān*, 2:98; Ibn Abū Dāwūd, *Kitāb al-maṣāḥif*, 204, 212; Makkī al-Qaysī, *al-Ibānah*, 61; see also al-Judayʿ, *Muqaddimāt al-asāsīya*, 121–22. Reportedly, he requested it shortly after Ḥafṣa's funeral, just after they had finished burying her.

123 Ibn Abī Dāwūd, *Kitāb al-maṣāḥif*, 212.

implications of Abū Bakr's contribution to the Qur'ān's preservation. It argues that through analysing the hadith and scholarly sources, a coherent picture emerges of how, when, and why Abū Bakr undertook this project. The compilation was meant to record the entirety of the Qur'ān in writing to ensure that Qur'ānic verses would not be lost with the death of those who had memorised them. Under Abū Bakr's stewardship, an official unified compilation was made through a rigorous process of verifying each verse through the combined attestation of written materials, memorisation, and direct testimony. This picture illustrates the deliberate and meticulous effort undertaken by the companions in assembling the first codex of the Qur'ān. The Islamic scholarly tradition contains a nuanced elaboration of many aspects of Abu Bakr's compilation which invites further research and investigation.

Bibliography

al-ʿAẓamī, Muhammad Mustafa. *The History of the Qur'ānic Text, from Revelation to Compilation: A Comparative Study with the Old and New Testaments.* Leicester: UK Islamic Academy, 2003.

al-Aʿẓamī, Muhammad Mustafa. *The Scribes of the Prophet*. London: Turath Publishing, 2020.

al-Bāqillānī, *al-Intiṣār lil-Qur'ān*. Beirut: Dār Ibn Ḥazm, 2001.

al-Bāqillānī. *Nukat al-intiṣār*. Alexandria: Manshàat al-Maʿārif, 1971.

al-Bayhaqī, *Dalā'il al-Nubuwwah*. Cairo: Dar al-Rayyān, 1988.

al-Bukhārī, Muḥammad Ibn Ismāʿīl. *Ṣaḥīḥ al-Bukhārī.*

al-Dānī, Abū ʿAmr. *al-Muqniʿ fī maʿrifah marsūm maṣāḥif ahl al-amṣār*. Riyadh: Dār al-Tadmurrīyah, 2010.

al-Dānī, Abū ʿAmr. *Al-Taysīr fī Qirā'āt al-Tisʿah*. Riyadh: Maktabah al-Rushd, 1998.

al-Fasawī, Yaʿqūb Ibn Sufyān. al-Maʿrifa wal-Tārīkh. Baghdad: Maktaba al-Irshad, 1974.

al-Ḥākim al-Naysābūrī. *al-Mustadrak ʿalā al-ṣaḥīḥayn*. Beirut: Dar al-Kutub al-ʿIlmiyya, 1990.

al-Jaʿbarī. *Jamīlah arbāb al-marāṣid fī sharḥ ʿaqīlah atrab al-qasāʾid*. Amman: Arwiqah, 2017.

al-Jaʿfarī, ʿAlī. *Jamʿ al-Qur'ān al-Karīm fī ʿahdi Abī Bakr al-Ṣiddīq*. Kuwait: Dar al-Ẓāhiriyyah, 2022.

al-Jaʿfarī, ʿAlī. *Jamʿ al-Qur'ān fī ʿahd ʿUthmān*. Kuwait: Dar al-Ẓāhiriyyah, 2022.

al-Judayʿ. *Muqaddimāt al-asāsīya fī ʿulūm al-Qur'ān*. Beirut: Mu'assasat al-Rayān, 2001.

al-Khaṭīb al-Baghdādī. *al-Faṣl li al-waṣl al-mudraj fī al-naql*. Riyadh: Dar al-Hijrah, 1997.

al-Kurdī, Muḥammad Ṭāhir. *Tārīkh al-Qur'ān al-Karīm*. Jeddah: al-Fath, 1946.

al-Naḥḥās. *al-Nāsikh wa-al-mansūkh*. Riyadh: Dar al-Asimah, 2009.

al-Qāḍī, ʿAbd al-Fattāh. *Tārīkh al-muṣḥaf al-sharīf*. Cairo: Maktaba Jundi, 1951.

al-Qurṭubī, Abū ʿAbdullāh. *al-Jāmiʿ li-aḥkām al-Qur'ān*. Beirut: Mu'assasāt al-Risālah, 2006.

al-Sakhāwī. *Jamāl al-qurrā wa kamāl al-iqrāʾ*. Beirut: Mu'assasat al-Kutub al-Thaqafiyyah, 1999.

al-Sakhāwī. *al-Wasīlah ilā kashf al-ʿaqīla*. Riyadh: Maktaba al-Rushd, 2003.

al-Shāṭibī. *ʿAqīlah atrāb al-qaṣāʾid*. Jeddah: Dār Nūr al-Maktabāt, 2001.

al-Sindhī, ʿAbd al-Qayyūm. *Jamʿ al-Qur'ān al-Karīm fī ʿahd al-khulafā al-rāshidīn*. Madinah: Majma Malik Fahd li-Tiba'ah al-Mushaf al-Sharif, 1421 AH.

al-Suyuṭī, Jalāl al-Dīn. *al-Itqān fī ʿulūm al-Qur'ān*. Beirut: Resalah Publishers, 2008.

al-Ṭabarī, Ibn Jarīr. *Tafṣir al-Ṭabarī*. ed. al-Turkī. Cairo: Dār Hajar, 2001.

al-Ṭāsān. *Taḥqīq mawqif al-ṣaḥābī al-jalīl ʿAbdullāh Ibn Masʿūd min al-jamʿ al-ʿUthmānī*. Riyadh: Kursī al-Qur'ān, 1435 AH.

al-Ṭāsān, Muḥammad Ibn ʿAbd ul-Raḥmān. *al-Masāḥif al-manṣuba lil-ṣaḥābah wa-al-radd ʿalā shubuhat al-muthārah*. Riyadh: Dar al-Tadmuriyyah, 2016.

al-Wāḥidī, *Tafsīr al-Basīṭ*. Riyadh: Al-Īmām university, 1430H.

al-Yaʿqūbī, *Tārīkh al-Yaʿqūbī*. Beirut: al-Aalami, 2010.

Abū Shāmah. *al-Murshid al-wajīz ilā ʿulūm tataʿallaq bil-Kitāb al-Azīz*. Beirut: Dar al-Kutub al-ʿIlmiyya, 2003.

Bell, Richard. *Introduction to the Qur'ān*. Edinburgh: University Press, 1953.

Catani, Leone. Annali dell'Islam. Milano: Hoepli, 1907.

al-Ḥamad, Ghānim Qaddūrī. *Aṣālah al-naṣṣ al-Qur'ānī waḥyan wa rasman wa lughatan wa qirā'atan*. Istanbul: Dār al-Ghawthānī 2019.

al-Ḥamad, Ghānim Qaddūrī. *Rasm al-muṣḥaf: Dirāsah lughawīyah tārīkhīyah*. Baghdad: al-Lajnah al-Waṭanīyah, 1982.

al-Ḥamad, Sālim Qaddūrī . *Athar rukhṣah al-aḥruf fī tadwīn al-naṣṣ al-Qur'ānī*. London: al-Furqan Islamic Heritage Foundation Centre for the Study of Islamic Manuscripts, 2018.

Ibn ʿAbd al-Barr. *al-Istidhkār*. Beirut: Dār al-Kutub al-ʿIlmiyya, 2000.

Ibn ʿAṭiyya. *al-Muḥarrar al-wajīz*. Beirut: Dār al-Kutub al-ʿIlmiyya, 1422H.

Ibn ʿĀshir. *Fatḥ al-Mannān al-marwī bi-mawrid al-ẓamān*.

Ibn Abī Dāwūd. *Kitāb al-maṣāḥif*. Kuwait: Mu'asassah Gharās li al-Nashr wa al-Tawzīʿ, 2006.

Ibn Ḥajar al-ʿAsqalānī. *Fatḥ al-Bārī*. Riyadh: Dar al-Ṭaybah, 2005.

Ibn Kathīr. *Faḍā'il al-Qur'ān*. Cairo: Maktabat Ibn Taymiyyah, 1416 AH.

Ibn Kathīr. *al-Bidāya wa-l-Nihāya*. Edited by al-Turkī. Riyadh: Dar ʿĀlam al-Kutub, 2003.

Ibn Khayyāṭ. *Tārīkh Khalīfa Ibn Khayyāṭ*. Edited by Akram Ḍiyā' al-ʿUmarī. Riyadh: Dār Ṭaybah, 1985.

Ibn Saʿd. *al-Ṭabaqāt al-Kubrā*. Cairo: Maktaba Khanji, 2001.

Ibn Taymiyya. *al-Fatāwá al-kubrā*. Beirut: DKI, 1987.

Jeffery, Arthur, ed. *Muqaddimatān fī ʿulūm al-Qur'ān: Wa-humā muqaddimāt Kitāb al-mabānī wa-muqaddimāt Ibn ʿAtiyya*. Cairo: Maktabat al-Khanji, 1954.

Khatib, Ammar, and Nazir Khan. "The ʿUthmānic Codex: Understanding how the Qur'ān was Preserved." Yaqeen, June 2022. https://yaqeeninstitute.org/read/paper/the-uthmanic-codex-understanding-how-the-qur'ān-was-preserved.

Makkī Ibn Abī Ṭālib. *al-Ibānah ʿan maʿanī al-qiraʾāt*. N.p.: Dar Nahdah Misr, n.d..

Muḥammad Muḥammad Abū Shahba, *al-Madkhal li-dirāsāt al-Qur'ān al-Karīm*. Riyadh: Dār al-Liwāʾ lil-Nashr wal-Tawzīʿ, 1987.

Mohar Ali, M. *The Qur'ān and the Orientalists*. Ipswich: Jamʿiyat ʾIḥyaaʾ Minhaaj al-Sunnah, 2004.

Schoeler, Gregor. "The Codification Of The Qur'ān: A Comment On The Hypotheses Of Burton And Wansbrough". In The Qur'ān in Context. Leiden, The Netherlands: Brill, 2009.

Sidky, Hythem. "On the Regionality of Qur'ānic Codices," Journal of the International Qur'ānic Studies Association 5 (2020):133–210.

Vahidnia, Ala. "Whence Come Qur'ān Manuscripts? Determining the Regional Provenance of Early Qur'ānic Codices," Der Islam 98, no. 2 (2021): 359–93.

Wahb, Yousef. "How the Qur'ān Was Preserved During the Prophet's Time: Mechanisms of Oral and Written Transmission". Yaqeen, December 5, 2022. https://yaqeeninstitute.org/read/paper/how-the-qur'ān-was-preserved-during-the-prophets-time-mechanisms-of-oral-and-written-transmission

CHAPTER SIX

Rasm (Qur'ānic Orthography): The Written Representation of the Recited Text of the Qur'ān

M.A.S. Abdel Haleem

'Quick! Help the Muslims before they differ about the text of the Qur'ān as the Christians and Jews differed about their scriptures.'

Thus demanded Hudhayfa ibn al-Yamān of 'Uthmān ibn 'Affān, the third Caliph, on returning from battles in Azerbaijan (25/645). Hudhayfa had become perturbed when he saw Muslim soldiers from different parts of Syria and Iraq meeting together and differing in their readings of the Qur'ān,[1] each considering his reading to be the correct one. Up to then the only complete official written rendition, which was collected under Abu Bakr, had remained unpublished, kept first with Abu Bakr, then with 'Umar ibn al-Khaṭṭāb, and after his death with his daughter Ḥafṣa, a widow of the Prophet.[2] Responding to the urgent demand for help, 'Uthmān sent word to Ḥafṣa, asking for the copy in her possession to be sent to him so that further copies could be made of it, to be sent far and wide as the only authorised Qur'ān in the different parts of the Muslim world. This circumvented

1 Muhammad ibn Ismail al-Bukharī, *Saḥīḥ Bukhārī*, *Faḍā'il al-Qur'ān*, 3.
2 Abū 'Amr al-Dānī, *Al-Muqni' Fi Marsūm wa-Maṣāḥif Ahl al-Amṣār Ma' Kitāb Al-Naqṭ*, (Damascus: Dār al-Fikr, 1983), 124-5.

the possibility of different oral versions evolving over time, a situation Hudhayfa feared, as he was aware of there being different Gospels and books of the Bible.

In the ʿUthmānic copies, the Qur'ān was written in a particular *rasm* (orthography) which became known as *al-rasm al-ʿUthmāni* (the ʿUthmānic way of writing the text of the Qur'ān) also referred to as *rasm al-muṣḥaf*. As the copies made at his orders and distributed to various parts of the Muslim world were meant to be authoritative, it is no wonder that the *rasm* with which they were written assumed authority as the correct way of writing the Qur'ān. Arabic orthography at the time had not yet developed in the way we have known for centuries, particularly in two important areas. Firstly, there was no distinction between letters of the alphabet of similar shape, and secondly there were no vowel marks. This may give the impression that such a system must have given rise to great confusion in reading. This was not actually the case, because the morphological patterns of words in Arabic, enable readers to read even very unfamiliar material without the short vowels being marked. More importantly, however, as far as the Qur'ān was concerned, learning and reading relied above all on oral transmission, indeed when these copies were dispersed across the expanding Islamic regions, they were accompanied with recitors. In the Islamic tradition, writing remained a secondary aid.[3] Nevertheless, to ensure correct reading of the written texts of the Qur'ān, particularly for those coming after the first generation of Muslims, steps were taken gradually to improve the orthography. This started with the two above-mentioned areas, by introducing dots to indicate different vowels and nunation (*tanwīn*). These were put in different coloured ink from that of the text. There were also dots to distinguish between

3 Abū ʿAmr ibn al-ʿAlā', one of the famous Qurrā' (d. 184/770) warned: *Lā ta'khudhū-l-Qur'ān ʿan muṣḥafiyy* – 'Do not learn the Qur'ān from a person who relies solely on what is written on the page.'

consonants of similar shape. This work was carried out chiefly by three men: Abū-l-Aswad al-Duʿalī (d. 69/688), Naṣr ibn ʿĀsim (d. 89/707) and Yaḥyā ibn Yaʿmur (d.129 /746). Understandably there was some opposition at first to adding anything to the way the Qur'ān was written. Ibn ʿUmar (73/692) disliked the dotting; others welcomed it, because it was, in fact, doing no more than ensuring proper reading of the Qur'ān as received from the Prophet, and this view was accepted by the majority of Muslims throughout the different parts of the Muslim world, from the time of the *Tābiʿūn* (successors). The people of Medina were reported to have used red dots for vowels - *tanwīn, tashdīd, takhfīf, sukūn, waṣl* and *madd* and yellow dots for the *hamzas* in particular. *Naqṭ* (placing dots on words in the *muṣḥaf*),[4] became a separate subject of study with many books written on it.[5] Al-Khalīl ibn Aḥmad (d.170/786) introduced the now traditional vowel signs into Arabic orthography instead of the dots, but the dotting system continued for distinguishing between consonants of similar shape.[6]

It was to serve the Qur'ān that Arabic orthography was developed. After all, the Qur'ān, as collected under Abū Bakr, became the first book in the Arabic language. It was in order to serve the Qur'ān that more and more people began to learn reading and writing, and that the art of calligraphy was developed, which became one of the chief arts of Islam. The Qur'ān, which unified the Arabic literary language and spread it into areas far beyond Arabia, was in fact the starting point of all Islamic and Arabic subjects of study. One of these subjects, in particular, has

---

4 al-Dānī, *Al-Muqniʿ*, 125-6.

5 Such as those by Abū Ḥātim al-Sijistānī (d.248/826) and al-Dānī (d.444/1502).

6 Jalāl al-Dīn al-Suyūṭī, *Al-Itqān Fi ʿulūm Al-Qur'ān*, vol. 1, (Beirut: Dār al-Kutub al-ʿIlmiyya, 1987), 484.

important bearing on Qur'ānic orthography:[7] that is Arabic phonetics, which was developed in *'ilm tajwīd al-Qur'ān*, the science of the proper articulation and reading of the Qur'ān. Among other things, this has minutely described and definitively prescribed for posterity the articulation of consonants and vowels singly and consecutively: the way of reciting the Qur'ān as received from the Prophet. This requires a degree of exactitude unmatched in reading any other material in Arabic. Qur'ānic orthographic signs had to be used with the Qur'ānic *rasm* and developed to a higher standard of representation than is known or needed in ordinary Arabic orthography.

Alongside the development of studies in Arabic grammar, Arabic orthography also developed for linguistic and literary material, and although the 'Uthmānic *rasm* was one of the sources of ordinary orthography the latter began to differ from the 'Uthmānic *rasm* of the Qur'ān.[8] The question was asked whether it was admissible to write the Qur'ān itself in the new orthography. Mālik ibn 'Anas (d. 179/795) was asked and said: 'No, the Qur'ān should be written only in the way of the first writing.' He was also asked whether the additional *wāw* and *alif* (as in the word أولوا) should be deleted since they were not pronounced, and he said no. Similarly, Aḥmad ibn Ḥanbal (d. 244/858) said it was unlawful to deviate in writing the *muṣḥaf* in *wāw, yā alif* or any other way.[9] In line with such views, it will be seen that adherence to the Qur'ānic *rasm* has persisted up to the present.

Along with numerous other aspects of the Qur'ān, its orthography was singled out as a separate branch of study known as *'ilm al-rasm*. Abū 'Amr al-Dānī (d.444/1052) examined in detail the characteristics of this *rasm*. His book *al-Muqni'* remains an important authority.

---

7 Jalal al-Dīn al-Suyūṭī, *Al-Itqān Fi 'ulūm Al-Qur'ān*, vol. 2, (Beirut: Dār al-Kutub al-'Ilmiyya, 1987), 348-56.

8 Hussain Wālī, *Kitāb al-Imlā'*, (Beirut: Dār al-Qalam, 1985), 42.

9 al-Suyūṭī, *Al-Itqān*, vol. 2, 470.

Al-Suyūṭī (d. 909/1503) reduced the rules of Qur'ānic *rasm* to 6 as follows:[10]

1. The rule of deletion, *ḥadhf*
2. The rule of addition, *ziyāda*
3. The rule of substitution, *badal*
4. The rule of the *hamza*,
5. The rule of joining and separating, *al-waṣl wa-l-faṣl*
6. The rule of cases where there are two readings, but the text is written according to one of them, *ma fīhi qirā'atan fa-kutiba ʿalā iḥdāhumā.*

I. Deletion (*ḥadhf*)

This involves deletion of an *alif* or *yā* or *wāw* or *lām*.[11]

Alif is deleted:

after vocative *yā'* as in يـٰأيها الناس
after *nā* of the plural as in أنجينـٰكم
in demonstrative pronouns as in هـٰؤلاء , هـٰذه , هـٰذا
in names of God as الله , الرحمـٰن
after a *lam* as خِلـٰف
between two *lams* as in كَلـٰلة
in proper names of more than three letters with
ابرٰهيم , اسمـٰعيل
in the dual of a noun or a verb, if it is not at the end of the letter, as in رجلـٰن , يعلمـٰن
in sound masculine and feminine plurals as in
والصـٰدقين والصـٰدقات
unless it is followed by a *hamza* as in والصـٰائمين والصـٰائمات

10 al-Suyūṭī, *Al-Itqān*, vol. 2, 471-82.
11 The deleted letter is actually replaced using an alternative sign, such as the so-called dagger-alif above the letter.

or a *shadda* as in الضـٰالّين
in plurals on the pattern مفاعل as in مسـٰجد
or a similar pattern as in مسـٰكين , نصـٰرى
in adjectives like عـٰلم
in the number ثلـٰث
in nouns with two or more *alifs* as in ءاخر , ءادم
in بسم الله and in the imperative of سأل as in وَسْئل

It should be noted here that normal orthography has retained the Qur'ānic *rasm* in many of these cases as in the demonstratives, and that Qur'ānic *rasm*, in some cases, caters for more than one *qirā'a* as in خلف which could be read as *khilāf* or *khalf*.

yā' can be deleted:

if it is a first-person pronoun at the end of a vocative noun as in يـٰقومِ instead of يـٰقومي

at the end of a word as the preceding *kasra* is deemed a sufficient indication of it, as in إذا يسْرِ , فارهبونِ , ولى دينِ instead of إذا يسْرِى , فارهبوني , ولى دينِى

where it is following another *yā'* in the same word, such as with الحواريّن , النبيّن instead of الحواريين , النبيين

in Sura 2 where it is written ابراهم which suggests a special reading;

at the end of every noun with a weak third radical in the nominative or genitive case as in غير باغٍ ولا عادٍ, and this is also deleted in normal orthography.

wāw is deleted when preceded by another *wāw* (to avoid repetition) as in فأوُا instead of فأووا and داوُد instead of داوود

In the last example it is also deleted in ordinary writing;

wāw is also deleted as the seat of the *hamza* with words such as رؤيا, as in الرءيا instead of الرؤيا and تـئويه instead of تؤويه

It is deleted as the third radical in verbs in the indicative mood as in سندعُ الزبانيه , يدعُ الانسان, instead of سندعوا , يدعو

lām is deleted when preceded by another *lām* in اليل , الائي , التي instead of الليل , اللائي , اللتي

nūn is deleted when repeated in تأمنا instead of تأمننا and نـجي[12] instead of ننجي

Avoiding repetition of the same shape is clearly an important factor in the rule of deletion.

II. Addition

This applies to three letters, *alif*, *wāw* and *yā'*, where the letter is written but not pronounced.

Alif is added:

- at the end of a word after the *wāw* of the plural as in ضربواْ , قالواْ
  This is also added in normal orthography to distinguish the plural from the singular.
- after the *wāw* in الربوٰاْ instead of الربا;
- after a final *hamza* written as a *wāw* as in تفتؤاْ , يبدؤاْ .
  Some Kufan scholars also used to add this in normal orthography.

---

12 The *nūn* is placed as a superscript above this word in 21:88.

- in مائة , مأئتين
- in لشأى instead of لشئ
- in لأوضعوا (9:47) لأاذبحنه (27:21) instead of لأوضعوا , لأذبحنّه
- between the *jīm* and *yā'* in جِأىء in (39:69; 89:23) instead of جيء
- in the word نبؤا instead of نبأ
- in تأيئسوا (12:87), يأيئس (13:31) instead of تيأسوا, ييأس

In the examples given above where an *alif* is added (apart from the first 3 words), it should be noted that a *hamza* is adjacent to the *alif*. This suggests that the addition has to do with the pronunciation of *hamza*. Al-Dānī suggests that *alif* is added to *hamza* 'to strengthen it'.[13]

wāw is added after the hamza as in سأوْريكم (7:145), instead of سأريكم, and in أوْلئك , أوْلوا , أوْلات. This is also added in normal orthography. Again, a *hamza* and *ḍamma* are adjacent. A variant pronunciation and a desire to avoid confusion between words of similar shapes account for the addition.[14]

yā' This is added in nine places[15] in the Qur'ān, as in أفإيْن مات , من نبإئ , instead of أفإن , نبأ. Again, in all the nine places it is adjacent to a *hamza* which suggests that the *hamza*, and the various ways it is pronounced in Arabic, accounts for the addition.

It has been observed that *alif*, *wāw* and *yā'* are involved in the rules of addition and deletion and will also be involved with the rule of *hamza*. This should not be surprising since in grammar

13 al-Dānī, *Al-Muqni'*, 140.
14 al-Dānī, *Al-Muqni'*, 108-9.
15 al-Suyūṭī, *Al-Itqān*, vol. 2, 475.

they are responsible for such classes of verb as the hollow, the final-weak and the hamzated.

III. The *hamza*

Hamza is peculiar in Arabic in many respects. Being a glottal stop, it is deemed more difficult to pronounce than other consonants. Accordingly, it takes one of four forms: distinctly pronounced, *taḥqīq*;[16] lightened, *talyīn*; changed, *ibdāl*; or deleted altogether, *ḥadhf*. These different ways are observed in *qirā'āt* and the various Arab dialects. Hamzated verbs are also treated in a separate section in Arabic morphology. It is no wonder that it affects the pronunciation and orthography of adjacent letters in the various sections dealt with so far. In the writing of the *hamza* itself, Qur'ānic and normal orthographies are similar in many ways. In some aspects, however, Qur'ānic *rasm* differs, as in the following cases:

- a medial *hamza* preceded by a *sukūn* is written without a 'seat' سوءة , بريـٔا , يسـٔل : instead of سوأة , بريئا , يسأل in normal orthography.
  It should also be noted that a medial *hamza* with *kasra* is written *under* a seat of *yā'* as in السرابِر instead of السرائر.
- A *hamza* is not written with an *alif* if preceded or followed by another *alif* as in شنـٔـان ,ءامنوا instead of شنآن , آمنوا. Avoiding repetition of shape is the factor involved here; in normal orthography this is achieved by writing a *madda*, i.e. (~) , but the *madda* sign is reserved in Qur'ānic orthography for further extending a long vowel, as will be seen later.
- It is not written on a *yā'* when preceded or followed by

16 Wālī, *Kitāb al-Imlā'*, 47.

yā' as in خسئين , متكئين instead of خاسئين , متكئين
- nor is it written on a *wāw* when preceded or followed by another *wāw* as in يئوده , يئوسا instead of يؤوده , يؤوسا . Again, avoiding repetition of shape is involved here and in general appears to carry more weight in Qur'ānic orthography than in ordinary orthography.[17]

IV. Changing

This involves changing *alif* into *wāw* or *yā'*, changing *nūn* into *alif*, and changing the final feminine *ha'* (*tā marbūta*) into an ordinary 'open' *tā'*.

In this connection it should be remembered that changing is an important feature of Arabic morphology, dealt with under the title *al-'i'lāl wa-l-'ibdāl*.

alif:

- the *alif* is written *wāw* for velarisation (*tafkhīm*) in some *qirā'āt* in صلوٰة, زكوٰة , ربوٰا, حيوٰة (without *idāda*) instead of صلاة , زكاة , ربا , حياة and as غدوٰة, مشكوٰة , نجوٰة , منوٰة instead of , غداة , مشكاة , نجاة , مناة
- It is written *yā'* if it has been changed from an original *yā'* as in يتوفىٰكم instead of يتوفاكم.
- The lighter *nūn* of *tawkīd* (emphasis) is written *alif* in ليكوناً and لنسفعاً. The *nūn* of إذن is written *alif* and pronounced *alif* in pausing, i.e., إذا, as in 17:73. This is in line with Basran grammarians; the Kufans write it as *nūn*.[18]
- The feminine *hā'* at the end of a noun is written *tā' marbūṭa* except for the following words: رحمت instead of

17 But it does sometimes carry weight in normal orthography. See, Wālī, *Kitāb al-Imlā'*, 78.
18 Wālī, *Kitāb al-Imlā'*, 92.

امرأت ; سُنّت instead of سُنّة ; نعمت instead of نعمة ; رحمت instead of رحمة ; امرأت instead of امرأة ; كلمت instead of كلمة (in four cases it is actually the *tā'* of the plural in some *qirā'āt*);[19] مرضات instead of مرضاة; معصيت instead of معصية, and لعنت instead of لعنة , all in a certain number of cases, and in isolated cases شجرت , ثمرت instead of شجرة , ثمرة but this could also be written as the ordinary *tā'* of the plural in some *qirā'āt*; in جنت , فطرت , بقيت instead of جنة , فطرة , بقية.[20] According to al-Dānī, in the above cases the *tā'* is written in regard to the fact that this is its origin form (*'ala-l-aṣl*).[21]

V. Joining and Separating

This involves a number of short particles when they are preceded or followed by another short particle to which they are attached. It includes such words as:

(إن ما) إمّا , (من ما) ممّا , (أن لا) ألّا , (في ما) فيما , (إن لم) إلّم , (أم من) أمّن , (أين ما) أينما , (كل ما) كلّما , (إنّ ما) إنّما , (حيث ما) حيثما , (عن من) عمّن , (أن لن) ألّن , (لكي لا) لكيلا

There are exceptions with some of these words fully surveyed in the Qur'ān and detailed in books and chapters on *rasm*; but some important factors have to be borne in mind in this connection. It should first be observed that even in normal orthography there are, in some cases, several opinions.[22] It is also observed that in

19 al-Dānī, *Al-Muqni'*, 79.

20 For details see al-Suyūṭī, *Al-Itqān,* vol. 2, 477.

21 Note that in modern Arabic *tā' marbūta* is pronounced and written an ordinary *tā'* in names like Midḥat, Ra'fat, Nash'at, Hayāt, in languages like Turkish and Urdu, *salāh* and *zakāh* are pronounced *salāt* and *zakāt.*

22 Wālī, *Kitāb al-Imlā'*, 143-151.

the words إنْ , أنْ , منْ , عنْ there is a *nūn* with *sukūn*; when added to many of the above words this incurs assimilation which strengthens the case for joining. The normal practice of joining, however, is sometimes set aside for such considerations as contrast. Thus, the joining of عمّن is set aside in يصيب به من يشاء ويصرفه عن من يشاء (24:43). أمّن is replaced by أم من in four places in the Qur'ān as in أفمن يلقي في النار خير أم من يأتي آمنا (41:40).

Moreover, in the examples cited for discussion, we find that various grammatical functions of words similar in sounds, entail different shapes. Thus, we find إنما أنا بشر in (18:110) but إن ما توعدون لآت (6:134). ما is *kaffa* (stops the grammatical function of أنَّ) in the former and a relative pronoun in the latter. Without taking such principles into account, hasty conclusions in regard to consistency can be reached about Qur'ānic orthography in the area under discussion.

VI. Variant Canonical Readings

'Uthmānic orthography made it possible from the beginning for some words to be read in more than one way, and the copies of the Qur'ān written and distributed according to the order of 'Uthmān are reported to have contained all the seven readings of the Qur'ān. In numerous cases, a word was written in such a way as to comply with more than one reading. Thus ملك in Sura 1 could be read as *mālik* or *malik*; وعدنا (2:51) is *wa'adnā* or *wā'adnā*; الغرفت (34:37) is *al-ghurufati* or *al-ghurfāti*; فكهين (52:19) is *fakahīn* or *fākihīn*.[23]

In some other cases the variant readings could not be contained in a single shape of a word and accordingly different forms were distributed in the 'Uthmānic copies. Thus وصى (2:132) is written *waṣṣā* according to Ḥafṣ' reading and *awṣā* according to

23 For further examples see al-Dānī, *al-Muqni'*, 83-92.

Warsh; وتوكل على العزيز (26:217) *wa-tawakkal* was written فتوكل *fa-tawakkal* in the copies sent to Madina and Syria.[24]

These are the six rules of Qur'ānic *rasm*. Rule IV of Variant Readings is exclusive to the Qur'ān in Arabic because of the canonical *qirā'āt* which were accommodated in the *rasm*. The five other rules of addition, deletion, *hamza*, change, and joining and separating are not in fact exclusive to the writing of the Qur'ān; they constitute normal chapters of books on *imla'* (orthography) in Arabic.[25] The difference lies in the fact that the features are much more limited in ordinary orthography; the Qur'ānic *rasm*, as we said, was one of the sources for ordinary orthography.

In addition to the abovementioned traditional six rules of *rasm*, I would add one more feature which has for long become a 'rule' of writing the Qur'ān, that is:

VII. Full Vocalisation

This is done to an extent unknown in the writing of any other material in Arabic. As Al-Dānī stated: 'Every letter should be given its due signs of vowel, *sukūn, shadda* and other signs.'[26] This becomes immediately obvious to anyone who opens the pages of the *muṣḥaf* and will be treated later under *iṣṭilaḥāt al-ḍabṭ* (conventional signs determining the proper pronunciation of Qur'ānic material).

The Qur'ān is unique in Arabic and is treated as such in various respects. According to some jurists, it is prescribed for anyone, when touching the text of the Qur'ān, to be in a state of ritual ablution. The way of reciting the Qur'ān is different from reciting any other text, including that age-old and most cherished art of the Arabs - poetry. When the Qur'ān is read, Muslims are enjoined to listen to it and keep silent so that they may

24 See al-Dānī, *Al-Muqni'*, 106 and al-Suyūṭī, *Al-Itqān*, vol. 2, 497.

25 See, Wālī, *Kitāb al-Imlā'*, 173-5.

26 al-Dānī, *Al-Muqni'*, 130.

obtain mercy (7:204). The Qur'ān is also written in a unique, fully-vowelled, calligraphy, different from writing even *ḥadīth* material, and immediately recognisable as Qur'ānic. Each chapter begins from the first verse and the material follows to the last without any paragraphing or blank spaces, to exclude the possibility of adding any non-Qur'ānic material. The traditional division into thirty parts (*juz'*) – for the benefit of those who wish to follow the tradition of reciting the entire text within a month – as well as markers for halves, quarters and eighths of each *juz'* are marked without interrupting the flow of the material.[27]

A Fine Example

The application of the above rules of *rasm*, is best exemplified in an edition of the Qur'ān which maintains the tradition more than any other, and now has more widespread circulation than any other edition. This is the Egyptian edition, printed originally in 1337/1918. It has been adopted as the primary model in the most important centres of publishing the Qur'ān in the Middle East: Egypt, Saudi Arabia (especially the King Fahd Complex for printing the Qur'ān in Medina)[28], Beirut and Turkey. This particular edition is, moreover, the one normally used as a base for translation of the Qur'ān into English[29] and is the one whose orthography I will discuss below.

---

27 In some earlier and current editions, a mark is added, showing the end of ten verses to be read in prayers.

28 See Appendix, pp. *alif-kāf* of copies printed - 1405/1984. The *muṣḥaf* printed in the King Fahd Complex is called *Muṣḥaf al-Madīna al-Nabawiyya*. Unlike the Egyptian edition, it has the convention of ending each page coinciding with the end of a verse. This concept was first introduced in Turkey.

29 Arberry's translation is an obvious exception, A.J. Arberry, *The Koran Interpreted*, (Oxford: Oxford University Press, 1955).

Unlike other editions, the Egyptian *muṣḥaf* states its credentials for the reproduction of the text of the Qur'ān. It was produced in 1337/1918 not by an individual, but by a committee of four, which appears more authoritative, headed, as it was, by the principal of the Egyptian Qur'ān reading institution, Shaykh al-Maqāri' al-Miṣriyya. In 1342/1923 it was adopted by a committee set up by King Fu'ād I, under the supervision of the Azhar authority, and was printed at the Official Būlāq Press. It became known as the *Amīrī Muṣḥaf* and became the model to be followed in Egypt and abroad. It contained an appendix, *ta'rīf bi-hādhā-l-muṣḥaf al-sharīf* (An explanatory statement on this noble *muṣḥaf*), which falls into three sections ending with the names and positions of members of the committee who checked it (in later editions given as Lajnat Murāja'at Al-Maṣāḥif - the Committee for checking copies of the Qur'ān) under the supervision of the Supreme Council of Islamic Research and Culture in Al-Azhar.

The first section of this Appendix cites in detail the authorities relied upon in the writing of the *muṣḥaf*. It was written, we are told at the beginning, according to the reading of Ḥafṣ as taken from 'Āsim, from ibn Ḥabīb, from the Companions 'Uthmān, 'Alī, Zayd ibn Thābit and Ubayy, as received from the Prophet.

The spelling was reproduced in accordance with what *'ulamā' al-rasm* (scholars of Qur'ānic orthography) determined to be the system used in the personal copy of 'Uthmān and the copies he sent to different Muslim cities, all as reported by the eminent authorities - Abū 'Amr al-Dānī (444/1052) and Sulaymān ibn Najāḥ (496/1103), giving the traditional authorities for this.

The specific way of vocalisation - *ṭarīqat al-ḍabṭ* in writing the *muṣḥaf* was the same as specified by scholars of *ḍabṭ* citing the traditional authoritative texts.

Places to pause in reading the verses of the Qur'ān are an important aspect of recitation. Commenting on 73:4 ورتّل القرءان ترتيلا- 'And recite the Qur'ān in slow, measured tones', the Caliph

ʿAlī ibn Abī Ṭālib is reported to have defined *tartīl* as 'proper pronunciation of letters and knowing the places of pausing'.[30]

Traditional authorities are given in the *taʿrīf* for determining places to pause as well as for the conventional signs for the different types of pauses. Related to this is a statement on places of ritual prostration *sajda* on reading certain verses of the Qur'ān. The system of numbering the verses in the Qur'ān is given as the Kufan system taken ultimately from ʿAlī ibn Abī Ṭālib, according to which the total number is 6236 verses, and traditional authorities are cited.

Determination of the beginning of each of the 30 parts (*juz'*) of the Qur'ān, their halves (*aḥzāb*), and quarters of the *aḥzāb* (*arbāʿ*) is a traditional aspect of the writing of the Qur'ān, which is observed in the edition. So is a statement at the head of each sura as to its title, whether it was wholly or partly revealed at Makkah or Madinah, and its number of verses. Traditional authorities are given.

The second section of the Appendix is dedicated mainly to a detailed specification and explanation of the conventional signs of vocalisation to ensure proper articulation, *iṣṭilāḥāt al-ḍabṭ*. This is in fact a most important aspect of Qur'ānic orthography. Here we see the basic *rasm*, which was sufficient to those early Muslims who knew the Qur'ān by heart anyway, transformed into a highly developed written system of representation, more exact than anything known in Arabic.

The section on *iṣṭilāḥāt al-ḍabṭ* in the Appendix includes 18 items, 14 of which are diacritical signs that affect the way words are pronounced.[31] We have seen earlier that the rules of *rasm* included addition, deletion and substitution of letters for certain

30 Husny Shaikh ʿUthmān, *Ḥaqq al-Tilāwa* (Jordan, Manshūrāt al-ʿAṣr al-Ḥadīth, 1971), 14.

31 See *Iṣṭilāḥāt al Ḍabṭ*, Egyptian *Muṣḥaf*, Appendix, and al-Dānī, *Al-Muqniʿ*, 123-143.

reasons. Signs in the present section ensure, nonetheless, the correct pronunciation in those cases.

1. Placing a small circle (o) above a weak letter (*ḥarf ʿilla*) indicates that such a letter is additional and should not be pronounced either in connection or pause position, e.g., قالوٓا *qālū*, أوْلئك *ulāʾik,* نبأىْ المرسلين *nabaʾi-l-mursalīn*. It should be noted that in ordinary orthography, additional letters are retained with nothing to indicate that they should not be pronounced; here the Qur'ānic orthography is seen to be more consistent and more precise.

2. Placing on oval sign (0) above an *alif* followed by a vowelled letter indicates that it is additional in consecutive reading but should be pronounced in a pause. e.g. أنا خير منه pronounced *ana* and *anā* respectively; لكنا هو الله pronounced *lākinna* and *lākinnā*.

3-5. Placing (ˆ) above any letter indicates that it is unvowelled and should be given a full, distinct pronunciation, e.g. منْ ; whereas writing the letter without the sign and placing a *shadda* on the following letter indicates that the two are fully assimilated e.g. يلهث ذّلك *yalhadhdhālik*, i.e. *th* has become *dh*. On the other hand, if the *shadda* is removed from the first letter of the second word, this indicates masking – *ikhfāʾ* – with nasalisation of the first letter, so that it is neither distinct nor fully assimilated into the second, e.g. من ثَمرات *miŋ thamarātim* - or is partially assimilated into the second, e.g. من والٍ *miŋ wālin*.

6. Placing a small *mīm* instead of the second vowel of *tanwīn* or instead of a *sukūn* above a *nūn* without a *shadda* on a following *bāʾ* indicates changing the *tanwīn* or *nūn* into a *mīm*: e.g. عليم بذات *ʿalīmun* becomes *ʿalīmum*; من بعد *min* becomes *mim baʿd*.

7-9. Placing the two vowel signs of a *tanwīn* one on top of the other ـًـٌـٍ indicates that it should be distinctly pronounced:

سميعٌ عليم *samīʿun;* شراباً *sharāban;* قومٍ *qawmin.* Placing the two signs in succession ـٍ ـً ـٌ with a *shadda* on the following letter indicates assimilation of a *tanwīn* e.g., in خشبٌ مُسنّدة *khushubummusannada* - *n* becomes *m*. On the other hand, placing them in succession without a *shadda* on the following letter indicates nasalising / masking or partial assimilation; thus: شهابٌ ثاقب - *bunth* becomes *buŋth,* and the same with *tanwīn* with *fatḥa* and *kasra.* It should be indicated that in normal orthography the *tanwīn* signs, like all short vowels, are dropped, and if at all written they will be in the first shape only and the fine distinctions in sound quality reading in the Qur'ān are obliterated in reading other material.

10. The small superscript letters ا / و / ى respectively indicate those omitted in the ʿUthmānic copies of the Qur'ān but which should be pronounced, thus ذالك *dhālika,* داوود *dāwūd* and وليّ *waliyyī.* Before the printing era these small letters used to be written in normal size but in red; smaller size now replaces the red colour. It should be noted that in normal orthography, the first two words are written in the abbreviated forms but without any sign to indicate the omitted letter. Qur'ānic orthography is thus more consistent and precise. If the omitted letter has a replacement in the word in the normal size it is still the added small letter that should be pronounced, thus: الصلوٰة is pronounced *aṣ-ṣalāh* and الزكوٰة *az-zakāh.*

11. Placing the *madda* sign (~) above a long vowel indicates that it should be lengthened more than its normal length. This is done before a *hamza* and an unvowelled letter as in قروٓء *qurū' : qurūū',* سيٓء بهم *sī'a bihim : sīī'a;* مآ أنزل *mā 'uŋzila: māā 'uŋzila*

The Signs 6-11 are particularly significant because they relate to two important features of Qur'ānic recitation: nasalisation and vowel length. Some manuals of *tajwīd* deal exclusively with *al-nūn wa-l-tanwīn wa-l-mudūd*. The Qur'ān has a high frequency of *nūn* and *tanwīn* and they have, when adjacent to other letters, different degrees of assimilation and nasality. In Sura 19 (chosen at random), the frequency of assimilation in *nūn* and *tanwīn* is about 6 times as great as without assimilation. This is important because assimilation increases the nasality, which has an emotional effect. The *madda* sign (~) adds extra length to vowels as required in certain situations. Prolongation is achieved not only by adding a *madda* to a long vowel before *hamza* or *sukūn*, as mentioned earlier, but third person masculine pronouns, with a *ḍamma* or a *kasra*, are also followed by a small *wāw* or *yā'* respectively, which gives them a length peculiar to the recitation of the Qur'ān, for example, 86:8 انهو على رجعة لقادر. These two features of assimilation and prolongation are characteristic of the Qur'ān and are not heard, to any similar extent, in recitation of Arabic poetry. The *nūn*, *tanwīn* and *mudūd*, together with the higher relative frequency of occurrence of the letters *alif*, *lām*, *mīm*, *wāw* and *yā'* in the Qur'ān[32] all have a slowing effect on the reading, more likely to make the reader and listener absorb the material, moreover they contribute a high degree of sonority to the recitation of the Qur'ān.

12. Placing a small circle under ر in بسم الله مجرٖاها indicates that the *fatḥa* should be inclined to a *kasra* and the *alif* to a *yā'*. Thus, instead of *majrāha* it becomes *majrayha*. This is known as *imāla* and normal Arabic orthography has no sign to represent it even though this sound is common in some Arab countries; Qur'ānic orthography is thus more developed in this respect.

13. Placing the same sign at the end of *mīm* in تأمَنّا indicates *ishmām* - giving the consonant a trace of the pronunciation of *ḍamma* according to Ḥafṣ' *qirā'a*.

32 See, 'Abd al-Raḥmān ibn al-Jawzī, *Funūn Al-Afnān fī 'Ajā'ib Al-Qur'ān*, (Baghdād, 1988), 104-106.

14. Placing a dot above the *alif* in ءأعجمي indicates that the second *hamza* should be pronounced lighter - *tashīl*. Thus instead of *'a'aʿjamiyyun* it becomes almost like *'aaʿjamiyyun*. These last three features are important in some *qirā'āt*, which explains an important function of Qur'ānic orthography.

15. The ornamental circle indicates the end of the verse (which is different from a sentence in Arabic) and affects the stress patterns in reading. Inside the circle is written the number of the verse always at the end (i.e., the full completion) and not at the beginning as in normal Arabic (and English) material.

16.* indicates the beginning of *rubʿ al-ḥizb* (an eighth of a *juz'*)

17-18. Placing a line above a word indicates that a ritual prostration is required by the reader/listener on reaching the end of that verse which is further marked by an ornamental sign after the verse number and a further sign in the margin, e.g., 96:19

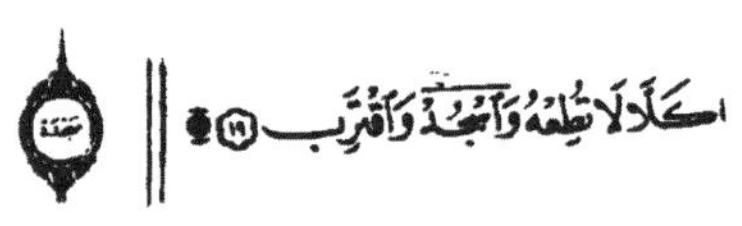

N.B. This edition uses one further sign, which is not listed here, that is, placing a *sīn* above the end of a word to indicate *saktah* (hiatus or slight interruption of reading), to separate two words, such as ولم يجعل له عوجا قيما 'and has not made in it [the Qur'ān] any crookedness; straight, to give warning...' (18:1,2). Without the hiatus, the meaning would be distorted.

The third section of the Appendix deals with the various signs for pauses *ʿalamāt al-waqf*. This is another area in which the writing of the Qur'ān is distinguished from the writing of any other Arabic material. Modern punctuation marks became known in Arabic only last century, and up to now they are not universally adopted in a systematic way. In any case, none of these marks appear in the writing of the Qur'ān. Six pausal signs (*'alamāt al-waqf*) are used in the *muṣḥaf*, placed higher than all other signs as follows:

م Sign for a mandatory pause *al-waqf al-lāzim*
e.g., إنّما يستجيبُ الّذين يسمعونَ ۘ والموتى يبعثهم الله
'... only those can accept who hear. As for the dead, Allah will raise them up' (6:36). The mandatory pause comes after 'who hear' in Arabic. This is followed by *wa-*, a conjunction which generally means 'and'; it retains the same form even in contexts where it means 'as for'. Without the mandatory stop, a reader may read the statement as: '... only those can accept who hear and the dead...' which would corrupt the sense.

لا Sign for prohibited pause - *al-waqf al-mamnū'*
e.g., الّذين تتوفّٰهم الملائكة طيّبينَ ۙ يقولون سلٰم عليكم ادخلوا الجنة
'Those whose souls the angels take while they are good, to them they say: "Peace be on you! Enter the Garden"' (16:32)
It is prohibited to pause at 'good' as it would leave the sentence unfinished and impair the sense.

ج Sign of optional pause - *waqf jā'iz jawāzan mustawiya-l-ṭarafayn*
e.g., ... نبأهم بالحقّ ۚ انّهم فتية ...
'We shall narrate to thee their story with truth. They were young men who believed in their Lord' (18:131). The optional pause comes after 'truth'.

صلى Sign of preferred non-pause *al-waqf jā'iz ma'a kawn al-waṣl awlā*
e.g., ... إلا هُوَ ۖ وإن يمسسك ...

> 'If Allah touches thee with affliction none can remove it but He; and if He touches thee with good, He is powerful over everything' (6:17).

This kind of pause comes after 'but He', since although it is allowable to stop here, in order to give a fuller meaning, it is preferable to pause at the end of the verse.

قلى Sign of preferred pause - *al-waqf jā'iz-wa awlā*
e.g., ما يعلمهم إلا قليلٌ فلا تمار ...

'Only a few have real knowledge about them [the seven sleepers of the cave], so do not argue, but stick to what is clear'. (18:22).

It is preferable to pause after 'them'

* * Sign of selective pause – *ta'ānuq al-waqf*. If you pause at either of the two places you may not pause at the other.
e.g. ذلك الكتاب لا ريب* فيه* هدىً للمتّقين
can be read, pausing to make the meaning either:
'This is the Book - no doubt. In it there is guidance for those who ...'
or
'This is the Book wherein is no doubt, a guidance to those who...' (2:2)

If you pause at both places, the material following the first pause will read 'in it', which would disrupt the sense.

The underlying principle in all these is whether the sense has reached final completion or remains incomplete; has reached an acceptable stage of completion; or would be more fully expressed if carried into a further stage.

Tradition or Change?

It was understandable that the 'Uthmānic *rasm* should be given such a high status through the ages. Indeed, some people took an extreme view that there were esoteric reasons for everything in it which could be grasped only by the very few endowed with esoteric knowledge. In the same way as there is *iʿjāz* (inimitability) in the linguistic structure of the Qur'ān, they argued, there is also *iʿjaz* in its *rasm*. Thus mystic explanations have been given, represented by such people as Abū-l-ʿAbbās al-Marākishī (d.721/1321).[33] It is clearly such views that led ibn Khaldūn (d.808/1405) to castigate those holding them:

> Do not pay attention to what some stupid people think that the Companions of the Prophet were masters of the craft of writing and what we find in their writing different from systematic orthography is not actually as we imagine but there is an explanation and wisdom behind it. Thus, they argue that the additional *alif* in لأاْذبحنّه (7:21) is there to indicate that Solomon did not slaughter the hoopoe, and the additional *yā'* in بأييْد (51:47) indicates how complete divine power is in building the sky.

Such people were led to this view, in ibn Khaldūn's opinion, by a desire to put the Companions above lack of knowledge in writing, when in fact this was a craft, the knowledge of which is relative and not necessarily indicative of innate perfection or otherwise. The Arabs at the time of writing the *muṣḥaf* were still closer to the Bedouin state which did not perfect crafts, and this, in ibn Khaldun's opinion, appeared in their writing of the *muṣḥaf* which was written by a number of people whose knowledge of

33 He still has followers now. See, Subhi al-Ṣāliḥ, *Mabāḥith fī 'Ulūm al-Qur'ān*, (Beirut, nd), 276-7.

writing was not excellent and they followed various orthographies.[34] It is understandable that ibn Khaldūn should have been so incensed by the imaginary and far-fetched explanation of al-Marākishī; what he said about the early stage of writing may have some justification but, on the other hand, he clearly did not pay regard to considerations of phonetics and *qirā'āt* and how they affect various aspects of *rasm*. For instance in the very examples he quotes (and we have seen many other instances earlier), he overlooks the fact that additional letters come only after a *hamza*; the real explanation has to be sought there, and in the desire to ensure specific pronunciation of *hamza* as explained above, not for esoteric reasons as argued by Al-Marākishī nor simply on the ground of inconsistency and lack of mastery of craftsmanship on the part of early scribes, as argued by ibn Khaldūn. His own views came to be dismissed out of hand by a modern authority on Qur'ānic *rasm* on the ground that he was a loner and not a *mujtahid* in the field.[35]

In the past and present,[36] some people (primarily non-traditionalists) have argued that there is nothing sacred about that particular Qur'ānic *rasm*. There is nothing in the Qur'ān or *ḥadīth* to make it obligatory or recommended and Muslims should use any specific system for writing the Qur'ān. The objective of writing the Qur'ān is surely to enable people to read it correctly and learn it correctly. Indeed, some argued that there was no reason that it should be written in an orthography that is not used for writing any other book of the time.[37] Desire to facilitate the reading and learning of the Qur'ān to each generation according to their contemporary orthography is an argument that non-traditionalists have always repeated. They regard

34 Ibn Khaldūn, *Al-Muqaddima*, (Cairo: Dār al-Sha'b, nd), 377-8.

35 Ḥifnī Nāṣif, *Al-Muqtaṭaf*, vol. 83, (Cairo, 1933), 206.

36 See, al-Ṣāliḥ, *Mabāḥith,* 287-9; Labīb el-Sa'īd, *Al-Jam' Al-Ṣawtī Al-Awwal Li'l-Qur'ān*, (Cairo, 1978), 291-2.

37 El-Sa'īd, *Al-Jam'*, 291-2.

traditional orthography as inadequate in this respect, citing especially the seeming inconsistency in the way some words are written in the ʿUthmānic *rasm*.

They were obviously unsuccessful, however, in citing such examples as لأاذبحنّه and بأييْد (always cited and highlighted in criticism of the *rasm*) even though there are valid considerations to do with the pronunciation of *hamza*. Critics do not seem to have noticed that such examples consistently have a *hamza* in them and no one asked whether this factor had any effect on the *rasm*. They were unsuccessful in citing بسم, written normally without an *alif*, but with an *alif* in 56:74, 69:52, 96:1, because in these three instances it is بٱسم ربك, whereas in all others (115 places) it is بسم الله; abbreviation (by omitting the *alif*) was clearly intended with the one most frequently used and with the name of Allah. Nor should they have an argument in the numerous examples where various *qirāʾāt* are involved or in examples where there is an intention of pointing out a contrast as explained earlier; this is a valid consideration in normal orthography.[38] However, they had a better argument in examples where there does not seem to be an obvious consideration of phonetics or *qirāʾāt* for variations. For instance, سبحٰن is written normally without an *alif* but in 17:93 it is written with an *alif* سبحان ربى ; similarly, اليل is written with one *lām* but اللهو و اللعب with two.

In such examples the explanation might legitimately be sought, not in mystical considerations nor necessarily in simple inconsistency but in the fact that Arabic orthography even after the period of ʿUthmān – as can be witnessed in older books on *imlāʾ* – knew more than one way of writing some letters within words. There were Kufan and Basran opinions and there was the question of *jawāz* (optional ways) in many cases.[39] Just as there were options in grammar, there were also options in orthography,

38 Wālī, *Kitāb al-Imlāʾ*, 94.

39 See, Wālī, *Kitāb al-Imlāʾ*, 147, 157-8.

but what was optional at an early stage of *rasm* became fixed because of the special status of things Qur'ānic.

Understandably the traditionalists have always had strong arguments for maintaining the status quo. After all, the early *rasm* was set by the Companions of the Prophet and sanctioned by no less figures than Abu Bakr, ʿUmar, ʿUthmān, ʿĀlī and others. It was adopted by their followers in what amounts to an *ijmāʿ*, so that Mālik, Aḥmad and other imams held that it should not be altered in any way.[40] Great care should also be taken to keep the Qur'ān as it originally was in pronunciation of the words and writing at that time. If the gate were to be opened, the traditionalists argue, to what was deemed desirable in *rasm*, it might in time become open to pronunciation. Thus, the juristic principle of *sadd al-dharā'iʿ* (blocking the way for unlawful or undecided things) was invoked. If changes in *rasm* are conceded, it is not unlikely that some might consider it desirable to write the Qur'ān in the Latin alphabet, or write abridgements of it, or write it in Arab dialects which the non-traditionalists could argue would make it more accessible.[41] Abandoning the *rasm* might also lead to abandoning many of the *ʿulūm al-adā'* (sciences of recitation). There are, moreover, many benefits in the ʿUthmānic *rasm* which should not be sacrificed:

(a) It indicates the origin of certain letters, as in صلوة and زكوة written with *wāw*;

(b) It indicates some *fuṣḥa* versions of Arabic such as in writing the feminine *ha'* as an ordinary open *tā'*; and the deletion of the final *yā'* of the indicative verb in يوم يأتِ (11:105);

40 See, El-Saʿīd, *Al-Jamʿ*, 297-300.

41 Nāṣif, *Al-Muqtaṭaf*, 206. See also Al-Shalabī, *Rasm Al-Muṣḥaf Wa-l-Iḥtijāj Bihi Fī-l-Qirā'at,* (Cairo, 1960), 152.

(c) It indicates a different meaning of a word in a certain context: thus أم من is written as two words in (4:109) to indicate that أم here is in the sense of بل (rather) unlike in 67:22;

(d) It indicates various *qirā'āt* of the same word – many examples can be cited here,[42] to quote but two: يخدعون (2:4) is written without *alif* and there are two *qirā'āt* of it: *yakhdaʿūna* and *yukhādiʿūna*; كلمت (6:115) is written with a regular *tā'* instead of a *tā' marbūṭa* and there are two *qirā'āt* of it: *kalimat* and *kalimāt*.

Traditionalists further argue that rules of ordinary orthography are themselves open to differences and changes and Qur'ānic *rasm* should not be made to follow them. Besides, it is not necessary in ordinary orthography that the writing of words should coincide with the pronunciation, thus we have words like, داود , لكن , هؤلاء , أولئك , يرى, to give but a few examples of 'irregular' orthography, where the orthography does not reflect the pronunciation and this is perfectly accepted by the non-traditionalists. Nor is this peculiar to Arabic: it is far more extensive and accepted in English and French, for instance. And, whereas the pronunciation of such 'irregular' words is not indicated by any signs in modern Arabic, all cases of additions, deletions or substitution of letters in the Qur'ānic *rasm* are indicated by signs of *iṣṭilāḥāt al-ḍabṭ* to guide the reader to their correct pronunciation. It should also be remembered that the 'Uthmānic *rasm* was one source of ordinary orthography[43] and came to differ from it only in certain aspects, all of which have been identified in detail, including every single exception from the rules, in a way not surprising from scholars of the Qur'ān, who counted even the occurrence of every single letter of the alphabet in the entire

42 El-Saʿīd, *Al-Jamʿ*, 304-6.
43 Wālī, *Kitāb al-Imlā'*, 44.

text.[44] They also supplied signs to guide the reader to pronounce every word, making the *rasm* a uniquely precise system of representation. This has always been supported by a tradition and an educational system that considers reception by word of mouth to be – as it was at the time of the Prophet – the primary way of teaching and learning the Qur'ān. In any case, in addition to *iṣṭilāḥāt al-ḍabṭ* and the guide printed in the Appendix of the *muṣḥaf*, some *muṣḥafs* are now printed with a further guide in the foot margin of every page containing the Qur'ānic and the modern orthographic ways of writing words where the two systems differ; but Muslims have evidently insisted that the text of the Qur'ān itself should remain written in the ʿUthmānic *rasm*. They apparently consider that this *rasm* has been an important way of ensuring that successive generations of Muslims have been faithful to the original writing and reading of the Qur'ān, ever since Hudhayfa ibn al-Yamān urged ʿUthmān, 'Quick! Help the Muslims before they differ about the text of the Qur'ān as the Christians and Jews differed about their scriptures.'

Bibliography

Arberry, A.J. *The Koran Interpreted*. Oxford: Oxford University Press. 1955.

al-Bukhārī, Muḥammad Ibn Ismāʿīl. *Saḥīḥ Bukhārī: Faḍā'il al-Qur'ān*, Book 61.

al-Dānī, Abū Amr. *Al-Muqniʿ Fi Marsūm Wa-Maṣāḥif Ahl Al-Amṣār Maʿ Kitāb Al-Naqṭ*. Damascus: Dār al-Fikr. 1983.

al-Jawzī, ʿAbd al-Raḥmān Ibn. *Funūn Al-Afnān Fī ʿAjā'ib Al-Qur'ān*. Baghdād, 1988.

al-Qaṭṭān, Mannāʿ Khalīl. *Mabāḥith Fī ʿUlūm al-Qur'ān*. Riyadh: Maktabah al-Maʿārif. 1992.

44 See Ibn al-Jawzī, *Funūn*, 104-6.

al-Suyūṭī, Jalāl-Al-Dīn. *Al-Itqān Fī ʿUlūm Al-Qur'ān*. Vols I and II. Beirut: Dār al-Kutub al-ʿIlmiyya. 1987.

al-Ṣāliḥ, Subhi Ibrāhīm. *Mabāhith fī cUlūm al-Qur'ān*, Beirut: Dar Al-ʿIlm li-l-Malayīn. 1981.

el-Saʿīd, Labīb. *Al-Jamʿ Al-Ṣawtī Al-Awwal Li'l-Qur'ān*, Cairo: Dār al-Kātib al-'Arabī. 1967.

Ibn Khaldūn, Abdur Rahman. *Al-Muqaddima*. Cairo: Dar al-Shaʿb. n.d.

Nāṣif, Ḥifni. *Al-Muqtaṭaf*. Vol. 83, Cairo. 1933.

Shalabī, ʿAbd al-Fattāḥ Ismāʿīl. Rasm Al-Muṣḥaf Wa-l-Iḥtijāj Bihi Fī-l-Qirā'āt. Cairo: Maktabat Nahḍat Miṣr.1960.

ʿUthmān, Ḥusny Shaikh. *Ḥaqq Al-Tilāwa*. Jordan: Manshūrāt al-ʿAṣr al-Ḥadīth, 1971.

Wālī, Hussain. *Kitāb al-Imlā'*, Beirut: Dār al-Qalam, 1985.

CHAPTER SEVEN

The View of 'Abdullāh ibn Mas'ūd on the 'Uthmānic Qur'ān Compilation

Zahed Fettah

The ease of reciting the Qur'ān is something that has been emphasised in several verses of the Qur'ān. For instance, the Qur'ān states, 'We have made this Qur'ān easy as a reminder. Is there, then, anyone who will take heed?'[1] One manifestation of this ease can be seen in the narrations which report a concession that the Prophet Muḥammad ﷺ sought for his followers, requesting that God allows the believers to recite in a variety of ways. This concession was granted with the notion of the seven *aḥruf* (variants). The Prophet's companions thus recited whatever they received from the Prophet directly or through other Companions. A number of Companions, including 'Umar[2], Ubay ibn Ka'b[3], 'Amr ibn al-'Āṣ[4], among others, reported that the Prophet said: 'The Qur'ān has been revealed according to seven *aḥruf*.' The ḥadīth of 'Umar also contains an important addition,

1 Qur'ān, Sūrat al-Qamar, 54:17.

2 Muḥammad al-Bukhārī, *Saḥīḥ al-Bukhārī* (Beirut: Al-Risalah Publishers, 2019), 2419; Muslim ibn al-Ḥajjāj, *Sahih Muslim* (Beirut: Al-Risalah Publishers, 2020), 818.

3 Muḥammad al-Tirmidhī, *Jami' al-Tirmidhī* (Beirut: Al-Risalah Publishers, 2017), 2944. Tirmidhī said after narrating it: 'This is an authentic Hadith.'

4 Aḥmad ibn Ḥanbal, *Musnad Aḥmad* (Beirut: Al-Risalah Publishers, 2001), 17821. Ibn Kathir said: 'This is a sound (*jayyid*) hadith.'

'so recite whatever is easy.' This is further clarified by the narration of 'Amr ibn al-Āṣ, which adds: 'According to whichever you recite, you have done well. Do not dispute regarding it.' I avoid discussing the precise meaning of the *aḥruf* here and the nature of this variation, for that is beyond the scope of our topic. However, it suffices us to show, through these reports, that these variations were viewed as acceptable ways of reciting the Qur'ān; not ones that contradict it.

Just as the concession of the seven *aḥruf* was brought about by a need, the two compilations of the Qur'ān, initially under the command of the first caliph, Abū Bakr, then followed by 'Uthmān ibn 'Affān, only came about due to a need. The main concern in the time of Abū Bakr was that the Qur'ān was scattered in writing, hence making its preservation more difficult in the long term. This became a particular problem when many memorisers and reciters of the Qur'ān were killed during the battle of Yamāmah.[5] In 'Uthmān's time, Hudhaifah ibn al-Yamān, a senior companion of the Prophet, warned 'Uthmān that the Muslims would be destroyed if they were allowed to continue to dispute and differ regarding their Book, urging him to do something. This was what prompted 'Uthmān's decision to compile a lead copy that would be enforced throughout the Muslim world.

After the compilation in the time of Abū Bakr, traditional sources report that 'Uthmān ordered the compilation of one lead copy (*al-muṣḥaf al-imam*) of the Qur'ān that would encompass, as much as possible, all the *aḥruf* of the Qur'ān, declaring it the standard.[6] 'Uthmān made the *ḥarf* (pl. *aḥruf*) of Quraysh the default if there was any difference during its inscription. Anyone that had a copy which opposed this lead copy was commanded to get rid of it. However, according to this model, one of the

5 al-Bukhārī, *Sahih al-Bukhārī*, 4679.

6 Behnam Sadeghi. The Codex of a Companion of the Prophet and the Qur'ān of the Prophet. *Arabica* vol. 57 (2010): 334.

problems with 'Uthmān's approach is that some of the variations that the Prophet taught would then be excluded from this grand copy of the Qur'ān. Nonetheless, the Prophet's Companions generally seemed to support 'Uthmān in his decision since the justification behind it was the greater good of the Muslims and the preservation of the Qur'ān itself. However, 'Abdullāh ibn Mas'ūd, a notable expert of the Qur'ān and senior companion of the Prophet, was unhappy with this decision. He ignored the third caliph's command to dispose of his personal copy of the Qur'ān, which differed from the lead copy in some verses.

'Uthmān's justification appears to have been that the seven *aḥruf* were merely equally valid ways to recite the Qur'ān, with each one presenting more or less the same meanings as the other. None of the meanings of the Qur'ān would thus be lost if some of the *aḥruf* were abandoned. However, it is understandable that some Companions struggled to accept this, since they were being asked to abandon verses that they had heard directly from the Prophet. Ibn Mas'ūd also opposed the majority of the Companions with his view that the last two chapters of the Qur'ān, Sūrat al-Falaq (ch. 113) and Sūrat al-Nās (ch. 114), were not meant to be included as part of the Qur'ān. This claim is arguably even more of a problem for Muslim scholars, as we shall see later. Hence, it will be given a larger share of the discussion in this chapter. Ibn Mas'ūd's dissent raises questions about the nature of the Qur'ān's transmission. Not only due to the severity of the dissent, but due to the status of 'Abdullāh among the Companions, as a leading scholar of the Qur'ān. The centrality of the idea of *tawātur* in the preservation and transmission of the Qur'ān is so essential, that several Muslim scholars throughout history ruled the reports of 'Abdullāh's dissent to be fabrications. This chapter seeks to discuss, and clarify, some of the problems that relate to the validity of these reports, the nature of this dissent, and what this means for the preservation and transmission of the Qur'ān in Islamic intellectual history.

Three Points of Contention

We can summarise the points of contention between 'Abdullāh ibn Mas'ūd and the majority of the Companions into three:

1. 'Uthmān's order to all Muslims to hand in their copies of the Qur'ān if they contain variants not consistent with the lead copy that was compiled under his supervision. These copies would then be burnt.
2. The appointment of young Companions to carry out the task of compiling the Qur'ān.
3. The last two chapters being part of the Qur'ān; the Muṣḥaf.

A lengthy report narrated by Anas ibn Mālik clarifies the first two matters. He says:

> Hudhaifah ibn al-Yaman came to 'Uthmān at the time when the people of Shām and the people of Iraq went to war to conquer Armenia and Azerbaijan. Hudhaifah saw that they each had different forms of recitation of the Qur'ān, so he said to 'Uthmān: 'O Commander of the Believers! Save this nation before they differ regarding the Book, as the Jews and Christians did before them.' So 'Uthmān sent a message to Hafsah, saying: 'Send us the manuscripts so that we may copy them into the maṣāḥif (plural of muṣḥaf: a written copy of the Qur'ān), then we shall return it to you.' Hafsah sent the manuscripts to 'Uthmān, who then ordered for Zaid ibn Thābit, Sa'eed ibn al-'As, Abdur-Raḥmān ibn al-Harith ibn Hisham, and 'Abdullāh ibn al-Zubair to copy the manuscripts in the maṣāḥif. 'Uthmān then said to the three Qurayshi men: 'In case you disagree with Zaid on anything, write it in

the dialect of Quraysh, for it was revealed in their dialect.' When they had copied the manuscripts, 'Uthmān sent one copy to every province.

Ibn Shihāb al-Zuhrī (d. 124 H) said: 'Ubaidullāh ibn 'Abdullāh ibn 'Utbah (d. 99 H) informed me that 'Abdullāh ibn Mas'ūd disliked that Zaid ibn Thābit was chosen for copying the maṣāḥif, and said: 'O Muslims, how can I be sidelined from recording the transcription of the Qur'ān and it is overseen by a man who, by Allah, when I accepted Islam, he was still in the loins of a disbelieving man?' This is why 'Abdullāh ibn Mas'ūd said: 'O people of Iraq, keep the copies of the Qur'ān that are with you, and conceal them, for Allah has said: 'Whoever conceals something, shall come with what he concealed on the Day of Judgement.' Meet Allah with your copies of the Qur'ān.'

Ibn Shihāb al-Zuhrī then said: 'I was informed that some of the most senior Companions of the Messenger of Allah disliked this view of ibn Mas'ūd.'[7]

This narration is reported at length in Jāmi' al-Tirmidhī who declared the report to be authentic. The narration shows that ibn Mas'ūd was unhappy with 'Uthmān's choice to give Zaid ibn Thābit the responsibility of such a great task. He felt that it was inappropriate for the Muslim community to be required to suffice with a recitation compiled by a junior Companion. Ibn Masʿūd would say, 'Whose recitation are you commanding me to read according to? I recited seventy chapters directly to the Prophet, while Zaid was still a boy playing with the children.'[8]

---

7 Al-Tirmidhī, *Jami' al-Tirmidhī*, 3104. He then said: 'This is an authentic Hadith.'

8 Aḥmad al-Nasā'ī, *Sunan al-Nasā'ī* (Beirut: Dar ibn Kathir, 2016), 5063.

We shall speak in more detail later about the rank of ibn Mas'ūd and his expertise in the Qur'ān; a status that other Companions accepted. However, it seems like ibn Mas'ūd was alone in questioning Zaid's appointment, bearing in mind that the Prophet himself testified to Zaid's competence when appointing him as one of his close scribes of the Qur'ān during the period of revelation. He also gained the trust of the two most senior Companions, Abū Bakr and 'Umar, who appointed him with the hefty task of compiling the whole Qur'ān into one place, at a time in which it was scattered. It was thus no surprise that 'Uthmān felt that Zaid would be a suitable choice for the task ahead. We also find that none of the Prophet's companions questioned any of the caliphs for appointing Zaid.

It should also be added that Zaid's efforts were under the supervision and approval of other senior Companions, including Abū Bakr, 'Umar, 'Uthmān, and 'Ali. It was thus not Zaid's recitation that people were left with, nor his lone efforts, but rather what seemed more of a consensus of the early Muslim community. Muṣ'ab ibn Sa'd (d. 103/721) said: 'I saw people's overwhelming approval of 'Uthmān when he burnt the copies of the Qur'ān. None of them rebuked him for it.'[9] Muṣ'ab here met many of the Companions and senior scholars and is the son of Sa'd ibn Abī Waqqās, who is himself a senior Companion.

It could even be argued that 'Abdullāh ibn Mas'ūd himself appreciated the justification of unity and reducing dispute regarding the Qur'ān. For he reports that he heard two people reciting a chapter of the Qur'ān – Sūrat al-Aḥqāf – differently from the way he was taught by the Prophet. Despite this, both claimed to have taken this recitation directly from the Prophet. When they took the matter to the Prophet, he became visibly angry and said: 'Do not dispute, for the people before you were

9 Abdullāh ibn Abī Dāwūd, *Kitāb al-Maṣāḥif* (Cairo: Al-Faruq al-Hadithah, 2002), 68.

destroyed by dispute.' He then said: 'Take the recitation of the most knowledgeable of you.'[10]

This incident sheds light on the nature of variety in Qur'ānic recitations. They seem to be viewed as equally valid and sufficient. Hence, the Prophet commanded each person to recite the Qur'ān as they had been taught. Not having knowledge of every variant, did not imply a deficiency in a person's own copy of the Qur'ān. This is the rule that appears to be taken from this *ḥadīth*. Even more explicit is the statement of ibn Mas'ūd himself: 'I have heard reciters, and found them to be similar, so just recite as you have been taught, and beware of exaggeration and dispute. It is like saying, *halumm* (come here) and *ta'āl* (come here).'[11] It thus seems unlikely that 'Abdullāh questioned the validity of the recitation compiled by Zaid; he was clearly aware that Zaid had accompanied the Prophet and took the Qur'ān directly from the Prophet. A more probable interpretation is that he felt that all recitations should be equally preserved. It may also have been that ibn Mas'ūd did not approve of 'Uthmān's decision to burn the copies, not that he rejected the idea of a united copy altogether. Alternatively, some early scholars, including Abū Bakr ibn Abī Dāwūd (d.316/927), claim that ibn Mas'ūd could have changed his view later on, eventually agreeing with the rest of the Companions. In which case, it seems like he came to terms with the initially burdensome order to abandon recitations that he had heard directly from the Prophet.[12]

Having discussed the first two areas of contention between 'Abdullāh ibn Mas'ūd and the majority of Companions, we should discuss the third in a little more detail in the upcoming

10 Ibn Ḥanbal, *Al-Musnad*, 3803, 3981. This Hadith was authenticated by Aḥmad Shākir and others.

11 Abū 'Ubaid ibn Sallām, *Fadhail al-Qur'ān* (Damascus: Dar ibn Kathir, 1995), 346; Muḥammad al-Tabari, *Tafsīr ibn Jarīr*, 13/77. The *isnad* of this Hadith appears to fit the condition of both al-Bukhārī and Muslim.

12 Ibn Abī Dāwūd, *Kitāb al-Maṣāḥif*, 82.

section. After doing so, we delve into the nature of mass transmission (*tawātur*) and the implications of 'Abdullāh's dissent on this.

The Debate on the Last Two Chapters of the Qur'ān

Some early reports, well-documented in ḥadīth works, imply that ibn Mas'ūd's copy of the Qur'ān did not contain the last two chapters of the Qur'ān, Sūrat al-Falaq and Sūrat al-Nas. He explicitly disagreed with those who included these two chapters into the Qur'ān, arguing that they were supplications that the Prophet would recite to seek protection (*isti'ādhah*) from harm, but not chapters of the Qur'ān. In fact, some reports go as far as claiming that he would scrape them out of copies in which they were found, and say: 'Do not mix with the Qur'ān that which is not from it.'[13]

This position of ibn Mas'ūd clearly has grave implications on the compilation and preservation of the Qur'ān, hence it was difficult for many scholars to accept these reports. Its problematic meanings were largely what led the Dhāhiri polymath, 'Ali ibn Aḥmad ibn Ḥazm al-Andalusī (d. 456/1063) to declaring all these reports to be fabrications and lies. After affirming the authenticity of every verse in the Qur'ān, he said:

> Whoever rejects a single letter of the Qur'ān is a disbeliever… and everything reported from ibn Mas'ūd about the *mu'awidhatain* (last two chapters) and *umm al-Qur'ān* (al-Fatiḥa) not being part of his *muṣḥaf* is a fabricated lie that is not authentic. In fact, what is authentically reported from him is the recitation of Asim from Zirr ibn

13 Muḥammad al-Shāfi'ī, *al-Umm* (Beirut: Dar al-Fikr, 1990), 7/199.

> Hubaish from 'Abdullāh ibn Mas'ūd, and it contains both the *mu'awidhatain* (chapters of refuge) and *umm al-Qur'ān*.[14]

Prior to ibn Ḥazm, al-Bāqillānī shared similar sentiments in his defence of the authenticity of the Qur'ān, *al-Intisar lil Qur'ān*. In his lengthy discussion of almost thirty pages, on the reports attributed to ibn Mas'ūd, he inclined towards the claim that declared them to be false reports. He says:

> Regarding the claim that 'Abdullāh ibn Mas'ūd rejected the last two chapters were from the Qur'ān revealed to Muḥammad, then this claim shows the ignorance and foolishness of whoever believes it. Such a person is distant from knowledge… How can 'Abdullāh ibn Mas'ūd, or any Companion, reject this, when this is something that the Prophet declared, repeated, and recited aloud in his prayers?... If these reports have reached us through mass transmission (*tawātur*), leading us to certainty beyond any doubt, what then of the generation of the Prophet who heard it directly from him?[15]

He then continued to explain how these reports simply do not fit with what is known of the Companions and their concern for preserving the Qur'ān. How could they allow him to hold such an opinion without harshly rebuking him for it? He argued that this was simply beyond imagination. He then comprehensively argued against the validity of the reports and argued that these chapters were clearly part of the Qur'ān in the Prophetic era.[16]

Another leading scholar, Abū Hāmid al-Ghazzālī (d. 505/1111) sought to make sense of the reports mentioned, saying:

---

14 Ali ibn Ḥazm, *al-Muḥallā bil Athār* (Beirut: Dar al-Fikr, 2002), 21.

15 Abū Bakr al-Bāqillānī, *al-Intisar lil Qur'ān* (Beirut: Dar ibn Ḥazm, 2001), 301.

16 Ibid, 303.

> Ibn Mas'ūd did not reject that they were from the Qur'ān. Rather, he believed that they should not be written as part of the copies of the Qur'ān, because the sunnah in his view was that only those chapters that the Prophet ordered to be recorded as part of the *muṣḥaf* could be recorded in it... This is not tantamount to rejecting their being from the Qur'ān, for doing so would be greatly evil (*fisq*); something that cannot be attributed to him, or any Companion.[17]

Al-Ghazzālī's interpretation was then adopted by other scholars including Mālikī jurist al-Maziri (d. 536/1141).[18] Qādī 'Iyād too agreed and added another possible explanation for the position of ibn Mas'ūd. In his commentary of Sahīh Muslim, he claimed that it could have been that the first and last two chapters of the Qur'ān were so short in size and known to all Muslims, that ibn Mas'ūd felt that there was no need to include them in the Qur'ān.[19] This argument is evidently problematic. However, as there are several chapters of the Qur'ān that are even shorter and similarly known to all Muslims, such as Sūrat al-Ikhlas and Sūrat al-Asr. Yet it has never been suggested that it was an option to exclude these from the *muṣḥaf*. Additionally, such a justification is not sufficient to exclude any part of the Qur'ān from the written copies, for the Muslims seem to be unanimous on the obligation of including all that is from the Qur'ān.

---

17 Abū Hāmid al-Ghazzālī, *al-Mustasfa min Ilm al-Usul* (Beirut: Dar al-Kutub al-Ilmiyah, 1993), 115.

18 Muḥammad al-Māzirī, *Idāḥ al-Maḥsul min Burhān al-Usul* (Tunisia: Dar al-Gharb al-Islami, 2001), 439.

19 Iyad al-Yaḥsubī, *Ikmāl al-Mu'lim bi-Fawā'id Muslim* (Egypt: Dar al-Wafa, 1998), 3/201.

A Study of the Authenticity of the Reports Attributed to Ibn Mas’ūd

The scholars quoted thus far are known to be authorities in Islamic scholarship, but we are far off from a consensus on the claims made here. In fact, it seems that the majority of earlier scholars accepted these reports as sound and understood them literally. I first narrate these reports, then discuss their authenticity using traditional ḥadīth principles, then refer to the comments of some early scholars on these reports.

1. Imam al-Shāfi’ī narrates that Waki told him, from Sufyān al-Thawrī, from Abū Ishāq al-Sabī’ī, that Abd al-Raḥmān ibn Yazīd said: ‘I saw ‘Abdullāh (ibn Mas’ūd) scraping the *mu’awidhatain* from the *muṣḥaf*. He would say, ‘Do not mix with it anything that is not from it.’[20]

This chain of transmission is authentic according to the apparent criteria of both al-Bukhārī and Muslim. All of its narrators are famously reliable narrators. Abū Ishaq narrates a lot from Abd al-Raḥmān, thus the problem of *tadlis* does not come up here, especially since one of the people who narrates this report from him is Shu’bah ibn al-Hajjāj who was strict on ensuring that the narrations of Abū Ishāq were completely connected.[21] A number of reliable narrators narrate it from Abū Ishāq, including al-A’mash, al-Thawrī, Shu’bah, and Abū al-Aḥwaṣ.

Given the soundness of this narration, it appears to discard the suggestions of al-Bāqillānī, al-Ghazzālī, al-Maziri, and Iyad,

20 Al-Shāfi’ī, *al-Umm*, 7/199; Abdullāh ibn Abī Shaybah, *Musannaf ibn Abī Shaybah* (Riyadh: Dar Kunuz Ishbiliya, 2015), 32207; Ibn Ḥanbal, *Al-Musnad*, 21188.

21 Al-Tabarānī, Sulaimān. *al-Mu’jam al-Kabīr* (Cairo: Maktabat ibn Taymiyyah, 1994), 9149.

who claimed that ibn Mas'ūd only believed that the last two chapters need not be written down for different reasons, not that they were not part of the Qur'ān. Here he explicitly negates their being part of the Qur'ān altogether.

2. 'Abdullāh ibn Aḥmad narrates in the Musnad that 'Abd al-Raḥmān ibn Yazīd said that 'Abdullāh ibn Mas'ūd would scrape the *mu'awidhatain* from his copies of the Qur'ān and say, 'They are not from the Book of Allah.'[22]

The narrators of this report are all reliable according to the consensus of ḥadīth critics. This narration is even more explicit in rejecting the claims of the aforementioned scholars. It makes it clear that ibn Mas'ūd believed that the last two chapters should not be written in the *muṣḥaf*, because they are not from the Qur'ān.

3. Ibrāhīm al-Nakha'i narrates from Alqamah that 'Abdullāh ibn Mas'ūd said: 'The Prophet only commanded us to seek protection through them, but he would not recite them (in prayers).'[23]

This is a different route to 'Abdullāh ibn Mas'ūd, which strengthens the previous narration further. Its narrators in al-Tabarani are deemed reliable.

4. Sufyān ibn Uyaynah narrates from both 'Abdah ibn Abī Lubābah and 'Asim ibn Abī al-Najūd, both from Zirr ibn Hubaish who said to Ubay ibn Ka'b: 'Your brother 'Abdullāh ibn Mas'ūd scrapes the *mu'awidhatain* from the

22 Ibn Ḥanbal, *Al-Musnad*, 21188.

23 Al-Tabarānī. *al-Mu'jam al-Kabīr*, 9152.

> *muṣḥaf.*' Ubay disagreed and explained that he himself simply says as he heard the Prophet say.[24]

All the narrators of this report are well-known. Imam al-Bukhārī narrates it in his Sahih without explaining exactly what ibn Mas'ūd said or did, but this is understood from the other narrations. However, it is not so clear why al-Bukhārī does so. It does not seem to be due to his hesitation about the authenticity of the report, since he narrates it in his book with a complete chain of transmission. It could be due to the severity of the action of ibn Mas'ūd which was not approved by the Muslims that he opted to allude to it, as opposed to explicitly mentioning it. This narration is also narrated by Aḥmad ibn Hanbal, from ʿAffān ibn Muslim, from Hammad ibn Salamah, from Asim; also, a strong and accepted chain of narration.

5. Abū Bakr ibn Abī Shaybah narrates from Waki', from ʿAbdullāh ibn ʿAwn, that Muḥammad ibn Sīrīn said: ʿAbdullāh ibn Mas'ūd used to not write the *mu'awidhatain*.'[25]

All the narrators in this chain of transmission are from the most reliable narrators of ḥadīth. Their reports are frequently found in both al-Bukhārī and Muslim. Muḥammad ibn Sīrīn did not meet ʿAbdullāh ibn Mas'ūd, so there is a slight break in the report. However, given that ibn Sirin is a senior scholar and student of the Companions, such a break in the chain is overlooked, especially given the previous narrations mentioned that support it.

These are some of the most important narrations that clarify the position of ibn Mas'ūd. They all seem to fit the criteria of traditional ḥadīth criticism for authenticity. What is attributed to ibn Mas'ūd is thus not claimed merely through a sole report of

---

24 Ibn Ḥanbal, *Al-Musnad*, 21181; al-Bukhārī, *Sahih al-Bukhārī*, 4977.

25 Ibn Abī Shaybah. *Muṣannaf ibn Abī Shaybah*, 32214.

questionable soundness, but through a number of famous chains of narration.

Those scholars who rejected these reports or claimed that they were lies did not provide a criticism of the reports using ḥadīth principles, but simply seem to have found issue with the content (*matn*) of these reports. Though clearly an easy way out of the problem, the soundness of this approach is questionable, given what has been mentioned about the evident strength of these reports. The narrations also pose a challenge for the various interpretations that al-Bāqillānī, al-Ghazzālī, and Iyad suggested. The reports appear to be quite explicit about 'Abdullāh's rejection of their being from the Qur'ān, despite him being fully aware of them. Instead, he understood that they were supplications through which the Prophet was taught to seek protection from God against harm, like many other supplications he was taught. In his view, they were never intended to be separate chapters of the Qur'ān. The second and third narrations mentioned above by Abd al-Raḥmān ibn Yazīd and 'Alqamah are quite unambiguous in this regard.

A number of early scholars thus accept what is attributed to 'Abdullāh ibn Mas'ūd, simply explaining it away as an error on his part. Besides the reports we have already quoted, Imam Aḥmad narrates in his Musnad, from his teacher, Sufyān ibn Uyaynah (d.198/814) that he said:

> They (the two chapters) are not in the copy of ibn Mas'ūd. He saw the Prophet reciting them as a means of protection for Ḥasan and Ḥusain, but did not hear him recite them in prayers, so he thought that they were merely supplications. He insisted on this opinion of his, but the rest of them (Companions) confirmed that they were indeed from the Qur'ān, so included them in their copies.[26]

26 Ibn Ḥanbal, *Al-Musnad*, 21189.

A similar explanation is provided by Muḥammad ibn Idrīs al-Shāfi'ī (d. 204/819) in his famous work, al-Umm. After reporting the Ḥadīth of Abd al-Raḥmān ibn Yazīd mentioned above, he explains:

> They (the Companions) narrated that the Prophet recited them in the morning (*Subh*) prayer. They are in the Qur'ān that was compiled in the time of the Prophet, was then kept with 'Umar, then Hafsah. 'Uthmān then gathered the people upon this copy. I also like to recite them in my prayers.[27]

'Abdullāh ibn Muslim ibn Qutaybah (d. 276/889), sometimes referred to as the orator of Ahl al-Sunnah, explains the position of ibn Mas'ūd:

> Ibn Mas'ūd had a reason for doing so (rejecting the two chapters), and people may believe things and err. If this can happen to the Prophets and Messengers, then even more so to others. The reason he left them out of his copy of the Qur'ān is that he saw the Prophet reciting them, as a form of seeking protection, upon Hasan, Husain, and others... he thus thought that they were not from the Qur'ān.[28]

The views presented by ibn 'Uyaynah, al-Shāfi'ī, and ibn Qutaybah thus put the harsh statements of al-Bāqillānī under question. In their view, the error of a Companion on a matter like this need not raise questions over the authenticity of the Qur'ān, whose compilation is a collective one, without the need to consider the view of every individual. Alongside the collective

---

27 Al-Shāfi'ī, *al-Umm*, 7/199.

28 Ibn Qutaybah, Abdullāh. *Ta'wil Mukhtalif al-Hadith* (Damascus: Al-Maktab al-Islami, 1999), 76.

agreement of the Companions, the following Ḥadīth further problematises their opinion. The Prophet said to Uqbah ibn Amir: 'Verses have been revealed to me, the like of which I have not seen before: Sūrat al-Falaq and Sūrat al-Nās.' Then he recited them.[29] In another report he said: 'O 'Uqbah, shall I teach you the best two chapters one can recite?' He then led the Muslims in the morning prayer and recited these two chapters in his prayer.[30] We should perhaps end this section by noting that the reports discussed above speak specifically of the last two chapters of the Qur'ān. The reports claiming that ibn Mas'ūd excluded Sūrat al-Fatiḥa from the Qur'ān seem to be questionable.

The Argument from Qur'ānic Recitations

As alluded to earlier, ibn Ḥazm also attempts to weaken these reports by arguing that the chains of transmission of the Qur'ānic recitations (*qira'at*) that go back to ibn Mas'ūd, all contain the last two chapters of the Qur'ān. He argues that it is a known fact that the recitation of Asim is taken from Zirr ibn Ḥubaish, who studied the Qur'ān with 'Abdullāh ibn Mas'ūd. This argument could have some standing if 'Abdullāh was Zirr's only teacher of Qur'ān. But this is not the case. Zirr ibn Hubaish was a student of at least two other Companions who were more senior than 'Abdullāh; they are 'Uthmān ibn Affan and 'Ali ibn Abī Tālib. Additionally, Zirr was not Asim's only teacher.[31] Asim also studied the Qur'ān with Abū Abd al-Raḥmān al-Sulami; another

29 Ibn al-Ḥajjāj, *Sahih Muslim*, 814; Ibn Ḥanbal, *Musnad Aḥmad*, 17303; Al-San'ani, Abd al-Razzaq. *Musannaf Abd al-Razzāq* (Riyadh: Dar al-Taseel, 2013), 6217.

30 Al-Sijistānī, Abu Dāwūd. *Sunan Abu Dāwūd* (Beirut: Al-Risalah Publishers, 2009), 1462; Al-Nasā'ī, *Sunan al-Nasā'ī,* 952.

31 Shady Hekmat Nasser. *The Second Canonization of the Qur'ān (324/936): Ibn Mujāhid and the Founding of the Seven Readings* (Leiden-Boston: Brill, 2020), 26.

scholar of recitation who was a student of 'Uthmān, Ali, Ubay ibn Ka'b, 'Abdullāh ibn Mas'ūd, and Zaid ibn Thābit.[32]

What this means is that the recitation of Asim is not necessarily restricted to 'Abdullāh ibn Mas'ūd. The nature of Quranic preferences (*ikhtiyarat*) is that a scholar of Qur'ān may pick and choose from the recitations of his teachers, eventually ending up with a recitation of his own. Since the Companions that Zirr and al-Sulami studied with all recited the last two chapters of the Qur'ān, it would make no sense for them to leave it out of their own recitations for 'Abdullāh's lone opinion. Essentially, when the Qur'ān was being transmitted in the first generations, this opinion of 'Abdullāh seemed to have simply been ignored and brushed aside. Hence, all the recitations that have reached us today are in line with the 'Uthmānic scripts and all contain the last two chapters.

What further supports the view that 'Abdullāh's opinion was simply ignored is that many of the chains of transmission of the current ten *qira'at* that are accepted today end up at 'Abdullāh ibn Mas'ūd. Along with Zirr and al-Sulamī, Asim also studied the Qur'ān with Sa'd ibn Iyās al-Shaybānī, another student of ibn Mas'ūd. None of these recitations exclude the last two chapters of the Qur'ān.[33] Similarly, Ḥamza ibn Ḥabīb narrates the Qur'ān from al-A'mash, who narrates it from Zaid ibn Wahb al-Juhani, a student of ibn Mas'ūd. Ḥamza also narrates the Qur'ān from Abū Ishāq al-Sabī'ī, a student of at least five of 'Abdullāh's senior students, all who studied the Qur'ān with him. They include 'Abīdah al-Salmānī, 'Amr ibn Shuraḥbīl, 'Alqamah ibn Qais, al-Aswad ibn Yazīd, and 'Amr ibn Maymun al-Awdī.[34] We see that every single recitation that has roots in the recitation

32 'Abdullāh ibn Mujāhid, *al-Sab'ah fi al-Qira'at* (Egypt: Dar al-Ma'arif, 1980), 69.
33 'Uthmān al-Dāni, *Jami' al-Bayan fi al-Qira'at al-Sab'* (UAE: University of Sharjah, 2007), 1/192.
34 Ibn Mujāhid, *al-Sab'ah fi al-Qira'at*, 71.

of 'Abdullāh ibn Mas'ūd, still includes the last two chapters of the Qur'ān.

Furthermore, Ibrāhīm al-Nakha'ī is reported to have asked al-Aswad about whether the *mu'awidhatain* are from the Qur'ān. He replied: 'Yes'.[35] Aswad was a senior student of 'Abdullāh, and Ibrāhīm was one of the most knowledgeable scholars in 'Abdullāh's opinion, though he never met him directly. The same position was upheld by al-Sha'bī, another student of 'Abdullāh.[36] There does not seem to be any dispute about this amongst any of the students of ibn Mas'ūd himself, nor any of the Companions or generations after them. This could be proof of a change of opinion by ibn Mas'ūd towards the end of his life. It is also possible that his view was simply accepted as a mistake, though he insisted on that view until he died.

The Problem of Tawātur

One of the problems al-Bāqillānī, ibn Ḥazm, and al-Rāzī faced when dealing with the view of ibn Mas'ūd, is that every verse of the Qur'ān must have been revealed through *tawātur*, such that it becomes common knowledge. If a Bedouin who accepted Islam towards the end of the Prophet's life can be excused for being ignorant of some verses, they felt it unreasonable to accept that a senior scholar of Qur'ān, one of the earliest Companions, and someone who witnessed the final recitation, be excused for rejecting two famous chapters of the Qur'ān. However, 'Abdullāh ibn Mas'ūd was not an ordinary Companion, and his dissent cannot simply be dismissed easily. He was one of four Companions the Prophet made teachers of the Qur'ān.[37] In fact, the Prophet

35 Ibn Abī Shaybah, *Musannaf ibn Abī Shaybah*, 32208.
36 Ibn Abī Shaybah, *Musannaf ibn Abī Shaybah*, 32205.
37 al-Bukhārī, *Sahih al-Bukhārī*, 3808; Ibn al-Ḥajjāj, *Sahih Muslim*, 2464.

specifically stated: 'Whoever wishes to recite the Qur'ān in the pure way that it was revealed, should read it according to the recitation of ibn Mas'ūd.'[38] According to a report attributed to 'Abdullāh ibn 'Abbās, ibn Mas'ūd was present during the final recitation of the Qur'ān between Gabriel and the Prophet, thus witnessing what was confirmed and what was abrogated.[39] Muḥammad ibn 'Umar al-Rāzī (d. 606/1209) recognised that this is further reason to make 'Abdullāh's dissent problematic for the principle of mass transmission. He comments:

> The ancient books mention that ibn Mas'ūd used to reject that Sūrat al-Fātiḥa and the Chapters of Refuge were from the Qur'ān. Know that this is highly problematic. For if we say that mass transmission existed in the time of the Companions for these chapters, then ibn Mas'ūd was aware of them. Rejecting them would thus constitute disbelief or a deficiency in intellect. If we say that mass transmission was not attained in that era, this would require us to say that the Qur'ān is not *mutawātir* to begin with. This would thus no longer make it a certain proof. The likelihood is that the reports attributing this opinion to ibn Mas'ūd are false, and this way we are able to get out of this problem.[40]

This problem noted by al-Rāzī is probably what led other scholars before and after him to resort to falsifying these reports. However, that would only seem necessary if we accept that the validity of these reports negates their quality of being *mutawātir.*

38 Ibn Ḥanbal, *Al-Musnad*, 35; Muḥammad ibn Majah, *Sunan ibn Majah* (Beirut: Al-Risalah Publishers, 2009), 138; Muḥammad ibn Khuzaimah, *Sahih ibn Khuzaimah* (Riyadh: Maktabat al-Azami, 2009), 1156.
39 Abu Ya'lā al-Mosili, *Musnad Abu Ya'la* (Cairo: Dar al-Hadith, 2013), 2562.
40 Muḥammad al-Rāzī, *Al-Tafsir al-Kabīr* (Beirut: Dar Ihya al-Turath al-Arabī, 2000), 1/190.

We should consider whether both the mass transmission of the Qur'ān and the reports attributed to ibn Mas'ūd can be accepted without any contradiction. We can take this even further and question the condition of mass transmission altogether. Is *tawātur*, as interpreted by various scholars, the only way to establish the validity of the Qur'ān? Perhaps delving into that requires a separate study, though it is a question worthy of investigation.[41] The concept of *tawātur* certainly did not go unchallenged, even with regards to the Qur'ān itself. We will however discuss the conditions of *mutawātir* laid down by various scholars to then see if it is possible to accept the reports narrated from ibn Mas'ūd without negating any of the conditions of mass transmission.

The Nature and Conditions of Tawātur

Ghazzālī clearly lays down four conditions for a *mutawātir* report[42]:

1. The narrators must have reported something with certainty, not probability.
2. This knowledge must relate to what can be observed by the senses.
3. That the aforementioned conditions are present in all stages of the transmission of the report, from beginning to end.
4. The required number of reporters and witnesses must be present. He then goes on to discuss the various opinions on what that number is. Juwayni preceded him in clarifying these conditions, admitting that the variety of

41 Akram Nadwi, *Foundation to Hadith Science: A Primer on Understanding & Studying Hadith* (Chicago: Qur'ān Literacy Press, 2021), 141.
42 Al-Ghazzālī, *al-Mustasfā*, 2/145.

> views regarding the required number to reach *tawātur* is 'horrible' (*fāḥish*).[43]

According to al-Ghazzālī, there seems to be no requirement of complete consensus for the validity of mass transmission. Other scholars who spoke about the conditions of *mutawātir* reports similarly describe the main condition being that a report is transmitted by a large enough number of people, such that it is normally impossible for them to have conspired to fabricate.[44] For example, al-Shāshī says in his Usul: 'The *mutawātir* [report] is one transmitted by a group from another group, such that it is unimaginable for them to conspire to lie. This includes the transmission of the Qur'ān, the number of units [of prayers], and the quantities of zakat.'[45]

Hanbali jurist, al-Mardāwi (d. 885/1480), defines *tawātur* as being 'the report of a group (*jama'ah*) which accords certain knowledge.'[46] He then goes on to list several matters of creed and law that ibn Hajar al-'Asqalānī (d. 852/1448) claimed to have been reported through mass transmission, including seeing God in the afterlife, wiping on the socks, and raising the hands in prayer.[47] The reader will note that some of these examples are ones which a minority of scholars have rejected. Abū Hurayra famously used to reject wiping over the socks, because he himself did not see the Prophet wiping over them during ablution, nor

---

43 Abd al-Malik al-Juwainī, *al-Burhan fi Usul al-Fiqh* (Beirut: Dar al-Kutub al-Ilmiyah, 1997), 1/569.
44 Ibid, 1/218.
45 Aḥmad al-Shāshī, *Usul al-Shashi* (Beirut: Dar al-Kitab al-Arabī, 1982), 272.
46 Sulaimān al-Mardāwī, *al-Tahbīr Sharh al-Tahrīr fī Usul al-Fiqh* (Riyadh: Maktabat al-Rushd, 2000), 1750.
47 Ibid, 1761.

did he hear him explicitly permitting it.[48] Yet, ibn Hajar, as well as scholars before him, did not hesitate in counting these reports as *mutawātir*, implying that consensus is not a condition for the validity of *tawātur*.

If the transmission of the last two chapters as being from the Qur'ān is tested in this way, it seems to fit the condition of *mutawātir*. An overwhelmingly large number of people transmitted this in every generation since the first with absolute certainty. This is not only suggested by the chains of transmission for the Qur'ānic recitations, but also by what is well known in the lives of ordinary Muslims. There therefore does not seem to be any contradiction for them between these chapters being mass transmitted and the dissent of 'Abdullāh ibn Mas'ūd. The negation of the condition of consensus is alluded to by al-Suyūṭī who says: 'It is not a condition of *tawātur* for every individual to memorise it all. It is enough for it (the whole Qur'ān) to be preserved, even collectively.'[49]

We are still left with the problem of those who argued that rejecting anything *mutawātir* negates one's faith and takes them out of the fold of Islam. As well as al-Rāzī, whose comment was quoted earlier, several other scholars also made this claim. 'Alā al-Dīn ibn al-'Aṭṭār, for example, says: 'It is obligatory to believe in the reality of the punishment and bliss of the grave. This is something the ummah has transmitted through *tawātur*. So whoever rejects the punishment or bliss of the grave is a disbeliever.' The justification for disbelief does not appear to have anything to do with the sanctity of the concept of mass transmission. Rather, rejection of a *mutawātir* report implies knowingly rejecting divine revelation, whether via the Qur'ān or Prophetic teachings.

---

48 Muslim ibn al-Ḥajjāj, *Kitab al-Tamyiz* (KSA: Al-Kawthar Publishers, 1990), 209.

49 Abd al-Raḥmān al-Suyuti, *Al-Itqan fi Ulum al-Qur'ān* (Cairo: al-Hay'ah al-Misriyyah al-Amma lil Kitab, 1974), 1/245.

This is clarified by Qādi 'Iyādh in al-Shifā where he requires that one is aware of something being from the Qur'ān before judgment about his disbelief can be made.[50] Similarly, ibn Taymiyyah says, 'Whoever rejects that which has been proven through *tawātur* and *ijmā'* (consensus) is a disbeliever, after the proof has been established against him.'[51] This would imply that rejection of something that the Muslims agree to and is reported through *tawātur* only necessitates disbelief if the denier is aware that a verse is from the Qur'ān, a report is correctly attributed to the Prophet, or a certain teaching is an Islamic one.

If these conditions on *mutawātir* and its implications are applied to our current discussion, there would be questions about the validity of faith if one rejected the last two chapters of the Qur'ān today. They were certainly transmitted through *tawātur* and everybody is aware or can easily find out that they are part of the Qur'ān. Hence, scholars today would probably agree that rejecting any chapter, in fact, even a single verse, of the Qur'ān, constitutes disbelief. However, it seems unreasonable to treat the early generation the same way as we would a generation in which the copies of the Qur'ān are widespread and known to all. The first generation was one in which people still largely relied on their own efforts to learn the Qur'ān directly from the Prophet. Most Companions did not memorise the whole Qur'ān, and many were unaware of some Prophetic teachings. 'Aisha says: 'It was revealed that ten breastfeeds prohibit [marital relations]. This was then abrogated by five breastfeeds. The Prophet passed away while these were still being recited as the Qur'ān.'[52] This report suggests that the Prophet died while some Companions were still unaware that these verses had been abrogated. There

50 Qadi Iyad al-Yaḥsubī, *al-Shifa* (Beirut: Dar al-Fikr, 1988), 2/615.

51 Aḥmad ibn Taymiyyah, *Majmu al-Fatawa* (Medina: King Fahd Complex for the Printing of the Holy Qur'ān, 2004), 1/109.

52 Ibn al-Ḥajjāj, *Sahih Muslim*, 1452.

are countless other examples of individual uncertainty in the early generation of matters that are viewed today as certain knowledge. Not that this knowledge was ever missing, but simply because new knowledge takes time to become settled and known to all. Given this, the issue of ibn Mas'ūd can be easier to accept.

Conclusion

It certainly would have been ideal if the Qur'ān was recorded in one copy under the supervision of the Prophet himself. However, this was not to be. Instead, the Prophet's senior Companions took on the hefty task of compiling the Qur'ān. The concession of the seven *aḥruf* made this compilation more difficult than it would have been. Despite that, Muslims reached an eventual consensus on what the Qur'ān is. All the Companions, including seemingly 'Abdullāh ibn Mas'ūd, supported the compilation of Abū Bakr. This compilation clearly would have contained the last two chapters of the Qur'ān. Given the soundness of reports about his dissent on these two chapters, it seems that his view was simply dismissed as an error. There was no need to view this as problematic for the sound transmission of the Qur'ān, nor the purity of the faith of the Companion involved. The Ḥadīth scholars of the second and third century, including Sufyān ibn Uyaynah, al-Shāfi'ī, and ibn Qutaibah, dealt with this matter in this way. They did not attack ibn Mas'ūd nor question his faith. They continued to affirm his great status in Islam, while admitting that he simply erred in this case.

In fact, it could be argued that the great status of ibn Mas'ūd actually gives further confidence in the transmission of the Qur'ān; and these two chapters in particular. Had there been any doubt regarding this, at least some of the students of ibn Mas'ūd would have followed his view, as they so often do on legal matters. But we find that no one really accepted his view and that his own students opposed him and believed his stance to be a mere error and slip-up. Abū Ja'far al-Taḥāwī too narrates the view of ibn Mas'ūd through various chains of transmission, then simply suffices with some authentic narrations in which the Prophet clearly described the last two chapters as being 'verses', 'revealed to me', 'chapters', as well as reciting them in prayer.[53] He did not seem to feel that there was a need for falsifying what was reported from ibn Mas'ūd, nor did he seem too bothered by his dissent. Hence, it seems as though it is only once the concept of *mutawātir* narrations and its implications makes its way into the Islamic tradition that we find many scholars struggling to deal with the reports attributed to 'Abdullāh ibn Mas'ūd. The rejection of any Companion would have caused an issue, let alone someone of the standing of 'Abdullāh. However, the role of *mutawātir* reports and their implication, particularly in the era of the Companions, is itself terminology that was not always accepted, and is still not by some.[54]

Bibliography

Al-Bāqillānī, Abū Bakr. *al-Intisār lil Qur'ān.* Beirut: Dar Ibn Ḥazm, 2001.

Al-Bukhārī, Muḥammad. *Sahih al-Bukhāri.* Beirut: Al-Risalah Publishers, 2019.

Al-Dabūsī, Ubaidullah. *Taqwim al-Adillah.* Beirut: Dar al-Kutub al-Ilmiyah, 2001.

Al-Dānī, 'Uthmān. *Jami' al-Bayan fi al-Qira'at al-Sab'.* UAE: University of Sharjah, 2007.

---

53 Abū Ja'far al-Taḥāwī, *Sharh Mushkil al-Athar* (Beirut: Al-Risalah Publishers, 1994), 118 - 128.

54 Mansur al-Sam'ānī, *Al-Intisar li Ashab al-Hadith* (KSA: Adwa al-Manar, 1996), 34.

Al-Farrā, Abū Ya'la. *al-Uddah fi Usul al-Fiqh*. Riyadh: Imam Mohammad Ibn Saud Islamic University, 1990.

Al-Ghazzālī, Abū Hamid. *al-Mustasfa min Ilm al-Usul*. Beirut: Dar al-Kutub al-Ilmiyah, 1993.

Al-Jassās, Aḥmad. *al-Fusul fi al-Usul*, Kuwait: Ministry of Awqaf and Islamic Affairs, 1994.

Al-Juwainī, Abd al-Mālik. *al-Burhan fi Usul al-Fiqh*, Beirut: Dar al-Kutub al-Ilmiyah, 1997.

Al-Mardāwī, Sulaimān. *al-Tahbir Sharh al-Tahrir fi Usul al-Fiqh*. Riyadh: Maktabat al-Rushd, 2000.

Al-Māzirī, Muḥammad. *Idah al-Mahsul min Burhan al-Usul*. Tunisia: Dar al-Gharb al-Islami, 2001.

Al-Mosili, Abū Ya'la. *Musnad Abū Ya'lā*. Cairo: Dar al-Ḥadīth, 2013.

Al-Nasā'ī, Aḥmad. *Sunan al-Nasā'ī*. Beirut: Dar Ibn Kathir, 2016.

Al-Rāzī, Muḥammad. *al-Tafsir al-Kabīr*. Beirut: Dar Ihya al-Turath al-Arabī, 2000.

Al-Sam'ānī, Mansur. *Al-Intisar li Ashab al-Ḥadīth*. KSA: Adwa al-Manar, 1996.

Al-San'ānī, Abd al-Razzaq. *Muṣannaf Abd al-Razzaq*. Riyadh: Dar al-Taseel, 2013.

Al-Shāfi'ī, Muḥammad. *al-Umm*. Beirut: Dar al-Fikr, 1990.

Al-Shāshī, Aḥmad. *Usul al-Shashi*. Beirut: Dar al-Kitab al-Arabī, 1982.

Al-Sijistānī, Abū Dāwūd. *Sunan Abū Dāwūd*. Beirut: Al-Risalah Publishers, 2009.

Al-Suyutī, Abd al-Raḥmān. *Al-Itqan fi Ulum al-Qur'ān*. Cairo: al-Hay'ah al-Misriyyah al-Amma lil Kitab, 1974.

Al-Tabarānī, Sulaiman. *al-Mu'jam al-Kabīr*. Cairo: Maktabat Ibn Taymiyyah, 1994.

Al-Tahāwī, Abū Ja'far. *Sharh Mushkil al-Athar*. Beirut: Al-Risalah Publishers, 1994.

Al-Tirmidhī, Muḥammad. *Jami al-Tirmidhī*. Beirut: Al-Risalah Publishers, 2017.

Al-Yahsubī, Iyad. *al-Shifa*. Beirut: Dar al-Fikr, 1988.

Al-Yahsubī, Iyad. *Ikmal al-Mu'lim bi-Fawa'id Muslim*. Egypt: Dar al-Wafa, 1998.

Ibn Abī Shaybah, 'Abdullāh. *Muṣannaf Ibn Abī Shaybah*. Riyadh: Dar Kunuz Ishbiliya, 2015.

Ibn Abī Dāwūd, 'Abdullāh. *Kitab al-Maṣāḥif*. Cairo: Al-Faruq al-Ḥadīth ah, 2002.

Ibn al-Ḥajjāj, Muslim. *Sahih Muslim*. Beirut: Al-Risalah Publishers, 2020.

Ibn al-Ḥajjāj, Muslim. *Kitab al-Tamyiz*. KSA: Al-Kawthar Publishers, 1990.

Ibn Anas, Mālik. *Al-Muwatta*. Beirut: Al-Risalah Publishers, 2019.

Ibn Hanbal, Aḥmad. *Musnad Aḥmad*. Beirut: Al-Risalah Publishers, 2001.

Ibn Ḥazm, Ali. *al-Muhalla bil Athar*. Beirut: Dar al-Fikr, 2002.

Ibn Jarīr, Muḥammad. *Tafsir al-Tabari (Jami' al-Bayan)*. Cairo: Dar Hajar, 2001.

Ibn Kathīr, Ismā'īl. *Tafsir Ibn Kathir*. Riyadh: Dar Taibah for Publishing and Distribution, 1999.

Ibn Khuzaimah, Muḥammad. *Sahih Ibn Khuzaimah*. Riyadh: Maktabat al-Azami, 2009.

Ibn Mājah, Muḥammad. *Sunan Ibn Mājah*. Beirut: Al-Risalah Publishers, 2009.

Ibn Mujāhid, Aḥmad. *al-Sab'ah fi al-Qira'at*. Egypt: Dar al-Ma'arif, 1980.

Ibn Qutaybah, 'Abdullāh. *Ta'wil Mukhtalif al-Ḥadīth*. Damascus: Al-Maktab al-Islami, 1999.

Ibn Sallām, Abū Ubaid. *Fadhail al-Qur'ān*. Damascus: Dar Ibn Kathir, 1995.

Ibn Taymiyyah, Aḥmad. *Majmu al-Fatawa*. Medina: King Fahd Complex for the Printing of the Holy Qur'ān, 2004.

Nadwi, Akram. Fou*ndation to Ḥadīth Science: A Primer on Understanding & Studying Ḥadīth*. Chicago: Qur'ān Literacy Press, 2021.

Nasser, Shady Hekmat. *The Second Canonization of the Qur'ān (324/936): Ibn Mujāhid and the Founding of the Seven Readings*. Leiden-Boston: Brill, 2020.

Sadeghi, Behnam. *The Codex of a Companion of the Prophet and the Qur'ān of the Prophet*. Arbīca vol. 57 (2010): 343-436.

CHAPTER EIGHT

An Alternative Opinion on the Reality of the 'Seven Aḥruf' and Its Relationship with the *Qirā'āt*

Yasir Qadhi

The topic of *aḥruf* and *qirā'āt*, and the relationship between these two concepts, is one that is integral to *'ulūm al-Qur'ān* (sciences of the Qur'ān), with both classical and modern scholarship postulating various opinions on this issue. Despite such scholarship, there still remains confusion and ambiguity with regard to specific aspects of these concepts and certain unanswered questions. Recently, several publications have sought to champion an alternative opinion which they claim is found in the earliest sources. This opinion, while perhaps solving many, if not all, of the perplexing questions on this issue, also raises its own challenges.[1]

1 The author would like to thank Hythem Sidky, Sohaib Saeed, Tulaib Zafir, Umer Khan, Suleiman Hani, Sharif Randhawa, and Andrew Booso for their feedback on this article. All views and errors are the responsibility of the author alone.

The most exhaustive and comprehensive analysis of this can be found in, al-Rājḥī, Ṣaliḥ b. Sulaymān. *Al-Masā'il al-Kubrā allatī Khālafa fīhā Qurrā' al-Muta'akhirūn Ijmā' al-Mutaqaddimīn min al-Qurrā'.* (Riyadh: Dar al-Ṣumay'ī, 2021); also see: al-Ḥārithī, Salwā, "Al-Qirā'āt 'alā Sab'at Aḥruf Bayn al-Ijtihād Wa-l-Tawqif," in *Majallat Kulliyat al-Dirāsāt al-Islāmiyya wa-l-'Arabiyya* (vol. 35, no. 5), pp. 99-158; al-Nūrī, 'Alī, "Al-Ṣaḥāba wa-l-Qirā'āh Bi-l-Ma'nā," in *Majallah Kuliyya al-Da'wa al-Islāmiyya* (vol. 11), pp. 9-23. Other works have also expressed similar views, such as: Shahīn, 'Abd al-Ṣabūr, *Tarīkh al-Qur'ān* (Cairo: Maṭba'ah al-Sa'ādah, 1995) and Jabal,

The purpose of this article is to present this opinion from the perspective of those who champion it, elaborate upon why it is seen by those that hold this position to be a stronger fit for the data available, and evaluate and respond to the possible objections that are made against this position.

A detailed discussion regarding the nature of the *aḥruf*, the controversy of the preservation of the *aḥruf* within the Uthmānic codices, and the hypotheses regarding the relationship between the *qirā'āt* and the *aḥruf* is obviously beyond the scope of this paper; however a brief summary might be useful. Ḥadīth literature is replete with references to the fact that the Qur'ān has been revealed in 'seven *aḥruf*', but the nature and reality of what these *aḥruf* are have been a source of controversy, and over forty opinions have been posited. Over time, the dominant opinions dwindled to three, namely that the *aḥruf* represent: specific variations of language and syntax, up to seven; or synonymous word changes; or specific tribal dialects that were prevalent amongst the Arabs of that time. Another major point of contention then occurred with respect to the 'Uthmānic project of preservation and compilation: did his compilation preserve all seven of these *aḥruf*, or an unspecified several based on an alleged 'final recitation' that the Prophet recited in front of the archangel Jibrīl, or one plus as many as the script devoid of vowels allowed, or precisely one? Based on a scholar's response to these first two controversies, the third and final question was then to posit a relationship between these original *aḥruf* and the actual documented recitations of the Qur'ān (meaning the *qirā'āt*), of

---

Muḥammad, *al-Qaḍiyya al-Qur'āniyya al-Kubrā: Ḥadīth Nuzūl al-Qur'ān 'alā Sab'ah Aḥruf* (Cairo: Maktabah al-Adāb, 2014); al-Ḥamad, Ghānim Qaddūrī, *Liqā Ma'a Shabakat Al-tafsīr* (online document at www.tafsir.net, last accessed Jul 2023). In English, one may refer to: Dutton, Yasin, "Orality, literacy and the 'seven aḥruf hadith', *Journal of Islamic Studies*, 23/1 (2012): 1-49; and Moqbel, Tarek, "The Emergence of the Qirā'āt : The Divine Permission Hypothesis" in *Journal of Islamic Studies*, 33(3), May 2022.

which seven (and then ten) were deemed to be *mutawātir* and equally authentic.[2]

For the purposes of this paper, it will be assumed that the current dominant view is that the *aḥruf* are primarily differences between the dialects of the Arabs, that the Caliph 'Uthmān intentionally discarded most of the *aḥruf* but intentionally preserved some that the script allowed, that these preserved variations eventually formed the basis of the *qirā'āt*, and that all of the variations within the *aḥruf* (and hence the *qirā'āt*) were recited by the Prophet. This view can be called the 'Dictation Model': The Prophet recited the Qur'ān in many different ways and from the composite of his recitations and through the 'Uthmānic codex, over time, the ten authentic *qirā'āt* developed. So, the phrase: '*unzil al-Qur'ān 'alā sab'at aḥruf*', according to this model, would be understood as: "The Qur'ān has been recited by the Prophet in different ways and wordings, up to seven."

Questions Regarding the Dictation Model

There are several key areas of concern that can be raised regarding the Dictation Model. These issues have, of course, all been addressed by those who follow this model. The question is not whether answers to these concerns exist, but rather whether

2 For an overview of the commonly held opinions, see: al-Zurqānī, Muḥammad 'Abd al-Adhīm, *Manāhil al-'Irfān fī 'Ulūm al-Qur'ān* (Makkah: Dār al-Bāz, 1996), vol. 1, pp.140-194; al-Juday', Abdullah ibn Yūsuf, *al-Muqaddimāt al-Asāsiyyah fī 'Ulūm al-Qur'ān*, (Beirut: Mu'sāsdah al-Rayāt, 2001) pp. 76-84; al-Qari, 'Abd al-'Azīz, *Ḥadith al-Aḥruf al-Sab'a* (Beirut: Mu'asah al-Risālah, 2002); Qadhi, Yasir, *An Introduction to the Sciences of the Qur'ān* (Birmingham: Al-Hidaayah Publishing, 1999), pp. 172-184. For a slightly modified view that may be classified as being between the models discussed in this paper, see: Khatib, A. and Khan, N.: "The Origins of the Variant Readings of the Qur'ān", published online at: https://yaqeeninstitute.org/read/paper/the-origins-of-the-variant-readings-of-the-Qur'ān (last accessed June 2023).

those answers are plausible, satisfactory, and reasonably fit the facts, or if they in fact raise even more questions and require unjustifiable presumptions. The purpose of raising these concerns is to demonstrate that, in the eyes of those who do not agree with the Dictation Model, there is a clear need to see if another opinion exists that can respond to these concerns in a more reasonable and holistic manner. While many questions can be asked, for the purposes of this article, fifteen questions will be raised, numbered Q1-Q15.

We begin with the genre of ḥadīth that mention the concept of 'seven *aḥruf*'. Several traditions explicitly mention that the very *raison d'être* (*ʿillah*) of the *aḥruf* is to make it easy for the Ummah to recite the Qur'ān, for '*...there are amongst them the old, and young boys and girls, and those who have never read.*'[3] The question arises as to (Q1) how exactly the Dictation Model facilitates this *ʿillah* for such categories of people: what difference do the variations make in the ease of reciting and memorizing? Also, (Q2) within these very traditions there are explicit examples that cannot be taken at face value and must be somehow interpreted, such as the Prophet's command: '*... all of the [aḥruf] are pure and complete, as if you are saying '[Allah is] Hearing and Seeing' or '[Allah is] Majestic and Powerful,' as long as you do not finish a verse of mercy with [Divine Attributes of] punishment or a verse of punishment with [Divine Attributes of] mercy.*'[4] This tradition, and others, seem to suggest a leeway that the Dictation Model does not allow for.

Within the early tafsīr and ḥadīth literature, we have hundreds of examples of *aḥruf* indicating word changes attributed to the Companions. There is the *ḥarf* of Ubayy ibn Kaʿb, and the *ḥarf* of ibn Masʿūd, and so forth. (Q3) If indeed the origins of these variant words is the Prophet, why attribute the entire *ḥarf* to only one Companion? And why wouldn't other Companions

3 Al-Tirmidhī, *Sunan*, ḥadīth no. 2944.

4 Abū Dawūd, *Sunan*, ḥadīth no. 1477.

at times alternate between these wordings to try to preserve the complete prophetic spectrum of recitation? After all, these same Companions would narrate multiple ḥadīth; surely *a fortiori* they should also have narrated multiple *aḥruf* emanating from the Prophet? To add to this, in the most famous tradition of the *aḥruf*, in which 'Umar bin al-Khaṭṭāb heard Hishām bin Ḥakīm recite Surah al-Furqān with different wordings, (Q4) why would two people from the exact same tribe be taught different 'dialects' if indeed the *aḥruf* were primarily about dialects? And why would Hishām – at this point a new convert – be given the privilege of a private lesson, unbeknownst to even 'Umar, on another unique *ḥarf*, while other Companions far senior to him were not given such a privilege? From this same incident, and 'Umar's surprise at learning of the existence of the *aḥruf*, (Q5) how does one explain that many senior Companions were not aware of the existence of the *aḥruf* during the period of Revelation? After all, if as the Dictation Model suggests, the Prophet was constantly reciting different wordings, why be puzzled with a different wording, especially at such a late stage of the *sīrah*? Even afterwards, 'Uthman in his caliphate had to ask people to publicly confirm that the Qur'ān was revealed in seven *aḥruf*. The ḥadīth literature also informs us that (Q6) this concession of the seven *aḥruf* began in the late Madinan period, so what does this imply of the earlier revelations before this concession was given? Were the chapters and verses that had been revealed earlier in only one *ḥarf* revealed all over again, such that each verse was dictated again? Regardless of the time of concession, (Q7) one of the perplexing realities of this field is the lack of evidence that the Prophet himself recited the same verse in different ways.[5]

5 There are a handful of reports, of dubious chains, that posit alternative readings back to the Prophet himself. Given that there are thousands of variations between the *qirā'āt*, this small quantity, even if some were to be claimed authentic, still raises the question of origin of the bulk of differences.

As every specialist is aware, to master even the ten *qirā'āt* requires an immense amount of time; the variations between the *aḥruf* were far more pronounced than the variations between the ten *qirā'āt*. Yet there does not seem to exist ḥadīth narrations in which the Prophet dedicated such time and effort to meticulously teach the differences in Qur'ānic recitation to the Companions and dictate variant readings.

Moving on from the time of revelation to the time of compilation, (Q8) if all seven *aḥruf* were divinely revealed and recited, why would 'Uthmān tell the committee, which was convened to *solve* the issue of the multiple *aḥruf* and the tensions that were being caused, to write '...in the dialect of the Qur'āysh, for *it was revealed in that dialect*?' Whence the specificity of only Qur'āysh if multiple wordings were revealed? And a classic controversy that remains perplexing: (Q9) by what justification did the Companions agree to discard the bulk of the remaining *aḥruf* (or according to another mainstream opinion, six of them), knowing their eagerness to preserve all matters prophetic? On what basis did they choose to discard some and leave others? Even if they felt that the other *aḥruf* were a concession and hence dispensable (as those who subscribe to the Dictation Model explain), it would make sense for them to have explicitly announced this concession and raised the bar of knowledge to preserve all of them, rather than leave it to later scholars to attempt to explain such a permanent and irreversible stance in which Divine Revelation is apparently discarded. And if they did discard the bulk of the *aḥruf* to unify the Ummah, (Q10) why are there still variations in the recitations post-'Uthmānic recension? The purpose of the 'Uthmānic project, by explicit testimony of the Caliph and the Companions, was to unify the entire Ummah on one recitation. The existence of the variations and the *qirā'āt* seems to conflict with that purpose. More perplexing still (Q11) the extremely minute differences between the 'Uthmānic codices[6] do not seem to have a reasonable explanation. If these differences were intentional, it would perhaps have been judicious for the committee to announce these differences so as not to cause any confusion. Instead, early literature seems to indicate that they were only later noticed, and eventually adopted into the ten *qirāʾāt*, depending on the regionality of the codex and its proximity to the geographic location of the reciter. Furthermore, why only preserve the most minute of variations (such as an added *wāw* or a missing *alif*), while leaving the far more substantive variations that were recorded to have been recited prior to the ʿUthmānic compilation? And if these differences were unintentional, this would seem to clash with the notion of Divine protection as understood by the proponents of the Dictation Model.

Moving on to the *qirāʾāt* phenomenon, (Q12) all scholars agree that there were numerous *qirāʾāt* in the second and third Islamic centuries, before the codification project of ibn Mujāhid. The 'seven' that ibn Mujāhid chose, were based on his personal choice from many reciters, and he was in fact criticised for a few of those choices, and for limiting the reciters to 'seven' which added to the confusion as it linked the *qirāʾāt* to the *aḥruf* in the minds of the masses. The three that ibn al-Jazarī added four centuries later were also somewhat arbitrary. Earlier chroniclers mention twenty, or twenty-five, or even forty *qirāʾāt*, and we

6 There are more than forty word-structure differences between the four known ʿUthmānic codices. All of these are orthographic variations of the type that, in any other scenario, would obviously be attributed as originating from the scribes who copied these manuscripts. However, this explanation is problematic, for obvious reasons, when discussing the original Qur'ānic codices. For a discussion of these differences, see: Cook, Michael, "The Stemma of the Regional Codices of the Koran," *Graeco-Arabica*, 9-10 (2004); Sidky, Hythem, "On the Regionality of the Qur'ānic Codices," *JIQSA* 5 (2020): 133-210; Vahidnia, Ala, "Whence Come Qur'ān Manuscripts? Determining the Regional Provenance of Early Qur'ānic Codices," *Der Islam* 98 (2): 359-393.

still have references to these abandoned recitations in works of language and exegesis. Ibn al-Jazarī himself remarks that anyone who knows this field has certain knowledge that the quantity of recorded recitations is but a drop in the ocean of those recitations that were prevalent in the earlier eras.[7] How does one explain this phenomenon if all *qirāʾāt* were equally divine and prophetic in origin, knowing that they no longer exist? Does this imply that some recitation is lost? Furthermore, (Q13) how does one explain the obvious and well-documented interplay between the scholars of *qirāʾāt* and Arabic grammarians in the earliest centuries in which they explained why they chose or rejected a particular recitation? How could so many giants in the field (such as al-Ṭabarī as one prominent example) consistently reject recitations that are now deemed *mutawātir* – surely, they cannot be accused of not knowing them? Or Aḥmad ibn Ḥanbal's problematising the recitation of Ḥamza – one of the 'seven' recitations eventually canonised by ibn Mujāhid – as another example?[8] At times, the back and forth between these scholars appears akin to the interplay between the various legal schools: each one claiming their opinion is correct and the other is not, and justifying grammatically or contextually why that is the case. Yet the Dictation Model tells us that all the *qirāʾāt* emanate from the Prophet, and so they are all equally correct. It is safe to say that almost all early scholars seemed to view the *qirāʾāt* with a very different lens than later ones: why is it that, according to the Dictation Model, so many scholars in early Islam seem to have made some mistakes

---

7 See: Ibn al-Jazarī, *Al-Nashr Fī Al-Qirāʾāt Al-ʿAshr*, vol. 1, p. 23.

8 This is a well-documented position from ibn Ḥanbal. Ibn Abī Yaʿlā reports that the Imam was asked about the recitation of Ḥamza, to which he remarked, "I despise it immensely (*akrahuhū ashadd al-karāhiyya*)…for it is an innovated recitation that no one before him recited. It is just 'ayh' and 'āh' [a reference to his unique *imālahs* and *mudūd*]." See: Ibn Abī Yaʿlā, *Ṭabaqāt*, vol. 1, p. 391.

in their adoption and rejection of recitations, but later scholars are all correct?

Another issue is that (Q14) early ḥadīth literature seems to indicate the exact *opposite*, as several scholars of the generation of codification (*zaman al-tadwīn*) wrote chapters or treatises in which they attempted to verify the precise recitation of the Prophet, under the genre of '*qirā'āt al-Nabī*'.[9] In fact, one of the ten famous reciters even authored one such work.[10] If all *qirā'āt* were equally from the Prophet, surely this entire genre seems superfluous? Lastly, (Q15) the obvious reality that the issue of *aḥruf* and *qirā'āt*, despite being so central and key to the religion of Islam and mentioned in *mutawātir* ḥadīths, remains perplexing to so many scholars. Surely a concept so integral to the Qur'ān and so central to its preservation and recitation should have a simple and obvious answer: an answer that is found in the earliest of sources, and not something 'discovered' after fourteen centuries of ambiguity.

These are merely some of the more prominent questions that come to mind, yet there are many more.[11] Of course, if one wishes to, one can find answers to all of these problems in earlier

9 See, as an example, the chapter "Kitāb al-Ḥurūf wa-l-Qirā'āt" in the *Sunan* of Abī Dawūd; and the chapter "Min Kitāb Qirā'āt al-Nabī" in the *Mustadrak* of al-Ḥākim.

10 See, al-Dūrī, Ḥafs ibn 'Umar, *Juz Fīhī Qirā'āt Al-Nabī*, ed. Ḥikmat Bashīr Yasīn (Madinah: Maktabah al-Dār, 1988).

11 Three more issues may briefly be referenced: 1) the numerous instances of what has been later termed *qirā'āt tafsīrīyyah* reported from the Companions; 2) the acceptance and proliferation of the *qirā'āt shādhah* pre-canonization, for these 'anomalous' recitations were some of the most popular ones recited by senior figures (such as al-Ḥasan al-Baṣrī or al-'A'mash) in their respective regions for decades, and recited in public, and in the prayers, centuries before later scholars opined that they should be considered anomalous and rejected during *ṣalāt*; 3) the genre of reports in which senior Companions allege regarding the canonized 'Uthmānic collection that '*na'is al-kātib*' or '*sahā al-kātib*' or '*fīhī laḥn*'; and more issues like these as well.

works. However, the question once again, is not whether answers exist, but how feasible those answers are, and how much unreasonable assumption (or '*takalluf*') needs to be employed to justify the Dictation Model paradigm. It is because these perplexing questions do not have easy answers that one wonders if there is an alternative explanation to the concepts at hand – an explanation which yields water-tight and obvious responses to all these questions without the need for unlikely assumptions. That is what proponents of the alternative view claim.

An Alternative: The Divine Permission Model

The alternative model claims that the 'seven *aḥruf*' is a Divine concession that allowed the Companions to recite the Qur'ān in accordance with their dialects and to the best of their memory as long as the meanings were correctly conveyed. In this model, the Prophet himself recited the Qur'ān in one manner (*ḥarf*), but permission was given to the Companions to recite it in 'several wordings' (which is the most obvious manner to translate the phrase '*sabʿa aḥruf*') as long as the meaning was conveyed. Some later scholars[12] coined the term '*qirāʾah bi-l-maʿnā*' (or: 'reciting according to the meaning') to explain this view; it has also been called the 'Divine Permission' model. According to this opinion, it was this original *ḥarf* that was preserved by ʿUthmān (i.e., only one *ḥarf* was preserved); since the other *aḥruf* were not recited, there was no 'discarding' of the others *per se*. Rather, the concession of *qirāʾah bi-l-maʿnā* was revoked because there was no need

12 The term is used in the fourth century by al-Bāqillānī (see his *al-Intiṣār*, vol. 2, p. 478) and ibn Jinnī (see his *Kitaāb al-Muḥtasab*, vol. 1, p. 27), both of whom mention the view but then disagree with it. A point to make here is that both authors are aware of such a view even if they disagree with it – as we shall see, some scholars attempt to deny that such a view ever existed.

for it. So, the phrase, *'unzil al-Qur'ān 'alā sab'at aḥruf*, according to this model, would be understood as: "The permission for the Qur'ān to be recited in several wordings has been revealed."[13]

There are numerous reports that can be used to demonstrate this claim. One of the earliest attempts to interpret the reality of the *aḥruf* seems to be the interpretation offered by the Successor Muḥammad bin Sirīn (d. 110 AH/729 CE) when he commented on the alternative recitation of ibn Mas'ūd who would recite '... it was not but a single cry (*in kānat illā* ***zayqah*** *wāḥida*),' in lieu of the 'Uthmānic wording: '...it was not but a single shout (*in kānat illā* ***ṣayḥah*** *wāḥida*). [36:29]. Ibn Sirīn explained, "It's like saying: *halumma*, *ta'āl*, and *aqbil* [synonyms for 'come']."[14] Ibn Sirīn seems to be insinuating that the *aḥruf* are synonymous words employed by the reciters.

---

13 This model would have to follow the opinion of al-Khaṭṭābī, al-Qāḍī 'Iyāḍ, and others, who understood 'seven' in the *ḥadīth* as 'several' and not the number seven exactly. While the default is that a number does represent a literal quantity, and the famous *ḥadīth* of Ubayy in the *Ṣaḥīḥ* of Muslim might seems to indicate a literal 'seven', proponents of the claim that 'seven' here means 'several' counter with two facts. Firstly, as a default no word or phrase in the Qur'ān has been recited in precisely seven ways, hence this fact alone would force us to view the word 'seven' as indicating 'several' rather than a literal 'seven'. In other words, an interpretation of a wording of one *ḥadīth* that might indicate an exact number 'seven' must be weighed against the observed and documented reality that 'seven' recitations do not actually exist for the entirety of the Qur'ān. Therefore, in light of the fact that there are not precisely seven variations narrated for any verse in the Qur'ān, we should take this concrete fact into account when attempting to understand the Arabic word *sab'a* as not actually indicating a literal 'seven'. Secondly, as is documented and mentioned by several classical linguists, 'seven' and 'seventy' and 'seven-hundred' are numbers commonly used by the Arabs to indicate a generic number within that region, similar to an English speaker saying 'ten' or 'a hundred' or 'a thousand'. See: al-Ḥamad, Ghānim Qaddūrī, *Liqā Ma'a Shabakat Al-Tafsīr* (online document at www.tafsir.net, last accessed Jul 2023), p. 31.

14 al-Qāsim ibn Sallām, *Faḍā'il al-Qur'ān*, vol. 2, p. 176.

Several reports from the earliest generations seem to corroborate this.[15] In one report, ibn Masʿūd was teaching someone to recite, "*The tree of Zaqqūm; is the food of the sinner* (*al-athīm*) [44:43-4]," but the man could not say it, and instead always

15 For the purposes of this article, a detailed *takhrīj* of each narration was not done, and is definitely a warranted and necessary next step. However, a few key points should be made here, as one of the objections made against the evidences in support of this model is to find fault with the *isnads* of some of these reports. Firstly, the total sum of arguments being made in support of this model brings diverse evidence from multiple genres, and not just specific isnads. Even if some *isnads* of some reports are deemed weak, the cumulative evidence substantiates that this model was held by some authorities in the past. Hence, the model itself is independent of whether a particular incident is narrated with a correct chain or not. Secondly, the bulk of our historical records in all genres of Islamic sciences are narrated with chains that have missing links in them. Such is the reality of all early works of exegesis, history, and *akhbār*. The point is not therefore in finding an *isnad* that would be deemed authentic by the scholars of ḥadīth, but rather to demonstrate that early authors were quoting such materials and deriving evidence or opinions from them. Factually speaking, if the standards of *ḥadīth* scholars were to be applied to the entirety of *tafsīr*, *sīrah* and history corpus, we would have very little left. There is, therefore, the issue of methodological consistency in wanting to apply the stricter standards of *ḥadīths* to only those narrations that one wishes to problematize while completely ignoring verdicts on all other narrations that one agrees with. Thirdly, it should also be emphasised, that an authentic *isnad* does not necessarily yield certainty that the quotation was actually uttered, and a weak *isnad* does not necessarily denote that it was not said by the one it is attributed to. The *isnad* is a tool, and its verification process, one aspect of many, in looking at reports and opinions of the past. Lastly, the awkward inconsistency must also be pointed out that when an *isnad* is actually deemed authentic, those who do not subscribe to this alternative view still find ways to re-interpret the obvious implications of this genre of reports (one such example will be given later in this article). Therefore, it appears that the issue is not as much about verifying a particular *isnad* than it is about disproving an opinion already deemed invalid. Nonetheless, this author reiterates that in this introductory article only so much can be done, and there is without doubt the need to write a far more detailed monograph on this complex topic, which would preferably include detailed *takhrīj* and a verdict on each *isnad*.

repeated, '*...the food of the orphan (al-yatīm)*'. Ibn Masʿūd said: "Can you say: '*...the food of the evildoer* (*al-fājir*)'"? The man said that he could; to which ibn Masʿūd replied: "Then recite it like this! It is not a mistake in the Qur'ān to say, 'The Forgiving, the Merciful (*al-Ghafūr al-Raḥīm*)', instead of 'The All-mighty, the All-Wise (*al-ʿAzīz al-Ḥakīm*). Rather, a mistake would be to read a verse of punishment like a verse of mercy, or a verse of mercy like a verse of punishment, or to add something to the Book of Allah that is not in it."[16] It would appear that ibn Masʿūd suggested a synonym based on the man's incapability to recite properly.

In another incident, al-ʿAʿmash reported that Anas bin Mālik recited: "*...they would rush headlong into it*" [9:57], which in the ʿUthmānic recension reads, "*la-wallaw ilayhī wa hum* ***yajmaḥūn***," as "*...wa hum* ***yajmizūn***." When informed that the verse actually reads '*yajmaḥūn*', he is reported to have said, "*Yajmaḥūn*, and *yajmizūn*, and *yashtaddūn* are all the same."[17] In yet another report, Anas bin Mālik recited [73:6], which reads "*...wa* ***aqwam*** *qīlā*," as "*...wa* ***aṣwabu*** *qīlā*." When he was told that the correct recitation is *aqwam*, he replied, "*Aṣwab*, *aqwam*, and *ahya'* are all the same."[18] Furthermore, Abān narrates that Anas recited "*And We lifted your burdens from you*" [94:2], which in the ʿUthmānic recension reads, "*wa* ***waḍaʿnā*** *ʿanka wizrak*," as "*wa* ***ḥaṭaṭnā*** *ʿanka wizrak*." When asked about this, he said, "It's all the same: *waḍaʿnā* and *ḥalalnā* and *ḥaṭaṭnā*. For Jibrīl came to the Prophet and said,

---

16 al-Shaybānī, *Kitāb al-Athār*, p. 44. Also see: Ibn Wahb, *Tafsīr*, vol 3, p. 54; Abū ʿUbayd, *Faḍā'il al-Qur'ān*, p. 311. Note that many later scholars interpret away the apparent meaning of what ibn Masʿūd seems to indicate – the point in this section of the article is to see what a possible alternative opinion is, and not how the Dictation Model has reinterpreted the evidence for any alternative opinion. We shall return to how this incident is understood by those who subscribe to the Dictation Model in a later section: 'Five Objections and Their Reponses'.

17 Ibn Jinnī, *al-Muḥtasab*, vol. 1, p. 415.

18 Ibid., vol. 2, p. 336.

'Recite the Qur'ān in *sab'a aḥruf* as long as you don't mix mercy and punishment, or punishment and mercy.'"[19] Note here the explicit linkage between the ḥadīth of the *aḥruf* and the synonymous wordings, along with the *raison d'être* of ease. In yet another example, Ubayy ibn Ka'b would recite [2:20], which reads, "*kullamā 'aḍā' lahum* ***mashaw*** *fīhī*" as, "...*kullamā 'aḍā' lahum* ***sa'aw*** *fīhī* ..." or "...*kullamā 'aḍā' lahum* ***marrū*** *fīhī*." Ibn 'Abd al-Barr comments, "Ubayy would recite all of these words."[20] Once again we find synonymous wordings used. In fact, the sheer quantity of narrations which chronicle word choices of the Companions that are different to the 'Uthmānic recension are too numerous to chronicle in any one article, and a reading of works of *tafsīr* or ḥadīth yields hundreds if not thousands of such examples.

Understanding such differences as a concession granted to the Companions would also explain ibn Mas'ūd's advice to his students regarding such differences. He is reported to have said, "I have listened to the reciters, and I found them to be similar (*mutaqāribīn*). Therefore, all of you should recite as you have been taught to recite, and I warn you against over-zealousness and differing amongst yourself (*al-ṭanaṭṭu' wa-l-ikhtilāf*), for all of these [differences] are just like someone saying, 'Please come to me' (*halumma*) or 'Can you come here?' (*ta'āl*)."[21] Note that ibn Mas'ūd, along with other Companions, would only recite in his manner; had they all viewed these synonyms as being prophetic (*viz.*, the Dictation Model), it would have made sense for the Companions to alternate between the wordings and recite with the wordings of other Companions. Yet, when pressure was put on ibn Mas'ūd to conform to the *ḥarf* of the 'Uthmānic compilation, as is well-known and documented in many narrations, he refused, claiming that he himself had heard the bulk of the Qur'ān

19 Ibid., vol. 2, p. 367.
20 Ibn 'Abd al-Barr, *al-Tamhīd*, vol. 5, p. 602.
21 Ibn Shabbah, *Tarīkh al-Madīnah*, vol. 3, p. 1007.

directly from the Prophet, while Zayd (who was tasked with the ʿUthmānic compilation) was still a child with braids playing with other children.[22] Thus, while he preferred his own recitation for himself and his students, he actively encouraged others to stick to what they had been taught by other Companions, and warned them against fanaticism and differing because of such differences. Had these variations been Prophetic in origin, this was the time to mention it; instead, he gave an example that they would all understand in their own usage of speech.

We also learn that even before the canonisation project of ʿUthmān, there was some discomfort regarding these variations. It is reported that ʿUmar heard a man recite '... *ḥattā ḥīn*,' as 'ʿ... *atā ḥīn*.' Upon questioning, he found out that ibn Masʿūd had taught the man this pronunciation, so he immediately sent a message to him from Madinah to Kufah, 'As to what follows. Allah revealed the Qur'ān in the dialect of the Qur'āysh, and not the dialect of Hudhayl, so when you receive this letter from me, teach the people in the dialect of Qur'āysh and not the dialect

---

22 There are many versions of this report, including in the *Ṣaḥiḥayn*. In the *Mustadrak* of al-Ḥākim, we find him saying, "I memorized from the Prophet over seventy chapters, and Zayd was still a child with two braids playing with other children" [*al-Mustadrak*, vol. 2, p. 228]. In another report, he was asked to recite according to the *ḥarf* of Zayd, to which he said, "And why should I recite according to his *ḥarf*? For I took directly from the mouth of the Prophet seventy chapters while Zayd was but a boy! Should I leave what I took (directly) from the mouth of the Prophet?" See: Ibn Shabbah, *Tarikh al-Madinah*, vol. 3, p. 1006. These reports, and others, would seem to indicate that ibn Masʿūd is arguing that his words (literally, his '*ḥarf*') is the more authentic one. While he did not claim that Zayd's *ḥarf* was invalid, he preferred his wordings. There is no notion that all wordings emanate from the Prophet; rather, ibn Masʿūd is arguing to preserve his wordings because those wordings (according to his memory) are the original Prophetic ones. As for why ʿUthmān decided to adopt Zayd's *ḥarf*, the answer is obvious and will be mentioned later in this article: ʿUthmān conditioned an actual written copy of the Revelation dictated by the Prophet himself, while ibn Masʿūd was relying on his memory. A written document is always preferred over oral recollection.

of Hudhyal, and peace be unto you!"[23] Here, 'Umar appears to want to discourage variant readings and pronunciations because those variants stem from the Companions' own dialects, and the Qur'ān came down in the Qur'āyshī dialect. The fact that the Companions, or at least some of them, would substitute words based on meaning is something that even ibn Ḥajar acknowledges: "It is established from a number of Companions that they would recite with synonyms even if they did not hear it [from the Prophet]."[24]

A similar interpretation of the *aḥruf* was offered by the iconic scholar ibn Shihāb al-Zuhrī (d. 127 AH/745 CE), who remarked, "I have heard that the seven *aḥruf* are all regarding the same matter (*al-amr al-wāḥid*); they do not differ about what is prohibited and permissible."[25] A student of al-Zuhrī, Abū Uways, said, " We asked al-Zuhrī about rearranging words (*al-taqdīm wa-l-ta'khīr*) in ḥadīth. He said: 'This is allowed with regard to the Qur'ān, so why should it not be allowed with ḥadīṭh as well? So long as you maintain the meaning of the ḥadīth, and you do not legalise what is unlawful and prohibit what is lawful, there is no issue.'"[26] In this statement we have another explicit endorsement of *qirā'ah bi-l-ma'nā*.

This position also seems to be explicitly stated by several prominent scholars of the second and third centuries. Yaḥyā bin Sa'īd al-Qaṭṭān (d. 198 AH/814 CE) said, commenting on narrating ḥadīths,[27]

> I am afraid that seeking out precise wordings (*tatabbu' al-alfāẓ*) will become burdensome upon people. After all,

---

23 Ibn Shabbah, *Tarikh al-Madinah*, vol. 2, p. 711, and ibn 'Abd al-Barr, *al-Tamhīd*, vol. 5, p. 589.

24 Ibn Ḥajr, *Fatḥ al-Bārī* vol. 9, p. 27.

25 Muslim, *Ṣaḥīḥ*, vol. 6, p. 101.

26 al-Bayhaqī, *Al-Madkhal Ilā 'Ilm Al-Sunan*, no. 519.

27 Al-Khaṭīb al-Baghdādī, *Al-Kifāya Fī 'ilm Al-riwāya*, p. 210; al-Isfahani, *Ḥilyat al-Awliyā'*, vol 8, p. 380–381.

> the Qur'ān is more sacred (*ʾaʿẓam ḥurma*), yet the concession was made (*wussiʿa*) that it can be read in different manners (*ʿalā wujūh*), so long as the meaning is one.

Perhaps one of the most seminal reports in this regard is that of Imam al-Shāfiʿī (d. 204 AH /820 CE) in his book *al-Risālah.* While discussing the proper wording of the *tashahhud* prayer at the end of the ritual *ṣalāt*, he claims that the reason why different wordings are found in the narrations is because the Companions narrated the gist of the prayer in their own wordings. He then justifies the variations of *tashahhud* by explicitly endorsing the notion of *qirāʾāh bi-l-maʿnā*:[28]

> [As a manifestation of] Allah's mercy towards His creation, He revealed His Book in seven *aḥruf*, *knowing that one's memory can be mistaken*, so He permitted them to recite it *even if they used a different word* if the different word did not change the meaning. Therefore, *a fortiori* it should be allowed to recite anything besides God's Book with different wording so long as the meaning is not changed.

This quote is telling in that he seems to take it as a given that his reader will be aware of this fact, since he uses it to prove that the *tashahhud* exists in multiple wordings. It is also pertinent to note that he links a word-change to a memory lapse, claiming this is a part of the concession of the 'seven *aḥruf*'. Linking the *aḥruf* to a memory lapse would seem to definitively rule out any other interpretation of this quote besides *qirāʾāh bi-l-maʿnā*: permission has been granted to overlook the exact word and convey the meanings of the Qur'ān as long as synonymous words are used and the same meaning is conveyed.

---

28 Al-Shāfiʿī, *Al-Risālah*, pp. 274-5. Emphasis added.

Another polymath of that era was ibn Qutaybah (d. 276 AH/ 890 AH). Commenting on the variant recitations ascribed to the Companions, he writes:[29]

> If someone asks, "Is it permissible for us to read according to all these modes (*wujūh*)?" The response is as follows: It is permissible for us to read whatever corresponds to our codex and conforms to the 'Uthmānic script, but we are not allowed to read anything contrary to that (i.e., the 'Uthmānic script). As for the predecessors from the Companions and the Successors (this does not apply), because they read in their dialects (*lughātihim*) and remained upon their habits and allowed their natural instincts to take over, so these (variations) were permissible for them, and for some of the reciters after them, who were trustworthy regarding the revelation and aware of its correct interpretation.

Ibn Qutaybah clearly allows for the first generations what he does not allow for his own and later generations: the ability to recite naturally and with a solid grasp of language, thereby expressing the meaning even if using different wordings.

This opinion is also narrated from one of the senior judges in Baghdad under the early Abbasids, al-Qāḍī Abū Isḥaq al-Jahḍamī (d. 282 AH/896 CE),[30] who was one of the earliest to write a treatise on the *qirā'āt* (which is unfortunately lost). He also

---

29 Ibn Qutayba, *Ta'wīl Mushkil Al-Qur'ān*, p. 34. The original is as follows (some license has been taken in translation but the meaning has been conveyed):

فإن قال قائل: فهل يجوز لنا أن نقرأ بجميع هذه الوجوه؟
قيل له: كل ما كان منها موافقا لمصحفنا غير خارج من رسم كتابه- جاز لنا أن نقرأ به. وليس لنا ذلك فيما خالفه، لأن المتقدمين من الصحابة والتابعين، قرؤوا بلغاتهم، وجروا على عادتهم، وخلّوا أنفسهم وسوم طبائعهم، فكان ذلك جائزا لهم، ولقوم من القرّاء بعدهم مأمونين على التنزيل، عارفين بالتأويل

30 Along with being a judge, he was a specialist in the science of *qirā'āt* and was known for his piety and scholarship. Al-Dhahabī says of him, "He was highly respected, visibly a man of honor, and greatly admired" (see: *Siyar*, vol 12, p. 128).

wrote a treatise entitled *Kitāb Aḥkām al-Qur'ān,* of which a portion remains. In that treatise, he mentions that 'Umar ibn al-Khaṭṭāb would recite '...so rush to the remembrance of Allah' (***fa-s'aw*** *ilā dhikr Allah*) [62:9] as '...so come to the remembrance of Allah' (***fa-mḍū*** *ilā dhikr Allah.*). He then comments:[31]

> The recitation of those who said *fa-mḍū ilā dhikr-illāh* is neither problematic nor rejected, since its meaning is like *fa-s'aw ilā dhikr Allah*. Before the unification of the people upon one *muṣḥaf*, the reciters from them [*viz.*, the Companions] would differ with one another in this verse, and in other verses, but all the meanings would be similar. And it has been narrated from the Prophet that the Qur'ān has been revealed in seven *aḥruf*, so *permission was given for the people regarding differing in some words if the meanings were similar*. Then, when the people were gathered together and united upon one *mushaf*, the recitation was only in accordance with its wording.

Here once again, similar to previous quotations, we find the sentiment that the 'seven *aḥruf*' represent word variations emanating from the Companions, as long as they were synonymous and the original meaning was conveyed. And, like his contemporary ibn Qutaybah, al-Jahḍamī understands that this concession applied to the past but is no longer applicable in his time. The sentiment was also expressed by Abū 'Awānah (d. 316 AH/927 CE), the author of the famous *Mustakhraj* on the two *Ṣaḥīḥ* work. He entitled his section on the ḥadīths of the *aḥruf* as follows: *The Chapter Explaining the Concession of Reciting the Qur'ān as Long as the Meaning is Not Changed And the Ḥalāl and Ḥarām are Not Affected.*[32]

---

31 Al-Jahḍamī, *Kitāb al-Tafsīr*, p. 20. Emphasis mine.

32 Abū 'Awānah, *Kitāb Al-Mustakhraj* (Madinah: The Islamic University, 2014), vol. 11, p. 66. The Arabic is:

باب بيان السعة في قراءة القرآن إذا لم يُحلِ المعنى ولم يختلف في حلال ولا حرام

In this chapter, he also quotes from Anas that the Prophet would allow the scribe to write a different verse ending and overlook it; see *ḥadīth* 4287.

Another icon of that era, the great Imam and codifier of Sunnī creed, Abū Ja'far al-Ṭaḥāwī (d. 321 AH/933 CE), also argued for this opinion. In his work *Sharḥ mushkil al-āthār*, he dedicates a section to comment on the reality of the *aḥruf*. He begins his discussion on the topic by affirming that Allah sent the prophets with revelation in the tongue of their people. In the case of the Prophet Muḥammad, that was the dialect of Qur'āysh. Given that many of Qur'āysh were unlettered and had to rely on their memory to retain the Qur'ān, it was difficult for even them at times to retain it in the original dialect. *A fortiori*, tribes that spoke in other dialects, found it even more difficult to retain the original dialect for every word. In light of this difficulty, al-Ṭaḥawī says, they were granted a divine concession to recite the Qur'ān by using different words so long as the original meaning was kept intact. He says:[33]

> It was difficult for them to memorize the exact wordings that would be recited to them, and writing it was not easy for them....so a concession was given for them to recite it by meaning *even if the words that they used to recite were different from the words the Prophet himself recited unto them*. Thus, a concession was given as we have mentioned.

Al-Ṭaḥawī continues and says that after some time, when these tribes became accustomed to the dialect of the Qur'āysh and scribes increased and could rely on the written word instead of memory, it became easier for them to retain the original reading of the Prophet, therefore this concession was abrogated and only one *ḥarf* remained. Hence, the allowance of the various *aḥruf* was a temporary concession out of necessity. Al-Ṭaḥāwī uses the incident of 'Umar and Hishām to emphatically reject any other

---

The point here is not whether this specific ḥadīth is authentic but rather how Abū 'Awānah is interpreting the meaning of *sab'a aḥruf.*

33 Al-Ṭaḥāwī, *Sharḥ Mushkil al-Athār*, vol. 8, p. 118.

interpretation of the concept of *aḥruf*, and states that it is clear that the two of them were reciting with different words, but these differences essentially conveyed the same meaning. He writes:[34]

> So this shows that the *sab'a aḥruf* that are mentioned do not differ in meaning even if they differed in the words they used. And this was a concession granted to them by Allah because their circumstances dictated it. *And thus what was revealed to the Prophet was only one wording (alfāẓ wāḥida).*

In all of these early narrations, there seems to be a consistent claim that the *aḥruf* represents a concession to convey the meanings of the Qur'ān with synonyms if a person, for a legitimate reason, did not use the original words; al-Ṭaḥawī's quote is perhaps of the most explicit in this regard.[35]

For those who subscribe to the Divine Permission model, it is obvious from these previous quotes that the origin of these synonyms is from the Companions; one can even claim that there is no hint of the Dictation Model in them. However, those who subscribe to the Dictation Model interpret these narrations as examples of variations emanating from the Prophet and repeated by the Companions. In other words, an assumption is made

---

34 Al-Ṭaḥāwī, *Sharḥ Mushkil al-Athār*, vol. 8, p. 117-8; also see: vol. 8, pp. 124-5. Emphasis mine.

35 Here, it must be mentioned that in other places of his work, (see for example vol. 8, p. 142) al-Ṭaḥāwī claims that variations in some of the *qirā'āt* were recited by the Prophet directly, and various Companions heard different recitations. Yet, in other places when discussing variant *qirā'āt*, he clearly picks and chooses between them based upon meaning, preferring between, and at times rejecting, recitations that are now deemed within the 'ten'. As with other early authors, it is necessary to be fair to all of their opinions and quotations, and to try to derive a cohesive idea of what they believed. Reconciliation between all of the quotes is ideal. However, if not, then it is unsound to use one quote in one place to negate the clear meaning of another. Rather, either one suspends judgment on the author's final opinion, or claims that the author had multiple opinions at various points in his writings.

that all of these variations were being transmitted by the Companions as they heard them from the Prophet. Hence, it can be said that the key distinction between the Dictation Model and the Divine Permission model is with respect to the origins of these variant synonyms.

The first explicit reference to the origin of the synonymous words stemming from the Prophet and not from the Companions seems to appear in the fourth Islamic century, and for a period of time, both opinions were propagated and viewed as being potentially legitimate. We find, for example, the famous Ḥanafī jurist and Qur'ān commentator Abū al-Layth al-Samarqandī (d. 373 AH/983 CE) mentioning both of these possibilities (*viz.*, the Dictation Model and the Divine Permission) with regards to the origin of the synonymous readings of the *sab'a aḥruf*:[36]

> People have differed about verses that are recited according to two readings. Some said that God has revealed one recitation but granted permission for both readings, and some have said He revealed both of them.

While he himself goes on to prefer the latter opinion, what is significant is that he appears rather nonchalant with respect to both opinions and considers them to be legitimate opinions. As well, the grammarian and linguist ibn Khālawayh (d. 370 AH/980 CE) explicitly mentions in his work on *qirā'āt* both of these opinions without himself offering his own preference:[37]

> If someone asks: 'Did all of these wordings descend down upon the Prophet with all of these differences and variations, or was it only revealed in one wording…' then the

36 Al-Samarqandī, *Bustān al-'Ārifīn*, p. 35.

37 Ibn Khālawayh, al-Ḥusayn ibn Aḥmad, *Kitāb 'Irāb Al-Qirā'āt Al-Sab'a wa 'Ilalihā*, ed. 'Abd al-Raḥman al-'Uthaymīn (Cairo: Maktabat al-Khānjī, 1992), p. 17-20.

> answer to this is that one group said: 'It was thus revealed, in seven *aḥruf* and from seven doors during the presentations that Jibrīl would bring down every year...' And others said, 'Rather, the Qur'ān was revealed in the dialect of the Qur'āysh, with one *ḥarf*...then the Prophet commanded, as a concession and ease upon his Ummah, that each group could recite in their dialect...'"

Ibn Jinnī (d. 391/1102), writing towards the latter part of the fourth century, also seems to vacillate regarding the origins of these different synonyms. Earlier in his seminal work on *qirā'āt*, in discussing Anas' variant recitation of [9:57], he writes,[38]

> It is possible for a critic to find fault regarding the recitation, and for one to say: these wordings are not all from the Prophet, since otherwise it would not be allowed to substitute a word for another...But our *assumption* regarding Anas is that *he must have heard* these three synonyms from the Prophet.

While acknowledging there is no actual evidence to suggest Prophetic origin, ibn Jinnī invokes a theological sentiment that suggests it would be improper to assume *qirā'ah bi-l-ma'nā*. In other words, despite any evidence to suggest this, ibn Jinnī states that one's religious notions regarding the Qur'ān would want us to prefer the Dictation Model over the Divine Permission one.[39]

---

38 Ibn Jinnī, *Kitāb al-Muḥtasab*, vol. 1, p. 415. Emphasis mine.

39 It is pertinent to point out that this same sentiment, noble as it may be, is perhaps the primary one that motivates those who subscribe to the Dictation Model to ignore (or reinterpret) all the evidence to the contrary. However, such an approach is problematic to say the least, and in the long run unsustainable.

However, later in the same book, when discussing Anas' variant recitation of [73:6], he writes: [40]

> And this leads us to believe that they (i.e., the Companions) would take into account the meanings and stick with that. Once they extracted the meaning and protected it, they permitted themselves to express it otherwise.

And when he discusses Anas' variant recitation of [94:2], in which Anas explicitly links *qirā'ah bi-l-ma'nā* with the ḥadīth of *sab'a aḥruf*, he adds, "A similar report has preceded from Anas in this regard, and it is this [incident] and similar ones which has allowed the proliferation of these *qirā'āt*."[41] It is clear that ibn Jinnī himself vacillated between the two models, and the later position he leaned towards was the Divine Permission model.

Another scholar who clearly advocated the Divine Permission model was the Qāḍī Abū Bakr ibn al-'Arabī (d. 543 AH/1148 CE), without a doubt one of the greatest minds that Muslim Spain produced. He wrote an entire treatise on the issue of the *aḥruf*. Sadly, that treatise is lost, but he did summarize his opinion in another famous work of his, *al-'Awāṣim min al-Qawāṣim*. He writes:[42]

---

40 Ibid., vol. 2, p. 336. The original reads: هذا يؤنّس بأن القوم كانوا يعتبرون المعانى، ويخلدون إليها، فإذا حصّلوها وحصّنوها سامحوا أنفسهم فى العبارات عنها

41 Ibid., vol 2, p. 367.

42 Abū Bakr ibn al-'Arabī, *al-'Awāṣim min al-Qawāṣim*, ed. Ammār Ṭālibī (Cairo: Maktabah Dār al-Turāth, 1974), p. 356. (It should be mentioned that the more common edition of this work, edited by Muḥibb al-Dīn al-Khaṭīb, is a severely condensed one and does not contain this section). Mention should also be made here of the other great Mālikī scholar ibn 'Abd al-Barr (d. 463 AH/1071 CE), who in his commentary on the *Muwaṭṭa*, discusses this topic and quotes al-Ṭaḥāwī extensively; however, his own final views and conclusions need further research. See his, *al-Tamhīd*, vol. 5, pp. 584-616.

> The meaning of this tradition [of the seven *aḥruf*] is that *Allah gave permission to the Companions* such that each one of them could recite in his own dialect...and this continued throughout the life of the Prophet, as a concession from Allah and an ease for the people, since if they had been commanded to recite the Qur'ān in the dialect it had been revealed in - *meaning the dialect of the Qur'āysh* - some people would have been turned away, and others would have found it difficult, but the Sharī'ah is ease...

Ibn al-'Arabī opines that only one *ḥarf*, in the Qur'āyshī dialect, was actually revealed, and a concession was given for the Companions and that first generation who encountered the Divine Revelation to recite the Qur'ān with alternative synonyms in their own dialects.

The opinion that each and every variation emanated directly from the Prophet (i.e., the Dictation Model) which as mentioned seems to have begun in the fourth Islamic century, became more and more widespread from the fifth century onwards, until eventually it supplanted the Divine Permission model. One of the most important figures whose fame and status helped spread the Dictation Model is the great icon in the field of *qirā'āt*, Abū 'Amr al-Dānī (d. 444 AH/1053 CE). Al-Dānī writes that Jibrīl recited the Qur'ān in multiple ways to the Prophet, and the Prophet then taught these ways to the Companions. The reason why one says 'The *ḥarf* of Ubayy', he claims, is *not* because the recitation originated from him but because he mastered and perfected this one method of recitation and took it as his custom, '...so the attribution is to his choice [of Prophetic recitation] and habit of continuity, not the attribution of inventing and a personal opinion and *ijtihad*'.[43]

43 al-Dānī, *Kitāb Al-Aḥruf al-Sab'a*, p. 61.

Even though this latter opinion eventually became the dominant one, the earlier opinion never disappeared entirely, and occasionally surfaced in various works on this topic. For example, Abū Shāma al-Maqdisī (d. 665 AH/1267 CE) in his listing of the opinions regarding the *aḥruf*, clearly references the opinion of *al-qirā'āh bi-l-maʿnā*. He explains:[44]

> So the meaning of this tradition that '*...there are amongst them the old, and young boys and girls, and those who have never read,*' is that a concession was made for them to substitute its wordings with other words that would give the same meaning or approximate its meanings – from one different synonym to up to seven. *And they were not required to protect one specific wording, since the Qur'ān was revealed to an illiterate nation that was not accustomed to being taught or rote memorization.*

Another famous scholar who clearly understood this position and perhaps held it as well was the exegete ibn Kathīr (d. 774 AH/1373 CE). In his work on the blessings of the Qur'ān, he has a section listing five opinions on the reality of the *aḥruf*. The first and most detailed, and the one that he himself appears to adopt, is al-Ṭaḥāwī's one, whom he cites by name. He then says:[45]

> Al-Ṭaḥāwī and others claimed that it was a concession for them to recite in several dialects since it would have

44 Abū Shāmah al-Maqdisī, *al-Murshid al-Wajīz* (Beirut: Dār al-Ṣādir, 1975), p. 89. Emphasis mine. His entire discussion on this matter is worth perusing, although it should be noted that it appears that he chooses another opinion as the more valid one. The point here is that he acknowledges – and his work was written in the seventh Islamic century – that this was an opinion that existed, that he chronicles it extensively, and he seems to consider it a viable one, even if he himself opts for another interpretation.

45 Ibn Kathīr, *Faḍā'il al-Qur'ān* (Cairo: Maktabah ibn Taymiyya, 1996), p. 134.

> been extremely difficult for many people to recite in the Qur'āyshī dialect, and in the recitation of the Prophet, due to their lack of knowledge of reading and capability of memorising perfectly. And al-Ṭaḥāwī ...claimed this was a concession in earlier times that was then abrogated once the excuse had been eliminated, and memorisation was easier, and people learned to write.

Ibn Kathīr goes on to explain that 'Uthmān decided to eliminate this concession and gather the people upon the recitation that Jibrīl did to the Prophet, and asked them to not take advantage of the concession that they previously had, since that concession was now causing disunity and even leading to accusations of heresy.

One also finds this opinion, or variations of it, scattered throughout the writings of later scholars, up until the modern era.[46] 'Abd al-Raḥmān ibn Yaḥya al-Mu'allimī (d. 1966), whose reputation as an ardent champion of the *Ahl al-Ḥadīth* school is known, explicitly wrote that the *aḥruf* represent word variations that indicate synonymous readings, and at times the Companions would substitute words that they had not heard from the Prophet: "...for the condition of the unlettered people [of that time] necessitated that a general concession be given to them that they 'recite with meaning' (*qad iqtaḍath al-tarkhīṣ lahum fī al-jumlah fī al-qirā'āh bi-l-ma'nā*), even though the wordings of the Qur'ān are intended in themselves since it is the Speech of the Lord of the worlds."[47]

---

46 Al-Rajḥī mentions quotations from many scholars, including ibn 'Ashūr, Dr. 'Abd al-Hādī Ḥamītū, Dr. Muḥammad Jabal, Dr. 'Abd al-Ṣabūr Shahīn, Dr. Ghānim Qaddūrī, and others. See, ibid., pp. 175-187.

47 'Abd al-Raḥmān ibn Yaḥya al-Mu'allimī, *al-Anwār al-Kāshifah* (Beirut: 'Alam al-Kutub, 1983), p. 76-7. It should be noted that his position is a modified one from that in this article. Al-Mu'allimī claims that one *ḥarf* was revealed as the original and default, and that some synonymous words were

But what of the reference works of *ʿulūm al-Qurʾān*, such as the *Burhān* of al-Zarkashī or the *Itqān* of al-Suyūṭī? Surely the Divine Permission model, even if they did not agree with it, could not have been ignored by them in their lists of opinions? When one re-reads these classics, it becomes apparent that this opinion *is* mentioned quite explicitly. For example, al-Zarkashī in his *Burhān* discusses the various interpretations of *aḥruf* and actually cites al-Ṭaḥawī by name, and mentions (in opinion five) that the reality of *aḥruf* are word synonyms. He cites many of the same examples of the variants of the Companions mentioned previously in this article, and he explicitly claims that ʿUthmān only preserved one *ḥarf*.[48] Al-Suyuṭī in his *Itqān* famously lists thirty-five opinions on what the *aḥruf* might be, of which number nine is precisely this opinion: that the *aḥruf* represents synonymous wordings. He too quotes al-Ṭaḥawī's claim that early generations could not read or write, so it would have been difficult for them to memorise one wording. He illustrates this opinion with the incident of ibn Masʿūd instructing the man to recite *ṭaʿām al-fājir* in lieu of *ṭaʿām al-athīm*.[49]

Perhaps because neither of these authors mentioned the phrase *al-qirāʾāh bi-l-maʿnā* nor explicitly stated where these synonyms originated from, it became easier to gloss over these explicit references and assume – as many later authorities did – that the reference here was to synonyms that the Prophet himself

---

also recited by Jibrīl to the Prophet who would then teach these variations to the Companions, but not all variations stemming from the Companions were from the Prophet; he explicitly states (p. 76) that at times Companions would substitute their own words even if they hadn't heard it from the Prophet.

48 Al-Zarkashī, *al-Burhān fī ʿulūm al-Qurʾān*, vol. 1, p. 220-2. The point being made here is that al-Zarkashī clearly understood the Divine Permission model and chronicles it: if only one *ḥarf* was preserved as al-Ṭaḥāwī claims, the reason is that it was the actual revealed *ḥarf*, and the other *aḥruf* were the concessions permitted to the Companions but not preserved.

49 Al-Suyūṭī, *al-Itqān fī ʿulūm al-Qurʾān*, vol.1, p. 62-3.

recited (i.e., the Dictation Model). But by quoting al-Ṭaḥawī, who states that only one wording was revealed and the rest came from the Companions, clearly these authorities did not intend what others seem to have understood from them.

Hence, the opinion that the *aḥruf* represent the permission granted to the Companions to recite with synonymous words (*al-qirā'āh bi-l-ma'nā*) is a well-attested view that is found in numerous references: early, medieval, pre-modern, and modern. However, as shall be explained later, these references are re-interpreted or glossed over by those who subscribe to the Dictation Model.

A question arises as to how the Divine Permission model understands the 'Uthmānic collection. According to proponents of this view, the recension of 'Uthmān takes on a different, and clear, reality.[50] When new converts who had been taught the choices (or *ḥarf*) of one Companion encountered the readings and choices of other Companions, they began rejecting those choices because they had never heard them nor been introduced to the concept of *aḥruf*. This ignorance on their part is why 'Uthmān had to publicly validate that indeed, the Qur'ān was revealed

---

50 A brief mention must be made here of the notion of the existence of a 'Final Presentation' (*'al-'Arḍah al-Akhīrah'*) to which all of the seven *aḥruf* and ten *qirā'āt* are linked. This concept seems to have begun during the second Islamic century, based on the narration that the Prophet recited to Jibrīl twice the year before he passed away (an incident that is authentically reported in numerous ḥadīth collections, but in and of itself is not linked to the concept of *aḥruf*). The notion of a particular Companion being present (the identity of whom is contested in the earliest of reports), and witnessing the entire recitation (no such claim is made by the Companions themselves who should have mentioned it when selecting the committee during 'Uthmān's time), and the claim that this 'Final Presentation' somehow cancelled all earlier ones and was the basis for the later recension of 'Uthmān (an idea that does not seem to be verbalized by the senior Companions and in particular by the committee commissioned by 'Uthmān), clearly developed over time, and is invoked with greater frequency and potency the later one goes in the works of *'ulūm al-Qur'ān*. This topic is worthy of a separate research paper.

in multiple *aḥruf*, and that no one should reject the recitations of the other Companions. As the situation worsened, the senior Companions realized that action had to be taken. Hence, they decided to canonise and codify the *original* wordings recited by the Prophet, and to eliminate the choices that were allowed in light of the concession of the *aḥruf* ḥadīth, but nonetheless were not the original wordings. Hence why 'Uthmān stipulated that only those who had written the verse directly from the Prophet should come, and hence why he ordered the committee to write in the dialect of the Qur'āysh '*...since it was revealed in that dialect*'. For this recension, 'Uthmān did not trust mere memorisation: he wanted written documentation and at least two witnesses who had heard that precise wording. And he wanted to stick as closely as possible to the original dialect – even down to the minute details of spelling words in the dialect of the Qur'āysh, since the Revelation had only occurred in this *ḥarf*. This is in all likelihood why he did not commission ibn Mas'ūd for such a monumental task, because ibn Mas'ūd, fully aware of the reality of *aḥruf* and also being a member of another tribe, had already established his own *ḥarf* and championed it based on his memory of the recitation he had been taught. Discarding the alternative recitations of the Companions required no explanation or justification: why keep substitutions when the original was available?

'Uthmān had some official copies made, and these were sent to the primary districts of the Caliphate. Some minor differences between these copies were overlooked and absorbed by the allowance of the *aḥruf* concession.[51] The project was an

51 Ibn al-'Arabī writes, "During the course of transcribing [the 'Uthmānic] *muṣḥafs*, the *muṣḥafs* differed in some letters, perhaps four or five, and then this issue increased until the reciters differed in over forty letters, including the *wāw*, the *alif*, and the *yā*. As for an entire word, this only occurred twice, once in [Surah] al-Tawbah, and the other in [Surah] al-Ḥadīd...and this is a trivial matter which neither affects the religion nor faults the concept of the preservation of the Qur'ān (*wa hādhā amr yasīr lā yu'athir fī al-dīn wa*

absolute success: all other variations were forgotten as a collective whole, and only a fraction of them remained in the memories of later people and were collected in works of history, grammar and exegesis.

Of course, the script available to 'Uthmān, along with the natural variations in the pronunciations of words that every

---

lā yaḥuṭṭu min ḥifẓ al-Qur'ān)". See: Ibn al-ʿArabī, *al-ʿAwāṣim min al-Qawāṣim*, p. 358-9. It is clear that ibn al-ʿArabī is ascribing the origin of these differences to the scribes and hence feels the need to state that this does not affect the concept of Divine preservation – this caveat is only needed, and such a reconciliation can only happen, if one believes in the Divine Permission model, which, as we quoted above, ibn al-ʿArabī does. It is important to note that some scholars characterize such differences as 'scribal errors' or 'mistakes' (as an example of a scholar who characterizes these differences as mistakes, see the comments of Dr. Bashār ʿAwwād Maʿrūf in his lecture on the *aḥruf*, where he remarks, "Today in the era of computers, when we write muṣḥafs, how many errors (*ghalat*) do we find, and this is in our times…so do you consider this a major issue upon those scribes [of 'Uthmān] that they made a mistake (*khaṭṭa*) in four or five or ten or fifteen places? These are not [intentional] differences, rather these are scribal mistakes (*khaṭṭa al-nāsikh*)…is it not possible for them to make mistakes, or is he (sic.) infallible and incapable of a mistake?" See his lecture and comments at: https://www.youtube.com/watch?v=dw_jknPwRdI (minute 26 onwards ; last accessed Jul '23). In the opinion of the author of this article, it is problematic to use the word 'error' or 'mistake', since describing these differences as 'mistakes' directly contradicts the explicit prohibition mentioned in the very *ḥadīth* of the *aḥruf*, such as 'Do not argue over the Qur'ān…' and 'All of them are pure and whole…' and other such phrases. In fact, interestingly, this sentiment of problematizing such differences and considering them mistakes was precisely the mindset of the new converts during the wars of 'Uthmān's time who almost excommunicated each other because of their differences. When one understands the Divine Permission model, these differences are perfect and trivial examples of it, and hence allowed by the *ḥadīths* of the *aḥruf*. Thus, in the opinion of this author they are not and should not be characterized as 'mistakes' or 'errors'. Notice as well, the precise wording that ibn al-ʿArabī uses to describes these differences. It is of course not impossible that these variations were intentional; if one holds this view, this point can be excluded from the fifteen concerns listed.

language has, did lead to a very small window of diversity in recitations. But this diversity, in comparison to the differences between the *aḥruf* pre-ʿUthmānic canonisation, was so utterly trivial as to be almost irrelevant in the minds of those who wished to preserve the revealed *ḥarf*. This explains why there was never the level of animosity or potential excommunication between the reciters post-ʿUthmān compared to the level of animosity that occurred amongst the various groups participating in the wars of Azerbaijan, which ultimately led to the ʿUthmānic compilation. It was in this narrow spectrum that the science of *qirāʾāt* began, flourished, and eventually closed with the canonisation projects. All of the *qirāʾāt* are therefore extrapolated from one *ḥarf*: the preserved *ḥarf* of the Prophet.

A fundamental question that needs to be asked is: what is the relationship between the *qirāʾāt* and the Qur'ān? For most scholars, the two are synonymous: the *qirāʾāt* collectively *are* the Qur'ān (and this is the logical corollary of the Dictation Model). But this was not the position of some of the most prominent scholars of the Qur'ān. Al-Zarkashī writes:[52]

> Know that the Qur'ān and the *qirāʾāt* are two separate, distinct realities (*ḥaqiqatān mutaghayirān*). The Qur'ān is the Divine Revelation that has come down as a miracle and clarification [for mankind]. And the *qirāʾāt* are the differences of the wordings of the Revelation within the letters, and enunciating them with, say, *takhfīf* and *tashdīd* and other such rules.

Hence, if one understands that the Divine Revelation is in fact manifested in the *qirāʾāt* but that they are not exactly the same, the question arises: how precisely would al-Zarkashī and those who held this distinction view the actual differences between the

52 Al-Zarkashī, *al-Burhān*, vol. 1, p. 318. Also see Shahīn, *Tarikh al-Qur'ān*, p. 40 onwards.

Revelation and the *qirā'āt*? Clearly, since the *qirā'āt* are not the exact same – at least in their minds – as the Revelation, they would allow for some minor areas of *ijtihad* in this science, as he explicitly states. And this is what many reports would seem to indicate if we take them at face value.

For example, in one narration it is reported that ibn Masʿūd advised his students, "If you differ about a consonant in the Qur'ān - if it is a *yā* or a *tā* - then recite it as masculine (*viz.*, with a *yā*), because the [default] of the Qur'ān is masculine."[53] If each and every letter were always recited with absolute precedence (*viz.*, the Dictation Model), this command would not make any sense. This of course would imply there is a level of independent reasoning that the first few generations of reciters employed, especially with respect to vocalising a skeletal word in the ʿUthmānic codex that allowed for multiple readings. Based on this model, the permissibility of variant recitations from the *ḥarf* preserved by ʿUthmān is under the purview of the concession of the *aḥruf*. The sources for the differences in the *qirā'āt* would then be three: firstly, the accents and pronunciations that Arab peoples from diverse regions and tribes differed over; secondly, the application of *ijtihād* by qualified grammarians and reciters of the first two centuries in deciphering a small percentage of the consonants (*tashkīl*) and the grammatical case (*'iʿrāb*) of a word; and lastly and most infrequent, the minute variations between the official ʿUthmānic codices. The evidence for this is too numerous to mention, since every single attempt to justify a recitation or explain it in light of broader meaning, or grammatical rules, or poetry, or via appealing to the enunciation rules of a tribe, is in fact a manifestation of this reality. One only needs to read *any* classical *tafsīr* or work on the *qirā'āt* to see examples of this. It is only later that scholars are forced to reinterpret every example as merely an explanation of *why* the Prophet would have

53 Ibn Wahb, *Tafsīr al-Qur'ān*, vol. 3, p. 44.

allegedly recited in such a manner (i.e., force the Dictation Model onto these reports), rather than the obvious fact that the reciter is justifying his *own* choice by appealing to grammar or poetry or meaning (i.e., the Divine Permission model).

The grammarian and reciter ibn Jinnī, after discussing Anas' variant recitation of [94:2], in which Anas explicitly links *qirā'ah bi-l-ma'nā* with the ḥadīth of *sab'a aḥruf*, comments, "...and it is this [incident] and similar ones which has allowed the proliferation of these *qirā'āt*."[54] In other words, the concession of the *aḥruf* is the precise concession that has allowed the proliferation of the *qirā'āt*, or to put it more bluntly: he is stating that if the first generation could substitute an entire word with another and this was considered valid, then these later *qirā'āt* may *a fortiori* differ in deciphering a skeletal word in the 'Uthmānic script, and these variants would all be considered valid.

Qāḍī Abū Bakr ibn al-'Arabī, the famous Andalusian scholar already quoted above, discusses the *qirā'āt* in the seventh century, well after the codification of ibn Mujāhid, and states plainly that these were the choices of these specific reciters; hence, he says, it is not obligatory to exclusively follow any one of them. Ibn Mujāhid's choices, he writes, were not better than those of al-Ṭabarī and other compilers, and all of them are valid, but some are stronger than others. After discussing some of the fundamental principles (*uṣūl*) and differences between the famous codified *qirā'āt*, he says, "And all of these principles, or most of them, in my view stem from dialects (*lughāt*), not from previous recitations (*qirā'āt*), *because none of them are confirmed as having originated from the Prophet and if you examine them, you will see that these are choices made based upon dialects and meanings*."[55] He then proceeds to explain why he himself – and recall his status as a master of *tafsīr*, *fiqh* and *qirā'āt* – actually chooses his own unique recitations, '...for there

54 Ibn Jinnī, *Al-Muḥtasab*, vol 2, p. 367

55 Ibn al-'Arabī, *al-'Awāṣim min al-Qawāṣim*, p. 364. Emphasis mine.

is no single reciter from all of these [famous] reciters except that they too recited with other recitations! None of them are infallible, and their recitations are merely their own choices (*ikhtiyārātuhum*), and no one else should be obliged to follow their choices.'[56]

It was precisely because the *qirā'āt* were flourishing and the bar was being pushed higher and higher (just as had occurred pre-'Uthmān with the proliferation of the concession of the *aḥruf*) that scholars had to intervene and attempt to chart out rules for which *qirā'āt* should be accepted and which rejected. The fact that rules are being debated, contested, and weighed against one another indicates that the *qirā'āt* as they existed in this era were not stemming from the Dictation Model, but rather from the Divine Permission model. In other words, the fact that scholars had to weigh in on the many dozens of *qirā'āt*, attempt to chart which ones should be accepted or rejected, and engage in debates over these rules, indicates the lived reality of the Divine Permission model rather than the Dictation Model.

Eventually, ibn Mujāhid's seminal work played a vital role in selecting which reciters' choices would live on, and which would not. The role of the state in enforcing this choice must also be mentioned, since ibn Mujāhid used the services of his friend, the vizier of the Abbasids ibn Muqlah (d. 941 CE), to accuse with heresy - and even punish - those who did not subscribe to his views.[57] In particular, the famous cases of ibn Shanabūdh and ibn Miqsam should be kept in mind: both of them attempted to defend their views (which clearly stem from the Divine Permission model) and claimed that earlier scholars also adopted their position. However, ibn Muqlah was successful in silencing them and others, either with actual punishments and torture or

56 Ibid., p. 362; also see his discussion in the previous pages.

57 Ibn al-Arabī explicitly mentions that the state enforced the choices of ibn Mujāhid on the people and it is because of this that only his seven became popular, even though others were more worthy of such acceptance. See: Ibn al-'Arabī, *al-'Awāṣim min al-Qawāṣim*, p. 360.

through threats of it.[58] From the second Islamic century to the fourth, the science of *qirā'āt* slowly shifted from being an active discipline where masters chose, debated and defended, to a passive one where students would memorise and preserve the choices of a specific group of reciters chosen by ibn Mujāhid, and then (in the ninth Islamic century) ibn al-Jazarī.

To summarise: the Divine Permission model champions the claim that the first generation was allowed a concession to recite as closely to the original as possible. 'Uthmān eliminated this concession and provided a skeletal framework that successfully preserved the Prophetic recitation (the one *ḥarf* actually revealed). However, a very small scope of variants continued, restricted to operating through and upon that skeletal framework. These variations were never deemed problematic as a whole because scholars differentiated between the *qirā'āt* and the Divine Revelation, and allowed for an extremely narrow field of *ijtihād* in the *qirā'āt* because of the Divine Permission granted via the *aḥruf* ḥadīths, while acknowledging that this did not impact the status of the *qirā'āt* being Divine as well.

Before proceeding to the next section, it is pertinent to point out that the claim that aspects of the *qirā'āt* are *ijtihād*-based is also the dominant opinion of the Muʿtazilites and Imāmī (Twelver) Shiʿites. Al-Bāqillānī chastises some of the *mutakallimūn* (*viz.*, some of the Muʿtazilites) of his time and states:[59]

> Some of them said: it is allowed to use one's judgment and *ijtihād* in affirming the (recitation of) the Qur'ān in its words and manners (*awjuh wa aḥruf*) as long as those manners were correct from a linguistic perspective and permissible to verbalize in such a manner, and as long as

58 For further details of this incident, see: Melchert, Christopher, "Ibn Mujāhid and the Establishment of Seven Qur'ānic Readings" in *Studia Islamica* No. 91 (2000), pp. 5-22.

59 Al-Bāqillānī, *al-Intiṣār lil Qur'ān* (Beirut: Dar ibn Ḥazm, 2001), vol. 1, p. 69

> there was no evidences that the Prophet himself recited the Qur'ān in a manner contrary to what the rules of language [they have used] would state. But the people of the truth (*ahl al-Ḥaqq*) rejected this opinion and refused to accept it, and they claimed that whoever holds this opinion is mistaken (*khaṭṭa'ūhū*).

Note that al-Bāqillānī appears to be writing about an opinion still held in his time. Furthermore, the language he uses is relatively mild compared to what later authors would hold – there is no accusation of heresy, or *kufr*, but merely the claim that this opinion is 'mistaken' and should be 'rejected' rather than accepted. Al-Zarkashī also informs us that this is the position of some of the Muʿtazilites: that the *qirā'āt* stem from choices the reciters made based on eloquence and the reasoning of qualified linguists.[60] The most famous Muʿtazilite exegete, al-Zamakhsharī (d. 1143 CE), in his *Kashshāf* deals with the entire genre of *qirā'āt* as a discipline that needed to be judged not on the basis of acceptance of the 'seven' or 'ten' but in accordance with the principles of Arabic grammar and the standards of eloquence.[61]

Al-Kulaynī (d. 329 AH/941 CE), whose work *Usūl al-Kāfī* is to the Twelvers what the *Ṣaḥīḥ* of al-Bukhārī is to the Sunnīs, attributes to their fifth Imam Muḥammad al-Bāqir (d. 114 AH/732 CE) the following statement, "The Qur'ān was revealed from The One [*viz.*, its recitation is also in one manner]. As for these differences (*ikhtilāf*), they come from the reciters (*qurrā'*)."[62] Similarly, the Grand Ayatollah Sayyid Abū al-Qāsim al-Musāwī al-Khoei (d. 1992), the most recognized jurist of the Imāmīs in the last century, wrote that the differences within the *qirā'āt* purely

60 Al-Zarkashī, *al-Burhān*, vol. 1, p. 321.

61 See the conclusions that Niḍāl al-Farāyah reached, and the many examples presented, in his doctoral dissertation on the subject: *al-Qirā'āt al-Qur'āniyyah fi Kitāb al-Kashshāf li-l-Zamakhsharī*, presented to the Department of Arabic Sciences and Literature, Mu'tah University, Jordan (2006).

62 Al-Kulaynī, *Usul al-Kāfī*, vol. 1, p. 203.

stem from the personal reasoning (*ijtihadāt*) of the reciters, and these differences cannot be traced back to the Prophet.[63]

Five Objections and Responses

In this section, five objections that have been raised against the Divine Permission model are listed, along with possible responses. It should be noted that of course this list is not exhaustive but serves as a sampling of key objections.

The *first objection* is that this opinion is completely invented by some modern authors, and that no earlier scholar has held it. All incidents or quotations that are mentioned in the previous section from authorities of the past, the claim goes, are invalid or have been misunderstood by those who propose this view.[64] To illustrate this objection, we can use the famous incident of ibn Masʿūd, and the opinion cited of al-Shāfiʿī, as examples. The incident of ibn Masʿūd in which he apparently substituted the word '*athīm*' with its synonym '*fājir*' when his student was unable to verbalize the former word is countered by those who object to the Divine Permission model in two ways. Firstly, the claim is made that the incident is narrated with a weak *isnad* and hence cannot be used as evidence. Secondly, it is interpreted as at attempt to *explain* the word (i.e., a *tafsīr*) rather than offer a *substitution* that was meant to be recited.

The response to the claim that this incident might have a weak *isnad* is preceded in an earlier footnote in which the issue of 'weak reports' was discussed. Ironically, and as a validation

---

63 Al-Shiblī, ʿAdawiyya Ḥayāwī, "Al-Qirā'āt Al-Qur'āniyyah Bayn Al-Tawātur wa-l-Ijtihād" in *Majallat al-Qādisiyyah fī al-Adāb*, vol. 8, (3) 2009, Kuwait.

64 See, for example, the website http://www.immutablequr'ān.com (last accessed Jul 2023), which appears to be dedicated to providing alternative interpretations to every incident or quote that is used to support the Divine Permission model.

of some of the points made in that footnote, this incident might perhaps not be authentically validated to ibn Masʿūd due to the presence of a particular narrator. However, it *is* narrated with authentic chains to another companion, Abū al-Dardāʾ.[65] Hence, the use of this example as evidence is not affected since it is substantiated that a Companion did this (in addition to the other points raised earlier about *isnad*s).

It is also claimed that the word substitution in this incident was merely an explanation, and not a recitation. Commenting on this incident, the famous Ḥanafī jurist Abū Bakr al-Jaṣṣāṣ (d. 370 AH/ 981 CE) states, "He (i.e., Ibn Masʿūd) wanted to explain to him the meaning of the word."[66] Ibn Taymiyyah writes, "What some have claimed – that ibn Masʿūd would allow reciting the Qur'ān with synonyms – is a fabrication against him ('*kadhib ʿalayhī*'). What he actually said was: 'I have listened to the reciters, and I found them to be similar (*mutaqāribīn*), for all of these [differences] are just like someone saying 'This way' ('*aqbil*'), or 'Please come to me' (*halumma*), or 'Can you come here?' (*taʿāl*). Therefore, all of you should recite as you have been taught to recite,' or [he said] something like that."[67]

To respond to this objection, one may state factually that there are indeed two groups of scholars: those who interpret these reports from within the Dictation Model (and this encompasses all those who object), and those who see these reports as examples of the Divine Permission model. If al-Jaṣṣāṣ and al-Qurṭubī

---

65 See, Saʿīd ibn Manṣūr, *Sunan* (Riyadh: Dār al-Ulūkah, 2012), vol. 7, p. 326; and al-Ḥākim, *al-Mustadrak*, vol. 4, p. 1380.

66 Abū Bakr al-Jaṣṣās, *Ahkām al-Qur'ān*, vol. 5, p 337. This same sentiment is expressed by many authorities who subscribe to the Dictation Model, such as ibn al-Anbārī and al-Qurṭubī

67 Ibn Taymiyyah, *Majmūʿ al-Fatāwā*, vol. 13, p. 397. Note here that ibn Taymiyyah is not actually commenting on the incident that is quoted here, but rather on another quotation attributed to ibn Masʿūd which was also referenced in the previous section of this article.

do not view these reports indicating *qirā'āh bi-l-ma'nā*, al-Ṭaḥāwī, Abū Shāmah, and other scholars did. Each group of scholars is making an assumption: it is up to each researcher to see which assumption is more reasonable and fits all of the other evidence regarding this issue. One may also add that the report itself does not actually give any indication that an explanation of the word '*al-athīm*' is being given. In fact in some reports, it is mentioned that the man was unable to pronounce Arabic properly, whereas in other reports (such as the one quoted earlier), an explicit mentioning of the concept of *aḥruf* is brought in; such details would only be pertinent if he were being taught an alternative recitation, and not an explanation of a word.

Moving on to the quote of al-Shāfi'ī that was previously cited to prove that he believed the *aḥruf* were a concession from Allah, and that the Companions could recite synonyms rather than the exact words if they conveyed the proper meanings, the claim is made by some[68] that one cannot understand this as an endorsement of *qirā'ah bi-l-ma'nā*. This is because in that passage, al-Shāfi'ī uses the concept of the *aḥruf* to demonstrate the permissibility of the variations in the *tashahhud* (meaning: he claims the *tashahhud* may be verbalized in different ways, for if Allah allowed the Qur'ān itself to be verbalized in different ways, then the *tashahhud* which is of lesser sanctity should *a fortiori* be allowed); however, in another location of the work, al-Shāfi'ī explicitly states that the *tashahhud* was taught in different ways to different Companions directly by the Prophet. Hence, they argue, one must understand the first passage of al-Shāfi'ī while also considering the second one.

The response to this is straightforward. Rather than try to force harmony between two obviously contradictory passages from two different locations of a work, it can be argued that

---

68 See, for example, Khatib and Khan, op. cit., under 'The Scope of the Concession'; and the website cited in the previous footnote.

al-Shāfiʿī's views on the *tashahhud* varied over time (as did many of his views), and at one instance he held one opinion, and at another he held a second. The quote of al-Shāfiʿī on the *aḥruf* cannot be easily dismissed since it explicitly links the concession of the *aḥruf* to memory lapse:

> [As a manifestation of] Allah's mercy towards His creation, He revealed His Book in seven *aḥruf*, *knowing that one's memory can be mistaken*, so He permitted them to recite it even if they used a different word if the different word didn't change the meaning.

Rather than interpret this passage to mean something its plain reading cannot justify, a more rational (and apparent) meaning is that he held two different opinions about the *tashahhud*. The same can be said of all the other quotations and references: for each one, scholars who subscribe to the Dictation Model and object to the Divine Permission model re-interpret all evidence offered even if, at times, it appears to belie the plain meaning of the incident or quotation. The irony is that by quoting scholars from the fourth century onwards who explicitly reject the validity of *qirāʾah bi-l-maʿnā*, this very refutation proves that the opinion existed! How else can one explain the angst of ibn al-Anbārī,[69] the denunciation of al-Dānī, and the claim of ibn Taymiyya that whoever believes ibn Masʿūd allowed *qirāʾah bi-l-maʿnā* is mistaken? At the very least, the cumulative evidence for the existence of those who advocated the Divine Permission model is undeniable. It is then up to each individual to see how best to interpret the evidence and which of the two models better fits the data available. Of course, if one accepts these objections to the evidence given, the Dictation Model still leaves all the difficult questions raised in the earlier section of this article, and one is

69 The quotation from ibn al-Anbārī is mentioned in the third objection.

left where one began with respect to the ambiguous aspects of this complex topic.

The *second objection* that is raised is that this opinion of *qirā'ah bi-l-ma'nā* seems to contradict the well-known and attested maxim, "Recitation is based on customary precedent" (*'al-Qirā'āh sunnah muttaba'ah'*). This maxim and variations of it have been narrated by many early reciters and is considered almost as a unanimous consensus; it is also the primary evidence of the Dictation Model. Al-Dānī writes:[70]

> The imams of the reciters do not rely in respect to the wordings of the Qur'ān upon what is widespread in language and analogies in Arabic. Rather, they rely on what is most accurately transmitted and reliably narrated in their opinion. This is not undercut by any linguistic reasoning (*qiyās*) or widespread grammar laws, since recitation is based on customary precedent.

What best illustrates this, according to those who state this objection, is the existence of detailed *isnad* and *ijāzāt* that continuously link living reciters to the Prophet. This objection can be answered by pointing out that the principle is in fact correct as a rule. In other words, it is precisely *because* the default has always been to conform to what has been previously recited that the variations within the *aḥruf* (in particular the post-'Uthmānic variations), and especially within the *qirā'āt*, has been so minimal. The concession of *qirā'ah bi-l-ma'nā* was *never* taught as a default or encouraged. Rather, it was always constricted, from its inception, as a necessary and unavoidable reality to the earliest of generations, and then the concession was done away with when there was no need for its continued existence. The 'Uthmānic compilation effectively eliminated the synonymous wording

70 Al-Dānī, *Jāmi' al-Bayān* vol. 1, p. 51.

variations, and reverted the recitation to its original, with only a very small spectrum left for variations.

As well, one can respond to this objection by pointing out all the evidence presented in the previous section that indicate the existence of *qirāʾah bi-l-maʿnā* and the views of early authorities on the *qirāʾāt*. It is logical, therefore, to combine this maxim alongside the evidence to the contrary to claim that the maxim is a general rule, and the concession of *qirāʾah bi-l-maʿnā* is an unavoidable concession that was never allowed to be taken as a norm. In fact, this is the most obvious interpretation of the famous statement of ibn Masʿūd himself that was quoted earlier: "I have listened to the reciters, and I found them to be similar (*mutaqāribīn*). Therefore, all of you should recite as you have been taught to recite, and I warn you against over-zealousness and differing amongst yourself (*al-ṭanaṭṭuʿ wa-l-ikhtilāf*), for all of these [differences] are just like someone saying 'Please come to me' (*halumma*) or 'Can you come here?' (*taʿāl*)."[71] Ibn Masʿūd teaches the rule and allows for the concession, while warning against fanaticism – had these variations been prophetic in origin, there would be no need for this warning against fanaticism nor the example at the end. Hence, the response to this second objection is explicitly encapsulated in this instruction from one of the most senior Companions of the Prophet.

The existence of *isnads* back to the reciters, and from them to the Prophet, is indeed a general testament to this maxim. However, the notion that before codification of the *qirāʾāt* the student imitated each and every choice of his teacher lacks evidence and contradicts the history of the evolution of the *qirāʾāt* during its golden era. Rather, what appears to be the case is that the first few names of the *isnads*, and in particular from the time of the Companions to the famous ten 'reciters', is a general chain of scholarship and mentorship, akin to *ijāzāt* in *fiqh* and other

71 Ibn Shabbah, *Tārīkh al-Madīnah*, vol. 3, p. 1007.

disciplines: the name of the teacher establishes a mentorship and a verification that the student is indeed qualified to teach, and that the student has mastered the basic principles and overall methodology of the teacher. It can also be shown that some reciters were more likely to imitate their teachers exactly than others. We know for a fact that the Companions themselves did not recite in the exact variations and choices of any of the 'seven' or 'ten', and we have documented evidence that some reciters chose variations different from their teachers.

Therefore, while the maxim does have a certain appeal and is valid as a general principle, it does not reasonably explain all the questions that arise from the Dictation Model, as demonstrated earlier, and contradicts known facts regarding the choices of the reciters, and of how the earliest icons of this discipline viewed *qirā'āt* choices as being worthy of 'accepted' or 'rejected' based on multiple factors.

A *third objection* that is raised is that the Divine Permission model would open the floodgates to any type of recitation, and the entirety of the Qur'ānic text would be destroyed. This objection can perhaps best be encapsulated by the fourth century grammarian ibn al-Anbārī (d. 328/940). Commenting on the narration of Anas ibn Mālik which appears to allow synonymous substitutions based on meaning, he states:[72]

> Some of those who are misguided may resort to such reports to cast doubts and state: whoever recites according to a reading that conforms to the meaning of a *ḥarf* from the Qur'ān is correct as long as he does not contradict the [original] meaning or bring forth other than what Allah

---

72 Ibn al-Anbārī's original work *Al-Radd 'Alā Man Khālaf Muṣḥaf 'Uthmān*, which was written as a refutation of ibn Shanabūdh, seems to be lost; however, al-Qurṭubī in his *tafsīr* occasionally quotes from it, and it is in that work that this quote is found. See, al-Qurṭubī, *al-Jāmi' li Aḥkām al-Qur'ān*, vol. 19, p. 40 (Beirut: Dār al-Kitāb al-'Arabī, 1997). Emphasis mine.

> intended and meant. They use as proof this statement of Anas ibn Mālik. But this argument is an empty claim that should not be relied upon, nor should the one making it be paid any attention. For if one were to recite according to words that differ with the wording of the Qur'ān as long as they approximate its meaning and general intent, it would be permissible to recite in place of "*al-ḥamdu lillāhi rabbi al-ʿālamīn*" the phrase "*al-shukru lil-bārī malik al-makhlūqīn*." And the flexibility in this regard would continue to increase *until the entire wording of the Qur'ān would be nullified and replaced with that which would be a fabrication upon God and a lie upon His Messenger.*

This objection can easily be responded to by pointing out that this 'floodgate argument' did not happen, and would never have happened, for the simple reason that *qirāʾah bi-l-maʿnā* was always a concession, and the default was following the maxim, "Recitation is based on customary precedent." In other words, no reputable scholar ever preached an open license to this concession, nor was it ever taught as a default. The customary practice since the very announcement of this concession during the Prophetic lifetime was to mandate adherence to precedence – this is why ʿUmar objected to Hishām's lapses! No Companion taught the concession of *qirāʾah bi-l-maʿnā* as a rule such that their students could make up their own words; rather, most variations occurred as an unintended manifestation of tribal Arabic dialects and regional pronunciations. Since this concession was always restricted and never taught, there was never an open license to intentionally substitute Qur'ānic words for others - especially after the ʿUthmānic codification project. Al-Ṭaḥāwī explicitly says this concession was only allowed for the Companions and that ʿUthmān sealed this door, and ibn Qutaybah, writing a century before ibn al-Anbārī, commented that this concession was only allowed for the first generation and a handful of reciters after them. As for later generations, he categorically stated that this concession no longer applied and there was no choice but to stick with the recitations of those in the past.[73] A further interesting point here is that the very fact that ibn al-Anbārī is refuting the notion of *qirā'ah bi-l-ma'nā* indicates that the idea was still around even in the fourth Islamic century such that it deserved an explicit refutation. This quote actually demonstrates the existence of an opinion that many modern researchers deny ever existed (*viz.*, the first objection).

The *fourth objection* is that this opinion is claimed to be an aberrant one, even if it is narrated by a handful of individuals. Hence, it is rejected (*'munkar'*), or singular (*'shādh'*), and not mainstream (*'mashhūr'*). In other words, the iconic figures of this field (i.e., the '*muḥaqqiqīn*'), like al-Dānī, ibn al-Jazarī, and others, clearly did not hold these views. Hence, an *appeal to authority* is made both in terms of status and quantity. A response to this is once again straightforward. The claim that proponents of the Divine Permission model make is that a shift occurred regarding the reality of the *aḥruf* and *qirā'āt* precisely *because* of the likes of al-Dānī, ibn al-Jazarī and others, and a position that would supplant the earlier one to become the new normative was championed by these later authorities. After the mainstreaming of the Dictation Model, it effectively became almost heretical to challenge it (Ibn Mujāhid's involvement of the state authorities was most definitely a catalyst in this regard). Hence, there is an obvious circularity in defining 'orthodoxy' based on the views of scholars who are considered iconic when we consider those very people as authorities and the icons of the field because they defined orthodoxy. Furthermore, all these icons lived in the fifth Islamic century and beyond: it does seem telling that one finds explicit quotations amongst earlier scholars that would seem to contradict their later views. In fact, the very title of the book

73 See Ibn Qutaybah's quotation in the previous section of this article.

on this issue by the modern author Ṣāliḥ al-Rajḥī is an explicit response to this objection: "*The fundamental principles that later reciters opposed the unanimous consensus of the earlier reciters (al-Masā'il al-kubrā allatī khālafa fīhā qurrā' al-muta'akhirūn ijmā' al-mutaqaddimīn min al-qurrā').*" For al-Rajḥī, this is no 'minority' opinion, it is the *default unanimous consensus* of the first generation of reciters! Or to phrase it differently, the Divine Permission model was the only opinion that the Companions and first generation of reciters even knew; over time the Dictation Model gained more currency until it became established orthodoxy. Lastly, and on this point, it is important to underscore the universal principle that operates both within the Islamic paradigm and outside of it: the validity of any opinion is not based on the fame of the people who say it, but rather on its evidence and its conforming to known facts.

The *fifth and final objection* is the claim that this opinion seems to contradict the Divine promise to protect the Qur'ān, and potentially destroys the miraculous nature (*i'jāz*) of the Qur'ān that is present in its syntax, style, and eloquence. Some might add to this point the claim that such an opinion also clashes with the belief that each and every word of the Qur'ān was recited by Allah to Jibrīl in the exact form found in the *qirā'āt*, which of course is the theological belief inherent in the 'Divine Dictation' model. This is an interesting point and was picked up by early authorities. For example, the Andalusian exegete ibn 'Aṭiyya (d. 468 AH/1075 CE), after quoting an example of Anas ibn Mālik's usage of synonyms while reciting, commented:[74]

> And this is how we must understand the narration of Anas [when he recited] *wa aṣwab qīla*: that this recitation is narrated from the Prophet. Otherwise, if it were allowed for anyone else to derive it, *the meaning of 'We have revealed this*

74 Ibn 'Aṭiyya, *al-Muḥarrar al-Wajīz*, vol. 1, p. 176. Emphasis mine.

> *Reminder, and We shall preserve it [15:9]' would be null and void (bāṭil).*

The earlier quote of ibn al-Anbārī also alludes to this objection. In both of these quotes, scholars objected to the opinion of *qirā'ah bi-l-ma'nā* precisely *because* it appears to clash with the Divine protection of the Qur'ān and its miraculous nature. At face value, this objection does appear quite incriminating, and this author was not able to find a detailed defence by those who subscribe to the Divine Permission model in countering this objection. Nonetheless, some points may be made. As a preliminary, it must be pointed out that these same authorities who championed the Divine Permission model clearly also believed in the Divine protection of the Qur'ān and its inimitable nature. Hence, in their minds, there was no inherent clash between the *qirā'ah bi-l-ma'nā* and the protection or miracle of the Qur'ān.

It can also be said that the 'Uthmānic compilation is the result of Allah's preservation and, as the original revealed *ḥarf*, is inherently inimitable by nature. The extremely miniscule variations within the established *qirā'āt*, especially when one compares those differences to the known pre-'Uthmānic ones, do not impact either the claim of preservation or the miraculous nature of the Qur'ān. Ibn Taymiyya himself claimed that many differences within the *qirā'āt* emanate from the differences of pronunciations between different speakers of Arabic, and that this was allowed by Allah.[75] The last part of the objection – that every letter was

75 See *Majmū' al-Fatāwā*, vol. 13, p. 399. Note that ibn Taymiyyah was not advocating for *qirā'ah bi-l-ma'nā* (he clearly did not subscribe to that opinion). This quote is in the context of explaining why words are pronounced differently in the established recitations. The point being made here is that ibn Taymiyyah, whose theology about the Qur'ān is known, did not consider the variations between the *qirā'āt* that originated from the first generations to clash with the notion of Divine Protection or inimitability or the Ḥanbalite belief of *kalām Allah* and that every word was recited verbatim by the Divine.

recited as is by the Divine to Jibrīl and then to the Prophet – can be deflected by emphasising that such a specific belief is not the mainstream belief of the broader Muslim community, but rather only the belief of the Ḥanbalite strand. No other theological school, from within or outside Sunnism, holds this doctrine as creed except for the Ḥanbalite school, hence this issue would only be of concern to them.[76] Furthermore, even the eponymous founder of that very school seems to have understood that the *qirā'āt* prevalent in his time were not the exact same as the Divine Speech (as referenced with his stance towards the recitation of Ḥamza); hence even ibn Ḥanbal's theological opinion itself needs to be understood in light of his own stance towards the *qirā'āt*.

To conclude, while the proponents of the Dictation Model view the Divine Permission model as a threat to the inimitability and preservation of Qur'ān, those who championed the Divine Permission model themselves clearly held no such beliefs, and also affirmed both the inimitability and the preservation of Qur'ān.

The Alternative Model's Answers to the Fifteen Questions

Now that the alternative opinion has been presented, and various objections responded to, let us return to the fifteen questions that were raised and see whether the responses to them based on this model are more *reasonable* and *plausible*, with no great stretch (or '*takalluf*') required. We shall respond to all the previous questions, Q1 – Q15, with answers A1 – A15.

---

76 For an exposition, and defence, of that school's position, the reader is referred to what this author himself wrote, in a younger phase of his life, in his work *An Introduction to the Sciences of the Qur'ān*, pp. 35-56.

The explicit *raison d'être* (*ʿillah*) of the *aḥruf* (A1) is obviously and clearly answered in this model, for the whole point of *qirāʾah bi-l-maʿnā* is that it allows the very old, the illiterate, and the uneducated, to recite to the best of their memory, forgiving any unintentional lapses. No other opinion regarding the reality of the *aḥruf* can explain this plainly stated Prophetic *ʿillah* more obviously than the Divine Permission model. Of course, the necessary condition would be that (A2) the appropriate meaning is conveyed; hence saying '[Allah is] Hearing and Seeing' instead of '[Allah is] Majestic and Powerful' would be such an example if the context of the verse allowed it. This also explains (A3) that various Companions chose certain words as synonyms, especially (but not exclusively) those who belonged to non-Qur'āyshī tribes like Ubayy ibn Kaʿb (who was from the Banū Khazraj) or ibn Masʿūd (who was from the tribe of Hudhayl); and these word choices (*viz.*, their unique *ḥarf*) were ascribed to them. Hence, only they and their students were known to recite with those choices, and other senior Companions would have no cause to recite the word choices of other Companions. At times, such as the case of ʿUmar ibn al-Khaṭṭāb and Hishām ibn Ḥakīm, (A4) the word variation might be due to a memory lapse, especially as Hishām was a new convert. There was no private lesson that Hishām was given to the exclusion of other senior Companions – hence why when he said, 'This is how the Prophet taught me,' the response was not a confirmation, 'Yes, I taught you these words,' but rather, 'It came down in this manner, for the Qur'ān was revealed in *sabʿa aḥruf*,' meaning in effect: 'Your recitation is also approved by Allah and is to be considered Qur'ān, because Allah allowed the Qur'ān to be recited in several wordings.'[77]

---

77 Note here that a fundamental difference in understanding between the Dictation Model and the Divine Permission model exists regarding the Prophet's response to both of them: '*hākadhā unzilat*.' For those who subscribe to the Dictation Model, this phrase would effectively translate as, 'Yes, Hishām and ʿUmār, you are both correct in that I taught you these exact

'Umar's surprise at learning of the existence of the *aḥruf* (A5) demonstrates that since it was a concession, the Prophet never actively encouraged the Muslims to exercise it, as the default was to conform to the original. Its allowance in the late Madinan period (A6) is understandable since it was at that time that more and more people of different tribes and backgrounds embraced Islam, and the quantity of believers increased exponentially. Hence, the Prophet was gifted the concession of the *aḥruf* when it was needed by the community, and there was no need for it in early Makkah. Since this concession was given to the laity of believers, there was no need to re-reveal all the verses that had been sent before this concession. This also explains why (A7) the Prophet himself never recited the same verse in different manners.

During the first two decades, as literacy increased and the Muslim empire expanded, the various *aḥruf* that were recited by the Companions became regional (depending on where the Companions or senior students of those Companions lived). New converts were typically unaware of the concession of the *aḥruf*, as this concession had never actively been propagated, hence the variant readings led to confusion and argument. Since the concession was no longer needed, (A8) 'Uthmān and the Companions agreed to preserve the original wordings of the Revelation, which also had the unique characteristic of being in the dialect of the Qur'āysh, and they agreed to (A9) discard all the variations that were allowed but did not have the sanctity of the original. There was no need to justify excluding the other *aḥruf* when the explicit goal and conditions of the committee were to meticulously preserve the wordings recited directly by the Prophet himself. In other words, why preserve the choices (*ḥarf*) of Ubayy or ibn Mas'ud (which were valid and allowed at their

---

wordings as you recall them.' In contrast, those who subscribe to the Divine Permission model would effectively translate this phrase as, 'Allah has sent down permission for both of your recitations to be considered valid.'

times) when they now had the capability of codifying the wordings of the Prophet himself? The 'Uthmānic project was successful in preserving the original *ḥarf* in which the Qur'ān was revealed. There would, however, be some minor caveats. (A10) Arabic, as is the case with any language, has a vast diversity of pronunciations and accents within its many tribal dialects and regional populations, and it is not humanly conceivable, nor even religiously required, to unify the enunciation of every minute vowel or letter. The rules of *tajwīd* and the differences between the specific rules of *ghunnah*, *imālah*, *idhghām*, and other specific issues are examples of this phenomena. As well, the script that was available at the time allowed for a multiplicity of readings of a given skeleton of a word, and (A11) the insignificant variations between the manuscripts contain no substantial differences and are divinely sanctioned by the concession of the *aḥruf*. The unification project of 'Uthmān was completely successful. It is conceivable that 'Uthmān aimed to eliminate the concession of the *aḥruf* in totality, yet still the concession was manifested in a narrow spectrum: in pronunciations of vowels and syllables, and word-variations that all conformed to the 'Uthmānic script, and the word differences between the four codices.

It was in this minuscule window that Qur'ān reciters and grammarians dedicated their energies to, and so (A12) for the first two centuries of Islam, much effort was expended in perfecting the art of recitation and codifying every single word, accent, and even pause. The default of precedence in recitation (*al-ittibāʿ*) was always maintained, but on relatively few occasions and for a small percentage of words, reciters differed over the specific vocalizations of the 'Uthmānic script, and in applying competing rules of the Arabic language as demonstrated by tribal dialects and recognized poetry. In these instances where reciters chose specific recitations, as long as general conditions were met, all recitations were accepted, but (A13) on rare occasions, there was debate and controversy. At times, some choices (*ikhtiyār*) of the reciters were deemed against the acceptable norms of Arabic, or as being not eloquent enough for the Qur'ān. Hence why great giants like al-Ṭabarī and a host of others of that era, fully aware of the reality of *qirā'āt*, felt no qualms in discrediting specific recitations from otherwise acceptable reciters. This continued back and forth between various authorities until the canonisation project of ibn Mujāhid and its eventual closure by ibn al-Jazarī. Concomitant to this project was also the effort of some (A14) to see if one could find ḥadīths that demonstrated the original way in which the Prophet might have recited a word, while acknowledging in light of the concession of *aḥruf* that alternatives were equally valid if the right conditions were met. Hence, even some of the scholars who compiled these very ḥadīth might themselves choose other recitations, since this concession allowed for these variant recitations.

This interpretation of the *aḥruf* (A15) explains these contentious issues and demonstrates the reality of the *qirā'āt* as being an extension of them, in a more obvious manner, without the need for unreasonable assumptions or interpretations. Furthermore, this is not some new or unprecedented opinion – one finds it in the earliest of explanations and explicitly quoted and championed by many early icons of this field, and throughout all eras of Islamic thought.[78] In fact, it can be said that one finds *only*

78 With respect to the three additional issues referenced in an earlier footnote: 1) all of the examples of the so-called '*qirā'āt tafsīrīyyah*' (and they are in the hundreds) are direct and explicit evidence of the entire 'Divine Permission' model; 2) the enforcement of the 'Uthmānic canon took some time, and hence in early Islam, especially in some regions far from the center of the Caliphate, some readings that existed before the canonisation project continued to be recited for a century or so, and the *qirā'āt shādhah* are the most famous examples of this; 3) the Divine Permission model permits such views from qualified experts like those senior Companions whose direct memory of the Prophetic recitation is a valid *ijtihād* against another Companion's memory, or even the committee convened by 'Uthmān, as the goal was always to revert to the original wording.

this opinion in the earliest of quotations and references of this field. All that one needs to do is to let the explicit quotations and evidence speak for themselves, rather than attempting to force a later perspective onto each and every point that appears to contradict it. Such an attempt to coerce the modern standard narrative onto the earlier data seems to inevitably leave more gaps than answered questions.

Ṣāliḥ al-Rājḥī writes, summarising the fundamental difference between the Dictation Model and the Divine Permission Model: [79]

> At the heart of all the aforementioned contentions is a premise upon which later reciters have based their opinion and methodology about the *qirā'āt*. It is a premise that is not supported by any evidence; rather, all evidence is contrary to it. That is why this premise was unheard of from the predecessors in general or the early reciters themselves, like the [canonical] ten reciters and others. This premise is the claim that all the aḥruf and *qirā'āt* are revealed: Jibrīl revealed it to the Prophet and taught it to him, and the Prophet in turn taught it to the Companions. Once this premise is accepted, you will find that the aforementioned contentions will take root and they will be a necessary outcome of that erroneous contrary position. *The truth of the matter is that Jibrīl only descended with one ḥarf and one qirā'ah. The remaining aḥruf and qirā'āt were only a concession from Allah.* Whatever amongst these are authentic such as the Ten [*qirā'āt*] enjoy the divine status of the Qur'ān since it was Allah Who intended that it be read as such.

79 Al-Rajḥī, *Masā'il al-Kubrā*, p. 460.

Conclusion

This article presented a model regarding the conception of the *aḥruf* and its relationship with the *qirā'āt* that is currently regarded as a minority one but has in recent times gained more traction. From the perspective of those who subscribe to the Divine Permission model, this understanding seems to be grounded in factual reality rather than simplistic, unfounded theological maxims, and was perhaps the default understanding of all earlier scholars, only becoming a minority opinion after the fifth century of Islamic history.

The Divine Permission model is straightforward. The meaning of the Qur'ān having been revealed in 'seven *aḥruf*' is that permission was given to a generation that could not read and write to recite it in 'several wordings' as long as the meaning was conveyed accurately. This concession was never actively taught nor propagated, since, as the default, one was expected to conform with precedence and transmit the original wording as faithfully as possible. Within half a generation, when both the level of literacy and the power of the government allowed for it, the Caliph 'Uthmān wished to eradicate this concession and preserve the original wordings revealed to the Prophet. Hence, his official recension did exactly that: it discarded all the variations that emanated from the other Companions and preserved the wordings recited by Jibrīl to the Prophet. Due to the reality of the dialects of the Arabic language, the deficiencies of the script at the time, and the variations between the 'Uthmānic codices, minute variations and differences in pronunciations remained for another two centuries: this was the era of the flourishing of the science of *qirā'āt*. All these minute variations were permitted by the Divine Permission of the *aḥruf*, hence the *qirā'āt* emanate from the same concept as that of *aḥruf*, the only difference being that the *qirā'āt* are far more restricted, based on the 'Uthmanic recension and precedents to the era of the first generations. One could also say that the *qirā'āt* are the codifications of the concession of the *aḥruf* as filtered through the skeletal *rasm* of the recensions of 'Uthmān (or, the *qirā'āt* are minute examples of the *aḥruf* concession applied upon the original *ḥarf* that 'Uthmān preserved). With the codification projects of ibn Mujāhid (and later ibn al-Jazarī), the flourishing of the era of *qirā'āt* came to an end, and the designation of the 'seven' and 'ten' with their strands ('*ṭuruq*') and sub-strands ('*awjuh*') acquired an acceptance within the Ummah. All these *qirā'āt* are equally Divine (based on the *mutawātir* ḥadīths of the *aḥruf* which state that '...*all of them are complete and whole*'), and all have the status of the Qur'ān, especially in light the community's agreement (*ijmā'*) about them. The concession of *qirā'ah bi-l-ma'nā* has been effectively sealed shut and made null and void by the unanimous consensus of the Companions and all later scholars, and with the closure of the door of *qirā'āt* by the codification projects of ibn Mujāhid and ibn al-Jazarī. As can be seen, this model reasonably solves all major areas of confusion with respect to the discussion of *aḥruf* and *qirā'āt*, with minimal conjectures and no imaginative assumptions. While this view does potentially solve many, or perhaps all, of the thorny questions that this much-debated topic raises, it simultaneously poses a smaller set of new questions as well.

Some further areas of study that would complement this topic should be mentioned.[80] Firstly, a thorough analysis of how

80 The author of this article reiterates: this topic is worthy of a much more detailed monograph, and an introductory article such as this can only present so much. There are obviously many other issues, topics, arguments and counter-arguments that need to be addressed, along with a detailed study of more reports and their *isnads*. It is hoped that others continue this conversation in the proper spirit of scholarly debate and with the sincere desire to contribute to Islamic knowledge. The author also wishes to state that while he is clearly sympathetic to the Divine Permission model, in the end ultimate truth lies with Allah, and these models are merely for academic discussions and do not and should not affect the basic belief of the Muslims in the Qur'ān being the protected and final Divine Revelation.

widespread this view was throughout the centuries, and how the earlier views were slowly supplanted by later views to redefine 'orthodoxy', is warranted. In other words, it is a worthy study to document the historical shift from the Divine Permission model to the Dictation Model. Such an analysis will go a long way in supporting the claim of those who champion this opinion as having been mainstream in early Islam. Secondly, a study of the development of the *qirā'āt*, and the linguistic and grammatical choices that some reciters made (including the non-canonical ones), in particular unique recitations, along with the acceptance or rejection of various reciters and their choices, would be a very welcome addition to this topic. While many studies have been conducted, almost all of them take the Dictation Model as the default, and hence spend much energy trying to reinterpret the data to fit their model. It would be a welcome addition for researchers to demonstrate how such choices were made and how simply and directly they support the Divine Permission model. Thirdly, a systematic and thorough extrapolation of how the *qirā'āh bi-l-ma'nā* paradigm is fully compatible with the normative belief in the preservation of the Qur'ān and its *'i'jāz* still requires further study.

Bibliography

al-'Arabī, Abū Bakr Ibn. *Al-'Awāṣim min al-Qawāṣim.* Edited by Ammār Ṭālibī. Cairo: Maktabah Dār al-Turāth, 1974.

al-Bāqillānī. *Al-Intiṣār lil Qur'ān.* Vol. 1. Beirut: Dar Ibn Ḥazm, 2001.

al-Baghdādī, Al-Khaṭīb. *Al-Kifāya fī 'Ilm al-Riwāya.* Hyderabad: Da'irah al-Ma'arif al-Uthamniyya, 1938.

al-Barr, Ibn 'Abd. *Kitāb al-Tamhīd li-Mā fī l-Muwaṭṭa' Min al-Ma'ānī wa-al-Asānīd.* Vol. 5. Morocco: Ministry of Islamic Affiars, 1967.

al-Bayhaqī. *Al-Madkhal ilā 'Ilm al-Sunan.* Beirtut: Dar al-Yusr, 2017.

al-Dānī. *Jāmi' al-Bayān.* UAE: Dar al-Shariqah, 2007.

—. *Kitāb Al-Aḥruf al-Sab'a.* Makkah: Matkatab al-Manarah, 1988.

al-Dūrī, Ḥafs Ibn 'Umar. *Juz fīhī Qirā'āt al-Nabī.* Edited by Ḥikmat Bashīr Yasīn. Madinah: Maktabah al-Dār, 1988.

al-Dhahabī. *Siyar A'lām al-Nubalā'.* Beirut: Mu'asasah al-Risalah, 1985.

al-Farāyah, Niḍāl. *Al-Qirā'āt al-Qur'āniyyah fi Kitāb al-Kashshāf li-l-Zamakhsharī.* Mu'tah University, Jordan, PhD Dissertation, 2006.

al-Ḥākim. *Al-Mustadrak.* Vol. 4. Beirut: Dar al-Ma'rifah (1989)

al-Ḥamad, Ghānim Qaddūrī. *Liqā Ma'a Shabakat al-Tafsīr.* www.tafsir.net (accessed July 2023).

al-Ḥārithī, Salwā. "Al-Qirā'āt 'alā Sab'at Aḥruf Bayn al-Ijtihād wa-l-Tawqif." *Majallat Kulliyat al-Dirāsāt al-Islāmiyya wa-l-'Arabiyya* 35, no. 5 (2020): 99-158.

al-Isfahani, Abu Nu'aym. *Ḥilyat al-Awliyā'.* Vol. 8. Beirut: Maktabah al-Khanji, 1996.

al-Jaṣṣās, Abū Bakr. *Aḥkām al-Qur'an.* Vol. 5. Beirut: Dar Ihya al-Turath, 1985.

al-Jahḍamī. *Kitāb Aḥkām al-Qur'an.* Beirut, Dar Hazm, 2005.

al-Jazarī, Ibn. *Al-Nashr fī al-Qirā'āt al-'Ashr.* Vol. 1. Beirut, Dar al-Kutub al-Ilmiyya, 1988.

al-Juday', Abdullah Ibn Yūsuf. *Al-Muqaddimāt al-Asāsiyyah fī 'Ulūm al-Qur'ān* . Beirut: Mu'sāsdah al-Rayāt, 2001.

al-Kulaynī. *Usul al-Kāfī.* Vol. 1. Tehran: Maktabat al-Saduq, 1962.

al-Maqdisī, Abū Shāmah. *Al-Murshid al-Wajīz.* Beirut: Dār al-Ṣādir, 1975.

al-Mu'allimī, 'Abd al-Raḥmān b. Yaḥya. *Al-Anwār al-Kāshifah.* Beirut: 'Alam al-Kutub, 1983.

al-Nūrī, 'Alī. "Al-Ṣaḥāba wa-l-Qirā'āh bi-l-Ma'nā." *Majallah Kuliyya al-Da'wa al-Islāmiyya* 11 (1994): 9-23.

al-Qari, 'Abd al-ʿAzīz. *Ḥadith al-Aḥruf al-Sabʿa.* Beirut: Mu'asah al-Risālah, 2002.

al-Qurṭubī. *Al-Jāmiʿ li Aḥkām al-Qur'ān.* Vol. 19. Beirut: Dār al-Kitāb al-ʿArabī, 1997.

al-Rājḥī, Ṣaliḥ b. Sulaymān. *Al-Masāʾil al-Kubrā allatī Khālafa fīhā Qurrā' al-Mutàakhirūn Ijmāʿ al-Mutaqaddimīn min al-Qurrāʾ.* Riyadh: Dar al-Ṣumayʿī, 2021.

al-Samarqandī. *Bustān al-ʿĀrifīn.* Beirut: Mu'asasah al-Kutub al-Thaqafiyya, 1993.

al-Shāfiʿī. *Al-Risālah.* Cairo :Mustafa Babi al-Halabi, 1938.

al-Shaybānī, Muhammad. *Kitāb al-Athār.* Beirut, Dar al-Kutub al-Ilmiyyah, 1993.

al-Shiblī, 'Adawiyya Ḥayāwī. "Al-Qirā'āt al-Qur'āniyyah Bayn al-Tawātur wa-l-Ijtihād." *Majallat al-Qādisiyyah fī al-Adāb* 8, no. 3 (2009).

al-Suyūṭī. *Al-Itqān fī ʿUlūm al-Qur'ān.* Beirut: Dar al-Ma'rifah, 1985.

al-Ṭaḥāwī. *Sharḥ Mushkil al-Athār.* Vol. 8. Beirut: al-Risalah al-Ilmiyyah, 2019.

al-Zarkashī. *Al-Burhān fī ʿUlūm al-Qur'ān.* Vol. 1. Beirut: Al-Maktaba al-Usayriyyah, 1979.

al-Zurqānī, Muḥammad 'Abd al-Adhīm. *Manāhil al-ʿIrfān fī ʿUlūm al-Qur'ān.* Vol. 1. Makkah: Dār al-Bāz, 1996.

'Awānah, Abū. *Kitāb Al-Mustakhraj.* Madinah: The Islamic University, 2014.

Cook, Michael. "The Stemma of the Regional Codices of the Koran." *Graeco-Arabica* 9-10 (2004).

Dutton, Yasin. "Orality, Literacy and the 'Seven Aḥruf Hadith'." *Journal of Islamic Studies* 23, no. 1 (2012): 1-49.

Ibn 'Aṭiyya. *Al-Muḥarrar al-Wajīz.* Vol. 1. Beirut: Dar al-Kutub al-Ilmiyyah, 1422.

Ibn Ḥajar. *Fatḥ al-Bārī.* Vol. 9. Cairo: al-Maktabah al-Salafiyyah, 1988.

Ibn Kathīr. *Faḍāʾil al-Qur'ān.* Cairo: Maktabah Ibn Taymiyya, 1996.

Ibn Qutayba. *Ta'wīl Mushkil al-Qur'ān.* Bierut: Al-Maktabah al-Ilmiyyah, n.d.

Ibn Jinnī. *Kitaāb al-Muḥtasab.* (no city) Dar Sezgin, 1986

Ibn Khālawayh, al-Ḥusayn ibn Aḥmad. *Kitāb 'Irāb al-Qirā'āt al-Sab'a wa 'Ilalihā.* Edited by 'Abd al-Raḥman al-'Uthaymīn. Cairo: Maktabat al-Khānjī, 1992.

Ibn Manṣūr, Sa'īd. *Sunan.* Vol. 7. Riyadh: Dār al-Ulūkah, 2012.

Ibn Sallām, Al-Qāsim. *Faḍā'il al-Qur'ān.* Damascus: Dar Ibn Kathir, 1985.

Ibn Taymiyyah. *Majmū' al-Fatāwā.* Vol. 13. Medinah: King Fahad Printing Press, 2004.

Ibn Wahb. *Tafsīr.* Vol. 3. Morocco: Dar al-Gharb al-Islami, 2003

Jabal, Muḥammad. *Al-Qaḍiyya al-Qur'āniyya al-Kubrā: Ḥadīth Nuzūl al-Qur'ān 'alā Sab'ah Aḥruf.* Cairo: Maktabah al-Adāb, 2014.

Melchert, Christopher. "Ibn Mujāhid and the Establishment of Seven Qur'ānic Readings." *Studia Islamica* 91 (2000): 5-22.

Moqbel, Tarek. "The Emergence of the Qirā'āt: The Divine Permission Hypothesis." *Journal of Islamic Studies* 33, no. 3 (2022): 299-330.

Qadhi, Yasir. *An Introduction to the Sciences of the Qur'ān.* Birmingham: Al-Hidaayah Publishing, 1999.

Ibn Shabbah, Umar. *Tarīkh al-Madīnah.* Vol. 3. Beirut: Dar al-Kutub al-Ilmiyyah, 1996.

Shahīn, 'Abd al-Ṣabūr. *Tarīkh al-Qur'ān.* Cairo: Maṭba'ah al-Sa'ādah, 1995.

Sidky, Hythem. "On the Regionality of the Qur'ānic Codices." *Journal of the International Qur'ānic Studies Association* 5, no. 1 (2020): 133-210.

Vahidnia, Ala. "Whence Come Qur'ān Manuscripts? Determining the Regional Provenance of Early Qur'ānic Codices." *Der Islam* 98, no. 2 (2021): 359-393.

Ya'lā, Ibn Abī. *Ṭabaqāt al-Ḥanābilah.* Vol. 1. Riyad: Ministry of Islamic Affairs, 1999.

'Ubayd, Abū. *Faḍā'il al-Qur'ān.* Beirut: Dar Ibn Kathir, 1999.

CHAPTER NINE

The Multifaceted Sanad Traditions of Extra-Muṣḥaf Qur'ānic Transmission

Khairil Husaini Bin Jamil

If one looks at the present Qur'ān in the form of a complete *muṣḥaf*, one may wonder how this *muṣḥaf* was conveyed or originated. Was the entire *muṣḥaf* conveyed as a whole, in chapters, or in verses, either in groups or in pieces? When one attempts to consult the academic study of the Qur'ān, one will encounter a plethora of literature on the history of the complete Qur'ān, i.e., the history of its compilation, particularly during the formative period, the study of *muṣḥaf* and Qur'ānic palaeography, the study of *tawātur* (widely translated as mass transmission) as the authoritative transmitting mechanism attached to Qur'ānic historicity, and the study of variant readings, particularly in relation to their connection to the integrity of the Qur'ānic texts.[1] The present study takes a different approach. It investigates the presence of Qur'ānic verses in circumstances and ultimately literary works unrelated to the aforementioned discourses. In general, it investigates the transmission of the Qur'ān not as a complete

1 See: 'Abd al-Fattāḥ al-Qāḍī, *Tārīkh Al-Muṣḥaf al-Sharīf* (Cairo: Maktabah al-Jundī, 1952); See particularly the chapter on 'Western Scholarship and the Early History of the Qur'ān: A Short History of Qur'ānic Studies in the West' in Seyfeddin Kara, 'In Search of 'Alī ibn Abī Ṭālib's Codex: Study of the Traditions on the Earliest Copy of the Qur'ān' (Doctoral Dissertation, Durham, University of Durham, 2014).

muṣḥaf, but as individual verses that are randomly repeated, practised, discussed, and/or transmitted for everyday rituals, religious and literary works, positive laws, etc. The purpose of the study is, therefore, not to investigate the veracity of the verses, but rather to highlight the silent transmission of Qur'ānic verses beyond the normative discussion of *muṣḥaf* and *tawātur*.[2] Furthermore, it has been observed that the Qur'ānic verses were imparted not only by Qur'ānic reciters and scholars, but also by jurists in their legal manuals, hadith scholars in chapters of their compendia, Sufis in their practises and epistles, theologians in their works and *summae*, and so on.[3] This approach may aid readers in observing the various living traditions associated with the Qur'ān and its texts. In terms of the academic endeavour, it is anticipated that advancing this thesis will shed light on the historical study of the multitudinous *sanad*s involved in the transmission of the aforementioned subjects, offering significant insights into the various networks and transmission mechanisms that have moulded the Qur'ānic heritage.

2 On the concept of *tawātur*, see: Suhail Ismail Laher, 'Twisted Threads: Genesis, Development, and Application of the Term and Concept of Tawatur in Islamic Thought' (Doctoral Dissertation, Harvard, Harvard University, 2014); and Khairil Husaini Bin Jamil, 'Traditional Sunnī Epistemology in the Scholarship of Al-Ḥāfiẓ al-Khaṭīb al-Baghdādī (463AH/1071CE)' (Doctoral Thesis, London, SOAS University of London, 2017); A critical position can be observed in: Shady Hekmat Nasser, *The Transmission of the Variant Readings of the Qur'ān: The Problem of Tawātur and the Emergence of Shawādhdh* (London: Brill, 2012).

3 'The very meaning of the word *summa* describes the goal of most encyclopaedias: it is a summation of knowledge presenting a particular view of the world both comprehensively and systematically. It is simultaneously an index of accumulated knowledge and a model that proposes a method for the organization of this knowledge.' See: Anna Sigrídur Arnar, *Encyclopedism from Pliny to Borges* (Chicago: University of Chicago Library, 1990), 1; Also: Mary Franklin-Brown, *Reading the World: Encyclopedic Writing in the Scholastic Age* (Chicago and London: The University of Chicago Press, 2012).

The Qur'ān's Self-Reference as a Complete Single or Piecemeal Revelation

Relying on the Qur'ān itself to answer questions about its own transmission may seem peculiar for sceptics, as it may give rise to the problem of circular reasoning, also known as *petitio principii*, in which the assertion is validated by reference to the Qur'ān itself, i.e., "it is such because the Qur'ān said so", thereby presenting self-proving evidence. Nevertheless, it is important to note that the Qur'ān has already implied that all forms of proof, including empirical evidence, are always subject to dispute. Verse 7 of al-Anʿām translates as follows, "Even if We had sent down to you [Prophet] a book inscribed on parchment, and they had touched it with their own hands, the disbelievers would still say, 'This is nothing but blatant sorcery' [Qur'ān 6:7]." After a number of verses, God tells the Prophet, "Say, 'Travel throughout the earth and see what fate befell those who rejected the truth.' Say, 'To whom belongs all that is in the heavens and earth?' Say, 'To God. He has taken it upon Himself to be merciful. He will certainly gather you on the Day of Resurrection, which is beyond all doubt [Qur'ān 6:11-12]."

These passages posit the possibility of discovering truth by accumulating corroborating evidence from accessible worldly experiences, from traversing the earth. It makes the case for the accumulation of piecemeal evidence and the epistemic possibilities they afford, especially when they are assured to be collectively free of conflict and contradiction. Therefore, it is not unexpected that Muslim scholars who draw upon the Qur'ān as their argument will reference the verse of al-Nisā' that says, "Will they not think about this Qur'ān? If it had been from anyone other than God, they would have found much inconsistency in it [Qur'ān 4: 82]." Analogously, if statisticians, when studying a specific population, contend that random sampling can provide unbiased estimates of population parameters, reduce bias and variance, and facilitate generalisation of results to the larger population;[4] the revelation of the Qur'ānic verses in a dispersed manner over a period of more than twenty years, involving random events and participants, is viewed as evidence for its divine origin, given the consistency of these verses and the underlying philosophy of induction out of randomness. This may be termed as the coherency argument.

Muslim scholars, from another point of view, would emphasise the significance of piecemeal revelations for a variety of reasons, including the gradual transformation of society, pedagogical purposes, and the sake of memorising and preservation. Verse 32 of al-Furqān is frequently referenced to explain this mode of revelation: "The disbelievers also say, 'Why was the Qur'ān not sent down to him all at once?' We sent it in this way to strengthen your heart [Prophet]; We gave it to you in gradual revelation [Qur'ān 25: 32]." The verse has been subject to extensive analysis within the exegetical tradition. Of particular interest here is the interpretation of this verse as an argument supporting the epistemic credibility of random piecemeal transmissions.

However, an inquiry emerges at this juncture - while it is well-established that each verse or group of verses were taught to the Companions of the Prophet upon revelation, a pertinent question arises: were these verses individually transmitted to subsequent generations through mass transmission, referred to later as *mutawātir*? The accounts of the official compilations by the caliphs, Abū Bakr and subsequently 'Uthmān, suggest retrieval from solitary sources. Nevertheless, it is essential to note that Muslim historical reports assert the establishment of *tawātur* for the 'Uthmānī *muṣḥaf*, with every verse of the Qur'ān being attributed with *tawātur* once its Qur'ānicity is established. There is no doubt about this agreement in classical literature as one can

4 Deborah Bennet, 'Defining Randomness', in *Philosophy of Statistics*, ed. Prasanta Bandyopadhyay and Malcolm Forster, 1st ed., vol. 7, Handbook of Philosophy of Science (North Holland: Elsevier, 2011), 633–40.

observe in the massive literature on *muṣḥaf* and variant readings (*qirā'āt*) of the Qur'ān.

To cut it short, as far as the *tawātur* discussion is concerned, the current study can be viewed as a valuable complement to the ongoing academic debate surrounding the Qur'ānic transmission. The above review of the Qur'ānic verses reveals that the Qur'ān itself argues for the acceptance of piecemeal evidence and its cumulative character as a means of establishing the consistency and integrity of the revelation.

Previous Studies on the History of Individual Qur'ānic Verses

As mentioned earlier, a considerable body of literature has emerged concerning the history of Qur'ānic transmission, particularly in relation to *muṣḥaf* studies. One prominent and widely acclaimed work in the Muslim world is *The History of the Qur'ānic Text from Revelation to Compilation: A Comparative Study with the Old and New Testaments*, authored by Muhammad Mustafa al-Azami. As observed from the title too, the work is concerned with the compiled Qur'ān, although the elaboration on the system of *sanad* is offered extensively to substantiate the historical vision adopted by the author. al-Azami presented an analogy where person C relies on eyewitness B to acquire knowledge about an action performed by person A in history, which, according to him, serves as the conceptual foundation for the *isnād* system. Though it may seem peculiar to attribute its origin to the lifetime of the Prophet, given that relying on eyewitness accounts is a universal phenomenon, al-Azami asserts that the *isnād* system developed into a proper science by the conclusion of the first century after Hijrah.[5]

5 Muhammad Mustafa al-Azami, *The History of the Qur'ānic Text from Revelation to Compilation: A Comparative Study with the Old and New Testaments* (Leicester, England: UK Islamic Academy, 2003).

Nonetheless, both *sanad*, which constitutes the chain of eyewitnesses and transmitters relating a particular piece of history, and *isnād*, representing the act of providing such a chain, significantly contribute to the subsequent discourse characterised by the binary classification of *mutawātir* (public knowledge) and *āḥād* (individual reports). The extensive nature of this discussion is apparent. What is most important here is the viewpoint that posits that information acquired through *sanad* is inherently *āḥād*, as *mutawātir*, according to this perspective, does not fall within the category of transmission. Hence, it is imperative to acknowledge and discern all nuances and distinctions associated with the subject of *sanad* in Qur'ānic transmission discussions, as they might serve to establish authenticity or simply to fulfil complementary objectives. Caution must be exercised not to automatically associate the *sanad* of Qur'ānic transmission with the notion that it is exclusively either not *mutawātir* or solely *āḥād*, as it can contain a wide range of possibilities and conditions.

Moving on to the works penned to interpret and elaborate specific verses of the Qur'ān, especially those written in Arabic, I have come across titles of several relevant scholarly works on such exercise. Here is a list of some of these works, preceded by chapter and verse numbers, alongside the respective titles and authors. To provide a full overview, the titles of the works begin with the relevant Arabic alphabet letter and the list covers most of the alphabet. The following are some examples:

1. Qur'ān 1:1 - *al-Ibānah wa al-Tafhīm ʿan maʿānī bism Allāh al-Raḥmān al-Raḥīm* by al-Zajjāj, Ibrāhīm ibn al-Sarī Abū Isḥāq al-Ḥanbalī (311AH/924CE).
2. Qur'ān 1:1 - *Sharḥ bi-ism Allāh al-Raḥmān al-Raḥīm* by al-Farazdaqī, ʿAlī ibn Faḍḍāl al-Mujāshiʿī al-Qayrawānī (479AH/1086CE).
3. Qur'ān 3:96 - *Iḥkām al-Asās fī Qawlihi Taʿālā Inna Awwala Baytin Wuḍiʿa li'l-Nās*, by al-Karmī, Marʿī ibn Yūsuf al-Ḥanbalī (1033AH/1624CE).

4. Qur'ān 13:39 - *Ittiḥāf Dhawī al-Albāb fī Qawlihi Ta'ālā Yamḥu Allāh Mā Yashā' wa Yuthbit wa 'Indahu Umm al-Kitāb*, by al-Karmī, Mar'ī ibn Yūsuf al-Ḥanbalī (1033AH/1624CE).
5. Qur'ān 11: 107 - *al-Istīfā' fī Qawlihi Ta'ālā Illā Mā Shā' Rabbuka*, by Makkī ibn Abī Ṭālib (437AH/1046CE).
6. Qur'ān 40:18 - *al-Iqnā' fī Tafsīr Qawlihi Ta'ālā Mā li'l-Ẓālimīn min Ḥamīmin walā Shafī'in Yuṭā'*, by al-Taqī al-Subkī, 'Alī ibn 'Abd al-Kāfī al-Shāfi'ī (756AH/1355CE).
7. Qur'ān 20:5- *Burhān al-Hudā fī Tafsīr al-Raḥmān 'alā al-'Arsh Istawā*, by al-Būrhanbūrī, Naṣīr al-Dīn 'Ubayd Allāh ibn Jalāl al-Dīn al-Ḥusaynī al-Hindī (1283AH/1866CE).
8. Qur'ān 41:11 - *Tafsīr Āyat al-Dukhān*, by Ibn Sīnā, al-Ḥusayn ibn 'Abd Allāh (428AH/1037CE).
9. Qur'ān 9:108 - *Juz' fī Qawlihi Ta'ālā Lamasjidun Ussisa 'ala al-Taqwā*, by Ibn 'Abd al-Hādī, Muḥammad ibn Aḥmad Abū 'Abd Allāh al-Ḥanbalī.
10. Qur'ān 22:52 - *Khulāṣat al-Bayān fī Dhikr mā Awradahu Mawlānā Ḥasan Afandī Shaykh Ẓādeh min al-Ishkāl fi al-Āyah wa mā Arsalnā min Qablika min Rasūl walā Nabiy*, by al-'Azīzī, Muḥammad ibn Muḥammad al-Shāfi'ī (c.1219AH/1804CE).
11. Qur'ān 96:1 - *Durr al-Tāj wa Insān al-Ḥadaq fīmā Yata 'allaq Iqra' bi-Ismi Rabbika Alladhī Khalaq*, by Abū al-Surūr ibn Aḥmad (possibly Ibn Abī al-Surūr who lived around 1050AH/1640CE).
12. Qur'ān 18:109 - *Risālah fī Tafsīr al-Āyah Qul Law Kāna al-Baḥr Midādā*, by al-Minqārī, Yaḥyā ibn 'Umar al-Rūmī (1088AH/1677CE).
13. Qur'ān 76:1 - *Ẓayn al-Fatā fī Tafsīr Hal Atā*, by al-'Āṣimī, Aḥmad ibn Muḥammad al-Khurāsānī (born 378AH/989CE).

14. Qur'ān 17:1 - *al-Sirr al-Asrā fī Maʿnā Subḥān Alladhi Asrā*, by Ibn ʿAqīlah, Muḥammad ibn Aḥmad al-Ḥanafī al-Makkī (1150AH/1737CE).

15. Qur'ān 6:158 - *Sharḥ Tawḍīḥ Ajwibat al-Qāḍī ʿAbd Allāh ibn ʿUthmān ʿalā Āyat (158) bi al-Anʿām*, by al-Dardīr, Aḥmad ibn Muḥammad al-Mālikī al-ʿAdawī (1201AH/1787CE).

16. Qur'ān 54:49 - *Sharḥ Qawlihi Taʿālā Innā Kulla Shayʾin Khalaqnāhu bi-Qadar,* by Makkī ibn Abī Ṭālib al-Qaysī al-Mālikī (437AH/1046CE).

17. Qur'ān 13:7 - *Ṭuruq Tafsīr Qawl Allāh ʿAzza wa Jalla Innamā Anta Mundhir wa li-Kulli Qawmin Hād*, by ibn ʿUqdah, Aḥmad ibn Muḥammad Abū al-ʿAbbās al-Shīʿī al-Kūfī (332AH/944CE).

18. Qur'ān 31:27 - *Ghāyat al-Ihtimām bi-Tafsīr Qawlihi Taʿālā Walaw Annamā fī al-Arḍ min Shajaratin Aqlām*, by al-Barzanjī, Muḥammad ibn ʿAbd al-Rasūl al-Shāfiʿī al-Ḥasanī (1103AH/1692CE).

19. Qur'ān 16:90 - *Fatḥ al-Raḥīm al-Raḥmān fī Tafsīr Āyat Inna Allāh Yaʾmuru bi al-ʿAdl wa al-Iḥsān*, by al-Khaṭīb al-Sharbīnī, ʿAlī ibn ʿAbd al-Raḥmān Abū al-ḤḤasan al-Shāfiʿī (1028AH/1619CE).

20. Qur'ān 3:8 - *Qatf al-Mustaṭāb Tafsīr al-Āyat Rabbanā lā Tuzigh Qulūbanā baʿda idh Hadaytanā … Innaka Anta al-Wahhāb*, by al-Barallusī, Nūr al-Dīn al-Muftī (possibly Muḥammad ibn ʿAbd al-Raḥmān al-Mālikī al-Barallusī who died in 1010AH/1601CE).

21. Qur'ān 28:85 - *Kitāb fī Inna Alladhī Anzala ʿAlayka al-Qur'ān La-rādduka ilā Maʿād*, by al-ḤḤḤallāj, al-Ḥusayn ibn Manṣūr (309AH/922CE).

22. Qur'ān 93:5 - *al-Mustarḍā fī Tafsīr Qawlihi Taʿālā wa-lasawfa Yuʿṭīka Rabbuka Fatarḍā*, by al-Ṭablāwī, Manṣur Sibṭ Nāṣir al-Dīn al-Shāfiʿī (1014AH/1605CE).

23. Qur'ān 3:144 - *Nukhbat al-Manqūl fī Qawlihi Taʿālā wa mā Muḥammadun illā Rasūl*, by al-Ḥalabī, Khalīl ibn ʿAbd al-Muḥsin (c.1252AH/1836CE).

24. Qur'ān 5:5 - *Hidāyat al-Albāb li-Tafsīr Āyat Wa-Ṭaʿāmu Alladhīn ʾŪtū al-Kitāb*, by al-Qāsimī, Jamāl al-Dīn ibn Muḥammad Saʿīd al-Dimashqī (1332AH/1914CE).
25. Qur'ān 3:55 - *Wabl al-Ghamāmah fi Tafsīr Qawlihi Taʿālā Wa-Jāʿilu Alladhīna Ittabaʿūka Fawqa Alladhīn Kafarū ilā Yawm al-Qiyāmah*, by al-Shawkānī, Muḥammad ibn ʿAlī (1250AH/1834CE).

The existence of a complete corpus dedicated to treating each of the individual verses in the Qur'ān, which exceeds six thousand in number, is currently very unlikely. Some of the titles mentioned above are only known through bibliographical references and have not been preserved in physical form. Others obviously reflect a focus on understanding a specific verse. Notably, the historical transmission of individual verses was not a subject of concern within the classical Muslim discourse, as there existed unanimous agreement on the *tawātur* status of the Qur'ān.

Finally, it is worth noting that when it comes to the *sanad*s associated with the Qur'ān, a considerable body of scholarly research has been dedicated to examining the *sanad*s of *qirāʾāt* (variant readings) and, more recently, the *sanad*s of early generation *tafsīr*s. Illustrative examples of the former include the doctoral thesis titled "*Asānīd al-Qirāʾāt wa Manhaj al-Qurrāʾ fī Dirāsatihā: Dirāsah Naẓariyyah Taṭbīqiyyah (The Sanads of Variant Readings and the Methodology of the Qurrāʾ in Their Studies: A Study on Methodology and Practices)*" advanced by Ahmad ibn Sa'ad al-Mutayri, and the book "*Awḍaḥ al-Dalālāt fī Asānīd al-Qirāʾāt (Clear Evidences for the Chains of Recitation)*," derived from a doctoral thesis composed by Yasir Ibrahim al-Mazru'i. Regarding the *sanad*s associated with early generation exegetical statements, an investigation of notable significance was conducted by Hikmat Bashir Yasin in the introductory section of his *tafsīr* work titled "*al-Ṣaḥīḥ al-Masbūr min al-Tafsīr bi al-Maʾthūr (The Established Sound Reports in Transmission-Based Exegesis).*"

To provide an example, the recitation of verse 3 of *sūrah* al-Kawthar presents variations among reciters. While the majority of reciters read it as "*inna shāniʾaka huwa al-abtar*," Abū Jaʿfar of Madinah reads it as "*inna shāniyaka huwa al-abtar*," replacing the *hamzah* following the *nūn* in "*shāniʾaka*" with a *yāʾ*. The rationale behind this particular variation is not the focus of our current study. What holds significance here is that Abū Jaʿfar acquired the modes of recitation from several Companions, including noteworthy figures such as Abū Hurayrah, ibn ʿAbbās, and his master ʿAbd Allāh ibn ʿAyyash, who, in turn, was reportedly a student of Ubayy ibn Kaʿb. This connection implicitly establishes a transmission lineage for verse 3 of al-Kawthar. The transmission chains connecting later generations to Abū Jaʿfar can be sourced from numerous *qirāʾāt* works, including the ones mentioned previously. Similarly, ʿAbd al-Razzāq of Sanaa reports from Maʿmar, who, in turn, reports from al-Kalbī that al-ʿĀṣ ibn Wāʾil scornfully referred to the Prophet as "*al-abtar*" (signifying being cut off from having offspring). Therefore, the verse proclaims, "it is the one who hates you who has been cut off." Although this *sanad* recounts a *tafsīr* statement for this verse, the above connection indirectly establishes another transmission chain for the verse.

Conclusively, an extensive array of *sanad*s is found within the genres of *qirāʾāt* and *tafsīr*, which is unsurprising given these genres' intimate connection to the Qur'ān. Nonetheless, an examination of selected examples reveals the existence of diverse networks and varying traditions in the transmission process, even when dealing with the same Qur'ānic verses. This chapter will further delve into the study of additional examples encompassing individual Qur'ānic verses in various contexts and domains.

The *Sanads* of Individual Qur'ānic Verses in Various Contexts

In this section, we shall examine various examples from the fields of theology, jurisprudence, and the hadith corpus found across different sects in Islam. It is pertinent to note that a significant portion of the early works on theology did not endure in tangible forms. In the authentically disputed work titled "*Masā'il Nāfi' ibn al-Azraq*," the distinguished figure, widely recognised in sectarian studies as one of the Kharijite leaders, is reported to have inquired ibn 'Abbās regarding the interpretation of "*innā a'ṭaynāka al-kawthar.*" In response, ibn 'Abbās expounded upon all three verses of this *sūrah*. Additionally, he referenced the poem of Ḥassān ibn Thābit, which eloquently reads: "*Wa-ḥabāh al-ilāhu bi al-kawthari al-ak * bari fīhi al-na'īm wa al-khayrāt* (And God bestowed upon him, i.e., the Prophet, the greatest Kawthar, brimming with blessings and goodness)."[6] In a subsequent work dedicated to the exposition of Sunnī creeds, an account is presented by 'Amru ibn Maymūn, wherein he narrates his experience of performing Hajj with 'Umar. The account mentioned an incident in which 'Umar was stabbed, leading to 'Abd al-Raḥmān ibn 'Awf assuming the responsibility of leading the prayer. During this prayer, ibn 'Awf recited two of the shortest *sūrahs* in the Qur'ān, namely *sūrah* al-Naṣr and *innā a'ṭaynāka al-kawthar*. The *sanad* accompanying this account, which implicitly conveys the transmission of the *sūrah*, is as follows: 'Alī ibn 'Umar < Aḥmad ibn al-Ḥasan < al-Ḥasan ibn 'Alī < 'Abbād ibn Mūsā al-Khuttalī < Ismā'īl ibn Ja'far < Isrā'īl < Abū Isḥāq < 'Amru ibn Maymūn.[7]

---

6 Muḥammad Aḥmad al-Dālī, ed., *Masā'il Nāfi' ibn Al-Azraq 'an 'Abd Allāh ibn al-'Abbās* (Cyprus: al-Jaffan & al-Jabi, 1993), 193–94.

7 Hibat Allah ibn al-Ḥasan al-Lālakā'ī, *Sharḥ Uṣūl I'tiqād Ahl Al-Sunnah Wa al-Jamā'ah*, ed. Aḥmad ibn Sa'd al-Ghāmidī (Riyadh: Dār Ṭaybah, 2003), 8: 1384.

In the Shīʿite text titled *Āʿlām al-Dīn*, dedicated to the discussion of the attributes of the believers, a notable statement is attributed to Jaʿfar al-Ṣādiq Abū ʿAbd Allāh, wherein he proclaims: "Whosoever recites *innā aʿṭaynāka al-kawthar* in both obligatory and supererogatory prayers shall be bestowed a libation from al-Kawthar in the Hereafter. Moreover, their dwelling shall be situated near the Prophet's abode at the heart of Ṭūbā in Paradise."[8] Although no specific *sanad* is provided in this source, it can be traced in another work titled *Thawāb al-Aʿmāl*. The following *sanad* is given by ibn Bābawayh al-Qummī: My father < Muḥammad ibn Yaḥyā < Muḥammad ibn Aḥmad < Muḥammad ibn Ḥassān < Ismāʿīl ibn Mihrān < al-Ḥasan < al-Ḥusayn ibn Abī al-ʿAlā' < Abū Baṣīr < Abū ʿAbd Allāh, i.e., Jaʿfar al-Ṣādiq.[9] The verse *innā aʿṭaynāka al-kawthar* is also referenced in another account where the Prophet conveys its meaning to ʿAlī. This account can be found in the work titled *Nawādir al-Akhbār fīmā Yataʿallaq bi-Uṣūl al-Dīn*, which primarily delves into theological subjects. The account is derived from *Tafsīr Furāt al-Kūfī*.[10] Notably, two distinct *sanad*s are presented within this *tafsīr*: Abū al-Qāsim al-ʿAlawī < Furāt al-Kūfī < ʿUbayd ibn Kathīr < Abū Jaʿfar Muḥammad ibn ʿAlī; and Furāt al-Kūfī < ʿUbayd ibn Kathīr in a *muʿanʿan* mode from < al-Mukhtār ibn Fulful < Anas ibn Mālik.[11]

It is pertinent to highlight that within the Shīʿite sources, an alternate interpretation of *al-kawthar* is presented to align with the third verse of the *sūrah*. As articulated by al-Ṭabāṭabā'ī, while

---

8 al-Ḥasan ibn Abī al-Ḥasan al-Daylamī, *Aʿlām Al-Dīn Fī Ṣifāt al-Muʾminīn* (Beirut: Mu'assasah Āl al-Bayt li-Iḥyā' al-Turāth, 2015), 385.

9 Muḥammad ibn ʿAlī ibn Bābawayh al-Qummī, *Thawāb Al-Aʿmāl*, ed. Aḥmad al-Māḥūzī (Qom: Dār Zayn al-ʿĀbidīn li-Iḥyā Turāth al-Maʿṣūmīn, 2014), 355.

10 Muḥsin ibn Murtaḍā al-Fayḍ al-Kāshānī, *Nawādir Al-Akhbār Fīmā Yataʿallaq Bi-Uṣūl al-Dīn*, ed. Mahdī al-Qummī, 1993rd ed. (Tehran: Muassasah-i Mutalaat va Tahqiqat-i Farhangi, n.d.), 356.

11 Furāt ibn Ibrāhīm al-Kūfī, *Tafsīt Furāt Al-Kūfī*, ed. Muḥammad al-Kāẓim (Tehran: Ministry of Culture and Islamic Guidance, 1990), 609–10.

the term *kawthar* linguistically signifies "abundance of goodness," interpreting it as "*kathrat al-dhurriyyah*" (the expansiveness of offspring, signifying the growth of the household of the Prophet and their followers) better complements the reference to "*al-abtar*" (cut off from having offspring), or alternatively, the notion of "*kathrat al-dhurriyyah*" can be encompassed within the concept of abundance of goodness.[12] Nonetheless, our primary focus lies on the *sanad*s that accompany the discourse pertaining to Qur'ānic verses within theological texts. It is conceivable that a considerable number of *sanad*s could be discovered if certain other texts, such as those produced by the Muʿtazilites, were extant. Notably, in the later works of the Muʿtazilites, such as Abū al-Qāsim al-Kaʿbī, a reliance on *sanad*s from early primary sources and Sunnī works on hadith can be observed.[13]

Shifting our attention to the jurisprudential and *fiqh* works, it is reasonable to posit that a wealth of insights awaits discovery concerning the incorporation and relevance of Qur'ānic verses in this specific field, particularly as we delve into the literature encompassing *āyāt al-aḥkām*, which pertains to the legislative commands found within the Qur'ānic verses. Considering the same examples in the above sections, the Qur'ānic injunction of *wa-nḥar* in *sūrah* al-Kawthar has been subject to diverse legal interpretations. For instance, within the Ḥanafī school, al-Qaddūrī views it as obligating the act of *uḍḥiyah* (sacrificing the livestock animal), drawing a parallel to the preceding command of *fa-ṣalli* (establishing the prayer).[14] Conversely, others maintain that the

12 Muḥammad Ḥusayn al-Ṭabāṭabā'ī, *Al-Mīzān Fī Tafsīr al-Qur'ān* (Beirut: Mu'assasah al-Aʿlamī li al-Maṭbūʿāt, 1997), 20: 428-429.

13 ʿAbd Allāh ibn Aḥmad al-Kaʿbī al-Balkhī Abū al-Qāsim, *Qabūl Al-Akhbār Wa-Maʿrifat al-Rijāl* (Beirut: Dār al-Kutub al-ʿIlmiyyah, n.d.), 1: 326; ʿAbd Allāh ibn Aḥmad al-Kaʿbī al-Balkhī Abū al-Qāsim, 'Dhikr Al-Muʿtazilah', in *Maqālāt Al-Islāmiyyīn*, ed. Fu'ad Sayyid (Tunisia: al-Dār al-Tūnisyiyyah li'l-Nashr, n.d.), 87.

14 Aḥmad ibn Muḥammad al-Qaddūrī Abū al-Ḥusayn, *Al-Tajrīd* (Cairo: Dār al-Salām, 2004), 12: 6319.

verse refers to the establishment of the *ʿīd* prayer and the act of sacrifice, i.e., *ʿīd al-aḍḥā*. Abū Jaʿfar al-Ṭaḥāwī in *Ikhtilāf al-Fuqahāʾ*, as presented by al-Jaṣṣāṣ, reports from ʿAlī ibn Abī Ṭālib that *fa-ṣalli li-rabbika wa-nḥar* signifies placing the right hand on the left-hand during prayer. This interpretation is supported by a transmission chain: From Ḥammād ibn Salamah < ʿĀṣim al-Jaḥdarī < ʿUqbah ibn Ṣuhbān < ʿAlī.[15] In similar fashion to the aforementioned instances, this implicitly establishes a transmission chain for the mentioned Qur'ānic verse. Additionally, other interpretations propose that the verse signifies placing both hands near the chest, close to the neck during prayer, given that the term for neck is *naḥr*. The *sanad* supporting this interpretation is found in the *tafsīr* of ibn Jarīr al-Ṭabarī: Ibn Ḥumyad < Mihrān < Hammād ibn Salamah < ʿĀṣim al-Jaḥdarī < ʿUqbah ibn Ẓuhayr < his father Ẓahīr < ʿAlī ibn Abī Ṭālib.[16]

Within Shīʿite *fiqh* works, various views have also been recorded. al-Ḥurr al-ʿĀmilī, in his *Wasāʾil al-Shīʿah*, cites *al-Majālis* by al-Ḥasan ibn Muḥammad al-Ṭūsī and *Majmaʿ al-Bayān* by al-Faḍl ibn al-Ḥasan al-Ṭabarsī, both relying on the narrations of Muqātil ibn Ḥayyān, which imply that *wa-nḥar* refers to raising the hands to the same level as the neck while transitioning from one state to another (such as from standing to bowing) during prayers. The *sanad* provided by al-Ṭūsī is as follows: From his father < Hilāl ibn Muḥammad al-Ḥaffār < Ismāʿīl ibn ʿAlī al-Daʿbalī < Muqātil ibn Ḥayyān < al-Aṣbagh ibn Nabātah < ʿAlī.[17] A similar account was also documented by al-Ḥākim al-Naysāburī in *al-Mustadrak*, with his *sanad* tracing

---

15 Aḥmad ibn ʿAlī al-Jaṣṣāṣ, *Mukhtaṣar Ikhtilāf Al-ʿUlamā Li-Abī Jaʿfar al-Ṭaḥāwī*, ed. ʿAbd Allāh Nadhīr Aḥmad (Beirut: Dār al-Bashāʾir al-Islāmiyyah, 1995), 1: 202.

16 Muḥammad ibn Jarīr al-Ṭabarī, *Jāmiʿ Al-Bayān ʿan Taʾwīl Āy al-Qurʾān*, ed. ʿAbd Allāh ibn ʿAbd al-Muḥsin al-Turkī (Giza: Dār Hajar, 2001), 24: 690.

17 Muḥammad ibn al-Ḥasan al-Ḥurr al-ʿĀmilī and Mīrzā Ḥusayn al-Nūrī, *Wasāʾil Al-Shīah Wa-Mustadarakuhā* (Qom: Mu'assasah al-Nashr al-Islāmī, 2013), 5: 377.

back to Muqātil as well.[18] ibn al-Jawzī claims that this chain is fabricated, while al-Suyūṭī disagrees and suggests that at worst, it can be evaluated as very weak.[19]

The primary focus of our research, however, does not centre on the scrutiny of these *sanads*. Instead, we are captivated by the collective implicit transmission of this particular Qur'ānic verse, despite the diverse legal interpretations presented in these *fiqh* works. Expanding our research to include *fiqh* works from other sects, we find interesting examples, such as in the Zaydite collection of hadith, which predominantly covers *fiqh* subjects. Here, it is reported that ʿAlī ibn Abī Ṭālib recited nine *sūrahs* in his *witr* prayer, including *innā aʿṭaynāka al-kawthar*. The *sanad* presented for this account in *Amālī Aḥmad ibn ʿĪsā* is as follows: Muḥammad ibn Jamīl < Muṣabbiḥ < al-Qāsim ibn ʿAbd al-Raḥmān < ʿAbd al-Rahmān ibn Ziyād ibn Zayd < Abū Juḥayfah < ʿAlī.[20] Thus, it becomes evident that the *fiqh* discourse among diverse sects also serves as a means for the implicit transmission of individual Qur'ānic verses.

Undoubtedly, hadith works represent the primary reservoir for obtaining and investigating the *sanads*. In light of this, we shall now proceed to enumerate some *sanads* provided by hadith compilers when presenting Qur'ānic verses in their compendia.

Firstly, in an account relayed by Anas ibn Mālik, the Prophet was in the company of his companions and momentarily dozed off. Upon awakening, he had a smile on his face, prompting his companions to inquire about the reason behind his amusement. The Prophet replied that a new *sūrah* had just been revealed to

---

18 Muḥammad ibn ʿAbd Allāh al-Ḥākim al-Naysābūrī, *Al-Mustadrak ʿalā al-Ṣaḥīḥayn*, ed. Yūsuf ʿAbd al-Raḥmān al-Marʿashlī (Beirut: Dār al-Maʿrifah, 1985), 2: 538.

19 ʿAbd al-Raḥmān ibn Abī Bakr al-Suyūṭī, *Al-La'ālī al-Maṣnūʿah Fī al-Aḥādīth al-Mawḍūʿah* (Beirut: Dār al-Maʿrifah, n.d.), 2: 20.

20 Aḥmad ibn ʿĪsā ibn Zayd ibn ʿAlī, *Al-ʿUlūm (Amālī al-Imām Aḥmad ibn ʿĪsā)*, ed. Muḥammad ibn Manṣūr al-Murādī (al-Sayyid Yūsuf ibn al-Sayyid Muḥammad al-Ḥasanī, 1981), 1: 229.

him, and he recited the verses: "*Bi-sm Allāh al-Raḥmān al-Raḥīm. Innā aʿṭaynāka al-kawthar. Fa-ṣalli li-rabbika wa-nḥar. Inna shāniʾa-ka huwa al-abtar* [Qur'ān 108: 1-3]." Subsequently, the Prophet asked if they knew the meaning of "*kawthar*," to which the companions replied that Allah and His Messenger knew best. The Prophet explained that it referred to a canal promised to him by his Lord, with an abundance of goodness within it. The *sanad* for this account is documented by Muslim ibn al-Ḥajjāj in his *Ṣaḥīḥ* work as follows: ʿAlī ibn Ḥujr al-Saʿdī < ʿAlī ibn Mushir < al-Muhktār ibn Fulful < Anas ibn Mālik. Additionally, Muslim reported it from Abū Bakr ibn Abī Shaybah, from ʿAlī ibn Mushir with the same *sanad*.[21] This *sanad* can be found in the work of ibn Abī Shaybah himself, titled *al-Muṣannaf*.[22]

Another compelling example comes from al-Tirmidhī, who recorded an account related by Yūsuf ibn Saʿd. In this narration, a man addressed al-Ḥasan ibn ʿAlī, who had pledged allegiance to Muʿāwiyah. The man said: 'You have made fools of the believers' or 'O you who has made fools of the believers.' In response, al-Ḥasan kindly requested the man not to scold him. He then explained that the Prophet had a dream in which he saw Banu Umayyah occupying his Minbar (pulpit), which caused him distress. Subsequently, *innā aʿṭaynāka al-kawthar* was revealed to console the Prophet. The *sanad* provided by al-Tirmidhī is as follows: Maḥmūd ibn Ghaylān < Abū Dāwūd al-Ṭayālisī < al-Qāsim ibn al-Faḍl al-Ḥuddānī < Yūsuf ibn Saʿd.[23] This account was also documented by al-Ṭabarī in his *tafsīr*, with a slightly different *sanad*: Abū al-Khaṭṭāb al-Jārūdī < Salm ibn

---

21 Muslim ibn al-Ḥajjāj al-Qushayrī al-Naysābūrī, *Al-Musnad al-Ṣaḥīḥ al-Mukhtaṣar Bi-Naql al-ʿAdl ʿan al-ʿAdl Ilā Rasūl Allāh*, ed. Muḥammad Fu'ād ʿAbd al-Bāqī (Beirut: Dār Iḥyā al-Turāth al-ʿArabī, 1954), 1: 300 no. 400.

22 ʿAbd Allāh ibn Muḥammad ibn Abī Shaybah Abu Bakr, *Al-Muṣannaf*, ed. Muḥammad ʿAwwāmah (Beirut: Dār Qurṭubah, 2006), 16: 395 no. 32312.

23 Muḥammad ibn ʿĪsā al-Tirmidhī Abū ʿĪsā, *Al-Jāmiʿ al-Kabīr*, ed. Bashshār ʿAwwād Maʿrūf (Beirut: Dār al-Gharb al-Islāmī, 1996), 5: 371 no. 3350.

Qutaybah < al-Qāsim ibn al-Faḍl al-Ḥuddānī < ʿĪsā ibn Māzin, narrating that he scolded al-Ḥasan ibn ʿAlī.[24]

The third noteworthy example coincides with the above example from the Zaydite collection of hadith, where it is recorded that ʿAlī ibn Abī Ṭālib recited nine *sūrahs*, including *"Innā aʿṭaynāka al-kawthar,"* in his *witr* prayer. This account is also preserved in ibn Ḥanbal's *Musnad* with the following *sanad*: Muḥammad ibn ʿAbd Allāh ibn al-Zubayr and Aswad ibn ʿĀmir < Isrāʾīl < Abū Ishāq al-Sabīʿī < al-Ḥārith < ʿAlī. However, it attests to the practice of the Prophet himself reciting nine *sūrahs*, including *"Innā aʿṭaynāka al-kawthar,"* in his *witr* prayer.[25] These diverse examples illustrate the intriguing phenomenon of how *sanads* for individual Qur'ānic verses can be traced within hadith works, even though their primary intention might not have been the intentional transmission of those specific verses.

Lastly, our examination will encompass certain examples from the realm of *taṣawwuf* or the writings of Sufi scholars. Among these, the work of al-Ḥārith al-Muḥāsibī, considered an early *taṣawwuf* text, provides instances of *sanads* being presented. For instance, in his *Māhiyat al-ʿAql wa Maʿnāhu wa Ikhtilāf al-Nās fīhi (The Quintessence of the Intellect and Its Meaning)*, al-Muḥāsibī conveys the interpretation of al-Ḥasan al-Baṣrī regarding verse 7 of sūrah al-Rūm: "*Yaʿlamūn ẓāhiran min al-ḥayāt al-dunyā wa-hum ʿan al-ākhirati hum ghāfilūn*" (Qur'ān 30:7). The *sanad* provided is as follows: ʿAffān < Ṣakhr ibn Juwayriyah < al-Ḥasan.[26] Another work by al-Muḥāsibī, titled *al-Riʿāyah li-Ḥuqūq Allāh*,

---

24 al-Ṭabarī, *Jāmiʿ Al-Bayān ʿan Taʾwīl Āy al-Qurʾān*, 24: 546-547.

25 Aḥmad ibn Ḥanbal, *Al-Musnad*, ed. Shuʿayb al-Arnaʾūṭ (Beirut: Muʾassasah al-Risālah, 1995), 2: 97 no. 678.

26 al-Ḥārith ibn Asad al-Muḥāsibī, *Māʾiyyat Al-ʿAql Wa-Maʿnāhu Wa-Ikhtilāf al-Nās Fīhi*, ed. Ḥusayn al-Quwwatlī (Beirut: Dār al-Fikr, 1971), 213; Part of the treatise was translated into English by Yasir Qadhi. See: Yasir Qadhi, 'Al-Harith al-Muhasibi (d. 243 A.H) – Part One', Muslim Matters, 31 May 2007, https://muslimmatters.org/2007/05/31/al-harith-al-muhasibi-d-243-ah-part-one/.

includes the interpretation of Mujāhid for three Qur'ānic verses: "*Wa-idhā qīla lahum ittaqū mā bayna aydīkum wa-mā khalfakum la'allakum turḥamūn* (Yet when they are told, 'Beware of what lies before and behind you, so that you may be given mercy)" [Qur'ān 36:45], "*Wa-liman khāfa maqam rabbihi jannatān* (For those who fear [the time when they will] stand before their Lord there are two gardens)" [Qur'ān 55:46], and "*Wa-mā tukhfī al-ṣudūr* (and of all that hearts conceal)" [Qur'ān 40:19]. The *sanad* for the first and third verses is as follows: Sunayd ibn Dāwūd < Ḥajjāj < ibn Jurayj < Mujāhid. For the second verse: Abū al-Naṣr < Shu'bah < Manṣūr < Ibrāhīm or Mujāhid.[27]

In a subsequent work authored by Abū Nu'aym under the title *Ḥilyat al-Awliyā' wa Ṭabaqāt al-Aṣfiyā' (The Beauty of the Righteous and Ranks of the Elite)*, we encounter a similar narration to the one previously mentioned, where 'Amrū ibn Maymūn reports that ibn 'Awf recited two of the shortest *sūrahs* in the Qur'ān, namely *sūrah* al-Naṣr and *innā a'ṭaynāka al-kawthar*. The *sanad* for this account is traced as follows: Abū Bakr ibn Khallād < al-Ḥārith ibn Abī Usāmah < Yaḥyā ibn Abī Bukayr < Isrā'īl < Abū Isḥāq < 'Amru ibn Maymūn.[28] It is worth noting that the majority of these works were composed at later periods, and their accounts may have relied significantly on the *muṣḥaf* as their primary source for the narrations presented therein.

al-Durr al-Manthūr as the Precursor for Advancing Studies

Throughout this study, a focus has been placed on examples primarily from *sūrah* al-Kawthar. This choice is motivated by several factors. Firstly, *sūrah* al-Kawthar is the shortest *sūrah* in the

27 al-Ḥārith ibn Asad al-Muḥāsibī, *Al-Ri'āyah Li-Ḥuqūq Allāh*, ed. 'Abd al-Ḥalīm Maḥmūd, 2nd ed. (Beirut: Dār al-Ma'ārif, 1990), 42.
28 Aḥmad ibn 'Abd Allāh Abū Nu'aym al-Iṣfahānī, *Ḥilyat Al-Awliyā' Wa-Ṭabaqāt al-Aṣfiyā'* (Beirut: Dār al-Kutub al-'Ilmiyyah, 1988), 4: 151.

Qur'ān, making it convenient for comparative analysis across different areas of scholarship concerning the *sanad*s connected to its verses. By employing this approach, a comprehensive exploration of the multifaceted nature of the *sanad*s involved in the endeavour becomes feasible. Moreover, the focus on *sūrah* al-Kawthar enables a direct comparison between the present research and the seminal work of al-Suyūṭī, titled *al-Durr al-Manthūr*.

al-Durr al-Manthūr is renowned for its exhaustive compilation of *sanad*s extracted from original hadith sources related to each verse of the Qur'ān. This comprehensive tradition-based exegesis serves as a valuable resource, elucidating the meanings of Qur'ānic passages through the inclusion of reports and narrations from Prophet Muhammad, his Companions, and succeeding generations. Notably, al-Suyūṭī's meticulous efforts encompassed gathering all available reports for each specific verse, even those that appeared to be contradictory. However, given the extensive nature of his work, dedicating significant space to the analysis of a single verse within the present research would be impractical. Thus, the strategic decision to focus on *sūrah* al-Kawthar allows for a pragmatic investigation into how *al-Durr al-Manthūr* can meaningfully contribute to the aims of this research. By examining the same verses as those elucidated in the preceding section, a valuable comparative analysis can be undertaken, shedding light on our subjects of concern. Let us now examine the treatment of *sūrah* al-Kawthar in the book.

al-Suyūṭī commences by presenting four traditions that address the *sūrah* in a general context. Among these, he recounts ibn Shubrumah's statement that there is no *sūrah* in the entire Qur'ān that consists of fewer than three verses. Then, he cites al-Ṭastī reporting the same dialogue between Nāfiʿ ibn al-Azraq and ibn ʿAbbās as previously presented. al-Suyūṭī proceeds to cite the hadith recorded by Muslim, narrated by Anas ibn Mālik, which pertains to the revelation of the *sūrah* to the Prophet, as we presented above. Furthermore, he references a narration wherein the Prophet recites the verse as *innā anṭaynāka al-kawthar*, substituting the *ʿayn* in *aʿṭaynāka* with *nūn*. An additional four accounts from Anas ibn Mālik are also brought forth, followed by several hadiths from ibn ʿAbbās and ʿĀʾishah, as well as others from Ḥuzayfah, Usāmah, and ʿAbd Allāh ibn ʿAmru concerning the meaning of *al-kawthar*. More than five accounts relating to the first verse are subsequently presented.[29]

With respect to the second verse, al-Suyūṭī gathers approximately seventeen reports regarding the meaning of establishing prayer and *wa-nḥar*. The interpretations of *wa-nḥar* encompass those aforementioned in our discussion above, with additional meanings introduced in al-Suyūṭī's work, such as *wa-nḥar* being construed as standing up straight after bowing in prayer, facing the *qiblah* with the neck, and expressing thankfulness to God. Finally, for the third verse, approximately sixteen reports are offered by al-Suyūṭī, sourced primarily from *tafsīr* and hadith works, as well as from historical and prophetological works. It is important to note that al-Suyūṭī's work does not consistently provide complete *sanad*s for the reports, necessitating reference to the sources mentioned by him to obtain them, though some of these sources are considered lost, such as the *tafsīr* of ibn Marduwiyah. Furthermore, it should be noted that the book does not include an evaluation of the reports cited therein.

Conclusion

Perhaps the simplest approach to depict the essence of the present research, albeit not entirely exhaustive, is to draw an analogy between the treatment of a particular verse in the Qur'ān and that of a hadith. This comparison leads us to inquire whether

29 ʿAbd al-Raḥmān ibn Abī Bakr al-Suyūṭī, *Al-Durr al-Manthūr Fī al-Tafsīr Bi al-Màthūr*, ed. ʿAbd Allāh ibn ʿAbd al-Muḥsin al-Turkī (Cairo: Markaz Hajar, 2003), 15: 695-710.

it is feasible to trace the *sanad*, or chain of transmission, for the transmission of this specific verse from the earliest generation of Muslims to subsequent ones. By pursuing this exercise, several significant observations have come to light.

First and foremost, the scarcity of reports or scholarly works specifically addressing the transmission of individual Qur'ānic verses serves as a clear indication of the unanimous acceptance and veneration of the *tawātur* (mass transmission or ubiquitous) status of the Qur'ān within the early Muslim generations. Moreover, although the hadith theorists such as al-Ḥākim al-Naysabūrī, al-Khaṭīb al-Baghdādī, ibn al-Ṣalāh, ibn Ḥajar al-'Asqalāni, and others, have been scrutinising and critically constructing the concept of *āḥād* (individual transmission), there has never been an elaboration on the *āḥād* transmission of the Qur'ān in their guidebooks for *sanad* criticism. Consequently, the present study assumes a role of peripheral evidence supporting the concept of *tawātur*, further corroborating the enduring and widely held position on the mass transmission of the Qur'ān.

Secondly, beyond the focus on *qirā'āt* (recitations) and *tafsīr* (exegesis) in studying the Qur'ānic verses, exploring the treatment of these verses in diverse fields such as hadith, theology, Sufism, jurisprudence, and literature can provide valuable insights into significant subjects and societal phenomena concerning the interpretation and interaction with these verses. This study has shed light on certain networks involved in the transmission of specific interpretations of the Qur'ān, with a notable concentration of *sanad*s related to *sūrah* al-Kawthar attributed to 'Alī ibn Abī Ṭālib. Although the status of these *sanad*s merits further evaluation, it is evident that this feature transcends across the literature of various sects within the Muslim world. However, it is essential to acknowledge that this study is, to some extent, preliminary in nature. With the discovery of additional manuscripts and materials from early periods and different sects, future research holds the promise of unveiling more intriguing findings.

Finally, this study serves as a valuable contribution to the exploration of the diverse forms and functions of the *sanad* tradition within the context of Islamic intellectual history. It delves into the intricate web of *sanad* practices surrounding the study of the Qur'ān, shedding light on its multifaceted nature. While it is true that esteemed figures such as al-Khaṭīb al-Baghdadī once emphasised that "for the narratives of the pious, the stories of ascetics and devout worshippers, the exhortations of skilled rhetoricians, and the sagacious wisdom of eloquent belletrists; *sanad*s serve merely as embellishments and do not constitute a criterion for establishing their authenticity," the present investigation stands as a distinctive tributary in the vast ocean of the multifaceted *sanad* tradition pertaining to Qur'ānic studies. Nonetheless, it is crucial to acknowledge that this study retains an academic essence. Throughout the Muslim world, the Qur'ān has perpetually resided in the hearts of individuals through memorisation, embodying a profound connection that extends beyond historical inquiry.

Bibliography

Abū Nuʿaym al-Iṣfahānī, Aḥmad ibn ʿAbd Allāh. *Ḥilyat al-Awliyāʾ Wa-Ṭabaqāt al-Aṣfiyāʾ*. Beirut: Dār al-Kutub al-ʿIlmiyyah, 1988.

ʿĀmilī, Muḥammad ibn al-Ḥasan al-Ḥurr al-, and Mīrzā Ḥusayn al-Nūrī. *Wasāʾil al-Shīah Wa-Mustadarakuhā*. Qom: Muʾassasah al-Nashr al-Islāmī, 2013.

Arnar, Anna Sigrídur. *Encyclopedism from Pliny to Borges*. Chicago: University of Chicago Library, 1990.

Azami, Muhammad Mustafa. *The History of the Qur'ānic Text from Revelation to Compilation: A Comparative Study with the Old and New Testaments*. Leicester, England: UK Islamic Academy, 2003.

Balkhī, ʿAbd Allāh ibn Aḥmad al-Kaʿbī al-, Abū al-Qāsim. 'Dhikr al-Muʿtazilah'. In *Maqālāt al-Islāmiyyīn*, edited by Fu'ad Sayyid. Tunisia: al-Dār al-Tūnisyiyyah li'l-Nashr, n.d.

———. *Qabūl al-Akhbār Wa-Maʿrifat al-Rijāl*. Beirut: Dār al-Kutub al-ʿIlmiyyah, n.d.

Bennet, Deborah. 'Defining Randomness'. In *Philosophy of Statistics*, edited by Prasanta Bandyopadhyay and Malcolm Forster, 1st ed., 7:633–40. Handbook of Philosophy of Science. North Holland: Elsevier, 2011.

Bin Jamil, Khairil Husaini. 'Traditional Sunnī Epistemology in the Scholarship of al-Ḥāfiẓ al-Khaṭīb al-Baghdādī (463AH/1071CE)'. Doctoral Thesis, SOAS University of London, 2017. https://eprints.soas.ac.uk/26670/1/4461_Jamil.pdf.

Dālī, Muḥammad Aḥmad al-, ed. *Masāʾil Nāfiʿ Ibn al-Azraq ʿan ʿAbd Allāh Ibn al-ʿAbbās*. Cyprus: al-Jaffan & al-Jabi, 1993.

Daylamī, al-Ḥasan ibn Abī al-Ḥasan al-. *Aʿlām al-Dīn Fī Ṣifāt al-Muʾminīn*. Beirut: Mu'assasah Āl al-Bayt li-Iḥyā' al-Turāth, 2015.

Franklin-Brown, Mary. *Reading the World: Encyclopedic Writing in the Scholastic Age*. Chicago and London: The University of Chicago Press, 2012.

Ibn Abī Shaybah, ʿAbd Allāh ibn Muḥammad, Abu Bakr. *al-Muṣannaf*. Edited by Muḥammad ʿAwwāmah. Beirut: Dār Qurṭubah, 2006.

Ibn Bābawayh al-Qummī, Muḥammad ibn ʿAlī. *Thawāb al-Aʿmāl*. Edited by Aḥmad al-Māḥūzī. Qom: Dār Zayn al-ʿĀbidīn li-Iḥyā Turāth al-Maʿṣūmīn, 2014.

Ibn Ḥanbal, Aḥmad. *al-Musnad*. Edited by Shuʿayb al-Arnāʾūṭ. Beirut: Mu'assasah al-Risālah, 1995.

Ibn Zayd ibn ʿAlī, Aḥmad ibn ʿĪsā. *al-ʿUlūm (Amālī al-Imām Aḥmad Ibn ʿĪsā)*. Edited by Muḥammad ibn Manṣūr al-Murādī. al-Sayyid Yūsuf ibn al-Sayyid Muḥammad al-Ḥasanī, 1981.

Jaṣṣāṣ, Aḥmad ibn ʿAlī al-. *Mukhtaṣar Ikhtilāf al-ʿUlamā Li-Abī Jaʿfar al-Ṭaḥāwī*. Edited by ʿAbd Allāh Nadhīr Aḥmad. Beirut: Dār al-Bashāʾir al-Islāmiyyah, 1995.

Kara, Seyfeddin. 'In Search of ʿAlī Ibn Abī Ṭālib's Codex: Study of the Traditions on the Earliest Copy of the Qur'ān'. Doctoral Dissertation, University of Durham, 2014.

Kāshānī, Muḥsin ibn Murtaḍā al-Fayḍ al-. *Nawādir al-Akhbār Fīmā Yataʿallaq Bi-Uṣūl al-Dīn*. Edited by Mahdī al-Qummī. 1993rd ed. Tehran: Muassasah-i Mutalaat va Tahqiqat-i Farhangi, n.d.

Kūfī, Furāt ibn Ibrāhīm al-. *Tafsīt Furāt al-Kūfī*. Edited by Muḥammad al-Kāẓim. Tehran: Ministry of Culture and Islamic Guidance, 1990.

Laher, Suhail Ismail. 'Twisted Threads: Genesis, Development, and Application of the Term and Concept of Tawatur in Islamic Thought'. Doctoral Dissertation, Harvard University, 2014.

Lālakāʾī, Hibat Allah ibn al-Ḥasan al-. *Sharḥ Uṣūl Iʿtiqād Ahl al-Sunnah Wa al-Jamāʿah*. Edited by Aḥmad ibn Saʿd al-Ghāmidī. Riyadh: Dār Ṭaybah, 2003.

Muḥāsibī, al-Ḥārith ibn Asad al-. *al-Riʿāyah Li-Ḥuqūq Allāh*. Edited by ʿAbd al-Ḥalīm Maḥmūd. 2nd ed. Beirut: Dār al-Maʿārif, 1990.

———. *Māʾiyyat al-ʿAql Wa-Maʿnāhu Wa-Ikhtilāf al-Nās Fīhi*. Edited by Ḥusayn al-Quwwatlī. Beirut: Dār al-Fikr, 1971.

Nasser, Shady Hekmat. *The Transmission of the Variant Readings of the Qur'ān: The Problem of Tawātur and the Emergence of Shawādhdh*. London: Brill, 2012.

Naysābūrī, Muḥammad ibn ʿAbd Allāh al-Ḥākim al-. *al-Mustadrak ʿalā al-Ṣaḥīḥayn*. Edited by Yūsuf ʿAbd al-Raḥmān al-Marʿashlī. Beirut: Dār al-Maʿrifah, 1985.

Naysābūrī, Muslim ibn al-Ḥajjāj al-Qushayrī al-. *al-Musnad al-Ṣaḥīḥ al-Mukhtaṣar Bi-Naql al-ʿAdl ʿan al-ʿAdl Ilā Rasūl*

Allāh. Edited by Muḥammad Fu'ād ʿAbd al-Bāqī. Beirut: Dār Iḥyā al-Turāth al-ʿArabī, 1954.

Qaddūrī, Aḥmad ibn Muḥammad al-, Abū al-Ḥusayn. *al-Tajrīd*. Cairo: Dār al-Salām, 2004.

Qadhi, Yasir. 'al-Harith al-Muhasibi (d. 243 A.H) – Part One'. Muslim Matters, 31 May 2007. https://muslimmatters.org/2007/05/31/al-harith-al-muhasibi-d-243-ah-part-one/.

Qāḍī, ʿAbd al-Fattāḥ al-. *Tārīkh al-Muṣḥaf al-Sharīf*. Cairo: Maktabah al-Jundī, 1952.

Suyūṭī, ʿAbd al-Raḥmān ibn Abī Bakr al-. *al-Durr al-Manthūr Fī al-Tafsīr Bi al-Ma'thūr*. Edited by ʿAbd Allāh ibn ʿAbd al-Muḥsin al-Turkī. Cairo: Markaz Hajar, 2003.

———. *al-Lầālī al-Maṣnūʿah Fī al-Aḥādīth al-Mawḍūʿah*. Beirut: Dār al-Maʿrifah, n.d.

Ṭabarī, Muḥammad ibn Jarīr al-. *Jāmiʿ al-Bayān ʿan Ta'wīl Āy al-Qur'ān*. Edited by ʿAbd Allāh ibn ʿAbd al-Muḥsin al-Turkī. Giza: Dār Hajar, 2001.

Ṭabāṭabā'ī, Muḥammad Ḥusayn al-. *al-Mīzān Fī Tafsīr al-Qur'ān*. Beirut: Mu'assasah al-Aʿlamī li al-Maṭbūʿāt, 1997.

Tirmidhī, Muḥammad ibn ʿĪsā al-, Abū ʿĪsā. *al-Jāmiʿ al-Kabīr*. Edited by Bashshār ʿAwwād Maʿrūf. Beirut: Dār al-Gharb al-Islāmī, 1996.

CHAPTER TEN

Multivocality, Variegation, and the Trajectories of "Text": *Ausgangstexte* as an Approach to Qur'ānic Pluriformity

Stephen Cúrto

The present work is grounded in the need to effectuate the reinterrogation of many of the implicit suppositions, and presuppositions, informing the conceptual paradigm of the category 'Qur'ān', and their entailments for the methodological approach towards Qur'ānic textual and historical criticism. We would adduce as illustrative examples thereof, the approach that would see this category exhausted by that of a singularity of Prophetic archetypical "autograph" or worse yet, the regrettable conflation of the narrowly delimited category of '*muṣḥaf*' with the plenary inexhaustibility of the category of 'Qur'ān'.

The Qur'ān, both in its Prophetic form, and as a communal enterprise instantiated through textual and recitational transmission, was one of tremendous fluidity of readings, and expansive pluriformity of exemplification. Any reconstructionist text-critical project beholden to epistemic and ontological commitments to the restoration of a Qur'ānic original recension *in the singular*, (as if it is to be rightly supposed that the author/composer/articulator of the Qur'ān would have recognized, or even entertained such categories), does violence to this Qur'ānic polysemy. What we have represented within the *amṣār maṣāḥif*, the manuscript tradition, or within the orality of the reading traditions themselves, are representative indexical instantiations of, but certainly not exhaustive for, the plenary category "Qur'ān."

Qur'ānic studies as a field, and, more pointedly, Qur'ānic textual criticism, would be well served by framing the text-critical project through borrowing the conceptual framework of *Ausgangstext*[1] as offered by Gerd Mink et al., in conjunction with a modified form of the "Living Text" framework articulated by D.C. Parker as applied to the New Testament, and, similarly, heeding what has been proposed in the works of Angelika Neuwirth, Shady Nasser, and Gary Martin. Whatever tensions adopting such methods concomitantly may introduce, it still affords us a far more productive state of affairs than the insoluble tensions imposed on Antiquity and her literatures by presuppositional insistence on authorial singularity of recension.[2] Antique and late antique audiences were demonstrably not beholden to such presuppositions, and antique texts are entirely unamenable to such paradigms.[3]

---

1 Operating under the definitional paradigm and semantic domain for this term offered by Gerd Mink, "It is the text *from which* the extant tradition originates." Peter J. Gurry, *A Critical Examination of the Coherence-Based Genealogical Method in New Testament Textual Criticism* (Leiden-Boston: Brill, 2017), p. 93. Emphasis in original. This is an important point to be delineated, as such a paradigm does not presume, nor does it require, access to holographic or autographic readings.

2 See D.C. Parker, *The Living Text of the Gospels* (Cambridge University Press, 1997), pp. 189-191.

3 See Gary D. Martin, *Multiple Originals* (Atlanta: Society of Biblical Literature Press, 2010), pp. ix, 11-76. The approach to scriptural discourse in Antiquity and Late Antiquity readily evidences a paradigm of variegation as normative, rather than exceptional; one can see examples of this in a well-attested phenomenon within the Greek NT, whereby the author(s) of many of the books contained therein, when proffering quotations of the Hebrew Bible, adduce citations comporting to variant readings present within the Septuagintal stream of textual tradition. See Timothy Michael Law, *When God Spoke Greek: The Septuagint and the Making of the Christian Bible* (New York: Oxford University Press, 2013), especially pp. 85-117. In the case of the Qur'ān, the recognition of polysemous normativity as an inherent feature of the ontology of

Indeed, noting the changing dynamics within the field, D.C. Parker has rightly observed, "Recent developments in *biblical criticism* have brought new challenges for *textual criticism*. There are even those who view it as a peculiarly obsolete aspect of western imperialism in its guise of the historico-critical method..."[4] Much of what has constituted the essential facets of such challenges centers around questions appertaining to methodological approach. On this question of methodology, Gary D. Martin has further rightly noted, "Modern text-critical editions of ancient literatures... typically strove to produce an Urtext...It has been the insistence of locating a single original text that has largely governed the textual studies of the Hebrew Bible as well as other ancient texts."[5]

Operating under such a paradigm, as described aptly by Martin above, variants within the streams of tradition of such ancient texts are largely appraised as textual corruptions,[6] rather than as attestation to pluriformity. As J.A. Bellamy remarks,

> ...I shall attempt to isolate several errors and then to emend the text in order to restore it as nearly as possible to its original form. In the Koran "original form" means, of course, the form the word or phrase had when it was first uttered by the prophet Muḥammad... It remains for modern scholars to...restore the text to the form it had when first spoken by the prophet Muḥammad.[7]

---

the Qur'ān, and Qur'ānic prophetology, is encountered in the work of Tareq Moqbel. See Tareq Moqbel, "The Emergence of the Qirā'āt: the Divine Permission Hypothesis," *Journal of Islamic Studies* vol. 33 no. 3 (2022): 299-330.

4 Parker, *The Living Text*, p. xi. Emphasis mine.

5 Martin, *Multiple Originals*, p. 12.

6 Corruption, it should be noted however, is not inherently a pejorative; "... corruption refers neutrally to any scribal change of a text." Bart D. Ehrman, *The Orthodox Corruption of Scripture: The Effect of Early Christological Controversies on the Text of the New Testament* (New York: Oxford University Press, 1993), p. 29.

7 James A. Bellamy, "Some Proposed Emendations to the Text of the Koran," *Journal of the American Oriental Society* vol. 113 no. 4 (1993): 562-573, pp. 563, 573. Emphasis mine.

This heuristic is methodologically equal parts undesirable, and untenable, for, to again invoke the observations of Martin, "The possibility of a multivalent tradition is immediately excluded. There is only one "original text."[8] It is certainly preferable to eschew the adoption of such a methodological approach when appraising the Qur'ān, for as Keith E. Small rightly observes, "One could legitimately speak of autographic text forms."[9]

Indeed, what Gary D. Martin so rightly notes about text-criticism generally, is especially apropos to Qur'ānic textual study. As Martin rightly contends:

> [there are] ...shortcomings in those practices of textual criticism that operate predominantly from a reductionist view of the text...Typically, a text-critical edition presents to the user a single primary text block thought to represent the closest possible approximation to a putative original text. The assumption is that, among variant extant textual witnesses, there can be only one correct reading...Current text-critical practices suppress multivalences as a result of a narrow *a priori* view of textual origins. In some cases multivalences can be demonstrated to be intended by the composer, in other cases multivalences of texts during the periods from which our earliest extant manuscripts derive simply fell within certain limits of acceptable variability by those who valued and transmitted those texts...Variant readings must not always be thought of as competing for the exalted status of singular original...[10]

Narrowing our scope to specifically the field of Biblical textual criticism for the moment, the works of scholars such as the

8 Martin, *Multiple Originals,* p. 15.

9 Keith E. Small, *Textual Criticism and Qur'ān Manuscripts* (Plymouth: Lexington Books/ Lanham: Rowman and Littlefield, 2011), p. 8

10 Martin, *Multiple Originals,* p. ix.

aforementioned Gary D. Martin and D.C. Parker have challenged this line of thinking, (i.e., the exclusion of concurrent, and concurrently valid multivalent text forms), on a variety of historical and methodological grounds.[11] As Parker notes "…precisely because it has been taken as axiomatic, the idea that there is an original text to be recovered is one that we must examine with the utmost care."[12] Further, we would note another "emergent shift" within the state of the field of text-criticism, one which has been effectuated by the 'CBGM' (Coherence-Based Genealogical Method) in Münster.[13] CBGM has entailed the need for the reinterrogation of many New Testament textual-critical norms and methodological approaches.[14] As to the nature of CBGM, Peter Gurry remarks,

> Michael Holmes, himself an editor of the Greek New Testament, hopes that the method can help editors and textual critics grasp the larger implications of their often atomistic decisions while David Parker, who is currently editing John, believes that the CBGM has finally resolved the longstanding problem of contamination… The CBGM is first and foremost a genealogical method and so it shares similar goals with other such methods. These goals are to help elucidate the development of a

11 Their studies had a profound influence upon the methodology of the approach adopted within the present work, and they are owed a deep debt of gratitude for what they have contributed to the field of text-criticism.

12 Parker, *The Living Text of the Gospels*, p. 4.

13 Gerd Mink, "The Coherence-Based Genealogical Method – What is it about?" https://www.uni-muenster.de/INTF/Genealogical_method.html Accessed January 14, 2023. See also, Tommy Wasserman and Peter J. Gurry *A New Approach to Textual Criticism: An Introduction to Coherence-Based Genealogical Method* (Atlanta: Society of Biblical Literature Press, 2017). Gurry, *A Critical Examination*.

14 Wasserman and Gurry, *A New Approach*, pp. 7-11. Gurry, *A Critical Examination*, pp. 1-21, 67-86, 90-93, 101-105.

> textual tradition and to help reconstruct the starting point of that development.[15]

CBGM has already markedly influenced the current text-critical landscape, as can be witnessed in textual decisions adopted by the Institut für neutestamentliche Textforschung within the ECM (*Editio Critica Maior*) project.[16] The principles inherent to the approach of CBGM include, as noted by Gerd Mink, and more recently by Wasserman and Gurry, the delineation between manuscripts as physical objects, and as textual witnesses,[17] which helps ground the 'fundamental principle' "... that *the relationship between witnesses can be determined by the relationship of their readings.*"[18] On this critical distinction, Gurry helpfully observes,

> The use of the term "witness" up to this point requires us to note one more very important distinctive of the CBGM. Unlike past methods, the CBGM consistently distinguishes between the texts of manuscripts (i.e., witnesses) and the manuscripts themselves and it is only concerned to relate the former.[19]

The CBGM is therefore methodologically occupied with this central question of the coherence[20] between 'witnesses'.[21]

15 Ibid., pp. 1, 36.
16 Ibid., pp. 1-2, 36-86.
17 Wasserman and Gurry, *A New Approach*, p. 3. Gurry, *A Critical Examination*, p. 38.
18 Ibid., p. 39. Emphasis in original.
19 Ibid., p. 38.
20 "...the main problems addressed by the CBGM...is [accomplished] through the use of coherence..." Wasserman and Gurry, *A New Approach*, p. 26.
21 "...a "witness" in the CBGM is simply the totality of its variant readings..." Gurry, *A Critical Examination*, 39. CBGM further distinguishes between a 'variant' proper, and a 'reading'. A reading could encompass *any* reading presented within the text, while a variant must be "grammatically and logically possible" to qualify as such. *Op. cit.*, p. 5. To properly function, a Qur'ān-specific CBGM, in accounting for a delineation between

However, as noted above, of significance for the CBGM "... is not a relationship between *manuscripts* but between the *texts* conveyed in them."[22] CBGM evaluates the 'pregenealogical coherence'[23] 'genealogical coherence'[24] and 'stemmatic

---

'reading' and 'variant' would need to take into account instances where Qur'ānic conventions violate later scholastic grammatical strictures and not retroject them as an imposition upon the text. See Mustafa Shah, "The Early Arabic Grammarians' Contribution to the Collection and Authentication of Qur'ānic Readings: The Prelude to ibn Mujāhid's *Kitāb al-Saba'a*," *Journal of Qur'ānic Studies* vol. 6 no. 1 (2004): 72-102, p. 73, see also Van Putten "When the Readers Break the Rules," pp. 448-449. This is especially true as there is already room for sustained and meaningful contestations over to what extent grammatical infelicities have encroached upon the transmission streams. Behnam Sadeghi, "Criteria for Emending the Text of the Qur'ān." in *Law and Tradition in Classical Islamic Thought: Studies in Honor of Professor Hossein Modarressi* ed. Michael Cook, Najam Haider, Intisar Rabb, and Asma Sayeed (New York: Palgrave Macmillan, 2013), pp. 24-25. See also, J.A. Bellamy, "More Proposed Emendations to the Text of the Koran" *Journal of the American Oriental Society* vol. 116 no. 2 (1996): 196-204, pp. 196-197, and Marijn van Putten, *Qur'ānic Arabic from its Hijazi Origins to its Classical Reading Traditions* (Leiden: Brill, 2022).

22 Wasserman and Gurry, *A New Approach*, p. 29. Emphasis in original. That the antiquity of a manuscript is to be delineated from the readings instantiated within that manuscript, which may attest to far greater antiquity, is a necessary entailment of this methodological approach. As Peter Gurry helpfully reminds us, "...a manuscript's text may be much older than its ink and parchment..." Gurry, *A Critical Examination*, p. 38. This phenomenon has been observed in relation to the Qur'ān by Sidky; "...the Cairo Edition's reliance on *rasm* works results in a text that is substantially more archaic and indeed more archetypal than many manuscripts over a millennium older." Hythem Sidky, Review of Daniel Alan Brubaker, *Corrections in Early Qur'ānic Manuscripts: Twenty Examples*, *Al-'Uṣūr Al- Wusṭā: The Journal of Middle East Medievalists* vol. 27 no. 1 (2019): 273-288, p. 276.

23 "Pregenealogical coherence is the percentage agreement between the texts of any two witnesses at all places of variation where both are extant and legible." Wasserman and Gurry, *A New Approach*, p. 27.

24 "Whereas *pre*genealogical coherence only tells us *how closely* two witnesses are related, genealogical coherence also tells us the *direction* of their relationship." Ibid., 28. Emphasis in original. In other words, genealogical

coherence'[25] between witnesses,[26] mapping "three types of stemmata"[27] the 'local stemma'[28] 'substemma'[29] and 'global stemma'.[30] Further, and of centrality to much of the textual transmission theory grounding CBGM is the 'Principles of Parsimony'.[31] The principles of parsimony (*à la* the famous philosophical dictum, which can be roughly summated as "One is not to effectuate the multiplication of entities beyond necessity"),[32] when applied to the text-critical project, results in "...four crucial assumptions..."[33] for CBGM. Perhaps the foremost being "*A scribe typically copies his source with fidelity*."[34]

---

coherence informs decisions regarding directionality of witness relationships. See *Op. cit.*, pp. 28-29.

25 "...simply another term for the relationships in an optimal substemma..." Gurry, *A Critical Examination*, p. 51.

26 See Ibid., pp. 1-15, 36-86.

27 See Wasserman and Gurry, *A New Approach*, pp. 29-35, and Gurry, *A Critical Examination* pp. 44-49.

28 "...a local stemma ...relates the variants at a single place or location (hence *local*) of variation. It is these stemmata that also form the basis for genealogical coherence..." Wasserman and Gurry, *A New Approach*, p. 29. Emphasis in original.

29 "The basic purpose of a substemma is to determine the minimal number of ancestors for a given witness... A substemma is simply one that relates any one witness to its ancestors." Ibid., p. 31.

30 "The global stemma is nothing more than the combination of all available optimal substemmata." Ibid., pp. 32-33. No such complete global stemma has yet been effectuated or adduced. See ibid., p. 33.

31 Gurry, *A Critical Examination*, pp. 40-42.

32 The sentiments of this maxim is alternatively conveyed, depending on the proposed provenance or attribution, by the Latin phrases "Entia non sunt multiplicanda, præter necessitatem" or "Non est ponenda pluralitas sine necessitate." See William M. Thorburn, "The Myth of Occam's Razor," *Mind* vol. 27 no. 107 (1918): 345-353, p. 345.

33 Gurry, *A Critical Examination* p. 40.

34 Ibid., p. 41. CBGM generally seeks to effectuate the trend towards "... sharpening the relationships between witnesses by *excluding* direct relationships wherever possible." *Op. cit.*, p. 40.

While CBGM remains a methodology largely (but neither prescriptively, nor exclusively) delimited to the domain of the study of the New Testament textual tradition,[35] we would suggest that the wider utilization of similar principles, procedures, and methodological approaches[36] promises to afford much benefit to text-critics outside of Biblical, and specifically New Testament, text-critical studies, and certainly this could apply to the felicity it can afford Qur'ānic studies .[37] This stands true, perhaps especially as appertaining to the 'Principles of

---

35 Ibid., pp. 1-2, 187-188.

36 As Hythem Sidky rightly notes, on the utility of similar such methodologies, and their use in his study, and the studies of others, "Within qur'ānic studies, Alba Fedeli and Andrew Edmondson have applied phylogenetic methods to a smaller corpus of manuscripts than present in this study but with a greater degree of granularity. Still in its infancy, we will have a lot to gain in terms of our understanding of the written transmission of the Qur'ān from such methods." Hythem Sidky, "On the Regionality of Qur'ānic Codices," *Journal of the International Qur'ānic Studies Association* vol. 5 (2020): 133-210, p.164.

37 The field of Qur'ānic studies in general is happily moving towards the more thoroughgoing integration of digital humanities, see "Preliminary Considerations on the Corpus Coranicum Christianum-The Qur'ān in Translation A survey of the State-of-the-Art Abstract Dossier" (Berlin: Freie Universität Berlin Chair of Byzantine Studies, 2018), 1-20, p. 13. Alba Fedeli, "Digital Humanities and Qur'ānic Manuscript Studies: New Perspectives and Challenges for Collaborative Spaces and Plural Views" *Journal of College of Shariah and Islamic Studies* vol. 38 no. 1 (2020): 147-158, pp.152-154. Alba Fedeli, "The Qur'ānic Text from Man_ uscript to Digital Form: Metalinguistic Markup of Scribes and Editors," in *From Scrolls to Scrolling: Sacred Texts Materiality, and Dynamic Media Cultures* ed. by Bradford Anderson, 213-245. (Boston: De Gruyter, 2020). Though rare, there is precedent for the application of CBGM to non-NT streams of textual tradition, and could very productively be marshalled in service of Qur'ānic text-criticism. Already, as Gurry notes, "Alberto Cantera has produced a version of the CBGM to work with the Avestan tradition…" Gurry, *A Critical Examination*, p. 187. A modified CBGM applicable to the Qur'ān holds tremendous potential for advancing the field, and establishing 'pre-genealogical' and 'genealogical coherence' for the Qur'ān manuscript tradition, in concert with effectuating a state of affairs very similar to Donner's *Qur'ān Manuscripts Database (QMD)*. See Fred Donner, "The Qur'ān in

Parsimony'.[38] One may rightly presume fidelity as the normative default informing scribal practice generally, for the Biblical text, and certainly for Qur'ānic textual transmission, especially of the 'Uthmānic text-type, as has been skillfully evidenced by Marijn van Putten's works.[39]

Turning our focus upon questions of the relationship between the *qirā'āt* with the transmission of the consonantal orthography of the Qur'ān, and Qur'ānic reception history, therefore raises a host of methodological and historiographical issues. The trajectory of the historical developments and processes whereby some of the *qirā'āt* were communally assented to as possessing "canonical status" and came by their presently recognized canonical form, and further, the interrelationships between recitational canonicity and orthographic canonicity, have received some very rigorous study within the works of Shady Nasser, Hythem Sidky, and Van Putten.[40]

Recent Scholarship: Challenges and Desiderata" in *The Qur'ān in its Historical Context* ed. Gabriel Said Reynolds (New York: Routledge, 2008), pp. 44-46.

38 Gurry, *A Critical Examination* pp. 40-42.

39 Observing the consistency of the distribution of the idiosyncrasies, Van Putten concludes: "...idiosyncratic spellings of certain words are not due to the whims of the scribe, but are reproduced with the same spelling in all early Quranic manuscripts. The only way that such a consistent reproduction can be explained is by assuming that all the documents that belong to the Uthmanic text type go back to a single written archetype whose spelling was strictly copied from one copy to the next, showing that these copies were based on a written exemplar." Marijn Van Putten "The Grace of God as Evidence for a Written Uthmanic Archetype: The Importance of Shared Orthographic Idiosyncrasies" *Bulletin of SAOS* (2019): 271-288, p. 286. This matter is discussed further below.

40 Shady Hekmat Nasser, *The Second Canonization of the Qur'ān (324/936): Ibn Mujāhid and the Founding of the Seven Readings* (Leiden-Boston: Brill, 2021). Shady Hekmat Nasser, *The Transmission of the Variant Readings of the Qur'ān: The Problem of Tawātur and the Emergence of Shawādhdh* (Leiden-Boston: Brill, 2013). Marijn van Putten, "Hišām's 'Ibrāhām: Evidence for a Canonical Quranic Reading Based on the Rasm" *Journal of the Royal Asiatic Society* Series 3, vol. 30 no. 2

The academic contestations regarding to what degree the field should privilege either orality, or textuality, in parsing the transmission history of the Qur'ān is complex, and certainly how one cashes out the ontology of the Qur'ān is directly germane to the positions adopted within this debate.[41] Van Putten especially has marshaled robust argumentation for what may be termed the "tenacity"[42] of specific spelling variations, and their distribution, as indicative of a standardised exemplar that functioned as the template for 'Uthmānic Qur'ānic apographa. Further, Van Putten militates strongly for the position that the oral tradition of the reciters itself may, at points, be either derived from, or influenced by, the consonantal text.[43] This facet of Van Putten's argumentation, which can be highlighted by his discussion of the distribution of the variants '*niʿmat/ niʿmah*' is twofold; that, "…there must have been a single written archetype from which all Quranic manuscripts of the Uthmanic text type are

(2020): 231-250. Sidky, "Regionality." Marijn van Putten "When the Readers Break the Rules: Disagreements with the Consonantal Text in the Canonical Qur'ānic Reading Traditions," *Dead Sea Discoveries* (2022): 438-462. Nasser rightly queries as to "How, when, and why were certain readings considered to be irregular/anomalous, while other readings were elevated to Canonical status, thus becoming divine revelation?" Nasser, *The Second Canonization*, p. 16.

41 Angelika Neuwirth has convincingly emphasised, and coherently presented argumentation in favor of, the significance of orality as a necessary concomitant to any sufficient accounting of Qur'ānic ontology, compilation, and transmission. Further, as Shady Nasser helpfully reminds us, "…written and oral transmission were intertwined, and… the exact mechanisms of *Qirāʾāt* transmission are more complex than we think." Nasser, *The Second Canonization* p. 159.

42 To borrow a turn of phrase from the Alands. See, Kurt Aland and Barbara Aland, *The Text of the New Testament: An Introduction to the Critical Editions and to the Theory and Practice of Modern Textual Criticism,* trans. Erroll F. Rhodes (Grand Rapids: William B. Eerdmans Publishing Company, 1995), pp. 56, 69-71, 280, 292.

43 See, Van Putten, "Hišām's 'Ibrāhām." Van Putten, "The Grace of God" See also, Van Putten "When the Readers Break the Rules," p. 447.

descended."[44] Further, that "Considering the early likely date of many of these manuscripts (second half of the seventh century), it is unlikely that the archetype of the "Uthmanic" text type post-dates the canonical date assigned to it in the tradition..."[45]

As for Van Putten's argumentation *vis-à-vis* Qur'ānic dating, this is developing into the normative consensus within the field, and indeed, rightly so; the revisionist (in some circles, problematically bordering upon mythicist) hyper-scepticism towards the date ranges afforded to us by radiography is highly unwarranted. The contention that there must be only one possible potential accounting, with sufficient explanatory power for this phenomenon, namely, "a *single* written archetype"[46] does raise certain questions, and present certain potential tensions. [47] We note the equally rigorous observations of Shady Nasser, who contends,

> ...the process of editing to which I believe the Qur'ān was subjected...was an oral process of correcting and standardizing the defective script of the early codices through the discipline of *Qirā'āt*...a collective, communal process that took place over decades and with multiple generations of scholars, rather than being conceived of as the

44 Van Putten, "The Grace of God", p. 279.

45 Ibid. Van Putten's observations are also discussed and cited in Sidky, "Regionality" pp. 135-136.

46 Van Putten "The Grace of God" p. 271. Emphasis mine.

47 Further however, as Sidky rightly notes, "With the dating and attribution of the standardization secure, there remain additional details in need of resolution. With electronic access to many first/ seventh century qur'ānic manuscripts readily available, it seems obvious that a comprehensive study of them is warranted at least to validate (or disprove) Nöldeke's and Cook's findings on the regional variants and codices. This is especially important considering that Edmund Beck, Déroche, and more recently Michael Marx have all expressed skepticism in some form towards the existence of the 'Uthmānic exemplars."Sidky, "Regionality," p. 136.

> final product of one individual or a few committee members who decreed and shaped its current form.[48]

These positions are, however, neither irreconcilable nor incommensurate. What Van Putten has documented indeed presents a very strong case for his argumentation "...that all Quranic manuscripts of the Uthmanic text type have been committed to writing not from memory, or copying from dictation, but copied from a previous written copy."[49] Much could yet be gleaned from the application of genetic studies[50] *à la* the approach of CBGM in service of pursuing further inquiry in this regard. If such a method were applied to the Qur'ān, it promises to afford a more defined picture of the state of affairs appertaining to the precursory stages of the Qur'ān's transmission, and provide resolution for many of the tensions in the field of Qur'ānic textual studies regarding orthography, orality, and transmission history.[51]

---

48 Nasser, *The Second Canonization* pp. 2-3.

49 Van Putten "The Grace of God" p. 280.

50 Note that CBGM is a specific genealogical and stemmatic method, however, it is not a perfectly synonymic identicality to Lachmannian phylogenetic stemmatic methodology, and CBGM affords decided improvements over purely Lachmannian stemmatics. See Gurry, *A Critical Examination*, pp. 139, 147. See also Leonardo Pessoa da Silva Pinto, "The CBGM and Lachmannian Textual Criticism," *TC: A Journal of Biblical Textual Criticism* vol. 27 (2022): 17-31, Klaus Wachtel, "The Development of the Coherence-Based Genealogical Method (CBGM), its Place in Textual Scholarship, and Digital Editing," in *The Future of New Testament Textual Scholarship*, ed. Garrick Allen, (Tübingen: Mohr-Siebeck, 2019), pp. 436-439, and Gerd Mink, Remarks on Carlson, "A Bias at the Heart of the CBGM," "INTF Blog" Accessed November 1, 2023 https://ntvmr.uni-muenster.de/intfblog/-/blogs/remarks-on-carlson-a-bias-at-the-heart-of-the-cbgm-guest-post-by-gerd-mink-

51 Upon this point Sidky correctly observes, "The amount of mixing of regional variants in manuscripts as well points to a complex and dynamic relationship between the *rasm* and the reading traditions—both influencing and interacting with each other, rather than one being completely dependent on the other. I anticipate that understanding this complex interplay between

The form of the earliest articulations of the Qur'ān, the question of multiple authorial or compositional hands, and the question of whether it should be situated within a period of Late Antiquity posterior to the 650's CE[52] (specifically, a chronology roughly contemporaneous to the period of Marwān ibn al-Ḥakam or ʿAbd al-Malik) have proved equally to be a well-spring of contestations.[53] These contestations have recently, and

qur'ānic written and oral transmission are apt to prove our richest source of insights into the shaping of the text of scripture during Islam's formative period." Sidky, "Regionality," pp. 184-185.

52 See John Wansbrough, *Qur'ānic Studies: Sources and Methods of Scriptural Interpretation* (Amherst: Prometheus Books, 2004). See also Charles J. Adams, "Reflections on the Work of John Wansbrough" *Method & Theory in the Study of Religion* vol. 9 no. 1 (1997): 75-90. Herbert Berg "The Implications of, and Opposition to, the Methods and Theories of John Wansbrough" *Method & Theory in the Study of Religion* vol. 9 no. 1 (1997): 3-22. As an aside, beyond the (admittedly untenable) extremity of his late dating, Wansbrough has articulated a host of exceptionally helpful observations on the situated history and nature of the Qur'ān as a discourse. This is especially true regarding his observation of '*Qur'ān*' as such, intending a pluriform *logia* tradition. Wansbrough, *Qur'ānic Studies* p. 51

53 Neuwirth has appropriately and coherently summated the tensions involved thusly: "...the problem underlying the present crisis in Western Qur'ānic scholarship-the seemingly unbridgeable divide between a tradition_ al position that regards the *Qur'ān* as the literary outcome of a prophetic mission in Mecca and Medina during the first half of the seventh century CE, and a skeptical position that ascribes its compilation to a later syncretistic Mesopotamian community -appears to reflect a mistaken premise... what Qur'ānic scholars should be looking for is not the whereabouts of a literary compilation called "*Qur'ān*," let alone asking "What the *Qur'ān* really says," but should instead be looking at the Qur'ānic text as a "medium of trans_ port," triggering and reflecting a communication. The *Qur'ān* in its emergent phase is not a pre-meditated, fixed compilation, a reified literary artifact, but a still-mobile text reflecting an oral theological-philosophical debate between diverse interlocutors of various late antique denominations. It is a text that first of all demands to be read as a drama involving multiple protagonists. What is demanded is a change in focus from the exclusive perception of a reified codex to a still-fluid pre-canonical text that can provide a solution to the historical problems that Qur'ānic scholarship addresses." Angelika Neuwirth,

productively, been revisited by Tommaso Tesei and Stephen J. Shoemaker.[54] Tesei's date-range, it should be noted, is still (relatively) conservative, entertaining a period between 661-680 of the Common era.[55]

Given the robust and lively nature of these contestations, and given some of the objections to various early dating schemes for the Qur'ān, [56] our position herein should be made clear: we are certainly in agreement with Shoemaker, Tesei, and others who have advanced similar positions, insofar as 'Uthmān, or his polity, would never have been logistically able to enforce the form of standardisation to which is normally attributed to him.[57] However, we would demur from the position advanced by some,

---

"Two Faces of the Qur'ān: *Qur'ān* and *Muṣḥaf*," *Oral Tradition* vol. 25 no 1. (2010): 141-156, p. 142.

54 Tommaso Tesei, "The Qur'ān(s) in Context(s)," *Journal Asiatique* vol. 309 no. 2 (2021):185-202. Stephen J. Shoemaker, *Creating the Qur'ān: A Historical Critical Study* (Oakland: University of California Press, 2022). Shoemaker expresses multiple concerns over the conclusions drawn from the radiographic dating of Qur'ānic manuscripts. While we by no means can aquiesce to the same degree of scepticism he entertains, many of the concerns broached by Shoemaker regarding regional variability within ^{14}C, and the occurrence of interindividual date ranges displayed between *individual* folios within certain codices warrants sustained accounting. See ibid., pp. 78-95. As has been oft-noted, however, palaeographic dating methodologies are far from grounds for establishing an unimpeachable epistemic surety. See William M. Schniedewind "Problems in the Paleographic Dating of Inscriptions" in *The Bible and Radiocarbon Dating: Archeology, Text and Science* eds. Thomas E. Levy and Thomas Higham (New York: Routledge, 2005), 405-412. Brent Nongbri "Paleographic Analysis of Codices from the Early Christian Period: A Point of Method" *Journal for the Study of the New Testament* vol. 42 no. 1 (2019): 84-97. Malcolm Choat, "Dating Papyri: Familiarity, Instinct and Guesswork" *Journal for the Study of the New Testament* vol. 42 no. 1 (2019): 59-83. See also, Nicolai Sinai "When did the Consonantal Skeleton of the Qur'ān Reach Closure? Part II" *Bulletin of the School of Oriental and African Studies* vol. 77 no. 3 (2014): 509-521. Hythem Sidky, "Regionality," pp. 133-136

55 Tommaso Tesei, "The Qur'ān(s) in Context(s)," p. 189.

56 *À la* Shoemaker; see *Creating the Qur'ān*, especially pp. 77-116.

57 Ibid., p. 68.

grounded upon an analyses of the features of specific Qur'ānic typologies, narratives, formal literary structural features, and mythemes, that such features of Qur'ānic content necessitate substantive redating.

Within such lines of argumentation, this position is often entailed in virtue of the companion assertion of the supposed reality that there was no meaningful Christian presence, (often taken to mean even sufficient "presence" via ideational influence), or sustained contact with Christianate communities and the Hijaz-prior or during- the presumed Prophetic period, to support Qur'ānic awareness of such mythemes and theologemes. Bracketing the multiple potential examples to the contrary[58] and adopting a wholistic chronological conservativism towards the ranges of ^{14}C dating,[59] we still have in the case of the *Qur'ān itself*, a document of 7th Century 'late antique Arabian' (LAA) provenance. That this document attests to tremendous familiarity and concern with Jews, "the Children of Israel," Christians, and Christianity,[60] (at the very least as topoi or mythemes), as

58 See Barbara Finster, "Arabia in Late Antiquity: An Outline of the Cultural Situation in the Peninsula at the Time of Muhammad" in *The Qur'ān in Context* edited by Angelika Neuwirth, Nicolai Sinai, and Michael Marx, (Leiden-Boston: Brill, 2010), esp. pp. 68-77, 81-100. Sidney H. Griffith, *The Bible in Arabic: The Scripture of the "People of the Book" in the Language of Islam* (Princeton: Princeton University Press, 2013), esp. pages 7-96.

59 See Sidky, "Regionality," pp. 148-153.

60 We are in accord with Juan Cole, Nicolai Sinai, and Behnam Sadeghi on the evidence attesting to early date of the Qur'ān, and a sole author. See Juan Cole "New Historicism: A Manifesto for Writing a History of the Qur'ān," Accessed September 17, 2023. https://www.juancole.com/2019/03/historicism-manifesto-writing.html

See also, Behnam Sadeghi "The chronology of the Qur'ān: A Stylometric research Program" *Arabica,* vol. 58 (2011): 210-299. Pluriformity of stylistic features need not entail of necessity a plurality of authorial or compositional hands post-composition; although we are happy to concede a rather robust communally driven redaction process. See Juan Cole "New Historicism: A Manifesto for Writing a History of the Qur'ān," Accessed September 17, 2023. https://www.juancole.com/2019/03/historicism-manifesto-writing.

well as late antique Biblical, and extra-Biblical topoi if anything, therefore, seems to militate against the author or author(s) of the Qur'ān not being situated within a milieu sufficiently permeated with such material to account for Qur'ānic familiarity therewith.[61]

---

html. See also, Behnam Sadeghi "The chronology of the Qur'ān: A Stylometric research Program" *Arabica*, vol. 58 (2011): 210-299.

61 Inter-and Intra-textual resonances between Biblical, Patristic, and Extra-Biblical literature, and the topoi, narrative, and theology of the Qur'ān are abound. The meta-textuality for instance, between the '*shema Yisrael*' (Duet. 6:4), and Q.112:1, and, likewise, the intertextual resonances between various creeds and confessions (esp. the Nicene and Athanasian Creeds), the Syriac and Cappadocian Fathers, and the Qur'ān (e.g., Q. 112:1, 4:171) have been exhaustively discussed, and documented. For Duet. 6:4 and Q. 112:1 see Abraham I. Katsh, *Judaism and the Koran: Biblical and Talmudic Backgrounds of the Koran and its Commentaries*, (New York: A.S. Barnes, 1962), pp. 4-5. For the Cappadocians, the School of Nisibis, et al. see Julian Decharneux, *The Cosmology of the Qur'ān and Its Late Antique Background*, (Berlin-Boston: De Gruyter, 2023), pp. 8-12. Further, in addition to the large narrative prose sections (such as *sūrah* Yūsuf), and smaller sections of late antique pericopæ- such as the more well-known interface with extrabiblical Gospel traditions (Q. 5:110, Q.19:23-26), or the 'Seven Sleepers of Ephesus' and the "Dhū l-Qarnayn" hagiographic harmonization of various Midrashic, Persianate, Syrian, and Byzantine cycles interwoven within the Qur'ānic text- there is much in the way of both documented, and perhaps more tentative, homiletic sub-textual references, and resonances between Biblical (including deutero-canonical), Parabiblical, (including talmudic midrashim, and Second Temple literature), and Qur'ānic material. E.g., Q. 2:98 (Jud. 1:9), Q. 9:30 (II Esdras 14:9-19, 3rd Enoch), Q. 17:1 (2nd Corinthians 12:1-5, Ezekiel 8:3, 40:1-3, 1st Enoch, 2nd Enoch, 3rd Enoch, and sundry articulations of the 'Assumption of Moses' traditions), Q. 2:79, 3:187 (2nd Corinthians 2:17), Q. 21:104 (Isa. 34:4, Rev. 6:14), Q. 32:5, Q. 22:47 (2nd Pet. 3:8), Q. 31:34 (Mat. 24:36). Looking at the Qur'ān *viz-à-viz* the antique and late antique tradition, we can see many of the "routes and roots," (to borrow the helpful phraseology of Daniel Boyarin) of Antiquity, and the matrices of transmission of antique tradition within the milieu of the Ḥijāz. For further relevant discussions, the reader is advised to consult the following: Tommaso Tesei, "The Prophecy of Ḏū-l-Qarnayn (Q 18:83-102) and the Origins of the Qur'ānic Corpus," *Miscellanea arabica* 2013–2014: 273-90. Daniel Boyarin, "Is Metatron a Converted Christian?" Judaïsme ancien/Ancient Judaism, vol. 1 (2013): 13–62,

The Qur'ān, and contact by its author with trans-Arabian Christianities, and late antique Platonisms, and Neoplatonisms, when the available data is coherently engaged in toto, certainly seems to antedate the sustained Byzantine contact concomitant

---

p. 13. Aleksandra Klęczar, "Alexander in the Jewish Tradition: From Second Temple Writings to Hebrew Alexander Romances," in *Brill's Companion to the Reception of Alexander the Great*, ed. K.R. Moore (Leiden-Boston: Brill, 2018), esp. pp. 391-392., Gabriel Said Reynolds, *The Qur'ān and its Biblical Subtext* (New York: Routledge, 2010). Mikhail D. Bukharin, "Mecca on the Caravan Routes in Pre-Islamic," in *The Qur'ān in Context* eds. Angelika Neuwirth, Nicolai Sinai, and Michael Marx (Leiden-Boston: Brill, 2010), esp. pp. 121-127. Emran Iqbal El-Badawi, *The Qur'ān and the Aramaic Gospel Traditions* (New York: Routledge, 2014). Joseph P. Schultz, "Angelic Opposition to the Ascension of Moses and the Revelation of the Law" *The Jewish Quarterly Review* vol. 61 no. 4 (1971): 282-307. E. Isaac, "1 (Ethiopic Apocalypse of) Enoch," in *The Old Testament Pseudepigrapha* vol. I ed. James H. Charlesworth, 5-89 (Peabody: Hendrickson Publishers, 2020). F.I. Andersen, "2 (Slavonic Apocalypse of) Enoch," in *The Old Testament Pseudepigrapha* vol. I ed. James H. Charlesworth 91-221, (Peabody: Hendrickson Publishers, 2020). P. Alexander, "3 (Hebrew Apocalypse of) Enoch," in *The Old Testament Pseudepigrapha* vol. I ed. James H. Charlesworth 223-315, (Peabody: Hendrickson Publishers, 2020). J.M Lindenberger, "Ahiqar: A New Translation and Introduction" in *The Old Testament Pseudepigrapha* vol. II ed. James H. Charlesworth 479-507, (Peabody: Hendrickson Publishers, 2020) especially p. 491. Juan Cole, "Dyed in Virtue: The Qur'ān and Plato's *Republic*," *Greek, Roman and Byzantine Studies* vol. 61 no. 4 (2021): 580-604. Juan Cole, "A Sickness in the Heart: Were the Qur'ān's Hypocrites a Late Antique Sect?" *The Muslim World* vol. 111 no. 3 (2021): 358-375. Juan Cole, "'It was Made to Appear to Them So': The Crucifixion, Jews, and Sasanian War Propaganda in the Qur'ān." *Religion* vol. 51 no. 3 (2021): 404-422. Juan Cole, "Paradosis and Monotheism: A late Antique Approach to the Meaning of Islam in the Qur'ān" *Bulletin of the School of Oriental and African Studies* vol. 82 no. 3 (2019): 405-425. Juan Cole, "Muhammad and Justinian: Roman Legal Traditions and the Qur'ān." *Journal of Near Eastern Studies* vol. 79 no. 2 (2020): 183-196. Juan Cole, "Infidel or Paganus? The Polysemy of Kafara in the Qur'ān." *Journal of the American Oriental Society* vol. 140 no. 3 (2020): 615-635. Jonathan Brown "The Qur'ān, the Jews and Ezra as the Son of God" Accessed March 21, 2023 https://drjonathanbrown.com/2016/the-qur'ān-the-jews-and-ezra-as-the-son-of-god/

with later Caliphal imperialist expansion; and yet, the Qur'ān is sufficiently cognisant of Christian motifs and ideologemes to pronounce meaningfully upon them. Shoemaker et al. are indeed correct to note that the true enforcement of the standardisation the Qur'ān did not, and could not, have occurred until well after 'Uthmān. However, it is concurrently true that, as Sadeghi and Goudarzi correctly note, "…the splitting off of the 'Uthmānic and other textual traditions occurred no later than the spread of the 'Uthmānic text type."[62] In point of fact, one could argue that this is attested by both by radiocarbon dating[63] and the witness of the manuscript tradition in its totality.[64]

It stands true, "The lower writing of Ṣan'ā' 1 clearly falls outside the standard text type. It belongs to a different text type..."[65] However, there remains much room for contesting the veracity of assertions that the lower text of San'ā'1 will suffer no comparisons whatsoever with the reading traditions *in toto*.[66] Further, as to the late-dating models, we note the observations of Hythem Sidky,

> A growing corpus of material evidence has also been fatal for arguments in favor of a late codification. Francois Déroche's seminal work on Qur'ānic scripts and detailed study of Umayyad-period Qur'āns, primarily through paleography and art history, places numerous manuscripts in the first/seventh century. His broad chronological classification is independently corroborated through

62 Behnam Sadeghi, and Mohsen Goudarzi, "San'ā'1 and the Origins of the Qur'ān," *Der Islam* vol. 87 (2012):1-129, p. 18.

63 Sidky, "Regionality," pp. 148-153.

64 See Sadeghi, and Goudarzi, "San'ā'1."

65 Ibid., p. 17.

66 Ibid., pp. 115-122.

radiocarbon dating of over a dozen of the earliest surviving Qur'āns.[67]

Finally, we would note the grounding of our present study upon the insistence that the transmission of the Qur'ānic streams of tradition, (irrespective of the views one adopts on the most felicitous historical-critical paradigm from which to situate the etiological genesis of the Qur'ān), was never one of ossified fixity, and rigid, univocal uniformity. Indeed, the concomitance of stability and variegation with the Qur'ān's transmission history itself is an indexicality that the provenance of such variegation is beholden to explanatory factors other than corruptions to an Urtext. The transmission and the production of the Qur'ān, when we rightly jettison certain 'Uthmānic hagiographical fictions, finds its provenance, not in the will of the state, but a communal shepherding process. As Shady Nasser helpfully reminds us,

"The eponymous readings were not static systems of recitation that were authored at one time in history and then transmitted from one generation to another. They were subject to revision, editing, polishing, and rigorous internal systemization that led them to their current state. One of the main objections of this study...is to overcome the misconception that the text was static and demonstrate that the Qur'ān, as an orally performed document, evolved and developed over time." [68]

Further, we note that, just as some voices in Biblical studies and textual criticism broadly, have begun moving toward the eschewal of the paradigm of reconstructing the 'original text', seeing the conceptual framework of 'initial text' (*Ausgangstext*)[69]

67 Sidky, "Regionality," p. 135.

68 Nasser, *The Second Canonization*, p. 257.

69 "Some believe that the term *original text* is simply too vague to be meaningful...Others go further and argue that the very notion of a single, authorial text for the New Testament is indefensible." Wasserman and Gurry, *A New Approach*, p. 11. See also Barbara Bordalejo, "The Genealogy of Texts: Manuscripts

as a more felicitous paradigm, we would likewise seek to advance that the same reframing is equally helpful for the discipline of Qur'ānic studies.

Polysemous Multivalence of Qur'ānic Ausgangstexte in the Early Prophetic Communities

The process of the 'evolutionary trajectory' of the development and the form of the Qur'ān, as discussed above, was the manifestation of a theistically sacralized religio-communal enterprise. What one encounters when engaging with the Islamic tradition therefore thoroughly lends itself to the paradigm of *Ausgangstext*.[70] Indeed, such is the nature of its formal polysemy, that it most fully, and perhaps more properly, is to be conceived as '*Ausgangstexte*'. *Ausgangstexte* accurately expresses what is an essential facet of the Qur'ān, from its most primitive formal and informal articulations, through the processes of codification, and unto its 'final form'.[71] Further, in the case of the Qur'ān, the paradigm of

---

Traditions and Textual Traditions *Digital Scholarship in the Humanities* vol. 31 no. 3 (2016):563-577, p. 564., Eldon Jay Epp, "In the Beginning was the New Testament Text, but Which Text? A Consideration of '*Ausgangstext*' and 'Initial Text'," in *Texts and Traditions: Essays in Honor of J. Keith Elliot* eds. Peter Doble and Jeffrey Kloha (Leiden-Boston: Brill, 2014), p. 60, and Eldon Jay Epp, "The Multivalence of the Term "Original Text" in New Testament Textual Criticism" *The Harvard Theological Review* vol. 92 no. 3 (1999):245-281.

70 "The *Ausgangstext* is the text from which the entire tradition originates and which directly precedes the first relationship in various branches of the tradition. When textual criticism speaks about the original text, this *Ausgangstext* is typically meant." Gerd Mink, "Eine umfassende Genealogie der neutestamentlichen Überlieferung," *NTS* vol. 39 no. 4 (1993):481-499, p. 482. Citation and translation in Gurry, *A Critical Examination*, pp. 92-93.

71 We are indebted to J.K. Elliot for this helpful, and necessary, observation on the need to transcend the singularity entailed by *Ausgangstext* to a more

'initial text'-or texts-is an especially helpful one, as such a term helps map a conceptual framework for a text where "...there is a methodological gap between the start of the textual tradition as we have it and the text of the autograph itself."[72] Further, we would contend in the case of the Qur'ān, there was never any *one* such singular autograph, and the communal enterprise cannot be divorced from the Prophetic recension; rather, it is inherent within the very ontology of the category of Qur'ānic revelatory discourse.

Before continuing in the discussion of these matters, however, it is indeed necessary to further ground this discussion on the Qur'ān, by asking the highly relevant frame question; when we invoke the term "Qur'ān" what do we intend to communicate?[73] What is the proper semantic domain for this term, and what are the ontolgical, methodological, and structural considerations that must rightly inform any such discourse? In his groundbreaking dissertation, Khalil Andani observes a critical point *vis-à-vis* Qur'ānic ontology, and its modality of formal annunciation.

---

expansive conceptual framework (*Ausgangstexte*). What he has said of NT streams of tradition from the 2nd century of the common era is certainly true (in modified form) of Qur'ānic streams of tradition in the 7th and 8th century, *vis-à-vis* the form(s) of the text(s) to which they are posterior, and their multivalence and pluriformity. Elliot rightly queries, "I wonder if we should not now speak in the plural, *Ausgangstexte*, and argue that all varying text-types of the New Testament could go back to forms already in existence in the second century." J.K. Elliott, "The New Testament Text in the Second Century: A Challenge for the Twenty- First Century," *New Testament Textual Research Update*. Citation in Eldon Jay Epp, "In the Beginning was the New Testament Text, but Which Text? A Consideration of '*Ausgangstext*' and 'Initial Text'," in *Texts and Traditions: Essays in Honor of J. Keith Elliot* eds. Peter Doble and Jeffrey Kloha (Lieden-Boston: Brill, 2014), p. 60.

72 Gurry, *A Critical Examination*, p. 93.

73 This critical epistemic and ontological question has been noted by Keith E. Small, and Andrew Rippin. See Small, *Textual Criticism*, p. 6. Andrew Rippin, "Foreword" in Wansbrough, *Qur'ānic Studies* pp. xiv-xv. Citation in Small, *Textual Criticism*, p. 12.

Specifically, he entreats the fluidity of the modality of the Prophetic conception of revelation, and the articulation of what Andani correctly notes were, ultimately,

> ...concurrent variant versions of a qur'ānic sūra and allowing substitutions of one formula with another – all in an ad hoc manner in response to his community's needs. ... the Qur'ān in its emergent phase was an orally dynamic and interactive revelatory event consisting of piecemeal qur'āns as opposed to a static written scripture; the concept of kitāb in the Qur'ān conveys the meaning of divine decree and prescription, represented in the active image of "divine writing", as opposed to a closed physical scripture...the Arabic Qur'āns, consisting of situated adaptations or tafṣīl from the Transcendent Kitāb, constitute the Revelatory Product...[74]

Approaching the revelatory process from this foundation, being appropriately cognisant of the multiple, concurrently valid, and concurrently articulated instantiations of variegation, grounds the approach of our present discussion. Not only could the paradigm of what comprised revelation, as interfaced with by the early Prophetic community, sustain robust variegation, but that variegation was the very nature of this discursive and polysemous revelatory platform.[75] So while the present work does not argue that there can be no concept whatsoever of the 'authorial text', or even the 'original text' as such, but rather, we insist *à la* Gary Martin and David Parker, that it would have to, by definition, incorporate authorial or original *texts*. It is the presupposition

74 Khalil Andani, "Revelation in Islam: Qur'ānic, Sunni and Shi'i Ismaili Perspectives" (PhD Diss., Harvard University, 2020), pp. 101,106-107.
75 See Yasin Dutton, "Orality, Literacy and the 'Seven Aḥruf' Ḥadīth," *Journal of Islamic Studies* vol. 23 no. 1 (2012):1-49, p.3.

of "...a single, authorial text..."[76] for the Qur'ān, the Bible, or any antique or late antique tradition, (scriptural or otherwise), as thoroughly, and rightly, argued by Martin, from which we rather sharply would demur.

The Prophetic normative "default position" for the Qur'ānic discourse was grounded upon such polysemy.[77] Indeed, as Aziz Al-Azmeh appropriately observes on the issue of Qur'ānic variegation, the entire paradigm behind even some usages of the language of "variant reading" as such "...is thus a misnomer, because such variants are integral to the Qur'ān, being an intrinsic part of the textual repertoire of the canon and not simply derivative of transmission."[78] Entreating the narrative discourse of this 'textual repertoire' (extending to both instantiations of orality, and orthography), and attestation to the pluriform multivalence that is to be found within the narrative discourse of the Qur'ān itself, one encounters multiple such assertions that attest to revelatory fluidity.[79] We find this evidenced within the well-known verses of Q. 15:87.[80] Further, verses such as Q. 35:31 likewise

76 Wasserman and Gurry, *A New Approach to Textual Criticism,* p. 11.

77 "...provided that you do not seal a verse of punishment with mercy or a verse of mercy with punishment..." Ahmad 'Alī al-Imām, *Variant Readings of The Qur'ān,* (Herndon: The International Institute of Islamic Thought, 2006), p. 8. "Related by Ahmed and Tabarani with a sound chain." Ibid., p. 117.

78 Aziz Al-Azmeh "Modeling the Paleo Qur'ān: Declamations, Reiterations, Fragments and Collations" in *The Making of Religious Texts in Islam: The Fragments and the Whole,* eds. Asma Hilali and S.R. Burge (Berlin: Gerlach Press, 2019), p. 39.

79 E.g., Q. 31:27, "And if all the trees on earth were pens and the ocean (were ink), with seven oceans behind it to add to its (supply), yet would not the words of God be exhausted (in the writing): for God Is Exalted in Power, Full of Wisdom." Yūsuf 'Alī trans. See 'Abdullāh Yūsuf 'Alī, *The Holy Qur'ān: Text, Translation, and Commentary.* (Elmhurst: Tahrike Tarsile Qur'ān, 2012), p. 1087.

80 The language of *sab'an mina l-mathānī* clearly invokes, or, at the very least can accommodate, a paradigm of highly polysemous Prophetic articulation for the formal annunciation of the Qur'ān. See, Edward William Lane, *Al-Qāmūs Madd: An Arabic-English Lexicon* (New Delhi: Asian Educational

proffer what is to be read most coherently as an internal assertion to an extra-mundane, multivalent fluidity; a fluid artifact of a transcendent reality, rather than of static fixity.[81] We similarly find many further instances of sundry notions of Qur'ānic variegation as ascribed to the early Prophetic community itself, documented within the writings of multiple pre-modern Muslim traditionalists and exegetes. This paradigm certainly comports for instance, with the discussion presented in al-Ṭabarī, recounting a hagiographic Prophetic pericope chronicling that the Qur'ān was revealed not only upon seven *aḥruf*, but likewise upon seven *abwāb*.[82] The integration of meaningful study of the Shīʿī traditional narratives and reception history regarding Qur'ānic variegation remains regrettably peripheral within the field. This rather infelicitous dimension of Qur'ānic studies has been observed by scholars such as Shady Nasser, Hossein Modarressi, Etan Kohlberg, and Mohammad Ali Amir-Moezzi.[83] Certainly,

---

Services, 2003), vol.1, pp.356-358, 360. While the identification of *sabʿan mina l-mathānī* conclusively with *sūrah al-fātiḥah* became normative exegetical gloss, we would caution against delimiting the intended meaning solely with *al-fātiḥah*. However, Neuwirth is correct to note that the idea of *sabʿan mina l-mathānī* comprising seven legendary accounts of punishment or divine retribution is rather strained, and rather untenable. See Angelika Neuwirth, *The Qur'ān and Late Antiquity: A Shared Heritage* (New York: Oxford University Press, 2019), pp. 282-283.

81 For a discussion of this see Andani, "Revelation in Islam", pp. 90-93.

82 Muḥammad ibn Jarīr al-Ṭabarī, *Tafsīr al-Ṭabarī: Jāmiʿ al-Bayān fī taʾwīl al-Qur'ān* (Beirut: Dār al-Kutub al-ʿilmīyah, 2014), vol.1, pp. 53-55. See also Dutton, "Orality," p. 1.

83 As Shady Nasser correctly notes, "Scholarship on the Qur'ān rarely considers the views of the *shīʿī* scholars on the subject, possibly because *shīʿī* have different and somehow complicated views on the topic. In the recently published *The Cambridge Companion to the Qur'ān* which claims to give a general historical, linguistic, and theological overview of the Muslims' holy book, there was no chapter designated for the *shīʿīs'* views on the history of the Qur'ān its transmission, its variant readings, its esoteric implications, and its integrity as a text." Nasser, Variant Readings, p. 31. See also Etan Kohlberg

the accepted narrative hagiographical accounts surrounding the 'form of the text' that comprised the 'Uthmānic recension, were not acquiesced to uncritically within Imāmī Shīʿīsm.[84] The Shīʿī tradition, broadly defined however, attests significant religio-cultural and socio-historical complexity in its engagement with Qur'ānic variants. The Shīʿī reception history appertaining to Qur'ānic variegation, as has been robustly documented by Etan Kohlberg and Mohammad Ali Amir-Moezzi, likewise evidences its own rich tradition of considerable consonantal and recitational variegation and multivalence .[85]

Al-Shahrastānī observes in his discussion on the subject, "Variations in readings are [in fact] countless and innumerable, some of them occurring in the transcription and others occurring in the pronunciation."[86] The Shīʿī exegete, traditionalist,

---

and Mohammad Ali Amir-Moezzi, Revelation and Falsification: The Kitāb al-qirā'āt of Aḥmad b. Muḥammad al-Sayyārī, Critical Edition with an Introduction and Notes (Leiden-Boston: Brill, 2009). Hossein Modarressi, "Early Debates on the Integrity of the Qur'ān: A Brief Survey." Studia Islamica no. 77 (1993): 5-39.

84 "...it is obvious that the discipline of *Qirā'āt* and the variant readings of the Qur'ān were used by the Shīʿīs to support their arguments that the Qur'ān was falsified and altered. Therefore, the notion of the seven or ten canonical Readings does not exist in Shīʿīsm." Nasser, *Variant Readings*, pp. 32-33.

85 See Kohlberg and Amir-Moezzi, *Revelation and Falsification*, esp. pp. 41-46, ١٠٢-٤١. Kohlberg and Amir-Moezzi document multiple exemplifications of variances in vocalisation, variegation of lexemes, and variant word orders; and these instances of variegation are substantive and worthy of equally substantive interrogation. Ibid., p. 41. See also, Seyfeddin Kara, "Contemporary Shiʿi Approaches to the History of the Text of the Qur'ān," in *New Trends in Qur'ānic Studies* ed. Mun'im Sirry (Atlanta: Lockwood Press, 2019), pp.123-124.

86 Muḥammad ibn 'Abd al-Karīm al-Shahrastānī, *Mafātīḥ al-Asrār wa-Maṣābīḥ al-Abrār Keys to the Arcana: Shahrastānī's Esoteric Commentary on the Qur'ān*, ed. and trans. Toby Mayer (New York: Oxford University Press in Association with The Institute of Ismaili Studies, 2009), p. 73. While there is some contestation on the matter, we concur with Daryoush Mohammad Poor on the evidence broadly attesting to al-Shahrastānī's Shīʿī identity. See Daryoush Mohammad Poor *Command and Creation a Shiʿi Cosmological Treatise*

and theologian Shaykh Abū Jaʿfar Muḥammad al-Ṭūsī, did not hesitate to effect a robust engagement with variegation, including what came to comprise the "canonical" variants presented in his discussions on these matters within al-Tibiyān.[87] Al-Ṭūsī lists multiple recitational variants and their implications for many verses, and even can be read as making theologically and exegetically significant assertions related to, or even based upon, these variants.[88]

Engaging holistically with the totality of both Sunnī and Shīʿī streams of tradition, we are confronted with the reality that (assuming certain constants) the most primitive form of the Qur'ān, whatever that would exactly comprise, would indeed present the *widest* diversity of multivalence whether by the felicity of de jure Prophetic fiat, or de facto communal living tradition.[89] The potential range of explanatory epistemic models for Qur'ānic pluriformity, and the historiographic, and heuristic frameworks behind such models, themselves present robust challenges and questions.

A Persian Edition and English Translation of Muḥammad al-Shahrastānī's Majlis-i Maktūb (London: I.B. Tauris in Association with The Institute of Ismaili Studies , 2021) esp. pp. 28-70.

87 See, Abū Ja'far Muḥammad ibn al-Ḥasan al-Ṭūsī, *al-Tibiyān fī Tafsīr al-Qur'ān,* 10 volumes, (Beirut: Dār al-ʿAmīrah, 2010).

88 For instance, in his discussion on the variants at Q. 1:4. See al-Ṭūsī, *al-Tibiyān* vol 1, p. 104. These matters are often complicated or obscured by the fact that within works of tradition, such as, for example, *Kitāb al-Kāfī*, one encounters certain statements (by now, becoming common knowledge within Islamic studies), that seem to negate, or even completely eschew, the liceity of Qur'ānic variegation. Traditions such as the following are often invoked: "… abu 'Abd Allah…said: 'If ibn Mas'ud does not read the Holy Qur'ān the way we read it he is straying…' We read the Holy Qur'ān as my father did" *Al-Kafi: Arabic Text and English Translation,* trans. Muhammad Sarwar (New York: The Islamic Seminary ICNYC, 2004), vol. 2, p. 491.

89 Yasin Dutton has a very helpful discussion on this point. See Dutton, "Orality," pp. 32-34. See also, Abū al-Ḥasan Muqātil ibn Sulaymān, *Tafsīr Muqātil ibn Sulaymān,* (Dār al-Kutub al-ʿilmīyah, 2020), vol. 1, p. 25.

One such potential accounting for at least some of the textual plurality evidenced by our manuscripts, and subsequently, within our surviving, attested, reading traditions is that "...when the copies of the Uthmanic codex were sent out to the provincial capitals, these variations were present in these initial copies."[90] The potential opinion that such readings were valid, and that the variegation attested in the apographa were contained in the *imām muṣḥaf*, was certainly a tradition known, and engaged, by traditionalists such as Abū ʿAmr al-Dānī.[91] This recognition, in turn, however, raises significant questions appertaining to the nature of the *imām muṣḥaf*. It may be the case that the *imām* codex comprised a collation of all the potential "ʿUthmānic" readings to be distributed.

Indeed, multiple rigorous stemmatological studies, especially those of Sidky, Van Putten, and Cook, have demonstrated that, antecedent both our Qur'ānic manuscript tradition, as is evidenced within the manuscripts themselves, and much of what traditional reports relate, stemmatics can coherently demonstrate an archetypal antecessor to which they are posterior.[92] A concomitant phenomenon, documented by Alba Fedeli (and invoked by Shady Nasser), is the presence of multiple variants, (representing different Qur'ānic textual and recitational witnesses) within a *single* manuscript![93]

90 Van Putten, "Hišām's ʾIbrāhām," p. 244.

91 See, al-Dānī, *al-Muqniʿ*, p.593.

92 See the following works: Sidky, "Regionality." Ala Vahidnia, "Whence Come Qur'ān Manuscripts? Determining the Regional Provenance of Early Qur'ānic Codices?" *Der Islam* vol. 98 no. 2 (2021): 359-393. Michael Cook "The stemma of the Regional Codices of the Koran." Van Putten, "Hišām's ʿIbrāhām." Van Putten, "The Grace of God," pp. 271-272, 286-287. Mayer, *Keys to the Arcana*, p. 71.

93 See Alba Fedeli, "Digital Humanities and Qur'ānic Manuscript Studies: New Perspectives and Challenges for Collaborative Spaces and Plural Views" *Journal of College of Shariah and Islamic Studies* vol. 38 no. 1 (2020): 147-158, p. 151. Alba Fedeli and Andrew Edmondson, "Early Qur'ānic

In light of this, we concur with those who have posited a definitional framework that asserts the position behind the *amṣār* apographa the ʿUthmānic *imām* likely represented an archetypal spectrum of licit '*variantium lectionum*'.[94] This paradigm has real explanatory power to reconcile the language surrounding the ʿUthmānic *imām* as an *aṣal* (exemplar) source tradition, from which descends the totality of variegation present in the *amṣār* codices.[95]

The nature of the ʿUthmānic text and its readings likewise raises some considerations for Qur'ānic orality and transmission history. In her profoundly important work on the Sanʿāʾ Palimpsest, [96]Asma Hilali has observed several phenomena that, she contends, suggest the production of at least some Qur'ānic manuscripts to be the artifact of what was *de rigueur* the concomitantly oral, aural, and scribal scholarly exercise. This certainly warrants much consideration, certainly more than it has perhaps received.[97]

Manuscripts and their Networks: A Phylogenetic Analysis project", (presentation, Paleo-Qur'ānic Manuscripts: State of the Field Conference, Budapest, May 2017). See also, the citation and discussion in Nasser, *The Second Canonization* p. 162. See also Sidky, "Regionality," p. 161.

94 As noted above, this was a tradition known to, and transmitted by, Abū ʿAmr al-Dānī. See al-Dānī, *al-Muqniʿ*, p. 593.

95 Nasser posits something very similar. See Nasser, *The Second Canonization*, pp. 151-152.

96 Dār al-Makhṭūṭāt MS 01-27.1 (DAM 01-27.1/MS 01-27.1).

97 This could stand true, even if one does not grant the rather unlikely proposal that such manuscripts would comprise mere teaching notes. See Asma Hilali, *The Sanaa Palimpsest: The Transmission of the Qur'ān in the First Centuries* AH palimpsest, p. 70-71. Nicolai Sinai has robustly engaged with her findings and their reception. See Nicolai Sinai, "Beyond the Cairo Edition: On the Study of Early Qur'ānic Codices" *Journal of the American Oriental Society* vol. 140 no. 1 (2020): 189-204, pp. 200-204. Sinai's discussion also makes note of the high degree of discrepancy between the reconstructions of Sadeghi and Goudarzi with those of Hilali. Sinai comments, "…the contrast between the amount of the lower writing that Sadeghi and Goudarzi, on the one hand,

The lower text of the San'ā' palimpsest is generally considered to represent not only a non-'Uthmānic text-type, but an idiosyncratic form, or "species unique" stream of tradition of non-'Uthmānic text-type.[98] The very coherent and compelling reconstructed readings offered by Sadeghi and Goudarzi,[99] however, if correct, not only provide attestation to what comports to established variant readings, or something perhaps formally very similar, being present in the San'ā' Palimpsest lower text,[100] but evidence the tenacity of these readings.

Hilali is right to note elsewhere that the codification of the *qirā'āt*, and the later mediaeval stratification of what the term itself came to represent, is a much later development, and should not be retrojected back onto the primitive form of the text.[101] However, this does not entail that the acceptance of textual or recitational plurality itself is a later phenomenon.[102] Rather, the weight of the evidence provided by studies such as that of Sadeghi and Goudarzi certainly would seem to indicate a contrary state of affairs, and the lower text of the San'ā' Palimpsest as a potential early witness to certain readings. Of profound interest

---

and Hilali, on the other, have been able to make out can be extremely striking..." Ibid, p. 193. See also Sidky, "Regionality", p. 148.

98 Sidky, "Regionality", p. 148. Hilali, *The Sanaa Palimpsest* pp. 22, 23.

99 Sadeghi, and Goudarzi, "San'ā'1 and the Origins of the Qur'ān," *Der Islam* vol.87 (2012):1-129, especially pp. 115-122.

100 The case for certain reconstructions, however, is certainly stronger than others. See Sadeghi and Goudarzi "San'ā'1," pp. 116, 117.

101 Hilali, *The Sanaa Palimpsest*, p. 22

102 "The Qur'ānic variants enshrined in the classical collections should be reimagined as reflections of what were once codices or portions of codices that, to their owners, readers, and students, represented *the single version of the Qur'ān*." Asma Hilali "The Qur'ān Before the Book: History and Concepts of Qur'ānic Variants (*qirā'āt*) *Journal of College of Sharia & Islamic Studies* vol. 38 no. 2 (2021): 233-245, p. 241 Emphasis mine. Hilali is indeed correct, however, in noting "The classical collections of variants should be viewed as the end result of multiple stages of canonization that entailed multiple actors and processes.These include readers, scholars and transmitters." ibid., 240.

for the sort of Qur'ānic textual and recitational variegation under discussion, is the stemmatic study[103] of Michael Cook.[104] Putting what Cook has observed surrounding the *amṣār maṣāḥif*,[105] in conversation with available collations of the traditional reports regarding the variant readings in the *qirā'āt*, can greatly inform us regarding both the commonalties, and the interindividuation evidenced among the *qurrā'* and their students' readings, and the implications for the trajectories and transmission of the Qur'ān.[106]

Especially of interest, are some of the readings from amongst the places of variation comprising what, as Cook has noted, represent Syrian textual isolates.[107] These instances of variegation present a very informative picture of the potential divergent trajectories within the nexus of Qur'ānic textuality and orality. For instance, Q. 2:116, (*qālū*, in contrast to *wa qālū*) expectantly finds Syrian attestation.[108] There is, however, the support from

---

103 "The very fact that the data admit a stemma free from contamination, Cook reasons, is sufficient to dismiss allegations of fabrication since it would require knowledge of stemmatics, which Muslim scholars certainly did not have." Sidky, "Regionality," p. 134.

104 See Michael Cook, "The stemma of the Regional Codices of the Koran," *Graeco- Arabica* 9–10 (2004): 89–104. See also Nasser, *The Second Canonization*, pp. 153-163 and Abū 'Amr al-Dānī, *al-Muqni' fī Ma'rifah Marsūm Maṣāḥif ahl al-Amṣār* (Riyadh: Dār al-Tadmuriyyah, 2010), esp. pp. 537-719.

105 Cook, grounds his observations largely upon the material offered within al-Dānī, Nöldeke, and ibn Abī Dāwūd in his data collation. As noted by Ala Vahidnia, Nöldeke does not have recourse to "...the more significant and earlier *al-Maṣāḥif* by al-Sijistānī..." See Vahidnia, "Whence Come Qur'ān Manuscripts," pp. 362-363.

106 This encompasses the binitarian ontology of both the Qur'ān as semiotic 'Text', both via the oral and written exemplifications thereof.

107 (See: Q. 2:116, Q. 3:184, Q. 4:66, Q. 6:32, Q. 6:137, Q. 7:3, Q. 7:43, Q. 7:75, Q. 7:141, Q. 10:22 Q. 17:93, Q, 39:64, Q. 40:21, Q. 55:12, Q. 55:78, Q. 57:10).

108 The reading is found in the the Syrian readings tradition of ibn 'Amir, as well as other exponents such as that of Shurayḥ and al-Dhamārī. See Aḥmad Mukhtār 'Umar, and 'Abd al-'Āl Sālim Mukram eds. *Mu'jam al-Qirā'āt*

a divergent source, that of the Madīnan ibn ʿAbbās.[109] We have then, granting the validity of this traditional attribution, a Syrian recitation, finding support with a reciter whose codex is of the Madīnan tradition, but who, at this point, follows a Syrian recitation, a recitation whose variant does not seem to enjoy attestation as a variant within what is reported regarding what is known of the content of his own codex.[110]

Marijn van Putten in his discussion of another such variant, that of Q. 10:22, sees the potential for scribal error behind the variegation.[111] This certainly could hold as a tenable option, and he argues convincingly noting the great parity in the consonantal orthography of the defective script between the two competing potential readings. We find in the reading traditions however, a great diversity of those who adopted the reading of the Syrian codex, with at least three different recitational variants that comport to some extent with the orthography of the Syrian reading.[112] Certainly, it could stand true there is a scribal error at work. However, one might also coherently entertain the potential that this is further attestation of the high degree of polysemous multivocality attested within the orality concomitant with the orthographic variegation of theʿUthmānic recensions.[113]

---

al-Qur'ānīyyah maʿa Muqaddimah fī al-Qirā'āt wa ashhar al-Qurrā' (Qum: Intishārāt Uswah, 2005), vol. 1 p. 106.

109 See ʿUmar and Mukram, *Muʿjam al-Qirā'āt*, vol.1 p. 106. See also ʿAbd al-Laṭīf al-Khatīb, *Muʿjam al-Qirā'āt* (Damascus: Dār Sʿad al-Dīn, 2002), vol. 1 p. 180.

110 Arthur Jeffery, *Materials for the History of The Text of the Qur'ān: The Old Codices* (Leiden, Brill: 1937), p. 195.

111 Which he notes presents a difficulty in ascertaining the directionality of the proposed scribal error. Van Putten "When the Readers Break the Rules," p. 450.

112 ʿUmar and Mukram, *Muʿjam al-Qirā'āt* vol.3 pp 66-67. Abd al-Laṭīf al-Khatīb *Muʿjam al-Qirā'āt* vol. 3 p. 521.

113 For an excellent discussion of the Syrian variants and the stemma of Cook see Sidky, "Regionality" and Vahidnia, "Whence Come Qur'ān Manuscripts?"

Therefore, the tensions such as those noted by Van Putten's excellent study regarding why Abū Jaʿfar adopted the Syrian reading,[114] can potentially be resolved by considering *yanshurukum* et al. as being among the licit range of communally accepted *Ausgangstexte*. This would be thoroughly substantiated by Nasser's contention that "The paradigm of associating one codex with one city...should be modified to a picture wherein multiple official and local copies of the Qur'ān were used and consulted."[115] In his profoundly important study of regional variation, Hythem Sidky makes some observations relevant to this assertion, noting,

> While many of the manuscripts included in this study were found to be in perfect agreement with a single region, a number of them are, as it were, contaminated with other variants and deserve discussion. For example, W1913 is an early and quite complete *muṣḥaf*... with a substantial degree of mixing between Syrian, Syrian/Medinan, and Iraqi variants. It has been extensively retouched by a later hand, or later hands, and contains ten scribal changes, outnumbered only by EH23. This latter manuscript has been systematically adjusted, in twenty-two instances, away from the Basran *rasm* towards the Syrian... More generally, the majority of manuscripts exhibit at least one scribal change, and there is an important observation to be made about the directionality of the changes. They are most often *not* in the direction of regional conformity. CPP, for example, which was originally a perfectly Syrian *muṣḥaf*, has had two corrections at S5 and S7 *away* from the Syrian variants ...A review of the canonical reading tradition reveals a picture not unlike the manuscript evidence where there is general consistency between regional orthography and reading, but with notable exceptions.

114 Van Putten "When the Readers Break the Rules," pp. 450-451

115 Nasser, *The Second Canonization*, p. 162.

> For example, Ḥafṣ, a Kufan reader, goes against his regional codex for M11 and K5, reading *tashtahīhi* (Q 43:71) and *ʿamilathu* (Q 36:35) respectively. Abū Jaʿfar as well, a Medinan reader, chooses to follow the Syrian-only variant S10. Interestingly, one of the few regional deviations in TOP, which is a decidedly Medinan codex, is also S10. The Basran reader Abū ʿAmr reads *wa-an* (Q 40:26) against the Basran *rasm*. Instances like these illustrate the complex interaction between oral and written transmission...One can account for the seemingly conflicting evidence through oral-written interaction.[116]

What Sidky has rigorously and rightly noted above, provides attestation of the highest order to the Qur'ān as a highly fluid tradition, and the degree to which this fluidity was embodied by, and exemplified within, the porous variegation encountered within the interleaving of scribal and reading traditions. Surely this state of affairs could not have come about if scribal communities felt universally beholden to their own regional form of the text-written or oral-as an immutable stricture necessitating unwavering conformity.

Granting, as earlier noted, the principles of parsimony, and the general fidelity of scribes, and further, the stability overall of the Qur'ānic text, it becomes readily apparent in view of the phenomena described above, that the category of 'Qur'ān' was both theologically and practically transcendent of merely the category of '*muṣḥaf*' for its seminal late antique transmitters, and their scribal and recitational communities. *Maṣāḥif*, therefore, comprised an indexicality and artifact of, or vehicle for, a given instantiation of this much broader category. Further, we may note Qur'ānic transmission history is beholden to a dyadic interrelationship between textuality, and orality, as the vehicle for instantiating this fluidity. When confronted by the totality of

116 Sidky, "Regionality," pp. 160-162.

the data, the malleability of the Qur'ānic discourse during its annunciation, and transmission, readily attests to its pluriformity.

Conclusive Remarks

Qur'ānic non-static fluidity is inherent not only within its reception and transmission history, but latent within the very nature of the charismatic Prophetic mission; an etiology inherent within the genesis of the milieu within which it was first annunciated as theolocutive enterprise. While the text critic should be disabused of the facile supposition that one may attain, with unqualified certitude, the "original" Prophetic *singular* text (as if, it should be supposed, such an ontological category ever existed); however, we *can* arrive at the range of Prophetically licit *Ausgangstexte*, and there is, indeed, much further, and highly productive text-critical endeavouring to be effectuated at that level of the transmission streams. There are, it should be noted, (looking at the oral transmission alone), "…eight hundred and fourteen (814) unique channels through which the ten eponymous Readings were transmitted…"[117] and over ten thousand documented places of recitational variegation of the oral tradition, amongst *qurrā' rāwīs,*and *ṭurūq.*[118]When one engages the transmission history of the Qur'ān, and specifically, Qur'ānic transmission history *qua* orality, with the concomitant transmission of the Qur'ān *qua* orthographic phenomena, the picture that emerges, despite high degrees of uniformity and stability in the consonantal orthography generally, remains a stream of tradition(s) likewise displaying a high degree of polysemous orality.

Indeed, at any given point, it makes more sense to speak of *'koranisch Ausgangstexte'* rather than it ever would to speak of any "autographic" original singular form of the text. We are,

117 Nasser, *The Second Canonization*, p 89.

118 The more exacting accounting gives the figure as 10,237. See 'Umar and Mukram, Muʿjam *al-Qirā'āt* vol. 8, p. 281.

then, primarily in agreement with Aziz al-Azmeh and others and on the "elasticity"[119] of the 'proto-Qur'ān'. As Nasser rightly contends, the "canonical" codification of the two *rāwī* system "…was retroactively developed in order to suppress the extent of the variants…What we today call the reading of Ḥafṣ *'an* 'Āṣim is but one variant among many that Ḥafṣ transmitted."[120]

The transmission history of the Qur'ān however, was likewise not a "controlled" textual transmission as such. Rather, it was, from its annunciation, the result of a democratized revelation *qua* communally driven multivocal theolocution; this was sustained through its transmission and development, and the contestations between both what *became* subaltern voices (the *shādh/shawādh-dh* readings), and what has been called an emerging scholarly "*haut monde*" enjoying the backing of Caliphal patronage.[121] In all this, we would note there is very little room to speak of "Urtext" proper. The ontology of the Qur'ān precludes such a goal being meaningful. We would likewise note the tenacity of specific readings even post-'Uthmānic recension, by adducing the case of Ubayy ibn Ka'b, the popularity of his codex in Syria,[122] namely, that "…Syrians made a Codex and came to Madinah to check it over with Ubai, and though at the time the standard text was in use, no one dared to dispute the peculiar readings that were derived from Ubai."[123]

Pluriformity remained of demonstrable centrality, both orally and orthographically, even post-'Uthmānic recension,[124] and

---

119 Al-Azmeh "The Paleo-Qur'ān", p. 35

120 Nasser, *The Second Canonization*, p, 3.

121 "…there was no single, well-defined System-Reading by 'Āṣim nor any of the Eponymous Readers…there existed multiple versions and renditions which were simultaneously circulating amongst the community of the Qurrā'." Ibid.

122 Jeffery, *Materials*, p. 114.

123 Ibid.

124 Ibid., p. 114.

"...if we adopt the traditional view that there was one main codex (*Imām*) in each city/region, it is difficult to explain discrepancies and variations we find in these accounts..."[125] Further, "...the fact that Readers of the same region adopted different readings that were based on different scribal traditions suggest that *multiple codices* were circulating in the same area."[126]

Ultimately, we argue that the borrowing and the application of some of the *principles* grounding the CBGM, and perhaps, more properly adopting a digital humanities approach to textual criticism in general, in concert with the proposed QMD project of Donner, and the application of 'Digital Philology' proposed by Fedeli and others[127] will have, no doubt, something particularly felicitous to contribute to these issues. The utility of the works of Hythem Sidky, Van Putten, and others on regionality and orthography have already amply demonstrated the merits of such transdisciplinary stemmatic studies. This is especially the case as it pertains to the question of the "directionality" of Qur'ānic readings.

It is here that the adoption of the principles grounding CBGM, delineating text as physical object from the 'witness' it contains, pursuing the potential for mapping Qur'ānic genealogical and pregenealogical coherence within the manuscript tradition, may prove most felicitous.

---

125 Nasser, *The Second Canonization*, p. 161.

126 Ibid. 162 Emphasis mine.

127 Alba Fedeli "*Early Qur'ānic Manuscripts, their Text, and the Alphonse Mingana Papers held in the Department of Special Collections of the University of Birmingham.*" (University of Birmingham, PhD Diss., 2015), pp. 38-45. See also Alba Fedeli, "Digital Humanities." Barbara Bordalejo and Adam Alberto Vázquez, "You're Collating Just Fine and Other Lies You've Been Telling Yourself," *Digital Medievalist* vol. 14 no. 1 (2021): 1-46.

Bibliography

ʿAbd Allah, ʿAhmed Alī Muhammad. *Variant Readings of the Qur'ān: A Critical Study of their Historical and Linguistic Origins*. Herndon: The International Institute of Islamic Thought, 2006.

Adams, Charles J. "Reflections on the Work of John Wansbrough." *Method & Theory in the Study of Religion* vol. 9 no. 1 (1997): 75-90.

Aland, Kurt, and Barbara Aland. *The Text of the New Testament: An Introduction to the Critical Editions and to the Theory and Practice of Modern Textual Criticism.* Translated by Erroll F. Rhodes. Michigan: William B. Eerdmans Publishing Company, 1995.

Alexander, P. "3 (Hebrew Apocalypse of) Enoch." In *The Old Testament Pseudepigrapha* Vol. 1, edited by James H. Charlesworth, 223-315. Peabody: Hendrickson Publishers, 2020.

ʿAlī, ʿAbdullāh Yūsuf. *The Holy Qur'ān: Text, Translation, and Commentary.* Elmhurst: Tahrike Tarsile Qur'ān, 2012.

Andani, Khalil. "Revelation in Islam: Qur'ānic, Sunni, and Shiʿi Ismaili Perspectives". PhD diss., Harvard University 2020.

Andersen, F.I. "2 (Slavonic Apocalypse of) Enoch." In *The Old Testament Pseudepigrapha* vol. I, edited by James H. Charlesworth, 91-221. Peabody: Hendrickson Publishers, 2020. Al-Azmeh, Aziz. "Modeling the Paleo Qur'ān: Declamations, Reiterations, Fragments and Collations." In *The Making of Religious Texts in Islam: The Fragments and the Whole*, e.dited by Asma Hilali, and S.R. Burge, 35-75. Berlin: Gerlach Press, 2019.

El-Badawi, Emran Iqbal. *The Qur'ān and the Aramaic Gospel Traditions*. New York: Routledge, 2014.

Bellamy, James A. "More Proposed Emendations to the Text of the Koran." *Journal of the American Oriental Society* vol. 116 no. 2 (1996): 196-204.

______, "Some Proposed Emendations to the Text of the Koran." *Journal of the American Oriental Society* vol. 113 no. 4 (1993): 562-573.

Berg, Herbert. "The Implications of, and Opposition to, the Methods and Theories of John Wansbrough." *Method & Theory in the Study of Religion* vol. 9 no. 1 (1997): 3-22.

Bordalejo, Barbara. "The Genealogy of Texts: Manuscripts Traditions and Textual Traditions." *Digital Scholarship in the Humanities* vol. 31 no. 3 (2016):563-577.

Bordalejo, Barbara and Adam Alberto Vázquez. "You're Collating Just Fine and Other Lies You've Been Telling Yourself." *Digital Medievalist* vol. 14 no. 1 (2021):1-46.

Boyarin, Daniel, "Is Metatron a Converted Christian?" Judaïsme ancien/Ancient Judaism, vol. 1 (2013): 13–62.

Brown, Jonathan "The Qur'ān, the Jews and Ezra as the Son of God" Accessed March 21, 2023 https://drjonathanbrown.com/2016/the-quran-the-jews-and-ezra-as-the-son-of-god/

Bukharin, Mikhail D. "Mecca on the Caravan Routes in Pre-Islamic." In *The Qur'ān in Context,* edited by Angelika Neuwirth, Nicolai Sinai, and Michael Marx, 115-134. Leiden-Boston: Brill 2010.

Choat, Malcolm. "Dating Papyri: Familiarity, Instinct and Guesswork." *Journal for the Study of the New Testament* vol. 42 no. 1 (2019): 59-83.

Cook, Michael. "The *Stemma* of the Regional Codices of the Koran." *Graeco- Arabica* 9–10 (2004): 89–104.

Cole, Juan. "A Sickness in the Heart: Were the Qur'ān's Hypocrites a Late Antique Sect?" *The Muslim World* vol. 111 no. 3 (2021): 358-375.

______, "Dyed in Virtue: The Qur'ān and Plato's *Republic*." *Greek, Roman and Byzantine Studies* vol. 61 no. 4 (2021): 580-604.

______, "Infidel or Paganus? The Polysemy of Kafara in the Qur'ān." *Journal of the American Oriental Society* vol. 140 no. 3 (2020): 615-635.

______, "'It was Made to Appear to Them So': The Crucifixion, Jews, and Sasanian War Propaganda in the Qur'ān." *Religion* vol. 51 no. 3 (2021):404-422.

______, "Muhammad and Justinian: Roman Legal Traditions and the Qur'ān." *Journal of Near Eastern Studies* vol. 79 no. 2 (2020): 183-196.

______, "New Historicism: A Manifesto for Writing a History of the Qur'ān." Accessed September 17, 2023. https://www.juancole.com/2019/03/historicism-manifesto-writing.html

______, "Paradosis and Monotheism: A late Antique Approach to the Meaning of Islam in the Qur'ān" *Bulletin of the School of Oriental and African Studies* vol. 82 no. 3 (2019): 405-425.

al-Dānī, Abū 'Amr. *al-Muqniʿ fī Maʿrifah Marsūm Maṣāḥif ahl al-Amṣār*. Riyadh: Dār al-Tadmuriyyah, 2010.

Déroche, François. *Qur'āns of the Umayyads: A First Overview.* Leiden-Boston: Brill, 2014.

Donner, Fred M. "The Qur'ān in Recent Scholarship: Challenges and Desiderata." In *The Qur'ān in its Historical Context*, 29-50, edited by Gabriel Said Reynolds. New York: Routledge, 2008.

Dutton, Yasin. "Orality, Literacy and the 'Seven Aḥruf' Ḥadīth." *Journal of Islamic Studies* vol. 23 no. 1 (2012): 1-49.

Ehrman, Bart D. *The Orthodox Corruption of Scripture: The Effect of Early Christological Controversies on the Text of the New Testament*. New York: Oxford University Press, 1993.

Epp, Eldon Jay "In the Beginning was the New Testament Text, but Which Text? A Consideration of '*Ausgangstext*' and "Initial Text'. In *Texts and Traditions: Essays in Honor of J. Keith Elliot,* eds. Peter Doble and Jeffrey Kloha 35-70. Leiden-Boston: Brill, 2014.

______, "The Multivalence of the Term "Original Text" in New Testament Textual Criticism." *The Harvard Theological Review* vol. 92 no. 3 (1999):245-281.

Fedeli, Alba. "Digital Humanities and Qur'ānic Manuscript Studies: New Perspectives and Challenges for Collaborative Spaces and Plural Views." *Journal of College of Shariah and Islamic Studies* vol. 38 no. 1 (2020): 147-158.

______, "Early Qur'ānic Manuscripts, their Text, and the Alphonse Mingana Papers held in the Department of Special Collections of the University of Birmingham." PhD Diss., University of Birmingham, 2015.

______, "The Qur'ānic Text from Manuscript to Digital Form: Metalinguistic Markup of Scribes and Editors." In *From Scrolls to Scrolling: Sacred Texts Materiality, and Dynamic Media Cultures* 213-245, edited by Bradford Anderson. Boston: De Gruyter, 2020.

Fedeli, Alba, and Andrew Edmondson. 2017. "Early Qur'ānic Manuscripts and their Networks: a Phylogenetic Analysis Project." Paper Presented at Paleo-Qur'ānic Manuscripts: State of the Field Conference, Budapest.

Finster, Barbara. "Arabia in Late Antiquity: An Outline of the Cultural Situation in the Peninsula at the Time of Muhammad." In *The Qur'ān in Context,* edited by Angelika Neuwirth, Nicolai Sinai, and Michael Marx 61-114. Leiden-Boston: Brill, 2010.

Griffith, Sidney H. *The Bible in Arabic: The Scripture of the "People of the Book" in the Language of Islam.* Princeton: Princeton University Press, 2013.

Gurry, Peter J. *A Critical Examination of the Coherence-Based Genealogical Method in New Testament Textual Criticism.* Boston: Brill, 2017. Hussain, Saqib "Q 63 (Sūrat al-Munāfiqūn): A Text-Critical and Structural Analysis." In *Unlocking the Medinan Qur'ān*, edited by Nicolai Sinai, 543-589, Leiden-Boston: Brill2022.

Hilali, Asma "The Qur'ān Before the Book: History and Concepts of Qur'ānic Variants *(qirā'āt) Journal of College of Sharia & Islamic Studies* vol. 38 no. 2 (2021): 233-245.

______, *The Sanaa Palimpsest: The Transmission of the Qur'ān in the First Centuries AH.* New York: Oxford University Press in Association with the Institute of Ismaili Studies, 2017.

Isaac, E. "1 (Ethiopic Apocalypse of) Enoch." In *The Old Testament Pseudepigrapha.* Vol. 1., edited by James H. Charlesworth, 5-89. Peabody: Hendrickson Publishers, 2020.

Jeffery, Arthur. *Materials for the History of The Text of the Qur'ān: The Old Codices.* Leiden: Brill, 1937.

Kara, Seyfeddin, "Contemporary Shiʿi Approaches to the History of the Text of the Qur'ān." In *New Trends in Qur'ānic Studies*, edited by Mu'nim Sirry, 109-124. Atlanta: Lockwood Press, 2019.

Katsh, Abraham I. *Judaism and the Koran: Biblical and Talmudic Backgrounds of the Koran and its Commentaries.* New York: A.S. Barnes, 1962.

al-Khatīb, ʿAbd al-Laṭīf. *Muʿjam al-Qirā'āt.* 11 volumes. Damascus: Dār Sʿad al-Dīn, 2002.

Klęczar, Aleksandra "Alexander in the Jewish Tradition: From Second Temple Writings to Hebrew Alexander Romances." In *Brill's Companion to the Reception of Alexander the Great*, edited by K.R. Moore, 379-402. Leiden-Boston: Brill, 2018.

Kohlberg, Etan and Mohammad Ali Amir-Moezzi, *Revelation and Falsification: The Kitāb al- qirā'āt of Aḥmad b. Muḥammad al-Sayyārī, Critical Edition with an Introduction and Notes.* Leiden-Boston: Brill, 2009.

al-Kulaynī, Muḥammad ibn Yaʿqūb ibn Isḥāq. *Al-Kafi: Arabic Text and English Translation.* 8 Volumes. Translated by Muhammad Sarwar. New York: The Islamic Seminary ICNYC, 2004.

Lane, Edward William. *Al-Qāmūs Madd: An Arabic-English Lexicon.* 8 volumes. New Delhi: Asian Educational Services, 2003.

Law Timothy Michael. *When God Spoke Greek: The Septuagint and the Making of the Christian Bible.* New York: Oxford University Press, 2013.

Lindenberger J.M, "Ahiqar: A New Translation and Introduction." In *The Old Testament Pseudepigrapha.* Vol. 2., edited by James H. Charlesworth, 479-507. Peabody: Hendrickson Publishers, 2020.

Martin, Gary D. *Multiple Originals: New Approaches to Hebrew Bible Textual Criticism.* Atlanta: Society of Biblical Literature Press, 2010. Mink, Gerd "The Coherence-Based Genealogical Method – What is it about?" https://www.uni-muenster.de/INTF/Genealogical_method.html Accessed January, 14 2023.

______, Remarks on Carlson, "A Bias at the Heart of the CBGM," "INTF Blog" https://ntvmr.uni-muenster.de/intfblog/-/blogs/remarks-on-carlson-a-bias-at-the-heart-of-the-cbgm-guest-post-by-gerd-mink-

Modarressi, Hossein. "Early Debates on the Integrity of the Qur'ān: A Brief Survey." *Studia Islamica* no. 77 (1993): 5-39.

Moqbel, Tareq. "The Emergence of the Qirāʾāt: the Divine Permission Hypothesis." *Journal of Islamic Studies* vol. 33 no. 3 (2022): 299-330.

Nasser, Shady Hekmat. *The Second Canonization of the Qur'ān (324/936): Ibn Mujāhid and the Founding of the Seven Readings.* Leiden-Boston: Brill, 2020.

______, *The Transmission of the Variant Readings of the Qur'ān: The Problem of Tawātur and the Emergence of* Shawādhdh. Leiden-Boston: Brill, 2013.

Neuwirth, Angelika. *The Qur'ān and Late Antiquity: A Shared Heritage.* New York: Oxford University Press, 2019.

______, "Two Faces of the Qur'ān: Qur'ān and *Muṣḥaf.*" *Oral Tradition* vol. 25 no 1. (2010): 141-156.

Nöldeke, Theodor, Friedrich Schwally, Gotthelf Bergsträßer, and Otto Pretzl. *The History of the Qur'ān,* translated by Wolfgang Behn, Leiden-Boston: Brill, 2013.

Nongbri, Brent. "Paleographic Analysis of Codices from the Early Christian Period: A Point of Method." *Journal for the Study of the New Testament* vol. 42 no. 1 (2019): 84-97

Parker, David C. *The Living Text of the* Gospels. Cambridge: Cambridge University Press, 1997.

______, "Is "Living Text" Compatible with "Initial Text"?" In *The Textual History of the Greek New Testament: Changing Views in Contemporary Research*, edited by Klaus Wachtel and Michael W. Holmes 13- 22. Atlanta: The Society of Biblical Literature Press, 2011.

Pinto, Leonardo Pessoa da Silva. "The CBGM and Lachmannian Textual Criticism." *TC: A Journal of Biblical Textual Criticism* vol. 27 (2022): 17-31.

Poor, Daryoush Mohammad. *Command and Creation a Shiʿi Cosmological Treatise A Persian Edition and English Translation of Muḥammad al-Shahrastānī's Majlis-i Maktūb*. London: I.B. Tauris in Association with The Institute of Ismaili Studies, 2021.

"Preliminary Considerations on the Corpus Coranicum Christianum-The Qur'ān in Translation A survey of the State-of-the-Art Abstract Dossier" Berlin: Freie Universität Berlin Chair of Byzantine Studies, 2018.

Puin, Gerd. R. "Observations on early Qur'ān manuscripts in Sanʿāʾ." In *The Qur'ān as Text*, edited by S. Wild 107-111. Leiden-New York: Brill 1996.

al-Qalānisī, Muḥammad ibn al-Husayn, *al-Kifāyah al-Kubrā fī al-Qirāʾāt al-ʿAshr*. Beirut: Dar al-Kutub al-ʿIlmīyah, 2007

Reynolds, Gabriel Said. *The Qur'ān and its Biblical Subtext.* New York: Routledge, 2010.

Sadeghi, Behnam. "Criteria for Emending the Text of the Qur'ān." In *Law and Tradition in Classical Islamic Thought: Studies in Honor of Professor Hossein Modarressi*, edited by Michael Cook, Najam Haider, Intisar Rabb, and Asma Sayeed, 21-41. New York: Palgrave Macmillan, 2013.

______, "The chronology of the Qur'ān: A Stylometric research Program" *Arabica*, vol. 58 (2011): 210-299.

Sadeghi, Behnam and Mohsen Goudarzi "Sanʿāʾ1 and the Origins of the Qur'ān" *Der Islam* vol.87 (2012):1-129.

Schniedewind, William M. "Problems in the Paleographic Dating of Inscriptions." In *The Bible and Radiocarbon Dating: Archeology, Text and Science*, edited by Thomas E. Levy and Thomas Higham 405-412. New York: Routledge, 2005.

Schultz, Joseph P. "Angelic Opposition to the Ascension of Moses and the Revelation of the Law." *The Jewish Quarterly Review* vol. 61 no. 4 (1971): 282-307.

al-Shahrastānī, Muḥammad ibn ʿAbd al-Karīm *Mafātīḥ al-Asrār wa-Maṣābīḥ al-Abrār Keys to the Arcana: Shahrastānī's Esoteric Commentary on the Qur'ān*, Edited and Translated by Toby Mayer. New York: Oxford University Press in Association with The Institute of Ismaili Studies, 2009.

Shah, Mustafa. "The Early Arabic Grammarians' Contribution to the Collection and Authentication of Qur'ānic Readings: The Prelude to ibn Mujāhid's *Kitāb al-Sabaʿa*." *Journal of Qur'ānic Studies* vol. 6 no. 1 (2004): 72-102.

al-Shāṭibī, Abū al-Qāsim. *Manẓūmah Ḥirz al-Amānī wa Wajh al-Tahānī Qirā'āt al-Sabʿ* ("al-Shāṭibiyyah"). Edited by Ayman Swed. Dār al-Ghūthānī, 2019.

Shoemaker, Stephen J. *Creating the Qur'ān: A Historical Critical Study.* Oakland: University of California Press, 2022.

Sidky, Hythem. "On the Regionality of Qur'ānic Codices." *Journal of the International Qur'ānic Studies Association* vol. 5 (2020): 133-210.

______, Review of Daniel Alan Brubaker, *Corrections in Early Qur'ānic Manuscripts: Twenty Examples*, *Al-ʿUṣūr Al- Wusṭā: The Journal of Middle East Medievalists* vol. 27 no. 1 (2019): 273-288.

Sinai, Nicolai "Beyond the Cairo Edition: On the Study of Early Qur'ānic Codices"

Journal of the American Oriental Society vol. 140 no. 1 (2020): 189-204

______, "When did the Consonantal Skeleton of the Qur'ān Reach Closure Part I." *Bulletin of SOAS* vol. 77 no. 2 (2014): 273-292.

______, "When did the Consonantal Skeleton of the Qur'ān Reach Closure Part II." *Bulletin of SOAS* vol. 77 no. 3 (2014): 509-521.

Small, Keith E. *Textual Criticism and Qur'ān Manuscripts.* Lanham: Lexington Books, 2011.

al-Ṭabarī, Muḥammad Ibn Jarīr. *Tafsīr al-Ṭabarī: Jāmiʿ al-Bayān fī taʾwīl al-Qur'ān.* 13 volumes. Beirut: Dār al-Kutub al-ʿilmīyah, 2014.

Tesei, Tommaso "The Qur'ān(s) in Context(s)." *Journal Asiatique* vol. 309 no. 2 (2021):185-202.

______,The prophecy of D̠ū-l-Qarnayn (Q 18:83-102) and the Origins of the Qur'ānic Corpus". Miscellanea arabica 2013–2014: 273-90

al-Ṭūsī, Muḥammad ibn al-Ḥasan. *al-Tibīyān fī Tafsīr al- Qur'ān.* Beirut: Dār al-ʿAmīrah,2010.

Thorburn, William M. "The Myth of Occam's Razor." *Mind* vol. 27 no. 107 (1918): 345-353.

ʿUmar, Aḥmad Mukhtār and ʿAbd al-ʿĀl Sālim Mukram eds '*Muʿjam al-Qirāʾāt al-Qur'ānīyyah maʿa Muqaddimah fī al-Qirāʾāt wa ashhar al-Qurrāʾ.* 8 volumes. Qum: Intishārāt Uswah 2005.

Vahidnia, Ala. "Whence Come Qur'ān Manuscripts? Determining the Regional Provenance of Early Qur'ānic Codices." *Der Islam* vol. 98 no. 2 (2021):359-393.

Van Putten, Marijn. "Hišām's ʾIbrāhām: Evidence for a Canonical Qur'ānic Reading Based on the Rasm." *Journal of the Royal Asiatic Society* Series 3 vol. 30 no. 2 (2020): 231-250

______, *Qur'ānic Arabic from its Hijazi Origins to its Classical Reading Traditions* (Leiden: Brill, 2022),

______, "The Grace of God as Evidence for a Written Uthmanic Archetype: The Importance of Shared Orthographic Idiosyncrasies." *Bulletin of SAOS* (2019): 271-288.

______, "When the Readers Break the Rules: Disagreements with the Consonantal Text in the Canonical Qur'ānic Reading Traditions." *Dead Sea Discoveries* vol. 29. (2022): 438-462.

Wachtel, Klaus. "The Development of the Coherence-Based Genealogical Method (CBGM), its Place in Textual Scholarship, and Digital Editing," in *The Future of New Testament Textual Scholarship*, edited by Garrick Allen 435-446. Tübingen: Mohr-Siebeck, 2019.

Wansbrough, John *Qur'ānic Studies: Sources and Methods in Scriptural Interpretation.* Amherst: Prometheus Books, 2004.

Wasserman, Tommy, and Peter J. Gurry *A New Approach to Textual Criticism: An Introduction to the Coherence-Based Genealogical Method* Atlanta: Society of Biblical Literature Press, 2017.

CHAPTER ELEVEN

The Recitations of the Shīʿah Imams and its Role in the History of the Qur'ān

Meysam Kohantorabi

The recitation and the variances of recitations of the Qur'ān is a topic that has been of immense interest among Muslim scholars. All classical scholars of the Qur'ān and its interpretation have, to some extent, addressed this issue in their writings. Some scholars have dealt with the recitations from the angle of which recitations are superior to others, and discussed the characteristics that make any particular recitation superior. Commentators have also discussed this topic due to the differences that arise in the meaning of verses on the basis of variant readings. The differences in the readings of the Qur'ān are so wide that the "*Dictionary of Qur'ānic readings*" - the most comprehensive work which collects the different variations in eleven volumes - lists more than ten thousand differences.

There are various approaches that have been adopted to the recitations of the Qur'ān. Some hold the recitations to be differences related to the words and expressions of the revelation, which have been narrated by reciters on specific letters and words of the Qur'ān, and their qualities such as reduction and intensification.[1] Various stages of development has also been

1 Badr al- Dīn Zarkashī, *Al-Burhān fī 'Ulūm al-Qur'ān* (Beirut: Dār al-Maʿārifah, 1989), 1: 318.

discussed. For example, ʿAbdulhādī Faḍlī consideres there to be sixteen stages in the formation of this discipline. He argues that the initial stages occurred in the presence of Prophet Muhammad. After receiving the revelation from Gabriel, the Prophet then recited it to the people, and since the various tribes had different accents, the criterion for reciting the Qur'ān was the Prophet's accent, which was heard from him while teaching the Qur'ān to the people. The next stages relate to the shortcomings of the writing style of the Qur'ān in the Uthmanic codex. The codification of the seven prominent reciters by ibn Mujāhid, as well as the difference of opinion around the superiority of certain lexical, acoustic, morphological and syntactic aspects of Qur'ānic words and sentences, represent the next steps in the development of this discipline.[2]

A historical study of the Qur'ān's recitations underscore that after the death of the Prophet, especially in the first and second century, certain people had their own recitations. They in turn had their own students who were taught these recitations, and who came to be called the reciters (Qurrā'). The Shīʿah Imams also adopted recitations that were different from the recitation of *Ḥafṣ*. Despite this variance in recitation, Shīʿah Imams never established themselves as reciters, nor actively promoted their own recitation. We will elaborate on the reasons for this in the following sections. However, it is clear from works on the science of recitation, *ḥadīth*, and exegesis – from both Shīʿah and Sunni sources – that recitations dissimilar from *Ḥafṣ* are attributed to the Shīʿah Imams. These readings are worth paying attention to for several reasons. One of these reasons is that Ali, the fourth Caliph and first Imam of Twelver Shiites, is traditionally considered to be one of the most important scribes during the Qur'ān's revelation. He is also described as having his own Muṣḥaf.[3]

2 ʿAbdulhādī Faḍlī, *Al-Qirā'āt al-Qur'āniah: Tārīkh wa Taʿrīf* (Beirut: Dār al-Qalam, 1984), 14-54.

3 Aḥmad ibn Abī Ya'qūb Yaʿqūbī, *Tārīkh Yaʿqūbī* (Beirut: Dār Ṣādir, 1959), 1: 113.

A described characteristic of Ali's Muṣḥaf is that it is in accord with the Prophet's own recitation.[4] Shīʿah ḥadīth state that this Muṣḥaf was inherited by the Imams after Ali and hence, they also had access to Ali's recitation.[5] Therefore, the recitations narrated by the other Shīʿah Imams are understood to be recitations contained in Ali's Muṣḥaf. Another important reason to focus on the recitations of the Shīʿah Imams, is because the Shīʿah Imams are traditionally considered to be among the most knowledgeable on the Qur'ān in their time. In fact, many authors of books relating to the science of recitation and exegesis who narrated the recitations of the Shīʿah Imams were Sunnis. Examples include figures such as ibn Jinni, al-Ṭabarī, al-Zamakhsharī, and al-Qurṭubī who repeatedly quote recitations from the Shīʿah imams in their respective works.[6]

With regards to the recitations transmitted by the Shīʿah Imams, the most important classical sources include:

1. "*Qirā'āt Amir al-Mu'minīn Alī*" authored by Zaid Bin Ali. This book, which purportedly contains Ali's recitation, is ascribed to Zayd, the son of Imam Sajjad, the fourth Shīʿah Imam, in the late first and early second century AH.[7]
2. "*Qirā'āt Amir al-Mu'minīn*" authored by Abu Ṭāhir al-Muqri', who was a Sunni and the slave of ibn Mujāhid who canonized the seven recitations.[8] This book was written in the fourth century AH.

4 Muḥammad Hādī Maʿrifat, *Al-Tamhīd fī 'Ulūm al-Qur'ān* (Qom: Tamhīd, 2007), 1: 293.

5 Muḥammad Bāqir Majlisī, *Baḥār al-Anwār* (Beirut: Dār Iḥyā' al-Turāth al-ʿArabī, 1982), 92: 42.

6 Mujīb Rafīʿī, *Qirā'āt Ahl al-Bait al-Qur'āniyah* (Qom: Dār al-Ghadīr, 2003), 7-144.

7 Muḥammad ibn Isḥāq al-Nadīm, *Al-Fihrist* (Beirut: Dār al-Maʿārifah, 1996), 328.

8 Ḥasan ibn Yūsuf Ḥillī, *Rijāl al-ḥilli* (Najaf: Maṭbaʿat al-Ḥaydariyah, 1961), 244.

3. Another "*Qirā'āt Amir al-Mu'minīn*" written by ibn Juḥām in the fourth century AH. Shīʿah sources consider ibn Juḥām to be a reliable narrator of Shīʿah ḥadīth.[9]
4. " *Qirā'āt Ahl al-Bayt*" was also written by ibn Juḥām in the fourth century AH.[10]

However, of these above-mentioned books, only their titles remain extant and we do not have the contents of these works.[11] Nevertheless, contemporary extant works include "*Qirā'āt Ahl al-Bait al-Qur'āniyah*" by Mujīb Rafīʿī.[12] Although the author attempts to collect the recitations attributed to the Shīʿah Imams, he does not mention all the recitations. My previous work in Persian titled "پژوهشی در قرائات منسوب به اهل بیت" (*Research on Recitations Attributed to the Ahl al-Bayt*) cites 407 recitations that are attributed to the Shīʿah Imams. In this work, in addition to categorising the recitations based on the difference in word structure - noun, verb and letter - or their position in the sentence, conceptual differences with *Ḥafṣ* are also elaborated upon. These previous works have only sought to collect and conceptualise readings attributed to the Shīʿah Imams and have not addressed the readings from a historical standpoint. Here we focus on the historical significance and impact of these recitations.

Typology of Recitations Attributed to Twelver Shīʿah Imams

In general, the recitations attributed to the Shīʿah Imams can be divided into two groups. The first group are recitations which

9 Aḥmad ibn 'Alī Najāshī, *Rijāl al-Najāshī* (Qom: Al-Nashr al-Islāmī, 1985), 379.
10 Ibn al-Nadīm, *Al-Fihrist*, 423.
11 Aqā Buzurq Tehrānī, *Al-Dharī'ah ilā Taṣānīf al-Shī'ah* (Beirut: Dār al-Aḍwā', 1982), 17: 54-55.
12 This book was published in 1993 in 144 pages by Dār al-Ghadīr Publication in Qom.

contain extra phrases or sentences from the traditional recitation of the Qur'ān. The second group relates to differences in the readings themselves, which include differences such as: accent, structure or syntactic function of the word, pronunciation of letters (especially the pronunciation of the letter Hamzah), pronouns, or, the verb being gramatically different (active or passive, singular or plural). Most contemporary Shīʿah scholars and commentators do not consider the first group of differences as readings *per se*, but consider them to be interpretations, hence we refer to this first group as "interpretative statements".

Interpretative Statements

A large number of recitations attributed to the Shīʿah Imams are short explanations that the Imams used to interpret and conceptualize certain words. This has created the impression among some[13] that these statements are part of the text of the Qur'ān from the perspective of the Shīʿah Imams. For example, with regards to the verse "إِنَّ الَّذِينَ كَفَرُوا وَ ظَلَمُوا لَمْ يَكُنِ اللَّهُ لِيَغْفِرَ لَهُمْ وَ لا لِيَهْدِيَهُمْ طَرِيقاً"[14] (Surely the unbelievers, who have done evil, God would not forgive them, neither guide them on any road),[15] Imam Sadiq is reported to have recited it as: "إِنَّ الَّذِينَ كَفَرُوا وَ ظَلَمُوا آلَ مُحَمَّدٍ حَقَّهُم لَمْ يَكُنِ اللَّهُ لِيَغفِرَ لَهُم وَ لاَ لِيَهْدِيَهُم طَرِيقاً" (Surely the unbelievers, who have done evil to the family of the Prophet Muhammad, God would not forgive them, neither guide them on any road).[16]

Another example can be found with the first two verses of *Sūrat al-ʿAsr*: "وَ الْعَصْرِ إِنَّ الْانسَانَ لَفِى خُسْر" (By the afternoon! Surely

13 Although narrations of this kind are present in some classical Shīʿah sources they have not explicitly confirmed them. The most prominent Shīʿah scholar who cited such reports is Ḥussain Nūrī, whose book will be mentioned later on.

14 *Al-Nisā'* 3: 168.

15 The English translations of the Qur'ān are taken from Arthur Arberry.

16 ʿAlī ibn Ibrāhīm Qummī, *Tafsīr al-Qummī* (Qom: Dār al-Kitāb, 1987), 2: 159.

Man is in the way of loss).[17] In his commentary, al-Ṭabarī reports that Imam Ali read these verses as: "وَ الْعَصْرِ وَنَوَائِبِ الدَّهْرِ انَّ الانسان لفى خَسِرَ وَ انه فيه الى آخِرَ الدَّهْرِ" (By the afternoon <u>and the troubles of this world!</u> Surely Man is in the way of loss <u>and it will be like this until the end of this world</u>).[18] As we can see from these examples, the traditional verses of the Qur'ān have additional phrases attached to them. Hence, among contemporary Shīʿah scholars and Shīʿah's in general, they are not considered to be actual recitations. Rather, it is generally upheld to be unacceptable that there are certain verses in the Qur'ān, as it is recited today, which are missing additional wordings. For example, we can see this approach adopted by Shaykh Ṭūsī in the beginning of his commentary. Just as he rejects the claim of distortion of the Qur'ān, he also rejects the claim of any additions and subtractions to verses to the Qur'ān, Furthermore, he considers the narrations which adopt such claims to be weak.[19] In a similar way, Ayatollah Maʿrifat lists the views of over twenty Twelver Shīʿah scholars regarding this issue and quotes their explicit opposition to the notion of deficiency to the Muṣḥaf.[20] However, despite the widespread adoption of this position, some scholars such as Ālusī, Ehsan Elahī Zahīr, Nasser al-Qafarī and Ṣalāḥ Abdul Fattaḥ Khalidī citing these reports, attribute the belief of distorting the Qur'ān to the Shīʿah.[21] We will elaborate on this issue later on.

---

17 *Al-ʿAsr* 103:1-2.

18 Muḥammad ibn Jarīr Tabarī, *Jāmiʿ al-Bayān fī Tafsīr al-Qur'ān* (Beirut: Dār al-Maʿārifah, 1991), 30: 188.

19 Muḥammad ibn Ḥassan Ṭūsī, *Al-Tibyān fī Tafsīr al-Qur'ān* (Qom: Al-Nashr al-Islāmī, 1999), 1: 3.

20 Muḥammad Hādī Maʿrifat, *Ṣiānat al-Qur'ān min al-Tahrīf* (Qom: Tamhīd, 2006), 11: 59-78.

21 Asad Allah Rezaei, "Wahhabis and the accusation against Kulainī about distorting the Qur'ā n," *Sirāj Munīr* 2, no. 7&8 (January 2013): 43-78.

Different Recitations

Most of the recitations attributed to the Shīʿah Imams are what I term as 'different recitations'. They are recitations that do not have additional wordings or phrases - such as the examples mentioned in the previous section – but rather are variant ways of reciting the Qur'ān (akin to the recitations attributed to the Seven Reciters). The number of these recitations is 407. These recitations are divided into two parts. The first part are recitations in which the root of the word is different from the root of the word in *Ḥafṣ*. The number of variants with respect to different roots numbers 46. With the remaining 361 differences, the root of the word remains the same, and the difference is related to other factors such as the accent, conjugation of the verb, definite and indefinite, and other structural and syntactic differences.[22]

We can see an example of differences stemming from the root of the word, with a recitation that is ascribed to Imam Ali regarding verse 182 of *Sūrat al-Baqarah*, in which he used the word "حَيْفاً" meaning 'deviation from moderation' instead of the word "جَنَفاً" meaning 'tend to'.[23] The root of these two words is not the same; the first comes from "جنف" and the second from "حيف". Another example is a recitation ascribed to both Imam Sajjad and Sadiq, who use the word "شَعَفَ" meaning 'to reach the top of something' in their recitations instead of "شَغَفَ " meaning 'removing the veil' in verse 30 of *Sūrat Yūsuf*.[24] In these two

22 Meysam Kohantorabi, "Investing the Quality of Reading of Hamzah in the Recitations Attributed to Ahl Al-Bayt," *Studies of Qurān Reading Journal* 8, no.15 (February 2021): 13.

23 Muḥammad ibn Aḥmad Qurṭubī, *Al-Jāmiʿ fī Aḥkām al-Qur'ān* (Tehran: Naser Khosrow, 1985), 2: 270.

24 Abulfatḥ Uthmān ibn Jinnī, *Al-Muḥtasab fī Wujūh Shawādh al-Qirā'āt* (Cairo: Al-Majlis al-Aʿlā li Shuʿūn al-Islāmiyah, 1994), 1: 339.

examples, the differences stems from the lack of a dot in the early writing script of the Qur'ān.[25]

The second type of differences are far more common. It is reported that Imam Ali recited the word "قِنْوَانٌ" as "قُنْوَانٌ" in verse 99 of *Sūrat al-An'ām.*[26] Difference in accent is the reason for the difference in this word's recitation. The former is the accent of the Hijaz region while the latter is the accent of the Qays tribe.[27] However, the root of both words remain the same. Another example is ascribed to Imam Sadiq's recitation of verse 159 of *Sūrat Āl 'Imrān*, in which he uses the verb "عَزَمْتُ" instead of the verb "عَزَمْتَ".[28] These two verbs also share the same root, but their difference stems from their conjugation. There are eighteen factors that account for the differences in recitations under this grouping, that is, differences where the words keep the same root. These eighteen factors include:

1. Differences in the triliteral or extra-triliteral verb
2. Verb conjugation
3. The simultaneous difference in the triliteral or extra-triliteral verb and conjugation
4. Active and passive verbs
5. The simultaneous difference in conjugation and active and passive verbs
6. The simultaneous difference in triliteral or extra-triliteral verb and active and passive verbs
7. Singular, dual and plural of the word
8. Word structure

---

25 To read all the examples, see: Meysam Kohantorabi, *Research on recitations attributed to the Ahl al-Bayt* (Qayen: Bozorgmehr, 2020), 30-57.

26 Ḥussain ibn Aḥmad ibn Khāliwaih, *Mokhtaṣar fī Shawādh al-Qur'ā'n min al-Kitāb al-Badī'* (Beirut: Al-Rayān, 2008), 45.

27 Muḥammad ibn Yūsuf Andulusī, *Al-Baḥr al-Muḥīt fī al-Tafsīr* (Beirut: Dār al-Fikr, 1999), 4: 591.

28 Faḍl bin Ḥassan Ṭabrisī, *Majma' al-Bayān fī Tafsīr al-Qur'ān* (Tehran: Tehran University, 1998), 2: 869.

9. Syntactic composition of the word
10. Differences caused by the different positions of the grammar schools
11. Pronouns
12. Difference in the letter "الف"
13. Accents
14. Final vowel of an Arabic word
15. Pronunciation of the Hamzah"ء"
16. Differences caused by the mutation of letters
17. Difference in letters used before verbs
18. Pronunciation of Arabicized words of the Qur'ān[29]

The Claim of Distortion to the Qur'ān and Its Relationship with the Recitations of Twelver Shīʿah Imams

Perhaps the most controversial issue related to the recitations of the Shīʿah Imams, which has created multiple challenges, is the claim that the Shīʿah believe in the Qur'ān's distortion. This is based on two issues: the first relates to Imam Ali's Muṣḥaf and the second on the 'interpretative statements' mentioned above. Due to the importance of these two issues and their connection with the history of the Qur'ān among the Shīʿah, we will discuss them below.

Imam Ali's Muṣḥaf and Claim of Distortion to the Qur'ān

According to various reports in Shīʿah sources and some Sunni books, the first person to collect the Qur'ān was Ali. For example, ibn Nadim states, "The first Muṣḥaf that was compiled was

29 For a closer elaboration of these differences, see: Kohantorabi, *Research on recitations attributed to the Ahl al-Bayt*, 58-225.

Ali's Muṣḥaf, and this Muṣḥaf was in the possession of the family of Ja'far. I saw a Muṣḥaf which was written in Ali's handwriting and some pages were missing from it, and the family of Hasan bin Ali (the second Shī'ah Imam) had taken it as a legacy".[30] In another report ibn Sirin states, "At the beginning of Abu Bakr's Caliphate, Ali stayed at home and collected the Qur'ān. No matter how hard I tried, I could not get this Qur'ān".[31] In another report, al-Suyūṭī states that Ali is said to have said when the Prophet died, "I swear that I will not wear a robe and will not appear in the crowd except for Friday prayers until I collect the Qur'ān".[32] Finally, in another report, ibn Abi al-Ḥadīd states, "everyone agrees that Ali memorized the Qur'ān during the time of the Prophet and [he] was the first to collect it".[33]

Most of the Shī'ah narrations on what occurred with Ali's Muṣḥaf can be summarised as follows: After finishing his collection, Ali placed his collection on a camel and brought it to the mosque while the people gathered around Abu Bakr and told them: "After the death of the Prophet, I have been busy collecting the Qur'ān. There is no verse unless the Prophet himself read it to me and taught me its interpretation. I brought this Qur'ān among you so that you may not say tomorrow that we did not know about it". Then one of the elders stood up and seeing what Ali had written on his Muṣḥaf said: "There is no need for what you have brought and what we have is sufficient". Ali replied: "Then you will never see it again". Ali then went inside his house, and no one saw this Muṣḥaf again.[34] Considering

30 Ibn al-Nadīm, *Al-Fihrist*, 47-48.

31 Muḥammad ibn Sa'd, *Al-Ṭabaqāt al-kubrā* (Beirut: Dār al-Kutub al-'Ilmīyyah, 1989), 2: 101.

32 Jalāl al-Dīn Suyūṭī, *Al-Itqān fī 'Ulūm al-Qur'ān* (Beirut: Dār al-Fikr, 1995), 1: 204.

33 .'Abd al-Ḥamīd ibn Hibah Allah ibn Abī al-Ḥadīd, *Sharḥ Nahjulbalāgha* (Qom: Maktabah Mar'ashī Najafī, 1983), 1: 27.

34 Ya'qūbī, *Tārīkh Ya'qūbī*, 2: 15; Muḥammad ibn 'Alī ibn Shahr Āshūb, *Manāqib Al Abī Ṭālib* (Qom: 'Allamah, 1999), 2: 41.

this narrative, and the rejection of Ali's Muṣḥaf because of what was written in it, Al-Qafārī claims that the Shīʿah believe that the real Qur'ān is Ali's Muṣḥaf, and the Qur'ān that is currently in circulation has undergone changes or hence is distorted.[35]

However, certain Shīʿah Imams have reacted against this claim. For example, it is reported that Imam Hasan said to Muʿāwīyah: "He who claims that a large part of the Qur'ān has been lost, has lied".[36] Other prominent Shīʿah scholars have also asserted that Ali's Muṣḥaf is no more or less than the popularly used Qur'ān. For example, Sheikh Mufīd states, "A group of Shīʿah say, 'No word, verse or chapter has been removed from the Qur'ān. However, the contents that were in Ali's Qur'ān were all related to the interpretation of the Qur'ān and were not considered from the Qur'ān'. In my opinion, this statement is closer to the truth than the statement of those who claim that some words have been removed from the Qur'ān itself." Sheikh Ṣadūq in a similar vein argues, "Our belief is this: the Qur'ān that God revealed to the Prophet is the one that is now between the covers and in the hands of the people. If he attributes it to us, he is a liar.[37] In addition to these early scholars, late Shīʿah scholars have also openly opposed the idea of distortion to the Qur'ān, which we will elaborate on in the next section.

To counter the claim of distortion to the Qur'ān and the claim that the text in the popularly adopted Qur'ān is different from Ali's Qur'ān, Shīʿah scholars have elaborated upon the characteristics of Ali's Muṣḥaf. Three characteristics are delineated which distinguish it from the current Qur'ān:[38]

---

35 Nāṣir Qafārī, *Usūl Madhhab al-Shīʿah al-Imāmyiah al-Ithnā ʿAsharyiah* (Beirut: Dar al-Riḍā, 1993), 2: 202.

36 Salīm Qays Ḥilāli, *Kitāb Sulaīm ibn Qays* (Tehran: Al-baʿthah, 1986), 396.

37 Muḥammad ibn ʿAlī Ṣadūq, *Al-Iʿtiqādāt* (Qom: Imām hādī, 2009), 59.

38 Maʿrifat, *Al-Tamhīd fī ʿUlūm al-Qur'ān*, 1: 293.

1. The arrangement of verses and chapters is in accordance with the chronology of the revelation to the Prophet. Hence, Ali's Muṣḥaf, is structured along the historical stages of revelation. Two early commentators underscore this chronology, Saʿīd bin Muṣayib and Muqātil bin Sulaimān.[39] Furthermore, there are traditions attributed to Imam Sadiq in which he had a Muṣḥaf where the verses and chapters were arranged in chronological order of their revelation to the Prophet.[40]
2. The verses of the Qur'ān are recorded in the Muṣḥaf of Ali according to the recitation of the Prophet. And although the recitation of *Ḥafṣ* is the closest recitation to this recitation, it does not fully correspond to it. For example, the pronunciation of Hamzah "ء" in the Qur'āysh dialect and in the recitation of the Prophet does not originate from the hoarseness of the throat. However, this is the case in the recitation of *Ḥafṣ*. [41]
3. It contains explanations in its margins detailing the occasion, place, and time of the various verses' revelation, as well as the person or people the verses are addressed to. For example, according to some Shīʿah sources that when Ali opened the Qur'ān in front of Abu Bakr at the mosque, some of the explanations of the verses were deemed to be scandalous, and hence they rejected Ali's Muṣḥaf.[42] Other explanations, include detailing verses that are *nāsikh* and *mansūkh*, or *muḥkam* and *mutashābih*. For example, one of Imam Reza's companions is

39 Ṭabrisī, *Majmaʿ al-Bayān fī Tafsīr al-Qur'ān*, 10: 613-614.

40 Muḥammad ibn 'Abdulkarīm Shahristānī, *Mafātiḥ al-Asrār wa Maṣābīḥ al-Abrār* (Tehran: Islamic Encyclopedia Foundation, 1898.), 292-298.

41 Kohantorabi, *"Investing the Quality OF Reading of Hamzah in the Recitations Attributed to Ahl Al-Bayt,"* 9-33.

42 Aḥmad ibn 'Alī Ṭabrisī, *Al-Iḥtijāj 'alā Ahl al-Lijāj* (Mashhad, Murtaḍā, 1982), 225.

reported to have said "I saw additional explanations to the text in the *muṣḥaf* that was in his possession".[43]

The Shīʿah commentator and jurist, Abul Qāsim Khū'ī elaborates after adhering to and enunciating the above contents, "The consensus of the scholars on the existence of Ali's Muṣḥaf makes it unnecessary to prove this book and therefore we will not enter into the discussion of this Muṣḥaf. However, the fact that some people have thought that this Muṣḥaf contains additions to the Qur'ān does not mean that there are additions to the text of the Qur'ān, but that it is an exegesis and interpretation."[44] This sentiment can also be found with some Sunni commentators. For example, ibn Jawzī writes in the introduction of his commentary, "During the Prophet's reign, the Qur'ān was scattered in scrolls and people's chests. When the Prophet died, Ali bin Abi Ṭalib stayed at home and collected the Qur'ān in the order of revelation. If his Muṣḥaf were to be found, there is much knowledge in it, but alas, it was not found."[45] He also states that additional information is expressed in the margins of verses.

Interpretative Statements and the Claim of Distortion to the Qur'ān

As stated earlier in this chapter, there are quotes attributed to the Twelver Shīʿah Imams relating to certain verses of the Qur'ān, which some understood to be the recitations of the Imams. The differences between these phrases and the standard recitation of the Qur'ān, is either that these phrases have additional

43 Muḥammad Bāqir Majlisī, *Bahār al-Anwār* (Beirut: Dār Iḥyā' al-Turāth al-ʿArabī, 1982), 52: 364-365.
44 Abulqāsim Khū'ī, *Al-Bayān Fī Tafsīr al-Qur'ān* (Qom: Iḥyā' Āthār Khū'ī, 2007), 222.
45 Aḥmad ibn Muḥammad Al-Kalbī, *Al-Tashīl li 'Ulūm Al-Tanzīl* (Beirut: Dār al-Arqam, 1995), 1: 7.

wording, or some of the words are missing from the standard Qur'ān. Sometimes the order of the words are also dissimilar from the standard Qur'ān. In the following, an example is mentioned for each of these three forms (increase, decrease and displacement in the text):

1. In the Shīʿah traditions, it is stated that Imam Baqir recited the verse, "إِنَّ اللَّهَ اصْطَفَى آدَمَ وَنُوحًا وَآلَ إِبْرَاهِيمَ وَآلَ عِمْرَانَ عَلَى الْعَالَمِينَ" (God chose Adam and Noah and the House of Abraham and the House of Imran above all beings)[46] as, "إِنَّ اللَّه اصْطَفَى آدَمَ وَنُوحًا وَآلَ إِبْرَاهِيمَ وَآلَ عِمْرَانَ وآل محمدٍ عَلَى الْعَالَمِينَ"[47] (God chose Adam and Noah and the House of Abraham and the House of Imran and the House of Muhammad above all beings). According to this narration, the phrase "آل محمدٍ" (the House of Muhammad) is in addition to the text of the standard Qur'ān.
2. A narration attributed to Imam Sadiq states that he reads the beginning of the first verse of *Sūrat al-Anfāl* as "يَسْأَلُونَكَ الأَنْفَال" (They ask you, [O Muḥammad], about the bounties [of war]) while in the standard Qur'ān it is recited as "يَسْأَلُونَكَ عَنِ الأَنْفَالِ".[48] In the recitation transmitted from Imam Sadiq, the "عَنَ" is omitted.
3. In a narration attributed to Imam Bāqir, he is said to have recited: "فَلَمَّا خَرَّ تَبَيَّنَتِ الْجِنُّ أَنْ لَوْ كَانُوا يَعْلَمُونَ الْغَيْبَ مَا لَبِثُوا فِي الْعَذَابِ الْمُهِين" (When he fell down, the jinn saw clearly that, had they only known the Unseen, they would not have continued in the humbling chastisement)[49] as "فَلَمَّا خَرَّ تَبَيَّنَتِ الإنس أنّ الْجِنُّ لَوْ كَانُوا يَعْلَمُونَ الْغَيْبَ

46 *Āl ʿImrān* 2: 33.
47 Furāt Kūfī, *Tafsīr Furāt al-Kufī* (Tehran: Ministry of Islamic Guidance, 1989), 78.
48 Ḥussain Nūrī, *Mustadrak al-wasāil fī Mustanbaṭ al-Masāil* (Beirut: Āl al-Bait li Iḥyā' al-Turāth, 1989), 7: 70.
49 *Saba'* 34: 14.

> مَا لَبِثُوا فِي الْعَذَابِ الْمُهِينِ"[50] (When he fell down, mankind saw clearly that, if the jinn had known the Unseen, they would not have continued in the humbling chastisement). In addition to the word "الإنس", the phrase also contains differences in the arrangement of the words.

Examples such as these, which are attributed to Shīʿah Imams, have perturbed Shīʿah scholars. Most notably the contention that the Shīʿah Imams adopted a Qur'ān that is different from the currently recited Qur'ān, and from this, the contention that the Qur'ān that Muslims currently recite today is incomplete or distorted.

In the context of such differences, Shīʿah scholars and commentators have adopted two approaches. Some scholars hold the view that these expressions indeed underscore distortion to the Qur'ān. This view is upheld by figures such as Ali ibn Ibrahim Qummī and Muhammad ibn Masʿūd ʿAyyāshī, who lived before the fourth century AH (and hence prior to the codification of the seven recitations by ibn Mujāhid and the writing of *al-Tibyān* by Sheikh Ṭūsī, a key work which rejects the position of the Qur'ān's distortion). Furthermore, certain Traditionalists (*Akhbārīyūn*), even in the modern period, who uphold the unquestioning acceptance of ḥadīths, also adopt the view of the Qur'ān's distortion. One of the first scholars to adopt this position was Seyyed Neʿmatullah al-Jazā'irī (d.1700). For him, the differences in readings indeed underscored the Qur'ān's distortion.[51] Two centuries later, the most detailed book on this issue was written by Mirzā Hussain Nūrī (d.1902), one of the most famous traditionalists Shīʿah scholars in his book "*Faṣl al-Khiṭāb fī Taḥrīf kitab Rab al-Arbāb*" (A Clear Word about the Distortion of God's Book). Mirzā Hussain Nūrī's work

50 Muḥammad ibn 'Alī Ṣadūq, *'Ilal al-Sharāiʿ* (Qom: Dāwarī, 2006), 1: 73-74.

51 Niʿmat Allah Jazāirī, *Al-Anwār al-Nuʿmāniyah* (Beirut: Dār al-Qārī, 2008), 1: 362-363.

was seen as particularly challenging and faced numerous responses from Shīʿah scholars and provoked numerous objections to his claims of distortion. The basis of such objections can be boiled down to two primary reasons. Firstly, what Nūrī considers to be the recitations of the Shīʿah Imams are not actually recitations, but interpretations and expression that give examples for such verses. Secondly, the numerous narrations cited by the author are inauthentic and hence invalid. For example, Mohammad Hādi Maʿrifat states: "Out of 1122 ḥadīths in this book, 815 ḥadīths are taken from unreliable books."[52] In Maʿrifat's work, he lists the eight reference works from which Nūrī narrated ḥadīths and discusses their inauthenticity in detail.[53]

In contrast to this position, the majority of Shīʿah scholars hold the position that these phrases are not actually recitations, but rather explanations of verses. The first scholar to adopt this position and to discuss it in detail was the famous Shīʿah scholar and commentator Sheikh Ṭūsī (d.1067). His Tafsir entitled *al-Tibyān fī Tafsīr al-Qur'ān* is considered to be the first complete exegesis of the Qur'ān written by a Shīʿah. The importance of this work is such that his interpretations are considered as a reference point for subsequent interpretations. In his commentary, he cites several examples of recitations attributed to the Shīʿah Imams under the title "Recitations of the Ahl al-Bayt". However, he does not discuss this issue under the title of "recitation" and among other aspects of recitation such as with the seven recitations, but discusses them in the context of his exegetical discussions. Sometimes he explicitly uses the title "Interpretation of Ahl al-Bayt" when referring to these sentences.[54] For example, he states with regards to verse 33 of *Sūrat Āl ʿImrān*, which we

52 Muḥammad Hādī Maʿrifat, *History of Holy Qur'ān* (Tehran: Samt, 2002), 175.

53 Maʿrifat, *Ṣīanat al-Qur'ān min al-Taḥrīf*, 1: 191-201.

54 Muḥammad ibn Ḥassan Ṭūsī, *Al-Tibyān fī Tafsīr al-Qur'ān* (Qom: Al-Nashr al-Islāmī, 1999), 6: 228.

mentioned previously," In the recitation of Ahl al-Bayt, this phrase is also mentioned 'آل محمدٍ'. The family of Muhammad is the same family of Abraham that God chose because they were pure and innocent and God was pleased with them."[55] From this, it is clear that Ṭūsī does not consider the additional phrase to be an addition to the text of the Qur'ān, but rather an interpretation of the phrase " آلَ إِبْرَاهِيمَ ". That is, since the Prophet Muhammad is a descendant of Abraham, then the Prophet Muhammad's family is also considered to be of Abraham's family. For Ṭūsī, this is the meaning of the recitation that is attributed to the Shīʿah Imams. The addition explains the verse by giving an example. This approach is adopted with other additions attributed to the Shīʿah Imams. Throughout his exegesis, Ṭūsī considers the recitations of the Shīʿah Imams as commentaries. Sheikh Ṭūsī's approach was adopted by most later Shīʿah scholars and commentators. After the writing of the *Tibyān*, very few Shīʿah scholars considered these to be actual recitations.

Scholars like Muhammad Hādī Maʿrifat, who also consider these phrases to be interpretations and not readings, further refer to the mode of interpreting the Qur'ān in the early years after the Qur'ān's revelation. Extensive and longwinded interpretations of the Qur'ān were not common. Rather, interpretations of the Qur'ān were expressed in short sentences, and these sentences were uttered by the interpreter while reciting the Qur'ān. In other words, while reciting the Qur'ān, a commentator would use a short sentences to explain specific sections of verses.[56] Ibn Jazarī, also makes this point: "At that time, the exegetes included their interpretations in the recitation because they knew what was revealed to the Prophet, and therefore they could distinguish between the Qur'ān and the explanatory sentences".[57]

55 Ibid, 2: 441.

56 Maʿrifat, *History of Holy Qur'ān*, 177.

57 Kamāl Ḥeydarī, *Ṣīanat al-Qur'ān min al-Taḥrīf* (Baghdad: Fārān, N.D), 49.

The View of the Shīʿah Imams on Public Recitation

Prior to discussing the views of the Shīʿah Imams on the public recital of the Qur'ān, it is important to elucidate their views on the Uthman's Muṣḥaf. According to the examples given in previous sections, the Muṣḥaf of Uthman did have differences from the Muṣḥaf of Ali – at least in certain readings and supplementary explanations. How do early sources portray Ali's position on the unification of the Muṣḥaf and his reaction to Uthman's collection? Certain narrations depict Ali as stating (in references to Uthman's codification): "By God, Uthman did not do anything about the Masāḥif except with our advice. He consulted us on the recitations, and said that they told me that some people say that my recitation is better than your recitation and this is something close to disbelief. I said to Uthman, 'What is your opinion?' He said, 'my opinion is that there should be only one Muṣḥaf at the disposal of the people and that there should be no division and disagreement in this field'. I said, 'it is a good idea'".[58] In another narration, Ali reported to have said: "If the work of Masāḥif was entrusted to me, I would have done what Uthman did".[59]

We also have examples of narrations in which Ali, when he became the caliph, encouraged people to adhere to the Muṣḥaf of Uthman. In one such example, a person recited verse 29 of *Sūrat al-Wāqiʿah* in the presence of Ali and came to the phrase "وَطَلْحٍ مَنْضُودٍ". Ali said: "What does "طَلْحٍ" mean? The correct word is 'طَلْعٍ' because this word is also found in another verse of the Qur'ān".[60] The people who heard this said to Ali, "Aren't you

58 Suyuṭi, *Al-Itqan fī 'Ulūm al-Qur'ān*, 1: 59.

59 Muḥammad ibn Muḥammad ibn Jazarī, *Al-Nashr fī Qirā'āt al-'Ashr* (Cairo: Maktabat al-ʿAṣrīyyah, 2012), 1: 8.

60 *Al-Shuʿarā'* 26: 148.

going to change it in the Qur'ān?" He replied, "From today, no changes should be made in the Qur'ān".[61]

Other Imams also seem to follow Ali's precedence. One narration mentions how a person asked Imam Sadiq about the revelation of the Qur'ān, to which he replied: "Recite the Qur'ān as you have learned".[62] In another narration from Imam Reza, a person was talking to Imam Reza about *Sūrat al-Ikhlāṣ* and asked him how to read it. He replied, "As all people read".[63] Such examples show how the Shīʿah Imams never sought to promote their own recitation among their followers.

Adherence to the General Recitation until the Appearance of the Promised Mahdi

There are certain ḥadīths in Shīʿah sources in which Shīʿah Imams are described as asking their followers to recite the Qur'ān as it is generally recited until the promised Mahdi appears. This notion plays an important role in the history of the Qur'ān among Twelver Shīʿah. On this particular issue, the recitations of Shīʿah Imams and the appearance of the promised Mahdi are intertwined. In one narration, a person is said to have recited the Qur'ān in the presence of Imam Sadiq in a way that was different from the general recitation. Imam Sādiq said to him: "Stop reading this! Recite like people until the promised Mahdi comes. When he rises, he will recite the Qur'ān as it was originally".[64] In another narration, a person came to Imam Kāzim and asked him, "We hear from you the verses of the Qur'ān that are different from other recitations and we cannot recite

---

61 Ṭabarī, *Jāmiʿ al-Bayān fī Tafsīr al-Qur'ān*, 27: 104.

62 Muḥammad ibn Ya'qūb Kulainī, *Al-Kāfī* (Tehran: Dār al-Kutub al-Islāmīyyah, 1986), 4: 666-667.

63 Muḥammad ibn 'Alī Ṣadūq, *Al-Tawḥīd* (Qom: Jāmiʿat al-Mudarrisīn, 1995), 284.

64 Kulainī, *Al-Kāfī*, 4: 671.

them as they have come down to us from you. Are we guilty?" He said, "no, recite as you have learned, the one who teaches you (as we recite) will come to you".[65] Here, 'the one who will come to you' refers to the promised Mahdi. This narration underscores some important points. Firstly, there is an implication that Imam Kāzim's recitation contained differences from the general recitation. Secondly, that Imam Kāzim used this particular recitation in the presence of his companions. Thirdly, the companions were ordered to recite in the general recitation and finally, the idea that when the promised Mahdi appears, he would then teach people the Qur'ān that is the recitation of the Prophet.

These two narrations in unison underscore two points: firstly, the Shīʿah Imams ordered their followers to recite the general recitation, and secondly, they postponed the recitation of their recitation until the time of the Mahdi's appearance. Other Shīʿah ḥadīth sources describe one of the actions of the Mahdi at the time of his appearance as 'teaching the Qur'ān as it was revealed'.[66] In such narrations, the Mahdi would also bring with him the Muṣḥaf of Ali, which was inherited by him and would teach people the Qur'ān according to it.[67] Hence, according to this model, the Shīʿah Imams' recitations among the Shīʿah has not reached its culmination. Rather, the Shīʿah are obliged to wait and recite the Qur'ān according to the general popular recitation - that is in *Ḥafṣ*, until the promised Mahdi appears who would then teach the authentic recitation.

With this model in mind – that the Shīʿah Imams ordered their followers to recite the Qur'ān of the common people, and oppose other recitations, including their own –how did Shīʿah scholars make sense of the fact that such variations were indeed

---

65 Ibid, 640.

66 Muḥammad ibn Muḥammad Mufīd, *Al-Irshād fi Maʿrifat Ḥujaj Allah ʿalā al-ʿIbād* (Qom: Āl al-Bait li Iḥyā' al-Turāth, 1992), 2: 401; Muḥammad ibn Ibrāhīm Nuʿmānī, *Al-Ghaybah* (Tehran: Ṣadūq, 1976), 318.

67 Muḥammad ibn Ḥassan Ṣaffār, *Baṣā'ir al-Darajāt fī Faḍā'il Āl Muhammad* (Qom: Maktabah Marʿashī Najafī, 1983), 1: 193.

subsequently discussed among the companions of the Imams? Why were such recitations not completely abandoned and negated? The justification for this is attributed to the notion of preserving unity and avoiding divisions among Muslims. The logic being that if the Shīʿah Imams taught their recitation to their followers and asked them to recite the Qur'ān with their recitation, the Shīʿah would be accused of separating from Islam and adhering to a Qur'ān that would be at odds with the general Qur'ān. Hence the rationale for preventing their followers from deviating from this reading. This can be seen from the aforementioned narration of Imam Ali on reading "طَلْحٍ". After stating the correct and incorrect reading of the word, Ali categorically rejects the questioner's request to change the Qur'ān.

A second rationale is also linked to this issue and linked to eschatology. A core tenet in the Shīʿah belief system is the emphasis on the coming of the promised Mahdi. Multiple narrations underscore the teachings of the Imams ordering their followers to wait for the appearance of the promised Mahdi and to pray for it to be hastened.[68] For example, we can see this in a narration attributed to Imam Ali: "The person who waits for this appearance is like someone who has lost his blood in the path of God".[69] Various signs are also recounted to the Shīʿah which signal the Mahdi's appearance and his actions so that the Shīʿah would have an awareness of him.[70] The Qur'ān that the Mahdi would bring and is understood to be the same Muṣḥaf of Ali falls under this genre. Hence, the Shīʿah Imams did not want the Shīʿah to be ignorant of this Qur'ān. Hence, they prepared their followers by familiarising them with their recitation and mentioning the attributes of Ali's Muṣḥaf.

---

68 Abū Muḥammad ibn Mas'ūd 'Ayyāshī, *Kitāb al-Tafsīr* (Tehran: *'Ilmiyyah*, 1960), 2: 155.

69 Muḥammad ibn 'Alī Ṣadūq, *Kamāl al-Din wa Tamām al-Ni'mah* (Tehran: Islāmīyyah, 1975), 2: 645.

70 Majlisī, *Baḥār al-Anwār*, 52: 337-348.

Conclusion

Narrations which attribute variant recitations to the Shīʿah Imams have been understood in two ways: as 'different recitations' or as 'interpretative statements'. The former refers to differences which include additional wordings or phrases and eighteen other factors identified in this article. With regards to the latter understanding, differences are not seen as recitations in the strictest sense, but rather as short sentences which clarify and interpret the Qur'ān. Furthermore, we have also examined the notion of the Qur'ān's distortion held by a small number of Shīʿah sources and mentioned in some Sunnī sources. However, this position is not held as the mainstream Shīʿah position. Finally, we have also examined the notion of the Shīʿah Imams prohibiting their followers from reading the Qur'ān with any differences that go against the general recitation. This was done in order to preserve unity and linked to eschatology such that the promised Mahdi would teach the Qur'ān according to the recitation of the Prophet. The Mahdi's recitation is understood to be inherited from Imam ʿAli, which is believed to be in accordance with the Prophet's original recitation.

Bibliography

al-Kalbī, Aḥmad ibn Muḥammad . *Al-Tashīl li ʿUlūm Al-Tanzīl.* Beirut: Dār al-Arqam, 1995.

Andulusī, Muḥammad ibn Yūsuf. *Al-Baḥr al-Muḥīt fī al-Tafsīr.* Beirut: Dār al-Fikr, 1999.

ʿAyyāshī, Abū Muḥammad ibn Mas'ūd. *Kitāb al-Tafsīr.* Tehran: *ʿIlmiyyah*, 1960.

Faḍlī, ʿAbdulhādī. *Al-Qirā'āt al-Qur'āniah: Tārīkh wa Taʿrīf.* Beirut: Dār al-Qalam, 1984.

Ḥeydarī, Kamāl. *Ṣīanat al-Qur'ān min al-Taḥrīf*. Baghdad: Fārān, N.D.

Ḥillī, Ḥasan ibn Yūsuf. *Rijāl al-ḥilli*. Najaf: Maṭbaʿat al-Ḥaydariyah, 1961.

Ibn Abī al-Ḥadīd, 'Abd al-Ḥmīd Ibn Hibah Allah. *Sharḥ Nahjul-balāgha*. Qom: Maktabah Marʿashī Najafī, 1983.

Ibn al-Nadīm, Muḥammad ibn Isḥāq. *Al-Fihrist*. Beirut: Dār al-Maʿārifah, 1996.

Ibn Jazarī, Muḥammad ibn Muḥammad. *Al-Nashr fī Qirā'āt al-'Ashr* .Cairo: Maktabat al-ʿAṣrīyyah, 2012.

Ibn Jinnī, Abulfatḥ Uthmān. *Al-Muḥtasab fī Wujūh Shawādh al-Qirā'āt*. Cairo: Al-Majlis al-Aʿlā li Shuʿūn al-Islāmiyah, 1994.

Ibn Khāliwaih, Ḥussain ibn Aḥmad. *Mokhtaṣar fī Shawādh al-Qur'ā'n min al-Kitāb al-Badīʿ*. Beirut: Al-Rayān, 2008.

Ibn Saʿd, Muḥammad ibn Saʿd . *Al-Ṭabaqāt al-kubrā*. Beirut: Dār al-Kutub al-ʿIlmīyyah, 1989.

Ibn Shahr Āshūb, Muḥammad ibn 'Alī. *Manāqib Al Abī Ṭālib*. Qom: ʿAllamah, 1999.

Jazāirī, Niʿmat Allah. *Al-Anwār al-Nuʿmāniyah*. Beirut: Dār al-Qārī, 2008.

Kariminia, Murtiḍa. "Differences in recitation or distortion of the Qur'ān", *'Ulūm Ḥadīth*, 40 (2006): 3-21.

Khū'ī, Abulqāsim. *Al-Bayān Fī Tafsīr al-Qur'ān*. Qom: Iḥyā' Āthār Khū'ī, 2007.

Kohantorabi, Meysam. *Research on recitations attributed to the Ahl al-Bayt*. Qayen: Bozorgmehr, 2020.

Kohantorabi, Meysam. "Investing the Quality of Reading of Hamzah in the Recitations Attributed to Ahl Al-Bayt", *Studies of Qurān Reading Journal* 8, no.15 (February 2021): 9-30.

Kūfī, Furāt. *Tafsīr Furāt al-Kufī*. Tehran: Ministry of Islamic Guidance, 1989.

Kulainī, Muḥammad ibn Yȧqūb. *Al-Kāfī*. Tehran: Dār al-Kutub al-Islāmīyyah, 1986.

Majlisī, Muḥammad Bāqir. *Baḥār al-Anwār*. Beirut: Dār Iḥyā' al-Turāth al-ʿArabī, 1982.

Maʿrifat, Muḥammad Hādī. *Al-Tamhīd fī 'Ulūm al-Qur'ān*. Qom: Tamhīd, 2007.

Maʿrifat, Muḥammad Hādī. *History of Holy Qur'ān*. Tehran: Samt, 2002.

Maʿrifat, Muḥammad Hādī. *Ṣiānat al-Qur'ān min al-Tahrīf*. Qom: Tamhīd, 2006.

Mufīd, Muḥammad ibn Muḥammad. *Al-Irshād fi Ma'rifat Ḥujaj Allah 'alā al-'Ibād*. Qom: Āl al-Bait li Iḥyā' al-Turāth, 1992.

Mufīd, Muḥammad ibn Muḥammad. *Awā'il al-Maqālāt fī al-Madhahib wa al-Mukhtārāt*. Tehran: Tehran University, 2003.

Najāshī, Aḥmad ibn 'Alī. *Rijāl al-Najāshī*. Qom: Al-Nashr al-Islāmī, 1985.

Nuʿmānī, Muḥammad ibn Ibrāhīm. *Al-Ghaybah*. Tehran: Ṣadūq, 1976.

Nūrī, Ḥussain. *Mustadrak al-wasāil fī Mustanbaṭ al-Masāil*. Beirut: Āl al-Bait li Iḥyā' al-Turāth, 1989.

Qafārī, Nāṣir. *Usūl Madhhab al-Shī'ah al-Imāmyiah al-Ithnā 'Asharyiah*. Beirut: Dar al-Riḍā, 1993.

Qays Ḥilāli, Salīm. *Kitāb Sulaīm ibn Qays*. Tehran: Al-baʿthah, 1986.

Qummī, 'Alī ibn Ibrāhīm. *Tafsīr al-Qummī*. Qom: Dār al-Kitāb, 1987.

Qurṭubī, Muḥammad ibn Aḥmad. *Al-Jāmiʿ fī Aḥkām al-Qur'ān*. Tehran: Naser Khosrow, 1985.

Rafīʿī, Mujīb, *Qirā'āt Ahl al-Bait al-Qur'āniyah*. Qom: Dār al-Ghadīr, 2003.

Rezaei, Asad Allah. "Wahhabis and the accusation against Kulainī about distorting the Qur'ān", *Sirāj Munīr* 2, no. 7&8 (January 2011): 43-78.

Ṣadūq, Muḥammad ibn 'Alī. *Al-I'tiqādāt*. Qom: Imām hādī, 2009.

Ṣadūq, Muḥammad ibn 'Alī. *Al-Tawḥīd*. Qom: Jāmiʿat al-Mudarrisīn, 1995.

Ṣadūq, Muḥammad ibn 'Alī. *'Ilal al-Sharāiʿ*. Qom: Dāwarī, 2006.

Ṣadūq, Muḥammad ibn 'Alī. *Kamāl al-Din wa Tamām al-Niʿmah*. Tehran: Islāmīyyah, 1975.

Ṣaffār, Muḥammad ibn Ḥassan. *Baṣā'ir al-Darajāt fī Faḍā'il Āl Muhammad*. Qom: Maktabah Marʿashī Najafī, 1983.

Shahristānī, Muḥammad ibn 'Abdulkarīm. *Mafātiḥ al-Asrār wa Maṣābīḥ al-Abrār*. Tehran: Islamic Encyclopedia Foundation, 1898.

Suyūṭī, Jalāl al-Dīn. *Al-Itqān fī 'Ulūm al-Qur'ān*. Beirut: Dār al-Fikr, 1995.

Tabarī, Muḥammad ibn Jarīr. *Jāmiʿ al-Bayān fī Tafsīr al-Qur'ān*. Beirut: Dār al-Maʿārifah, 1991.

Ṭabrisī, Aḥmad ibn 'Alī. *Al-Iḥtijāj 'alā Ahl al-Lijāj*. Mashhad, Murtaḍā, 1982.

Ṭabrisī, Faḍl bin Ḥassan. *Majmaʿ al-Bayān fī Tafsīr al-Qur'ān*. Tehran: Tehran University, 1998.

Tehrānī, Aqā Buzurq. *Al-Dharīʿah ilā Taṣānīf al-Shīʿah*. Beirut: Dār al-Aḍwā', 1982.

Ṭūsī, Muḥammad ibn Ḥassan. *Al-Tibyān fī Tafsīr al-Qur'ān*. Qom: Al-Nashr al-Islāmī, 1999.

Yaʿqūbī, Aḥmad ibn Abī Ya'qūb. *Tārīkh Yaʿqūbī*. Beirut: Dār Ṣādir, 1959.

Zarkashī, Badr al- Dīn. *Al-Burhān fī 'Ulūm al-Qur'ān*. Beirut: Dār al-Maʿārifah, 1989.

CHAPTER TWELVE

Shaping the Qur'ān's Journey: A Global History of Translation

Afsan Redwan

The history of Qur'ān translation is a complex and multifaceted topic that scholars from various disciplines have explored. Qur'ān translation is the intersection of multiple domains, ranging from having an important role in unlocking intellectual history to understanding diverse translation methodologies. The translation of the Qur'ān has a rich and complex history that spans centuries and encompasses various languages and cultures. Scholars have delved into this topic from different perspectives, shedding light on the linguistic, hermeneutic, and theological aspects of Qur'ān translation. Within this also lies continual challenges such as those highlighted by Abdullah, who, in a recent study, describes this through the continuous challenges authors face in dealing with polysemy in different languages such as French Qur'ān translations.[1] Qur'ān translation has also been argued to require a distinct hermeneutic, such as those asserted by Atmojo, who claims a disconnect from Western models of sacred translation.[2] The development of Qur'ān translation in specific languages has also been explored, such as translating the Qur'ān

1 J. Abdullah., 'The Term (كلمة) in the Holy Qur'ān Between Translation and Interpretation', *Al-Adab Journal*, 1 (2001), 21-42.

2 M. Atmojo et al., 'Development of Islamic Teachings Through the Translation of the Qur'ān in Various National Languages' *Randwick International of Social Science Journal* 3(1), (2022), 168-175.

into Malay,[3] Bengali,[4] and Indonesian.[5] This current chapter will explore the history of Qur'ān translation, describing and engaging with critical moments in its discourse. The topics will develop from early Islamic legal issues around the use of Qur'ān translation to the appearance of Qur'ān translations in South Asia, the translation of the Qur'ān in Latin Europe, English Qur'ān translations and a final part discussing modern-day challenges and prospects. It is worth pointing out that Qur'ān translation is a global discipline, and some notable mentions could not be addressed in this chapter. It would be pertinent for readers to be aware that Qur'ān translation has a rich history and debate among Javanese, Somali, central African, Japanese, and Chinese languages; these are underrepresented areas.[6]

Qur'ān translation contains numerous linguistic challenges. Abdullah discusses the term "word" in the Qur'ān and the difficulties in translating it accurately.[7] The difficulty, though, in translation, is not restricted to one language; in an interview with the academic Bruce Lawrence in 2016, he details the challenges in translating the *basmala*[8] in finding an apt English rendering.

---

3 For a detailed discussion on Malay see, Hussin and Kamal, 'Translation of Al-Qur'ān into Malay Language in the Malay World', *International Journal of Islamic Studies and Humanities*, 4(1), (2021), 32.

4 For a detailed discussion on Bengali Qur'ān translations see, M Rahman, 'The History of the Translation of the Holy Qur'ān in Bengali: The Translation Example of Gulam Azam', *International Journal of Social Political and Economic Research*, 8(1), (2021), 152-172.

5 F Utomo et al, 'Stemming Impact Analysis on Indonesian Qur'ān Translation and their Tafsir Classification for Ontology Instances', *Iium Engineering Journal*, 21(1), (2020), 33-50.

6 For an overview of the political and societal impact of various Qur'ān translations, see, S. Taji-Farouki, *The Qur'ān and its Readers Worldwide: Contemporary Commentaries and Translations* (New York: Oxford University Press/Institute of Ismaili Studies, 2015).

7 Abdullah, The term (كلمة), 24.

8 The Muslim invocation mentioned at nearly the beginning of every Qur'ānic chapter. For the lecture see the video: B. Lawrence, "Bruce

Another aspect of Qur'ān translation is the role of the translator and their hermeneutic positioning. Elass and Bennoudi explore the hermeneutic implications of the Qur'ān translator and exemplify a middle way approach.[9] A rising trope in Qur'ān translation is to consider the contextual place of the source text and the translation. Professor Abdel Haleem, a known translator of the Qur'ān in his work, advances the importance of context required when translating the Qur'ān.[10] Haleem emphasises the need to be cognisant of several areas to employ correct contextual practice when translating. The development of Qur'ān translation in different national languages is another crucial aspect. Saleh discusses the challenges and controversies surrounding the history of Qur'ān translation in Islamic theology. Saleh's discussion is centred around the Islamic concept of *ijaaz* (Qur'ānic inimitability), which claims that the Qur'ān cannot be translated into another language.[11] The debates and discussions around Qur'ānic inimitability have recently led to encyclopedic products in English Qur'ān translations. Davary highlighted that 'The Study Qur'ān is the first actual comprehensive English translation that is useful for students and academics' when reviewing The Study Qur'ān.[12] However, could such a monumental work exist had it

---

Lawrence - language of the Qur'ān," YouTube video, 2016, https://www.youtube.com/watch?v=_IggjGshTjA (accessed November 6, 2023).

9 H. Elass and H. Bennoudi, 'Hermeneutic positioning of the translator in Qur'ān translation,' *International Journal of Language and Literary Studies* 5(2) (2023), 61-80.

10 M. A. Haleem, *Exploring the Qur'ān: Context and Impact*, (London: I. B. Tauris, 2017). 2-4.

11 Throughout their work they make use of English Qur'ān translations as examples of not being able to capture the full Arabic. Bassam Saleh, *The Miraculous Language of the Qur'an: Evidence of Divine Origin* (London: International Institute of Islamic Thought, 2015).

12 B. Davary, 'The Study Qur'ān: A New Translation and Commentary', *Horizons* 43(2), (2016), 397-401.

not been for the hotly contested debates among Islamic scholars during early Islamic history?

Early Juristic Debates on the Use of Alternative Languages in Islamic Prayer (7th-13th Century)

In the early 20th century, debates among Egyptian Islamic scholars contested the validity of translating the Qur'ān, especially into English. Early among the *fatwas*[13] was by Muhammad Habib Shakir (d.1939), an Egyptian Islamic judge prohibiting the translation of the Qur'ān into any foreign language.[14] The fatwa examined the tension between maintaining the sanctity of Arabic, the language of the Qur'ān, and circulated translations at the time, mainly from an Ahmadiyya viewpoint. However, legal debates around Qur'ān translation have been part of an ongoing discourse, with evidence indicating juristic discussions as early as the 7th century. This discussion coincided with the early Islamic period, which witnessed the rapid expansion of Islam beyond the Arabian Peninsula, attracting people from diverse linguistic backgrounds. The Qur'ān, considered the literal word of Allah, revealed in Arabic, became the central text for Islamic worship, making reciting its verses a fundamental requirement during prayer. However, the linguistic diversity of the Muslim *ummah*

13 Legal rulings given by Muslims, usually by a Mufti or judge.

14 Shakir gave a damning verdict regarding Qur'ān translations in his Fatwa published in 1925, one reason cited for his significant opposition was the spread of Ahmadiyyah and Orientalist translations, as well as following on from Rashid Rida's earlier Fatwa outlawing translations, for Rashid Rida's Fatwa see: Al-Munajjid and Khkri, *Fatawa al-Imam Muhammad Rashid Rida*, Vol. 2, (Beirut: Dar al-Kitbal-Jadid, 1970), 642-650. For Shakir's see, M. Shakir, *Al-Qawl al-Fasl fi Tarjamat al-Qur'ān al-Karim ila al-Lughat al-Ajamiyyah*. (Egypt: Matba'ah al-Naddah, 1925).

(community) posed a significant challenge in that how could non-Arabic-speaking communities engage meaningfully with the Qur'ānic text during worship?

There are reports of an early mention regarding the translation of the Qur'ān into Persian by the famous companion Salman, the Persian. The incident explores the relationship between access to a religious text and its function as a sacred language for worship. The account is recorded in the well-known Hanafi work by Sarakhsi (d.1090), *al Mabsut.*[15] This mention, however, is only of an account wherein Salman was asked to write the verses of *Fatiha* in Persian. Sarakhsi uses this account in the text to justify Abu Hanifa's (d.767) viewpoint that alternative languages can be used for ritual prayer. The report has been criticised by later Shafi scholars such as Fakhr al-Din al Razi (d.1209) and Al-Nawawi (d.1277), who both dispute that such an incident ever occurred. This account, though appearing in Sarakhsi's juristic work, would indicate that, at the least, the question around the use of translations was an early debate. It can be viewed in subsequent discussions as the crux of this ongoing argument used by early Hanafi jurists to respond to its criticisms. The debate is amplified in that the entire translation of the Fatiha attributed to Salman does appear in Hanafi texts such as, Al-Mustaghfri's work *fadail* Qur'ān.[16] The whole prayer is quoted in full; the chain of narration, however, does not trace back to the prophet's time, bringing the integrity of this translation and report into some disrepute. Translations after that became a hallmark in Hanafi works and were even used by scholars such as Isfahani (d.1038) from a Shafi background to justify using translations.

Exploring how the translation of the Qur'ān led to such central debates brings us to pose questions regarding Imam Abu

---

15 al-Sarakhsi, *Kitab al-Mabsut*, vol. 1 (Egypt: Matba'ah al-Sa'adah, 1906).

16 al-Mustaghfiri, *Fada'il al-Qur'ān*, ed. Ahmad ibn Faris al-Sallum, 2 vols. (Beirut: Dar ibn Hazm, 2006).

Hanifa's reasoning and justification for this opinion. As one of the earliest and most influential Islamic jurists, the evidence does indicate that the ruling was given by Abu Hanifa when considering the linguistic diversity within the Muslim ummah and the challenges faced by non-Arabic-speaking Muslims.[17] His approach to accommodation was pragmatic, emphasising the importance of understanding the content of the prayer. Imam Abu Hanifa proposed that if an individual did not understand Arabic, they could use their native language for supplications during prayer. This accommodation was rooted in the principle of accessibility, seeking to make Islamic rituals understandable and accessible to a broader range of individuals while maintaining the sanctity of the Arabic language. Imam Abu Hanifa's primary argument was grounded in intention (*niyyah*).[18] He believed that if an individual intended the Arabic content of their prayers, supplicating in their native language was permissible. This accommodation aimed to foster understanding and engagement with the Qur'ānic message, even if the linguistic barrier was not entirely overcome. Imam Abu Hanifa's approach demonstrated an attempt to preserve the sanctity of Arabic and the Qur'ān's language and ensure that the message was accessible to the diverse Muslim population. Imam Abu Hanifa's approach to accommodation profoundly impacted Islamic jurisprudence. It demonstrated the early recognition of the linguistic diversity within the Muslim ummah and the necessity of making Islamic worship accessible. This perspective also laid the groundwork for later debates on language in Islamic prayer. The legacy of Imam Abu Hanifa's approach can be observed in the Hanafi school of jurisprudence. Hanafi scholars attempted to preserve Abu Hanifa's earlier understanding of translation by adopting flexible positions

17 Z. 'Uthmān ibn 'Alī and A. 'Izzū 'Ināyah, *Tabyīn al-Ḥaqā'iq Sharḥ Kanz al-Daqā'iq: Wa-ma'ahu Ḥāshiyat al-Imām al-'Allāmah al-Shaykh al-Shalabī 'alá Hādhā al-Sharḥ* (Beirut: Dār al-Kutub al-'Ilmīyah, 2010).

18 Bazdawī, *Kanz al-Wuṣūl ila Ma'rifat al-Uṣūl* (Beirut: Sharikat Dār al-Bashā'ir, 2009), 24.

regarding language accessibility. Some examples include writing verses of the Qur'ān in Persian with the Arabic text and using interlinear translations. This is also clearly viewed in the rise of Persian exegetical literature from the 10th century onwards.[19] While there are clear traces back to Abu Hanifa's opinion, there has been an attempt within the school to minimise how much of a discussion this caused. Subsequent Hanafi works have wrestled with Abu Hanifa's opinion and taken two approaches to address this. The first has been to emphasise Abu Hanifa's having retracted this position and returning to the opinion of his students of its impermissibility. Ala' al-Din al Bukhari (d.1332), a prominent Hanafi scholar appearing almost 500 years after Abu Hanifa, cites that 'the authentic view is that Abu Hanifa withdrew to the view of the majority'.[20] He then quotes several scholars to support this approach. Abu Hanifa's opinion is then briefly discussed in later Hanafi scholarship; interestingly, the argument is maintained in these works, with some supported by a few Hanafi scholars that he did and does maintain this viewpoint. The late Shaykh of the Ottoman Empire, Mustafa Sabri (d.1954), is also an excellent example of this Hanafi argumentation as despite arguing for why the Hanafis would not primarily take this view, he still evidences for how Abu Hanifa came to this conclusion. He argues and justifies that Abu Hanifa's view either stemmed from his causal understanding that the Qur'ān has been revealed for ease or that the meaning itself is isolated from the Qur'ān and ultimately is not the Arabic Qur'ān. Sabri concludes, however, in the same way as many previous scholars that Abu Hanifa returned to the authentic position of the school, in that reciting for prayer in other languages would be impermissible.[21]

---

19 T. E. Zadeh, *The Vernacular Qur'ān: Translation and the Rise of Persian Exegesis* (Oxford: Oxford University Press, 2012).

20 A. Muhammad, and N. Awadi, *Al-Muntakhab fī uṣūl al-Madhhab, al-Mashhūr bi Al-Muntakhab al-Ḥusāmī*, (2002), 55-57.

21 M. Sabri, *Mas'alah Tarjamat al-Qur'ān*, (Dār al-Lubāb, 2010) 117-8.

Medieval Islamic Period (10th-16th Century CE): Embracing Linguistic Diversity and Regional Adaptations

During the medieval Islamic period, regions where Persian was the dominant language, such as the Indian subcontinent and Persia, saw the prominent use of Persian in interlinear Qur'ān translations.[22] This practice illustrated the adaptability of Islamic jurisprudence to regional linguistic contexts while upholding the principles of faith. However, the first complete translations of the Qur'ān into Persian were done between the 10th and 12th centuries by a group of scholars from Khorasan, whom the Samanid emperor, Mansur I (d.976), commissioned.[23] These translations were based on the Tafsir al-Tabari, a famous commentary on the Qur'ān by al-Tabari (d.923), and they aimed to make the Qur'ān accessible to Persian-speaking Muslims who were not fluent in Arabic. One significant development during this time was the introduction of ample space layouts in Persian Qur'ān manuscripts,[24] which was a feature also found in West African Islamic manuscripts.[25] This layout allowed for translating the Qur'ānic text into Persian below each line of the Arabic text. This practice can be observed in Persian translations of the Qur'āns dating back to the 11th and 12th centuries. Including Persian translations alongside the Arabic text provided accessibility to

22 Zadeh, *The Vernacular Qur'ān.*

23 K. Fleet et al., *The Encyclopaedia of Islam Three* (Leiden: Brill, 2022), 'Mansur Ia.'

24 Keith E. Small, *Qur'āns: Books of Divine Encounter* (Oxford: Bodleian Library, 2015).

25 D. Bondarev, A. Brigaglia, and M. Nobili, 'Islamic Education and Ample Space Layout in West African Islamic Manuscripts', in *Islamic Manuscripts from Mali*, ed. Ghislaine Lydon (Leiden: Brill, 2020), 105-142.

Persian-speaking audiences and facilitated a deeper understanding of the Qur'ānic message.

The early juristic debates regarding alternative languages in Islamic prayer from the 7th to the 13th century provide essential insights into the formative period of Islamic jurisprudence. The tension between maintaining the sanctity of Arabic and accommodating the linguistic diversity of the Muslim ummah shaped the foundational arguments and justifications that would influence later developments in Islamic thought. The early accommodation presented by the Hanafi school laid the groundwork for discussions on language in Islamic prayer, emphasising the importance of understanding the content of the prayer. The clear rejection by early scholars in the Maliki and Shafi schools highlighted the complexities of preserving Arabic purity while accommodating regional linguistic variations.

Several prominent figures played significant roles in translating the Qur'ān into Persian from the 11th to the 17th century. One such figure is Abu Sa'id Abi al-Khayr (d.1049), a renowned Sufi poet and scholar who produced a poetic rendition of the Qur'ān known as Tarjumān al-Qur'ān.[26] This translation emphasised spiritual and mystical interpretations, reflecting Sufi influences. Another important figure is Shah Ni'matullah Wali (d.1431), an eminent Persian mystic who translated the Qur'ān into Persian prose.[27] His translation aimed to make complex religious concepts more accessible to a broader audience, emphasising moral and ethical teachings.

---

26 P. O'Donnell, 'Ibn Abi'l-Khayr, Abu Sa'id Fadlullah,' in *The Biographical Encyclopaedia of Islamic Philosophy*, (accessed October 21, 2023), https://www-oxfordreference-com.abc.cardiff.ac.uk/view/10.1093/acref/9780199754731.001.0001/acref-9780199754731-e-165.

27 M. Zolfaghary and H. Omid Ali, 'An Analysis of Functions of Qur'ānic Ayahs in Shah Nimatullah Wali's Poetry', *Literary Qur'ānic Researches* 5(1), (2017), 151-171.

Another influential translation which rose during this time was the work of Rashid Ad-din Maybudi, whose commentary is written in Persian.[28] He was a renowned Sufi scholar and theologian in the 12th century, and wrote his commentary to promote a traditionalist form of Sufi hermeneutics. He aimed to show that Sufi hermeneutics are compatible with the Qur'ān, not in opposition. The commentary was formed in a dialogue format, with a narrator asking questions and Maybudi responding.[29] He discusses topics such as piety, faith, knowledge, the soul, and the afterlife. He also focuses on the importance of reflection and contemplation in understanding the Qur'ān. He emphasises that one should not only read the words of the Qur'ān but also reflect on their meaning. He explains that the words of the Qur'ān are powerful and should be revered but that they should not be interpreted literally. Instead, as Keeler emphasises, Maybudi argues that one should draw on spiritual insight to decipher the text.[30]

While the medieval Islamic period witnessed the embrace of linguistic diversity and regional adaptations in Qur'ān translations, South Asia, with its diverse cultural and linguistic landscape, took this evolution to new heights. These translations, shaped by the rich tapestry of South Asian traditions, are a testament to the region's vibrant intellectual and spiritual heritage. This chapter now shifts its focus to provide a historical analysis of the evolution and transformation of Qur'ān translation in South Asia. In doing so, it places particular emphasis on the pivotal role played by Shah Waliullah al-Dihlawi (d.1762), a renowned scholar and reformer whose contributions have left an indelible

---

28 W. C. Chittick, *Kashf al-Asrār The Unveiling of the Mysteries Rashīd al-Dīn Maybudī* (Louisville, KY: Fons Vitae, 2015).

29 Keeler, *Sufi hermeneutics: The Qur'ān commentary of Rashid al-Din Maybudi* (Oxford: Oxford University Press, 2017)

30 Keeler, *Sufi hermeneutics*. Keeler has also discussed the role of al-Ghazali and al-Maybudi's teachings in the commentary. Keeler highlights the importance of Rashid al-Din Maybudi's commentary on Persian Qur'ān translations.

mark on the landscape of Qur'ānic translation in the subcontinent. From the early attempts at translation to contemporary interpretations, this will offer an insight into the multifaceted nature of this dynamic region's engagement with the Qur'ānic text.

Qur'ān translation in South Asia: Early Modern Era

South Asia, with its diverse cultural and linguistic landscape, has produced many Qur'ānic translations, each influenced by the region's unique historical and religious dynamics. This section explores the development of Qur'ān translations in South Asia, tracing their evolution from early attempts to the vibrant landscape of contemporary interpretations. The central theme revolves around the significant influence of Shah Waliullah al-Dihlawi, a renowned scholar and reformer, on Qur'ānic translation in the subcontinent. His scholarly contributions, particularly in Qur'ānic translation and exegesis, are examined in the context of their impact on Islamic scholarship and reform movements in South Asia. Finally, we explore contemporary interpretations of the Qur'ān, including the transition of Qur'ān translations into English translations in India and the influence of colonialism on the output of English Qur'ān translations in India.

With its distinct cultural and linguistic landscape, South Asia has given rise to Qur'ān translations ranging from Persian, Bengali, Tamil, Urdu and English. Venjara describes how these languages and the rise of their respective translations interact with the shift in geographical boundaries and demographics.[31] This cultural and linguistic landscape includes Muslim converts

31 A. Venjara, 'Qur'ān Translation in South Asia' in *Islam, Judaism, and Zoroastrianism*, edited by Z. R. Kassam, Y. K. Greenberg, and J. Bagli, (Dordrecht: Springer, 2018).

and born Muslims, wherein, according to Lawrence, their concern with the lack of access to translations led to this unexpected rise.[32] As stated previously, increasing accessibility to the Qur'ān is a consistent theme amongst these communities. However, South Asia also witnessed an evolution from interlinear translations to exegetical translations. This introduced a different challenge, wherein tensions surrounding theological verses and their proposed explanations were increasingly charged.[33] The translation of the Qur'ān into Tamil was at the time viewed by the population as a novelty and an unique approach which had not been widely viewed in the 19th century. When examined under scrutiny, however, an issue arose regarding the translation of the disjointed letters, which, even within the Qur'ānic Arabic, are not fully understood.[34] In addition, the development of Qur'ān translations in South Asia can be characterised as a shift from scholarly endeavours to accessibility for the public. Tareen makes a strong case for how these languages, significantly Urdu, represent proliferation and concern for laity access to the sacred text.[35] Over time, these translations have developed to meet the needs and wants of the South Asian population, providing a rich source of knowledge and understanding of the Qur'ān.

Focussing on Persian translations in South Asia and their influence, translations from the 14th century came into criticism for their theological stances. This led to tensions around the translation being taken as potential replacement for what is considered a divine language in that the Qur'ān was initially

32 B. Lawrence, *The Koran in English: A Biography* (Princeton, NJ: Princeton University Press, 2017).
33 A. Venjara, Qur'ān Translation.
34 T. Tschacher, ''Extraordinary Translations' and 'Loathsome Commentaries': Qur'ānic Translation and the Politics of the Tamil Language, c. 1880–1950,' *Religion* 49(3) (2019), 458-480.
35 S. A. Tareen, 'South Asian Qur'ān Commentaries and Translations: A Preliminary Intellectual History,' *ReOrient* 5(2), (2020), 233-256.

revealed in Arabic. This is further compounded, leading to difficulties in translating the text into other languages. Moreover, multiple text interpretations have further complicated the process of translating the Qur'ān. For example, some translations lean towards a more literal approach, while others use a more interpretive approach. One of the earliest instances of trying to rectify this was works written on Qur'ānic hermeneutics. In South Asia this was headed by the work of Shah Waliullah Dihlavi, a prominent scholar who translated the Qur'ān into Persian, the language of the elite and the literati at the time. One work of his, titled *al-Fawz al-Kabir fi Usul al-Tafsir* (The Great Victory in the Principles of Interpretation), was based on his commentary and aimed to convey the spiritual and moral meanings of the Qur'ān. He also wrote a shorter translation, called *al-Tafhimat al-Ilahiyyah* (The Divine Instructions), which was more accessible to the common people. These works were essential to answering the earlier questions posed about how to conduct an acceptable translation and exegesis.

Shah Waliullah al-Dihlavi, a prominent writer, left a legacy with his Persian Qur'ān translation *Fathur Rahman*.[36] He attributed the decline of Indian Muslims to their lack of knowledge about the Qur'ān and believed that making it more accessible was crucial. As a result, he played a pivotal role in translating the Qur'ān into a popular version that the masses could easily understand. In addition, he aimed to revive the study of the Qur'ān by promoting interpretations that closely adhered to its literal meaning and by encouraging a contextual approach.[37] Furthermore, he sought to spread the teachings of the Qur'ān to a broader audience in South Asia. He advocated for a direct understanding

36 S. Waliullah, *Fathur Rahman*, (King Fahd Qur'ān Printing Complex, 2017).
37 H. Khan, 'Shah Wali Allah (Qutb al-Din Ahmad al-Rahim) (1703–62),' in *Routledge Encyclopedia of Philosophy* (Taylor and Francis, 1998).

of the Qur'ān, which further solidified his position as a critical figure in Qur'ān translation in the region.

Post-Shah Waliullah, colonialism ensured that English would greatly influence the production of future Qur'ān translations in India. The British Empire imposed their language and culture upon the region, marginalising Indian languages and cultures.[38] As a result, English-language translations of the Qur'ān became popular among all communities in India as well as a form of missionary work targeting the West. The influence of colonialism is also evident in the writings of Muhammad Jamal al-Din al-Qasimi, who wrote Tafsir al-Qasimi, a modern Muslim exegesis of the Qur'ān.[39] He incorporated aspects of Buddhism into his interpretations of the Qur'ān, reflecting colonialism's influence in India. Colonial power can also be seen in re-interpreting the Qur'ān to fit the current age and focusing on the socio-ethical core of the Qur'ān.[40] In addition, there has been a focus on English as a modern approach to translating according to the Qur'ān and Sunnah.[41] This highlights the impact of colonialism on the production of English Qur'ān translations in India. Colonialism has had a far-reaching effect on interpreting, receiving, and presenting English Qur'ān translations. In the English language, this continued to develop with the production of literal translations, which attempted to render the words and syntax of the Arabic text as closely as possible in another language without adding any interpretation or commentary. Paraphrastic translations rephrased or restructured the Arabic text

38 M. Campanini, *The Qur'an: Modern Muslim interpretations* (London: Routledge, 2011).
39 J. Pink, 'Modern and Contemporary Interpretation of the Qur'ān,' in *The Wiley Blackwell Companion to the Qur'ān*, ed. A. Rippin and J. Mojaddedi, (2004).
40 A. Saeed, *Interpreting the Qur'ān Towards a Contemporary Approach* (London: Routledge, 2009).
41 M. Ayoub, *Contemporary Approaches to the Qur'ān and Sunnah* (London: International Institute of Islamic Thought, 2012).

in another language, using idioms or expressions that were more familiar or natural to the target audience. Examples of this style are the English translations by Abdul Majid Daryabadi (1941)[42] and the English translation of Abul Ala Maududi's (1967) Urdu translation.[43] Interpretive translations incorporate commentary or explanation within the translation, either in brackets or footnotes. Examples of this style are the English translations by Muhammad Ali and Yusuf Ali.

While South Asia presented a diverse and rich landscape for Qur'ānic translations, the history of Qur'ān translation in Latin Europe unfolds a distinct narrative shaped by complex interactions between various religious and cultural traditions. In stark contrast to the linguistic diversity of South Asia, for many centuries, Europeans had limited access to the Qur'ān's original text and its true meaning. Instead, they relied on Latin translations and often encountered polemical accounts that frequently distorted or misrepresented the Islamic faith. The following section delves into the fascinating history of Qur'ān translation in Latin Europe, shedding light on early efforts, such as Flavius Mithridates' (d.1489) translation, and the significant impact of figures like Alexander Ross (d.1654) in shaping European perceptions of Islam.

The Qur'ān translations in Latin Europe

The translation of the Qur'ān in Latin Europe holds a significant position in the history of Qur'ānic scholarship. The earliest known translations of the Qur'ān in Latin occurred during the early medieval period. These translations were primarily

42 A. Daryabadi, *Tafsir-ul-Qur'an: Translation and Commentary of the Holy Qur'an* (Karachi: Darul-Ishaat, 2014).

43 A. Mawdudi, Z. I. Ansari, and A. R. Kidwai, *Towards understanding the Qur'ān* (Leicestershire: Islamic Foundation, 1988).

produced by Christian scholars who sought to study and critically oppose the Islamic faith. The first recorded translation of the Qur'ān in Latin Europe was completed in the 12th century by Robert of Ketton, a well-known scholar of Arabic language and culture. This translation served as a foundation for other Latin translations of the Qur'ān, which were further refined and developed by subsequent scholars.

Translating the Qur'ān into Latin remains critical to studying Islamic history, facilitating cross-cultural understanding and scholarly pursuits. The translation of the Qur'ān in Europe elucidates the intricate interplay and ongoing polemics between diverse religious and cultural groups. Throughout numerous centuries, most Europeans could not access the original text or comprehend its significance and hence depended on Latin translations or polemical depictions that frequently distorted or misconstrued the tenets of the Islamic religion. Flavius Mithridates, a Christian convert from Judaism who hailed from Sicily, attempted one of the first translations of select passages from the Qur'ān into Latin. Specifically, he translated suras 21 and 22 for Federigo da Montefeltro, the Duke of Urbino, between 1480 and 1481. Mithridates' translation was accompanied by a commentary and presented alongside the original Arabic text in a lavishly produced manuscript now held in the Vatican.[44] Notably, Mithridates' translation was characterised by its absence of polemic yet contained serious mistakes compared to the Arabic. This approach, which focused on the decor of work, may have distorted the attempt of the Renaissance's humanist values, as the inclusion of Arabic was supposed to emphasise the return to the original texts. This early endeavour set the stage for the academic study of the Qur'ān in Europe.

---

44 T. E. Burman, *Reading the Qur'ān in Latin Christendom, 1140-1560* (Philadelphia, PA: Univ. of Pennsylvania Press, 2007).

During the 12th century, Robert of Ketton, an English scholar employed by Peter the Venerable, abbot of Cluny, produced the most widely circulated Latin translation of the Qur'ān in Europe. Robert's translation was part of a larger project aimed at compiling and translating various works on Islam to refute and convert Muslims. Although polemical, Robert's translation constituted a significant milestone in European engagement with the Qur'ān. Despite being based on a single Qur'ānic manuscript, Robert's translation contained numerous misconceptions and errors. It also included a preface and marginal notes that condemned Islam as a violent and heretical religion and Muhammad as a false prophet. Despite these limitations, Robert's translation was frequently copied and printed until the 16th century and translated into Italian in 1547, thus contributing to the dissemination of Islamic knowledge in Europe. André du Ryer, a French Orientalist who had lived in Egypt and Syria, was responsible for producing the first complete translation of the Qur'ān into a European vernacular language. In 1647, he published his French translation based on an Arabic manuscript he had acquired in Aleppo. Du Ryer's translation proved to be more precise and polished than Robert's earlier attempt; however, it was not without a few errors and omissions. Furthermore, the translation had a polemical tone and aimed to expose the contradictions and irrationalities in the Qur'ān.

In 1649, Alexander Ross, chaplain to Charles I, translated du Ryer's work into English. Ross added his preface and notes, which were even more hostile and disparaging than du Ryer's, indicating the prevailing attitudes of the time. The translations of the Qur'ān in Europe that were produced during its early stages exhibit the influence of prevailing political, religious, and cultural circumstances of the time. Furthermore, these translations reveal the different translators' divergent motives, methods, and attitudes towards the Qur'ān. While some endeavoured to comprehend and appreciate the Qur'ān as a literary and religious text, others aimed to undermine and discredit the Qur'ān as a source of untruths and inaccuracies. Thus, the history of Qur'ān translations in Europe during this period records linguistic and cultural intersections, conflicts, and dialogues between Islam and Christianity.

Between the 17th and 20th centuries, there were numerous attempts to translate or study the Qur'ān in Europe. In addition to those motivated by religious purposes, such as Christian missionaries seeking to convert Muslims, there were also endeavours driven by academic interest and scholarly curiosity. One such example is Ludovico Marracci, an Italian priest and professor of Arabic at La Sapienza University in Rome. In 1698, he published a translation of the Qur'ān into Latin, accompanied by a comprehensive commentary and refutation.[45] Marracci's translation was based on several Arabic manuscripts and incorporated quotes from Muslim commentators, which marked a significant advancement in Qur'ānic scholarship within Europe. While Alexander Ross may be held as the first translator of the Qur'ān into English, George Sale, a British Orientalist and legal professional, could be viewed as the first contextual discursive translator. In 1734, Sale published an English translation of the Qur'ān, which included notes and an introductory discourse. His translation, which drew on du Ryer's French version and other sources, aimed to present the Qur'ān to English readers more objectively, unbiasedly, and respectfully.[46] While not without some errors and prejudices, Sale's translation was widely read and was influential throughout Europe and America until the 20th century. It played a crucial role in shaping the Western understanding of Islam.

---

45 T. E. Burman, *Reading the Qur'ān in Latin Christendom, 1140-1560* (Philadelphia, PA: Univ. of Pennsylvania Press, 2007).

46 G. Sale, *The Koran: Commonly Called the Alcoran of Mohammed: Translated into English Immediately from the Original Arabic, with Explanatory Notes Taken from the Most Approved Commentators, to which is Prefixed a Preliminary Discourse* (London: Printed for L. Hawkes, W. Clarke, and R. Collins, 1764).

During the 19th century, various translations of the Qur'ān were produced in European languages to improve previous translations or offer alternative perspectives on Islam. Gustav Flügel, an Orientalist from Germany employed at the Imperial Library in Vienna, published a Latin version of the Qur'ān in 1834. Flügel's translation was aimed at scholars, and it included variations from several manuscripts, providing valuable insights into the textual differences of the Qur'ān.[47] As a result, it has contributed significantly to the academic study of the Islamic scripture. Furthermore, in 1861, John Rodwell, an English clergyman and scholar, produced an English translation of the Qur'ān, organised according to the suras' revelation dates. Rodwell's translation, which was based on Flügel's Latin version and other sources, aimed to clarify the development of the Prophet Muhammad's ideas and doctrines throughout his prophetic career. This approach emphasised the historical and chronological dimensions of the Qur'ānic text. The translation of the Qur'ān into European languages during the period spanning the seventeenth to the twentieth century constitutes a natural progression and extension of the translation of the Qur'ān that occurred during the medieval era. In addition, this historical development also represents a record of the discourse and interaction between the Islamic and European civilisations. Moreover, this progression is also a testament to the diversity and multiplicity within the expressions of the Islamic faith in a European context. Throughout the 20th century, Qur'ān translations into European languages would continue to increase, reflecting the intricate and multifaceted nature of the Muslim world and its interactions with the West.

---

47 H. Bobzin, 'Koran,' in *Encyclopaedia of the Qur'ān*, ed. Johanna Pink. (Accessed 2023).

The English translation of the Qur'ān and its modern development

The English translation of the Qur'ān has been a topic of great interest and intensive research, especially in the 20th and 21st centuries. Advances in technology and multicultural interactions have driven the need for accessible and nuanced English translations of the Qur'ān. This section explores the developments and innovations in the English translation of the Qur'ān during this dynamic period. We will examine features of translators, methods, and trends that have influenced English translations of the Qur'ān, emphasising traditional and contemporary voices. The impact of access, technology, and multicultural and interreligious interactions on Qur'ān translation is also explored. Finally, the section discusses the development of the English translation of the Qur'ān and its implications for the future.

Focussing on those translations produced in English, the early half of the 20th century was heavily influenced by the Ahmadiyya movement. Muhammad Ali had the first translation and commentary from a missionary perspective.[48] This translation and writing would go on to influence subsequent English translations in their layout, format, and structure, a clear example being Arabic parallel to English. Later, Muslim translators such as Yusuf Ali clearly adopted similar layouts to Muhammad Ali's; however, they used different linguistic tools to present their interpretations and understandings of the Qur'ān to an English audience.[49] One prominent example is Muhammad Marmaduke Pickthall, a British convert to Islam and a notable Muslim leader who, in the 1940s, published an English translation of the Qur'ān with

48 M. Ali, *The Holy Qur'ān: Arabic Text with English Translation and Commentary* (Dublin: Ahmadiyyah Anjuman Isha'at Islam, 2002).

49 A. Y. Ali, *The Qur'ān: Text, Translation and Commentary* (Elmhurst: Tahrike Tarsile Qur'ān, 2002).

a focus on making Arabic accessible to English. Based on his Arabic language proficiency and consultations with Muslim scholars, Pickthall's translation was a notable departure from earlier polemical translations, presenting the Qur'ān with English words suitable for the public.[50] It was the first translation of the Qur'ān by a native English speaker and remains popular today. Pickthall's translation was ground-breaking because he was the first to use Arabic and English sources to produce a translation that he claimed was accurate and faithful to the original text going against the English trend of lengthy footnotes and commentary. Furthermore, Pickthall's translation was the first to be written in a more easy to follow English, rather than earlier translators' more formal and archaic language use of English. His work is credited with making the Qur'ān better understood in the English-speaking world and impacting all subsequent translations. Pickthall's work is still considered one of the most influential translations of the Qur'ān, as it provides a comprehensive overview of the text and helped shape understandings of the Qur'ān till today. Another noteworthy translation is that of Muhammad Asad, a Jewish convert to Islam and renowned Islamic scholar who, in 1980, published an English translation of the Qur'ān with extensive commentary and notes. Based on his personal experiences of living in the Muslim world and his study of various sources, Asad's translation aimed to convey the Qur'ān's universal message and relevance to modern times, emphasising its message's inclusive and contemporary aspects.[51] His translation aims to give readers a deeper understanding of the Qur'ān's message in a contemporary context.

This critique attempted to clarify and elucidate the various interpretations that have emerged and examined how the

50 M. M. Pickthall, *The Meaning of the Glorious Qur'ān* (Gulberg, Lahore, Pakistan: Books on Islam, 2001).

51 M. Asad, *The Message of the Qur'ān* (Gibraltar: Dar Al-Andalus, 1993).

English translation of the Qur'ān was an attempt to meet the needs of a growing and diverse audience. The Qur'ān has been translated by Muslims and non-Muslims with varying accuracy and style. During the 19th and 20th centuries, most translations were in conversation as they included critical comments regarding each other in their introductions. While their comments indicate discussions around poor renditions, the lack of a standardisation process[52] and increased proliferation in English led to an organic discourse amongst English translations documented in their prefaces and introductions. Early English translations of the Qur'ān were motivated by a desire to refute Christian claims, while later translations were inspired by an impulse to answer. During the 20th century, many English translations of the Qur'ān were published, most of them by non-Muslims. However, Muslim translators also took up the task of translating the Qur'ān into English with pious enthusiasm. During the 20th and 21st centuries, several new English translations of the Qur'ān appeared, reflecting different approaches and perspectives. Some of them were conducted by Muslim scholars or converts, such as Muhammad Marmaduke Pickthall (1930), Abdullah Yusuf Ali (1934), Muhammad Asad (1980) and Muhammad Abdel Haleem (2004). Others were conducted by non-Muslim Orientalists or missionaries such as Richard Bell (1947), Arthur Arberry (1955), and N.J. Daoud (1956). These translations vary in style, accuracy, interpretation, and annotation, depending on the translator's goals, methods, and sources. Alongside these discourses, there existed external discussions. For more recent translations, however, those in the 21st century, permissibility was given via the endorsement and direct involvement of the scholarly class which became of critical importance to the translations and the

52 A. M. Halimah, 'Translation of the Holy Qur'ān: A Call for Standardization,' *Advances in Language and Literary Studies* 5 (2014), 122-133.

influence of state actors.[53] In addition, the question has arisen regarding whether translating the Qur'ān into English has become exhaustive. Finally, there is a question about the incorporation of technology and how this will affect translation processes and translator visibility.

Al-Azhar University, the oldest and most prestigious Islamic university in the world, has a complex and evolving stance towards translating the Qur'ān. On the one hand, Al-Azhar has traditionally maintained that the Qur'ān is a unique and inimitable text that cannot be adequately translated into any other language. This view is based on the belief that the Qur'ān is not simply a collection of words and phrases but rather a divine revelation with its own unique linguistic and rhetorical style. On the other hand, Al-Azhar has also recognised the importance of translation in making the Qur'ān accessible to Muslims who do not speak Arabic.[54] As a result, Al-Azhar has endorsed and published several Arabic-to-language translations of the Qur'ān, including translations into English, French, Urdu, and Persian. In recent years, Al-Azhar has taken a more nuanced approach to the issue of Qur'ān translation. In 1936, the university issued a decree stating that Qur'ān translations are permissible if they are faithful to the original Arabic text and are accompanied by appropriate commentary and guidance. This decree reflects Al-Azhar's recognition that translation can be a valuable tool for understanding and disseminating the Qur'ān, but that it must be done with care and caution. Azhar's nuanced approach to translation has been praised by some scholars, who argue that it reflects a deep understanding of the challenges and opportunities of translation in the modern world. Other scholars have

---

53 See the endorsement of certain translations by Fatwa bodies such as Egypt's Dār al-Iftā' on translations such as Abdel Haleem, Mustafa Khattab and Musharraf Hossain.

54 Muḥammad Farīd Wajdī, *al-Adillat al-'Ilmiyyat 'Alā Jawāz Tarjamat an-Qur'ān ilā al-Lugāt al-Muḥammad* (2004).

criticised Al-Azhar for its cautious approach, arguing that it has hindered the spread of the Qur'ān and the understanding of Islam among non-Arabic speakers.

Al-Azhar scholars also emphasise the importance of consulting qualified scholars and authoritative sources when researching translations of the Qur'ān. While Al-Azhar does not explicitly discuss the permissibility of translations of the Qur'ān into English, it plays a vital role in supporting and overseeing Qur'ān translation projects in various languages, including English. Al-Azhar's participation in these projects reflects an awareness of the importance of exposing a broader audience to the Qur'ān and promoting their understanding of its teachings.[55] It is worth noting that individual scholars associated with Al-Azhar may differ in their views and opinions on specific translation issues. However, the agency supports efforts to translate the Qur'ān into various languages, including English, to facilitate the understanding and disseminating its message. Saudi Arabia is another country with the largest printing press that distributes translations of the Qur'ān in multiple languages.

The impact of Saudi Arabia on English Qur'ān translation is difficult to ascertain over a long period; in recent times, there is more evidence of their impact. In 1996, the Saudi government financed a new translation of the Qur'ān called 'the Hilali-Khan Qur'an'. This translation was distributed by the Saudi government's publishing and distribution company, The King Fahd Printing Complex. Criticised previously for being in line with a strict interpretation of the Qur'ān, this translation is distributed free of cost to many countries worldwide as part of the Saudi government's mission to spread the Qur'ān. It can be concluded

55 A. Adeleke, N. Samsudin, and N. Nawi, 'Comparative Analysis of Text Classification Algorithms for Automated Labelling of Qur'ānic Verses', *International Journal on Advanced Science Engineering and Information Technology* 7(4), (2017): 1419.

that Saudi Arabia has had a significant impact on the financing and distribution of a debated English translation of the Qur'ān. Additionally, they have used their publishing and distribution company to spread Qur'ān translations to many countries worldwide. This has resulted in the distribution of several translations of the Qur'ān. Furthermore, the translations of the Qur'ān by British authors had a considerable influence on the official English translation of the Holy Qur'ān in the country. The most popular and influential English translations of the Qur'ān, Pickthall and Yusuf Ali translations, have been distributed by the King Fahd Printing Complex. In addition to state-funded sponsorship, publishing houses in Saudi Arabia, such as Darul Abul Qasim's particular translation, the Saheeh International Qur'ān translation, published by three female converts in Saudi Arabia in 1997, remains to this day one of the most popular and widely distributed translations. This translation was popularised due to its faithful adherence to the original Arabic text, as well as its easy-to-understand English translation that was accessible to a wide range of readers. A new area of challenge is whether translation methods in English can attain or reflect Qur'ānic meanings.

Previous studies have adopted exegetical translation models to compare Yusuf Ali (1934) with Al-Hilali and Khan in translating a series of collocations. In addition, research has examined the advantages and disadvantages of the translation methods used by translators. Professors Abdel Haleem and Musharraf Hossein discuss specific topics in footnotes or introductions to provide readers with a comprehensive overview of the religion. They also comment on the translation of God's names in the Qur'ān, considering the general problems faced by translators of divine attributes. This sparked an ongoing trend of English translations of the Qur'ān, with many authors trying to capture the meaning and spirit of the Qur'ān. This has been attempted through partial or select translations, such as that of Abdur Rahim Kidwai, who attempted to translate the Qur'ān into English based on selected theological verses. In addition, Muslims have developed multilingual Qur'ān software to provide Qur'ān commentary in Arabic and English. This allows for a fuller understanding of the sacred text. Scholars have discussed the difficulties of translating the richness and nuances of Arabic into other languages, especially English, which is still a challenge.[56] Differences between the Arabic and English language systems create challenges in accurately translating the Qur'ānic text. This debate highlights the need for translators to exercise caution and consider linguistic factors when translating the Qur'ān. This challenge is particularly exemplified by Islamic institutions in the UK, which recently passed a fatwa in 2016 banning the publication of translations of the Qur'ān without an Arabic text.[57] One of the advantages is that multiple support agencies are available for Qur'ān translation. However, this approach also has limitations; for example, Al-Azhar emphasised that the translator must have an in-depth understanding of the Arabic language, Islamic theology, and Qur'ānic exegesis to ensure an accurate translation. Another area of discussion focuses on the interpretation and hermeneutics of the Qur'ān. Muslim thinkers have participated in conversations about applying hermeneutic methods to the Qur'ān.[58] This debate explores different approaches to understanding and interpreting the Qur'ānic text, considering historical, cultural, and linguistic contexts.

Differing views within Muslim scholarship have led to ongoing discussion and debate regarding appropriate methods and

---

56 A. Siddiek, 'Linguistic Precautions to be Considered When Translating the Holy Qur'ān,' *Advances in Language and Literary Studies* 8(2) (2017), 103.

57 *Is it permissible to publish an English translation of the Qur'ān without the Arabic text?* (2021) *Islamic Portal.* Available at: https://islamicportal.co.uk/is-it-permissible-to-publish-an-english-translation-of-the-quran-without-the-arabic-text/ (Accessed: 06 November 2023).

58 N. Zainol, L. Majid, and M. Saad, 'An Overview on Hermeneutics Method Application to the Qur'ān by Muslim thinkers,' *International Journal of Engineering and Technology* 7(4), (2018), 167.

principles for translating and interpreting the Qur'ān. The issue of wording in the translation of the Qur'ān has also been a subject of debate. Scholars have studied the impact of translating Qur'ānic wording units and the challenges of maintaining consistency and accuracy.[59] The fragmented documentation and inconclusive evidence in this debate highlight the need for further research and exploration of effective strategies for translating Qur'ānic wording.

Contemporary translation of the Qur'ān into English is a dynamic field of study covering various topics and new areas of study. A prominent theme is developing an automatic labelling system for Qur'ānic verses. Adeleke et al. (2017) studied a comparative analysis of text classification algorithms for automatically labelling Qur'ānic verses. The purpose is to identify the verses' corresponding themes, which helps organise and classify the Qur'ānic text. Another area of research focuses on applying translation theory to the translation of the Qur'ān. Jabak studied the application of Eugene Nida's translation theory in the English translation of 'Surah Ash-Shams'.[60] This study demonstrates the need for further research on the applicability of translation theory to the English translation of the Qur'ān.

The socio-cultural and historical aspects of Qur'ān translation are also examined. Farah discusses a corpus of recorded content from the English-language Qur'ān about the Prophet and his people.[61] This study highlights the need for further research to understand Semitic religions' representation in Qur'ān translations. Muwafi explores the field of English translation of

59 H. Hassan and K. Menacere, 'Demystifying Phraseology: Implications for Translating Qur'ānic Phraseological Units,' *Advances in Language and Literary Studies* 10(1), (2019), 28.

60 O. Jabak, 'Application of Eugene Nida's Theory of Translation to the English Translation of Surah ash-Shams,' *Transcultural a Journal of Translation and Cultural Studies* 12(2), (2020): 3-18.

61 F. Amjad and M. Farahani, 'Problems and Strategies in English Translation of Qur'ānic Divine Names,' *International Journal of Linguistics* 5(1) (2013).

Qur'ānic meanings and analyses the socio-cultural and socio-political forces that shape this field.[62] This study provides insights into the social aspects of Qur'ān translation due to a combination of factors such as the advent of the printing press, an increase in political disputes that cast a shadow over the translation process and the development of modern technology. Furthermore, an increasing number of contemporary translations have produced new interpretations of Islamic texts that are more accurate and faithful to their original context. This enables English readers to understand the message of the Qur'ān better. On the other hand, improving translation by introducing standardisation also raises some issues. These include misrepresentations, misunderstandings, and inconsistencies in translation. Overall, using English has allowed Qur'ān translation to bring about its academic state, become an essential part of state influence and raise questions over methodology.

Conclusion

In summary, contemporary English translations of the Qur'ān cover a wide range of topics and emerging areas of study. These include automatic tagging systems, applications of translation theory, challenges in translating Qur'ānic heads and synonyms, phrases, socio-cultural and historical aspects, social dynamics, euphemisms, and translation changes. While this field offers great promise for improving the understanding and accessibility of the Qur'ān, it also poses challenges related to linguistic complexity, cultural differences, and meaning preservation. Further

62 D. Muwafi, 'Translation as a Social Activity: Towards a Bourdieusian Understanding of Pickthall's Translation of the Qur'ān,' *International Journal of Arabic-English Studies* 21(2),(2021): 65-84.

research in these areas may help translate the Qur'ān into more accurate and nuanced English.

The translation process of the Qur'ān reveals the many historical, linguistic, and cultural nuances that influenced the dissemination of the Qur'ān from the original Arabic into various languages, especially English. This exploration spans centuries and reveals a rich history of encounters, conversations, and disputes. We began our journey to understand the central role of the Qur'ān in the Islamic faith and the sanctity of its Arabic text. The Qur'ān is rooted in the unique linguistic structure of classical Arabic, which poses a significant challenge to its translation into other languages. This language barrier presents the translator with the task of understanding the complexity and richness of the Qur'ān to convey its message and, at the same time, preserve core integrity. Here, we see the earliest attempts at translating the Qur'ān in South Asia, where the interplay between religious tradition and cultural context unfolds. This section explores the impact of Persian and Urdu translations and their effects on different audiences. It highlights the dynamic relationship between language, faith and culture when translating sacred texts. When we turn our gaze to Latin Europe, we find a fascinating history of translation that embodies both scholarly endeavour and polemical intent. Translators such as Flavius Mithridates and Alexander Ross proposed different approaches to Qur'ān translation, some based on humanistic values, while others serving polemic purposes. Their efforts illustrate the complex interplay between religion, politics, and the East/Western context during the Renaissance. This section takes us back to the development of Qur'ān translation in medieval and modern Latin Europe. The contributions of translators such as André du Ryer, George Sale, and their contemporaries resulted in different interpretations and approaches to the Qur'ān. Their efforts are evidence of ongoing dialogue and exchange between Islamic and Christian traditions.

As we ventured into the English-speaking world, a new chapter in Qur'ān translation began, marked by scholars, theologians, and Orientalists. Translations by Pickthall, Yusuf Ali, Asad, and others reveal the variety of interpretations available to English readers. Their works paved the way for future developments in Qur'ān translation and highlighted various scholarly perspectives and linguistic nuances. The final chapter explores the prospects and challenges facing the field of Qur'ān translation. Topics such as linguistic differences, cultural interpretations and theological dimensions are at the centre of debate. The role played by supporting organisations such as Al-Azhar and Saudi Arabia in translating the Qur'ān demonstrates a shared commitment to accuracy and accessibility. Ongoing debates over hermeneutics, phrasing, and specific modes of expression illustrate the evolving dynamics of translation methods. Contemporary translation of the Qur'ān into English is a dynamic field that blends technology, linguistics, and interpretive theory to bridge the gap between the sacred Arabic text and an increasingly diverse audience. Automatic tagging systems, application of translation theory, and phrasing studies broaden the horizons of Qur'ān translation.

Taken together, the history, challenges, and innovative journey of Qur'ān translation illuminate the deep and complex nature of this undertaking. It is a journey fraught with language barriers, cultural differences, and theological nuances. Ongoing debate and developments in this area portend a dynamic future in which access to and understanding of the Qur'ānic message will continue evolving. Within scholarly inquiry, translation efforts, and literary engagement, one stands at the intersection of history and modernity, poised to navigate the multifaceted landscape of Qur'ān translations. This journey entails traversing linguistic and cultural nuances while safeguarding the profound essence of the sacred text. This is a testament to an enduring commitment to articulating the message of the Qur'ān across borders, languages, and cultures, thereby fostering a bridge of understanding in our increasingly interconnected global landscape.

Bibliography

Abdullah, J. "The Term (كلمة) in the Holy Qur'ān between Translation and Interpretation." *Al-Adab Journal* 1, no. 136 (2021): 21-42.

Adeleke, A., N. Samsudin, and N. Nawi. "Comparative Analysis of Text Classification Algorithms for Automated Labelling of Qur'ānic Verses." *International Journal on Advanced Science Engineering and Information Technology* 7, no. 4 (2017).

Albanon, R., and M. Abdul-Wahid. "Translation of Qur'ānic Euphemism into English: A Critical Review of Four Translations." *Kufa Journal of Arts* 1, no. 54 (2023): 653-672.

Alduhaim, A. "Translating Near-Synonyms in the Qur'ān: A Semantic Analysis of Three Near-Synonyms and their English Translations." *The Southeast Asian Journal of English Language Studies* 27, no. 1 (2021): 76-89.

Alhaj, A. "The phenomenon of (Un)translatability Dilemma of Translating the Qur'ānic Heart Words into English in (Repentance) Sūrat al-Tawbah." *Arab World English Journal for Translation and Literary Studies* 6, no. 3 (2022): 99-112.

Ali, A. Y. *The Qur'ān: Text, Translation and Commentary*. Elmhurst, NY: Tahrike Tarsile Qur'ān, 2002.

Ali, M. *The Holy Qur'ān: Arabic Text with English Translation and Commentary*. Dublin, OH: Ahmadiyyah Anjuman Isha'at Islam. 2002.

'Alī, Z. 'Uthmān ibn, and A. 'Izzū 'Ināyah. *Tabyīn al-Ḥaqā'iq Sharḥ Kanz al-Daqā'iq: Wa-ma'ahu Hāshiyat al-Imām al-'Allāmah al-Shaykh al-Shalabī 'ala Hādhā al-Sharḥ*. Beirut: Dār al-Kutub al-'Ilmīyah, 2010.

al-Mustaghfiri. *Fada'il al-Qur'ān*, edited by Ahmad ibn Faris al-Sallum. 2 vols. Beirut: Dar ibn Hazm, 2006.

al-Sarakhsi, *Kitab al-Mabsut*. Vol. 1. Egypt: Matba'ah al-Sa'adah, 1906.

Amjad, F., and M. Farahani. "Problems and Strategies in English Translation of Qur'ānic Divine Names." *International Journal of Linguistics* 5, no. 1 (2013).

Asad, M. The Message of the Qur'ān. Gibraltar: Dar Al-Andalus, 1993.

Atmojo, M., et al. "Development of Islamic Teachings through the Translation of the Qur'ān in Various National Languages." *Randwick International of Social Science Journal* 3, no. 1 (2022): 168-175.

Ayoub, M. *Contemporary Approaches to the Qur'ān and Sunnah*. London: International Institute of Islamic Thought, 2012.

Bazdawī. *Kanz al-Wuṣūl ila Ma'rifat al-Uṣūl*. Beirut: Sharikat Dār al-Bashā'ir. 2009.

Bin-Hariz, M. "Problems of Translating Synonyms and Homonyms in the Holy Qur'ān: A Comparative Study of Two Qur'ānic Translations by Yusuf Ali and Ahmed Ali." *Electronic Journal of University of Aden for Humanity and Social Sciences* 4, no. 1 (2023): 129-136.

Bobzin, H. "Koran. Flügel. 1834." In *Encyclopaedia of the Qur'ān*, edited by Johanna Pink.

Bondarev, D, Brigaglia, A, and Nobili, M, 'Islamic Education and Ample Space Layout in West African Islamic Manuscripts', in *Islamic Manuscripts from Mali*, ed. Ghislaine Lydon (Leiden: Brill, 2020), 105-142.

Burman, T. E. *Reading the Qur'ān in Latin Christendom, 1140-1560*. Philadelphia: University of Pennsylvania Press, 2007.

Campanini, M. *The Qur'an: Modern Muslim Interpretations*. London: Routledge, 2011.

Chittick, W. C. "Kashf al-Asrār the unveiling of the mysteries Rashīd al-Dīn Maybudī." Louisville, KY: Fons Vitae, 2015.

Daryabadi, A. *Tafsir-ul-Qur'an: Translation and Commentary of the Holy Qur'an*. Karachi: Darul-Ishaat, 2014.

Davary, B. "The study Qur'ān: a new translation and commentary." *Horizons* 43, no. 2 (2016): 397-401.

Elass, H., and H. Bennoudi. "Hermeneutic Positioning of the Translator in Qur'ān Translation." *International Journal of Language and Literary Studies* 5, no.2 (2023): 61-80.

Farah, R., P. Sumarsono, and . Sukarma. "Prophets and People of the Semitic Religion in English Translated Qur'ān: Corpus and CDA over Western Power Dominance." *Englisia Journal of Language Education and Humanities* 9, no. 2 (2022).

Fleet, K., et al. "The Encyclopaedia of Islam Three." Leiden: Brill, 2022.

Haleem, M. A. *Exploring the Qur'ān: Context and Impact.* London: I. B. Tauris, 2017.

Halimah, A. M. "Translation of the Holy Qur'ān: A Call for Standardization." *Advances in Language and Literary Studies* 5 (2014): 122-133.

Hassan, H., and K. Menacere. "Demystifying Phraseology: Implications for Translating Qur'ānic Phraseological Units." *Advances in Language and Literary Studies* 10, no. 1 (2019): 28.

Hussin, M., and M. Kamal. "Translation of al-Qur'ān into Malay language in the Malay world." *International Journal of Islamic Studies and Humanities* 4, no. 1 (2021): 32.

Jabak, O. "Application of Eugene Nida's Theory of Translation to the English Translation of Surah ash-Shams." *Transcultural a Journal of Translation and Cultural Studies* 12, no. 2 (2020): 3-18.

Keeler, A. *Sufi Hermeneutics: The Qur'ān Commentary of Rashid al-Din Maybudi.* Oxford: Oxford University Press, 2017.

Khan, H. "Shah Wali Allah (Qutb al-Din Ahmad al-Rahim) (1703–62)." In *Routledge Encyclopedia of Philosophy.* Taylor and Francis, 1998.

Lawrence, B. Bruce Lawrence - language of the Qur'ān. YouTube, 2016. Available at: https://www.youtube.com/watch?v=_IggjGshTjA (Accessed: 06 November 2023).

Lawrence, B. *The Koran in English: A Biography.* Princeton, NJ: Princeton University Press, 2017.

Mawdudi, A., Z. I. Ansari, and A. R. Kidwai. *Towards Understanding the Qur'ān*. Leicestershire: Islamic Foundation, 1988.

Muwafi, D. "Translation as a Social activity: Towards a Bourdieusian Understanding of Pickthall's Translation of the Qur'ān." *International Journal of Arabic-English Studies* 21, no. 2 (2021): 65-84.

O'Donnell, P. "Ibn Abi'l-Khayr, Abu Sa'id Fadlullah." In *The Biographical Encyclopaedia of Islamic Philosophy*. Retrieved October 21, 2023, from https://www-oxfordreference-com.abc.cardiff.ac.uk/view/10.1093/acref/9780199754731.001.0001/acref-9780199754731-e-165.

Rahman, M. "The History of the Translation of the Holy Qur'ān in Bengali: The Translation Example of Gulam Azam." *International Journal of Social Political and Economic Research* 8, no. 1 (2021): 152-172.

Pickthall, M. M. *The Meaning of the Glorious Qur'ān*. Gulberg, Lahore, Pakistan: Books on Islam, 2001.

Pink, J. "Modern and Contemporary Interpretation of the Qur'ān." In *The Wiley Blackwell Companion to the Qur'ān*, edited by A. Rippin and J. Mojaddedi. 2004.

Rodwell, J. M. *The Koran Translated*. London: Phoenix, 2003.

Sabri, M. *Mas'alah Tarjamat al-Qur'ān*. Dār al-Lubāb, 2010.

Saeed, A. *Interpreting the Qur'ān Towards a Contemporary Approach*. London: Routledge, 2009.

Sale, G. *The Koran: Commonly called the Alcoran of Mohammed: Translated into English Immediately from the Original Arabic, with Explanatory Notes taken from the Most Approved Commentators, to which is Prefixed a Preliminary Discourse*. London: Printed for L. Hawkes, W. Clarke, and R. Collins, 1764.

Shakir, A. M. *Al-Qawl al Fasl fi Tarjamat al-Qur'ān al-Karīm ila al-Lughat al-Ajamiyyah*. Egypt Matba'ah al-Naddah, 1925.

Siddiek, A. "Linguistic Precautions that to be Considered when Translating the Holy Qur'ān." *Advances in Language and Literary Studies* 8, no. 2 (2017).

Small, Keith E. *Qur'āns: Books of Divine Encounter*. Oxford: Bodleian Library, 2015.

Taji-Farouki, S. *The Qur'ān and its Readers Worldwide: Contemporary Commentaries and Translations*. New York: Oxford University Press/Institute of Ismaili Studies, London, 2015.

Tareen, S. A. "South Asian Qur'ān Commentaries and Translations: A Preliminary Intellectual History." *ReOrient* 5, no. 2 (2020): 233-256.

Tschacher, T. "'Extraordinary Translations' and 'Loathsome Commentaries': Qur'ānic Translation and the Politics of the Tamil Language, c. 1880–1950." *Religion* 49, no. 3 (2019): 458-480.

Utomo, F., N. Suryana, and M. Azmi. "Stemming Impact Analysis on Indonesian Qur'ān Translation and their Tafsir Classification for Ontology Instances." *IIUM Engineering Journal* 21, no. 1 (2020): 33-50.

Venjara, A. "Qur'ān Translation in South Asia." In *Islam, Judaism, and Zoroastrianism*, edited by Z. R. Kassam, Y. K. Greenberg, and J. Bagli. Encyclopedia of Indian Religions. Springer, Dordrecht, 2018.

Zadeh, T. E. *The Vernacular Qur'ān: Translation and the Rise of Persian Exegesis*. Oxford: Oxford University Press, 2012.

Zainol, N., L. Majid, and M. Saad. "An Overview on Hermeneutics Method Application to the Qur'ān by Muslim Thinkers." *International Journal of Engineering & Technology* 7, no. 4.9 (2018): 167.

Zolfaghary, M., and H. Omid Ali. "'An Analysis of Functions of Qur'ānic Ayahs in Shah Nimatullah Wali's Poetry'." *Literary Qur'ānic Researches* 5, no. 1 (2017): 151-171.